Achieving
TABE® Success
in Reading

Level A

Mc
Graw
Hill
Education

Cover photo: C. Zachariasen/PhotoAlto

MHEonline.com

Send all inquiries to:
McGraw-Hill Education
8787 Orion Place
Columbus, OH 43240

ISBN: 978-0-07-704462-6
MHID: 0-07-704462-2

Printed in the United States of America.

16 17 18 19 20 QVS 20 19 18 17 16 15

Table of Contents

Table of Contents

To the Learner

If reading has never been easy for you, Contemporary's *Achieving TABE Success in Reading* will help. The workbook will explain basic comprehension skills. The reader will let you practice those skills on a short, interesting story. *Achieving TABE Success in Reading* will build your confidence in your ability to read.

Using Contemporary's *Achieving TABE Success in Reading* is a good way to improve your reading comprehension skills. The workbook covers
- vocabulary
- recalling information
- using graphic information
- constructing meaning
- extending meaning

Included in the workbook are a Pretest and a Posttest. The Pretest will help you find your reading strengths and weaknesses. Then you can use the workbook lessons to improve your skills. When you have finished the lessons and exercises, the Posttest will help you see if you have mastered those skills. Usually mastery means completing 80% of the questions correctly.

Achieving TABE Success in Reading will help you develop specific reading skills. Each workbook is self-contained with the Answer Key at the back of the book. Clear directions will guide you through the lessons and exercises.

Each lesson in the **workbook** is divided into four parts:

- The **first page** clearly defines, explains, and illustrates the skill. The examples prepare you for the work in the following exercises.

- **Practice** lets you work on the skill just introduced.

- **Apply** gives you a different way to practice the comprehension skill.

- **Check Up** provides a quick test on the skill covered in the lesson.

Each selection in the **reader** will let you practice reading. The article or story will grab your interest and keep you reading to the end. When you finish reading, you will

- check your understanding of the story

- apply the workbook lesson's skill to the story

How to Use This Workbook

1. Take the Pretest on pages 7–15. Check your answers with the Answer Key on page 16. Refer to the Evaluation Chart on page 16 to find the skills on which you need to work.

2. Take each four-page lesson one at a time. Ask your teacher for help with any problems you have.

3. Use the Answer Key, which begins on page 264, to correct your answers after each exercise.

4. At the end of each unit, complete the Review and Assessment. These will check your progress. After the Assessment, your teacher may want to discuss your answers with you.

5. At the end of some lessons, you will see a Read On note about a selection in the reader for *Achieving TABE Success in Reading*. Take a break from the workbook and read the story or article. Answer the comprehension questions and the skill questions at the end of the story.

6. After you have finished all five units, take the Posttest on pages 253–262. Check your answers on page 263. Then discuss your progress with your teacher.

Pretest

Circle the word that is spelled correctly and best completes each sentence.

1. _____ is the science that deals with the composition and properties of substances.
   A Cemistry
   B Kemistry
   C Chemistry
   D Chemestry

2. They lived in a simple _____ high in the Alps.
   F challet
   G shalet
   H chalet
   J shallet

3. Jane hoped her preteen son was just going through a rebellious _____.
   A fase
   B phase
   C faize
   D phaze

4. The defendant _____ the charges made against him.
   F denied
   G dennied
   H denyed
   J denide

Circle the answer that is a synonym for the underlined word.

5. <u>cordial</u> greeting
   A forced
   B hostile
   C aloof
   D friendly

6. <u>towering</u> pine trees
   F tall
   G steep
   H minute
   J lush

7. <u>sweltering</u> summer weather
   A hot
   B cool
   C chilly
   D warm

8. <u>thoughtless</u> comment
   F observant
   G inconsiderate
   H kind
   J angry

9. <u>coax</u> a reluctant child
   A admonish
   B discourage
   C persuade
   D reprimand

10. striking color <u>scheme</u>
    F unit
    G tune
    H suggestion
    J plan

Circle the answer that is an antonym for the underlined word.

11. kindle a fire
    A extinguish
    B fan
    C build
    D ignite

12. expensive furnishings
    F overstuffed
    G extravagant
    H costly
    J cheap

13. permissive parent
    A tolerant
    B indulgent
    C strict
    D forgiving

14. animals native to North America
    F common
    G foreign
    H peculiar
    J indigenous

15. murky river
    A dark
    B clear
    C dim
    D muddy

16. reminisce about her childhood
    F forget
    G recall
    H review
    J memorize

Circle the answer to each question.

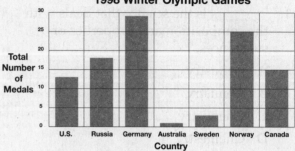

Distribution of Medals in the 1998 Winter Olympic Games

Source: *Time Almanac, 1999*

17. Which country won about twice as many medals as the United States?
    A Germany
    B Norway
    C Sweden
    D Canada

18. Which countries together won as many medals as Russia?
    F Germany and Sweden
    G United States and Australia
    H Canada and Sweden
    J Norway and Australia

Chicago, Illinois

19. Which of the following is south of Grant Park?

   A   Petrillo Music Shell

   B   Chicago Cultural Center

   C   Shedd Aquarium

   D   Civic Opera House

20. In which direction would you travel to get from the Art Institute to the Merchandise Mart?

   F   northeast

   G   northwest

   H   southeast

   J   southwest

21. Which pronunciation matches the word *architect*?

   A   är′chi•tekt

   B   är′ki•tekt

   C   ärch′i•tekt

   D   är′ki•techt

22. Which words are in alphabetical order?

   F   arid, arise, aristocracy, arithmetic

   G   because, beautify, bedding, bedlam

   H   chowder, chromium, chubby, chrysanthemum

   J   education, eerie, ego, eggshell

23. Which pair of words would be the guide words on a dictionary page that has the word *imperative* on it?

   A   imperfect/impetus

   B   impedance/impiety

   C   immorality/impel

   D   impatient/impede

Index

Mayflower Compact, 420
   See also Mayflower
   Democracy, 136
   Massachusetts, 400
   Plymouth Colony, 664
   United States (history of), 789

Mayfly, 427
   Insect, 305
Mayo, William Dr., 456
Mayo Clinic, 468
   Mayo, William Dr., 456
   Minnesota, 522

24. What subject is both an entry and a subentry in the index?

  F Minnesota

  G Mayflower Compact

  H Mayfly

  J Dr. William Mayo

25. Under what other entry might you find information about the mayfly?

  A Plymouth Colony

  B *Mayflower*

  C Democracy

  D Insect

26. The card catalog does **not** include

  F the author of the book

  G the date of publication

  H the price of the book

  J the publisher

27. In which reference source would you find a list of hardcover and paperback books by title, author, and subject?

  A an encyclopedia

  B *Bartlett's Familiar Quotations*

  C World Atlas

  D *Books in Print*

28. Which information would **not** be required on an Authorization to Hold Mail form?

  F begin holding date

  G credit card number

  H address

  J resume delivery date

29. When filling out a catalog order form, you would provide all of the following information except

    A item number

    B price

    C date of birth

    D shipping and handling charge

30. The best place to find a comparison of the performance and price of big-screen televisions would be a

    F consumer magazine

    G newspaper advertisement

    H television program guide

    J billboard

31. All of the following information would probably be covered in a consumer rating of a big-screen television except

    A favorite show of viewers

    B picture quality

    C price

    D size of the screen

Frostbite is an injury that results from overexposure of the skin to the extreme cold. Ice crystals form in the tissues and restrict blood flow to the affected area. The most frequently frostbitten areas are the toes, fingers, nose, and ears. The first sign of a frostbitten area is that the skin turns very pale or grayish-blue. The body parts feel cold and painful. As the frostbite progresses, body parts become numb. Frostbite should be treated by restoring circulation and warmth to the affected area as quickly as possible. First wrap the victim in a blanket, and bring him or her indoors if possible. Do not rub or manipulate frostbitten parts with snow or ice. Handle the affected areas very gently. Soak the affected parts in warm water (102° to 105°). Because of the heat they generate, do not use a hot water bottle, heating pad, or heat lamp to warm the body parts. Finally, place gauze or cloth between fingers or toes before loosely bandaging them. For serious frostbite, seek medical attention for thawing because it is very painful and extensive tissue damage may occur.

32. How does frostbite affect the body?

    F   The skin breaks on affected areas and a victim bleeds to death.

    G   A victim's body temperature rises to between 102° and 105°.

    H   Affected body parts become brittle.

    J   Ice crystals form in the tissues and restrict blood flow to affected areas.

33. You can conclude that frostbite should never be treated with a hot water bottle, heating pad, or heat lamp because

    A   such treatment might produce temperatures that can damage frostbitten tissue

    B   such treatment will put the victim into shock

    C   it would take too long to thaw tissues using this kind of treatment

    D   most people do not have access to this kind of treatment

34. What is the purpose of soaking the affected area in warm water?

    F   to keep infection from spreading

    G   to thaw the tissues

    H   to clean the damaged skin

    J   to relax the victim

What does a stick of dynamite have to do with the world's most famous peace prize? The story begins in the 19th century with Alfred Nobel, a Swedish chemist and engineer. The Nobel family owned an explosives plant in which both Alfred and his younger brother worked. The plant manufactured liquid nitroglycerin. After his brother was killed in an experiment that went awry, Alfred became determined to develop a safer explosive. In 1867 he was granted a patent for a new explosive he named "dynamite." The invention of dynamite turned Alfred Nobel into a rich man but not a happy one, for he regretted the often warlike application of the explosive. He had meant for dynamite to be used in safe and peaceful endeavors, but he lived to see it employed as a tool of aggression. Because he was a pacifist at heart, he used his dynamite fortune to establish the Nobel Prize for Peace.

35. What caused Alfred Nobel to find a way to minimize the danger of handling nitroglycerin?

    A his sorrow over the death of his younger brother in an industrial accident

    B pressure from the Swedish government

    C his humanitarian instincts

    D the promise of financial gain

36. What is a pacifist?

    F an inventor

    G a person who opposes violence

    H a soldier of fortune

    J a scientist

37. Compared to nitroglycerin, dynamite is

    A more dangerous

    B less dangerous

    C less noisy

    D more costly

38. Which phrase best describes Alfred Nobel?

    F interested in helping others peacefully

    G interested in becoming a millionaire

    H determined to avenge his brother's death

    J determined to build safe bombs for use in war

Before using the answering system on your telephone, you will need to record an announcement that callers will hear when the system answers an incoming call. Prepare an announcement that reminds your callers they will hear a beep before the system begins recording. First press and release the *Change* button. Then press and release the *Announcement* button and wait for the beep. After the beep, speak toward the front about 10 inches away from the speaker. A humorous announcement is the best kind to record. Finally press and release *Play* when you are finished. The tape will reset automatically and play the announcement.

39. When do you begin recording your announcement?

    A before pressing and releasing *Change*

    B after pressing and releasing *Announcement*

    C after pressing and releasing *Play*

    D after the phone rings

40. What is the author's purpose in this paragraph?

    F to inform the reader about how to set the day and time on a telephone answering system

    G to explain how a telephone answering system works

    H to persuade the reader to purchase a telephone answering system

    J to tell the reader how to record an announcement on a telephone answering system

41. Which of the following is an opinion?

    A Prepare an announcement that reminds your callers they will hear a beep before the system begins recording.

    B First press and release the *Change* button.

    C After the beep, speak toward the front about 10 inches away from the speaker.

    D A humorous announcement is the best kind to record.

Many tales about great discoveries are interesting and exciting to hear. For example, the English mathematician and physicist Sir Isaac Newton saw an apple fall from a tree. At the time, there was a crescent moon in the sky. Newton looked up at the moon and wondered if the same force that pulled the apple to the ground held the moon near Earth. Newton himself admitted that the apple helped him to discover the force of gravity. However, the apple did not, as some people think, fall and hit him on the head.

42. What is the main idea of this paragraph?

   F   Sir Isaac Newton came upon the idea of gravity after observing the falling of an apple and relating it to the force that holds the moon near Earth.

   G   Most tales of scientific discoveries aren't true.

   H   The story of how Sir Isaac Newton discovered gravity is false.

   J   Sir Isaac Newton wondered how the moon stayed near Earth.

43. This paragraph would most likely be found in

   A   a social studies textbook

   B   an almanac

   C   a magazine article

   D   a government report

44. Based on this paragraph, which generalization can be made?

   F   Stories about scientific discoveries are always factual.

   G   Scientific discoveries are usually made in a research lab.

   H   A scientific principle must be completely understood when it is discovered.

   J   Stories about scientific discoveries may be embellished to make them more interesting.

Pretest Answer Key and Evaluation Chart

This Pretest has been designed to help you determine which reading skills you need to study. This chart shows which skill is being covered with each test question. Circle the questions you answered incorrectly and go to the practice pages in this book covering those skills. Carefully work through all the practice pages before taking the Posttest.

Key

#	Ans
1.	C
2.	H
3.	B
4.	F
5.	D
6.	F
7.	A
8.	G
9.	C
10.	J
11.	A
12.	J
13.	C
14.	G
15.	B
16.	F
17.	B
18.	H
19.	C
20.	G
21.	B
22.	F
23.	B
24.	J
25.	D
26.	H
27.	D
28.	G
29.	C
30.	F
31.	A
32.	J
33.	A
34.	G
35.	A
36.	G
37.	B
38.	F
39.	B
40.	J
41.	D
42.	F
43.	C
44.	J

Tested Skills	Question Numbers	Practice Pages
synonyms	5, 6, 7, 8, 9, 10	21–24, 25–28
antonyms	11, 12, 13, 14, 15, 16	29–32, 33–36
context clues	36	37–40, 41–44
spelling	1, 2, 3, 4	45–48, 49–52
details	34	59–62, 63–66
sequence	39	67–70, 71–74
graphs	17, 18	89–92
maps	19, 20	93–96
dictionary	21, 22, 23	97–100
index	24, 25	101–104
card catalog	26	105–108
reference sources	27	109–112
forms	28, 29	113–116
consumer materials	30, 31	117–120, 121–124
characters	38	131–134, 135–138
main idea	42	139–142, 143–146
compare and contrast	37	147–150, 151–154
drawing conclusions	33	155–158, 159–162
cause and effect	35	163–166, 167–170
identifying fact and opinion	41	201–204, 205–208
author's purpose	40	209–212, 213–216
generalizations	44	225–228, 229–232
genre	43	233–236
applying passage elements	32	245–248

Correlation Chart

Correlations Between Contemporary's Instructional Materials and TABE® Reading

Test 1 Reading

Subskill	TABE® Form 9	TABE® Form 10	TABE® Survey 9	TABE® Survey 10	Practice and Instruction Pages			
					Achieving TABE Success in Reading, Level A*	The Complete GED	Essential GED	GED Language Arts, Reading
Interpret Graphic Information								
maps		1, 3, 33		1, 3, 19	W: 93–96 R: 35–40	283–284, 427–440	193–200	
reference sources	8, 9, 10, 12		5, 6, 7, 9		W: 88, 97–112 R: 41–45, 46–50	657–676	326–338	128–134
graphs		2		2	W: 89–92 R: 35–40, 41–45	275–282, 403–425	396–399	
Words in Context								
same meaning	1, 46	24, 32	1, 22	14, 18	W: 21–28 R: 5–10	217–224		31–33
opposite meaning	47		23		W: 29–36 R: 5–10			
appropriate word	11	8, 16	8	7, 10	W: 20, 37–44, 87 R: 11–15			
Recall Information								
details		13, 17, 22		11	W: 59–66 R: 20–24	237–239	41–43	23–30
sequence	17	12, 37, 47, 48		9, 23	W: 67–74 R: 25–29	254–255	48–50	72–76
stated concepts	13, 14, 24, 26, 37, 38, 43	6, 8, 21, 39, 40	13, 14, 19, 20	5	W: 75–82 R: 30–34	213–216, 217–221	32–37	

* W = Workbook; R = Reader.

TABE® Forms 9 and 10 are published by CTB/McGraw-Hill. TABE is a registered trademark of The McGraw-Hill Companies.

Correlation Chart continued

Subskill	TABE® Form 9	TABE® Form 10	TABE® Survey 9	TABE® Survey 10	Practice and Instruction Pages			
					Achieving TABE Success in Reading, Level A*	The Complete GED	Essential GED	GED Language Arts, Reading
Construct Meaning								
character aspects	5, 27, 31	26, 28, 31, 46	3, 15	17	W: 130–138 R: 56–59	594–598, 647–653	293–294, 322–324	179–192, 263–266
main idea	20, 21, 42	4, 41, 45	10. 11	4, 22	W: 139–146 R: 56–59	237–239	33–37, 41–42	15–23
summary/ paraphrase	7, 49	9, 14, 43	25		W: 171–178 R: 66–71, 72–76	221–230	34–36	
cause/effect	32, 36, 45	7		6	W: 163–170 R: 66–71	259–261	51–52	81–82
compare/ contrast	22, 23, 30	50	12, 17	25	W: 147–154 R: 60–65	256–258	48–50	89–95
conclusion	29	15, 20, 27, 38		12, 15	W: 155–162 R: 60–65	245–248	45–47	47–56
supporting evidence	2, 18, 44	42	2		W: 179–186 R: 72–76	243–248	43–46, 121–122	23–30
Evaluate/Extend Meaning								
fact/opinion	33, 40, 50		21		W: 201–208 R: 77–81, 87–91	242–244	42–44	111–113
predict outcomes	4, 16	23		13	W: 193–200 R: 77–81			
apply passage elements		5, 10, 19, 34, 35, 36		20, 21	W: 245–248 R: 92–96	231–235, 263–269	312–316, 318–320	28–29, 39–46, 117–128
generalizations	6, 39, 41	30	4	16	W: 225–232 R: 82–86	605–606	298–299	47–52
effect/ intention	15, 19, 25	25			W: 241–244 R: 92–96	593–594, 626–636	290–293, 300–302, 312	176–196
author purpose	28, 35, 48		16, 18, 24		W: 209–224 R: 82–86	605–606, 655–656	325–326	99–105
style techniques	3	11, 29, 49		8, 24	W: 57–58, 192, 237–240 R: 92–96	249–250, 599–604, 607–612, 619–623	292, 297–298, 308–311	57–71, 113–116, 230–237
genre	34	44			W: 233–236 R: 87–91, 92–96	589–593, 615–619, 637–641, 657–676	289–293, 304–307, 317–321, 326–335	109–110, 166–175, 217–226, 249–260

* W = Workbook; R = Reader.

TABE® Forms 9 and 10 are published by CTB/McGraw-Hill. TABE is a registered trademark of The McGraw-Hill Companies.

Analogies

An **analogy** compares the relationship between one pair of words to the relationship between another pair of words. There are different kinds of relationships.

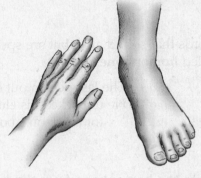

Here is an example of a **part/whole analogy**

finger : hand : : toe : foot

This is read "finger is to hand as toe is to foot." The relationship between finger and hand is the same as the relationship between toe and foot. That is, a finger is a **part** of a **whole** hand the same way a toe is a **part** of a **whole** foot.

Other analogies include the following:

cause/effect analogy: bacteria : pneumonia : : fire : heat

worker/product analogy: painter : picture : : sculptor : statue

opposite analogy: laughing : crying : : comedy : tragedy

Complete each analogy.

1. minute : hour : : _____ : week

2. bee : hive : : _____ : nest

3. sun : shine : : _____ : rain

4. Moscow : Russia : : Paris : _____

5. students : school : : diners : _____

6. baker : bread : : _____ : bouquet

7. paycheck : job : : _____ : schoolwork

8. pass : fail : : _____ : penalty

9. hammer : tools : : shirt : _____

10. life jacket : swimmer : : _____ : skydiver

11. tennis : sport : : Spanish : _____

12. guest : hotel : : _____ : hospital

13. athlete : gym : : scientist : _____

14. biology : science : : algebra : _____

Homophones

Words that sound alike but are spelled differently and have different meanings are called **homophones**.

> The last person out of the house will **close** the door. (shut)
> He unpacked his **clothes** and hung them in the closet. (coverings for a person's body)

Write the homophone from the box that correctly completes each sentence.

weight	stake	hour	peace	bored	their	board
there	piece	wait	loan	our	lone	steak

1. The people cheered when _____ candidate appeared on stage.

2. He served each of his guests a _____ of apple pie.

3. The customer insisted that she wanted her _____ well done.

4. The pillars support the _____ of the roof.

5. After the war ended, a _____ treaty was signed.

6. The trip downtown took less than one _____.

7. A _____ house stood on the top of the mountain.

8. I was so _____ by the speaker that I found myself dozing off.

9. We had to _____ an hour before boarding our plane.

10. We traveled to Mexico for _____ vacation.

11. The news said _____ was flooding on Highway 32.

12. The carpenter sawed the _____ in half.

13. The strong wind pulled every tent _____ out of the ground.

14. I went to the bank to apply for a home-improvement _____.

Recognizing Synonyms

Read this sentence.

The dancers *(spin, twirl)* across the stage.

You could use either *spin* or *twirl* in the sentence because *spin* and *twirl* have similar meanings. Words with meanings that are the same or almost the same are called **synonyms**.

Match pairs of words in the box that are synonyms. Then write the pairs of words.

make	odd	village	cost
bad	build	hard	shout
firm	price	town	road
ill	evil	answer	sick
yell	reply	strange	street

1. _____ _____

2. _____ _____

3. _____ _____

4. _____ _____

5. _____ _____

6. _____ _____

7. _____ _____

8. _____ _____

9. _____ _____

10. _____ _____

Practice

Recognizing Synonyms

Think of a synonym for each underlined word. Write the synonym on the line.

You are probably familiar with the tale of Johnny Appleseed. He traveled the American frontier in the 1840s. To reforest the earth, he carried sacks of apple seeds and planted them wherever he went. In his own odd way, he was as much of a polluter as a conservationist. In addition to planting apple seeds, Johnny planted a weed called dog fennel. He believed that this weed could be brewed into a tea to cure malaria. Good-hearted Johnny was wrong. Dog fennel spreads like any other weed, and it stinks. For years after Johnny Appleseed passed by, angry farmers held their noses and desperately rooted out the dog fennel he had planted by their homes.

1. tale _____

2. traveled _____

3. earth _____

4. sacks _____

5. odd _____

6. believed _____

7. Good-hearted _____

8. wrong _____

9. angry _____

10. homes _____

Apply

Find a word in the box that is a synonym for the underlined word in each sentence. Then write the word on the line.

homelike	hub	factories	alternate	schooling
salary	stayed	identical	improved	valuable

1. By 1825 Lowell, Massachusetts, had become the manufacturing <u>center</u> of the young American nation.

   _____

2. Most of the workers in the <u>mills</u> were teenage girls.

   _____

3. Most of the girls left their family farms for the promise of <u>better</u> lives.

   _____

4. The young women were housed in <u>comfortable</u> dormitories.

   _____

5. Older women acted as <u>substitute</u> mothers.

   _____

6. The girls' <u>education</u> was provided by visiting teachers.

   _____

7. However, the girls worked 11 hours a day, 6 days a week. Their <u>pay</u> was $3 a week each.

   _____

8. It was more than they would have earned if they had <u>remained</u> on the farms.

   _____

9. Men doing the <u>same</u> work were paid twice as much.

   _____

10. Factory jobs were considered <u>important</u>.

    _____

Check Up

Find the synonym for each underlined word. Then circle the answer.

1. Make a list of your <u>ideas</u>.
   A equipment
   B thoughts
   C names
   D clothes

2. Mr. Albert will <u>train</u> us to work at the restaurant.
   F teach
   G event
   H tell
   J help

3. The <u>odor</u> of the cleaner was unpleasant.
   A touch
   B taste
   C sound
   D smell

4. Step to the <u>rear</u> of the bus.
   F front
   G back
   H middle
   J top

5. Her <u>reply</u> was incorrect.
   A story
   B answer
   C explanation
   D thought

6. I'm going to <u>exchange</u> the gift.
   F buy
   G wrap
   H trade
   J sell

7. The staff raised a <u>commotion</u> when they heard the new <u>schedule</u>.
   A disturbance
   B question
   C shout
   D speech

8. The <u>professors</u> planned the course.
   F parents
   G friends
   H teachers
   J principals

9. We fish in the deep <u>brook</u>.
   A ocean
   B stream
   C lake
   D sea

10. I <u>realize</u> that the meeting is very early.
    F understand
    G share
    H agree
    J disagree

Using Synonyms

Read these two words.

quiz   *test*

The words have almost the same meaning. Words that have the same or almost the same meaning are called **synonyms.** You could use each word in the same sentence.

Find a word in the box that is a synonym for the numbered word. Write the word. Then choose one of the two words to complete the phrase.

instantly	brief	manual	sporty	shrewd
certain	crisp	society	dispute	evening

1. handbook or _____

   the _____ of

   instructions

2. immediately or _____

   taken home _____

3. twilight or _____

   the coolness of _____

4. casual or _____

   the _____ jacket

5. short or _____

   the _____ report

6. absolute or _____

   the _____ answer

7. culture or _____

   our American _____

8. cunning or _____

   the _____ liar

9. brittle or _____

   the _____ bacon

10. argument or _____

    an unresolved _____

Practice

Read the following passage. Then find and write words from the passage that are synonyms for the words below.

From earliest times, people have reported the ability to go into states of consciousness that were different from the usual waking self. In some early cultures, priests or healers were respected for their talents while in a special trance. In ancient Egypt, soothsayers put themselves in a detached state to try to predict the future.

Tribal peoples around the world often had spiritual leaders who were able to go into a trance. In this state they were expected to cure diseases and to communicate with members of distant tribes.

Often the special state was caused by the actions of a second person or was induced by self-suggestion. Today these practices continue to attract widespread interest.

1. heal   _____

2. common   _____

3. currently   _____

4. faraway   _____

5. honored   _____

6. gifts   _____

7. condition   _____

8. groups   _____

9. foretell   _____

10. illnesses   _____

Apply

In each question, find the synonym for the underlined word. Write the synonym on the line.

1. You <u>admire</u> your friend's courage.

   Do you approve or admit? _____

2. The desserts look <u>appetizing</u>.

   Do they look desirable or fattening? _____

3. The song was <u>monotonous</u>.

   Was it repetitious or exciting? _____

4. She was <u>bewildered</u> by the question.

   Was she amazed or confused? _____

5. The material was <u>coarse</u>.

   Was it smooth or rough? _____

6. The stomach <u>digests</u> food.

   Does it absorb food or destroy food? _____

7. The host was <u>gracious</u>.

   Was he rude or courteous? _____

8. We listened to a <u>renowned</u> scientist.

   Was she famous or unknown? _____

9. You <u>submit</u> an application.

   Do you offer it or desire it? _____

10. Turkey is a <u>traditional</u> food at Thanksgiving.

    Is it customary or unusual? _____

11. My suitcase was <u>unwieldy</u>.

    Was it cumbersome or inexpensive? _____

12. The knife was <u>blunt</u>.

    Was it sharp or dull? _____

Check Up

All of the words in each group are synonyms except one. Circle the word that is **not** a synonym of the others.

1. A stare
    B gaze
    C gawk
    D grip

2. F attractive
    G beautiful
    H expensive
    J lovely

3. A attentive
    B cowardly
    C spineless
    D gutless

4. F deduce
    G criticize
    H reason
    J infer

5. A courage
    B bravery
    C fearlessness
    D honesty

6. F defeat
    G defect
    H conquer
    J overcome

7. A increase
    B enlarge
    C expand
    D affect

8. F knowledge
    G information
    H wisdom
    J article

9. A disloyal
    B distaste
    C dislike
    D disgust

10. F guide
    G allow
    H direct
    J lead

Recognizing Antonyms

Read these two words.

dirty *clean*

The words have opposite meanings. Words that have opposite meanings are called **antonyms.**

Notice how the meaning of the sentence changes.

The horse's stall was very <u>dirty</u>.
The horse's stall was very <u>clean</u>.

Choose the antonym for each word. Then write its letter on the line.

1. morning _____   **A** never

2. victory _____   **B** frequently

3. innocent _____   **C** flabby

4. always _____   **D** evening

5. seldom _____   **E** whisper

6. muscular _____   **F** defeat

7. grin _____   **G** serious

8. hero _____   **H** guilty

9. shout _____   **I** proud

10. drowsy _____   **J** alert

11. humorous _____   **K** villain

12. humble _____   **L** frown

Practice

On the line, write an antonym for the word given below the line.

The black bear has a relatively _____ play period,
short

_____ at four months and lasting four years. It starts with
ending

_____ play with its mother. _____ that comes
rough   Before

rough-and-tumble play with its siblings. Through their play, bears learn the

_____ behavior that is expected of them.
simple

If a black bear has a bone snatched from it, it must instantly see if the attacking cub

holds its mouth _____ or if the lips are tightly shut, and whether
closed

the eyelids are wide open or shut. It must also notice if the ears stand erect

and face _____.
backward

Each cub must learn how to send out the _____ messages and
wrong

how to understand the messages that are _____. It must also
taken

react _____.
slowly

Apply

Use a different pair of antonyms to complete each sentence.

1. The movie was _____, but the book was _____.

2. The amusement park _____ at 10:00 A.M. and _____ at 10 P.M.

3. The first statement was a _____, but the witness told the _____.

4. My brother is very _____ and my sister is _____.

5. The orchestra was _____, but the audience was _____.

6. The new car is _____, but the old car is _____.

7. Last week the weather was _____, but this week it is _____.

8. Gabriel was _____ with the decision, but June was _____.

9. It took a _____ time to prepare the meal, but it took a _____ time to eat it.

10. The jacket was _____, but the pants were _____.

11. The kitchen was _____, but the dining room was _____.

12. Ben was _____ in the morning and _____ in the afternoon.

Check Up

Find an antonym for each word. Then circle the answer.

1. idle
   - A lazy
   - B confused
   - C busy
   - D bashful

2. least
   - F most
   - G greater
   - H medium
   - J small

3. listless
   - A tired
   - B energetic
   - C weak
   - D poor

4. normal
   - F even
   - G correct
   - H average
   - J unusual

5. fancy
   - A dressy
   - B informal
   - C proper
   - D expensive

6. vital
   - F valuable
   - G important
   - H unnecessary
   - J unfortunate

7. departure
   - A delay
   - B disappearance
   - C absence
   - D arrival

8. illusion
   - F reality
   - G spirit
   - H disappearance
   - J error

9. inaccurate
   - A correct
   - B wrong
   - C simple
   - D easy

10. immense
    - F huge
    - G tiny
    - H superb
    - J awesome

Read On As you read "America's Natural Wonders," look for synonyms and antonyms. Then answer the questions.

Using Antonyms

Read this sentence.

The hat was <u>cheap</u>, but the gloves were <u>expensive</u>.

In this sentence the words *cheap* and *expensive* have opposite meanings. Words that have opposite meanings are **antonyms**, so *cheap* and *expensive* are antonyms.

Write an antonym for the underlined word to complete the phrase.

1. a <u>big</u> dog with a(n) _____ tail

2. a <u>wealthy</u> king with a(n) _____ kingdom

3. an <u>eager</u> teacher with a(n) _____ student

4. an <u>orderly</u> room with a(n) _____ desk

5. a <u>gloomy</u> story with a(n) _____ ending

6. a <u>polite</u> child with a(n) _____ friend

7. a <u>knowledgable</u> speaker with a(n) _____ audience

8. an <u>exhausted</u> babysitter with a(n) _____ child

9. a difficult <u>problem</u> with a simple _____

10. a <u>permanent</u> house with a(n) _____ porch

11. a <u>strict</u> teacher with a(n) _____ assistant

12. a long <u>question</u> with a short _____

13. an <u>ornate</u> pendant with a(n) _____ chain

14. an <u>interesting</u> plot with _____ characters

15. a <u>coarse</u> outside with a _____ inside

Practice

Write a synonym and an antonym for each word.

Remember: Antonyms are words that are opposites.
Synonyms are words that have the same or almost the same meaning.

	Synonym	Antonym
1. whisper	_____	_____
2. cruel	_____	_____
3. ashamed	_____	_____
4. enemy	_____	_____
5. frequently	_____	_____
6. identical	_____	_____
7. delicate	_____	_____
8. confusion	_____	_____
9. authentic	_____	_____
10. dependable	_____	_____
11. agree	_____	_____
12. violent	_____	_____
13. attractive	_____	_____
14. courage	_____	_____
15. increase	_____	_____

Apply

Use each of the following pairs of antonyms in a sentence.

1. positive   negative

_____

2. create   destroy

_____

3. horizontal   vertical

_____

4. question   answer

_____

5. mundane   unusual

_____

6. fact   opinion

_____

7. aggressive   passive

_____

8. fantasy   reality

_____

9. accept   reject

_____

10. vital   unnecessary

_____

Check Up

Find the antonym for each underlined word. Then circle the answer.

1. Can you <u>bend</u> your knee?
   - A shorten
   - B straighten
   - C move
   - D flex

2. What is the <u>length</u> of the table?
   - F width
   - G perimeter
   - H area
   - J angle

3. I don't want to <u>confront</u> the problem.
   - A solve
   - B face
   - C avoid
   - D understand

4. We were <u>energetic</u> after the hike.
   - F motivated
   - G refreshed
   - H excited
   - J exhausted

5. The stones in the necklace are <u>unique</u>.
   - A special
   - B common
   - C precious
   - D unusual

6. The rope was very <u>taut</u>.
   - F stressed
   - G firm
   - H relaxed
   - J stretched

7. The <u>selfish</u> child kept all the crayons.
   - A giving
   - B concerned
   - C desirable
   - D personable

8. We ironed the <u>rumpled</u> clothes.
   - F unwrinkled
   - G unkempt
   - H creased
   - J dirty

Recognizing Context Clues

Context is the "frame" for a word in a sentence. It is the words, phrases, and sentences that surround a word. Context can give you clues to the word's meaning.

> Use the context to figure out the meaning of the word *itinerary*.
>
> My travel agent helps me plan my itinerary.

The other words and the meaning of the sentence help you know that an itinerary is a travel plan.

Use context clues to figure out the meaning of the underlined word. Write the meaning. Then look the word up in a dictionary and write a short definition.

1. The disappearance of the ocean liner *Waratah* is a mystery in <u>nautical</u> history.

   Your definition: _____

   Dictionary definition: _____

2. The ship left the <u>port</u> of Durban, South Africa, in 1909 bound for London.

   Your definition: _____

   Dictionary definition: _____

3. Early during the voyage, the ship <u>vanished</u> without a trace.

   Your definition: _____

   Dictionary definition: _____

4. Ships steamed to the area but found neither survivors nor <u>flotsam</u>.

   Your definition: _____

   Dictionary definition: _____

5. To this day, no one has been able to offer a <u>plausible</u> explanation.

   Your definition: _____

   Dictionary definition: _____

Practice

Sometimes words in a nearby sentence will provide context clues.

Use context clues to determine the meaning of the underlined word. Write the meaning of the word. Then write the context clues that helped you figure out the word's meaning.

1. J.R.R. Tolkien spent 14 years writing the three books of *The Lord of the Rings*. The popular fantasy <u>trilogy</u> is about life in Middle Earth.

   Meaning of *trilogy:* _____

   Context clues: _____

2. The novels are inhabited by creatures called <u>hobbits</u>. Hobbits have brown furry legs and live underground.

   Meaning of *hobbits:* _____

   Context clues: _____

3. The hobbits <u>engage</u> in great universal struggles. They also take part in simple daily pleasures.

   Meaning of *engage:* _____

   Context clues: _____

4. The author <u>disclaims</u> the idea that his story has symbolic significance. He refuses to accept the idea, saying "It is not about anything but itself."

   Meaning of *disclaims:* _____

   Context clues: _____

5. The books have inspired countless groups of devoted readers. In the United States, a <u>cult</u> has developed around Tolkien's tales of creatures in another world.

   Meaning of *cult:* _____

   Context clues: _____

Apply

Sometimes a word will be defined within the paragraph.

Use context clues to figure out the meaning of each underlined word. Choose its definition from this list and write the letter of the definition beside the word.

guess	dull	rabbit
male mallard ducks	spoiled	guard
mistreated	bullying	

In some London parks, male mallard ducks, which are called drakes, have become a bunch of delinquents. Experts theorize, or guess, that the birds are suffering from "character collapse." The males have abandoned their drab mates and offspring. They have grouped themselves into roving gangs that go about the parks terrorizing other wildlife by picking on them. Bird experts say that tourists are to blame. They have overindulged the birds, feeding them too much and giving them whatever they want.

1. drakes _____

2. theorize _____

3. drab _____

4. terrorizing _____

5. overindulged _____

Some people thought that using a rabbit as a sentinel was a bad idea, but not the ASPCA (American Society for the Prevention of Cruelty to Animals). Their suggestion was that Harvey was perfect for the guard job, for he would bite and thump anyone who got too close to him. The hare behaved in such a manner because he had been abused, or treated badly, by human owners when he was young. The black-and-white rabbit became a mascot for the ASPCA. He was taken on a tour and even had his picture printed on T-shirts.

6. sentinel _____

7. hare _____

8. abused _____

Check Up

Read each selection and use context clues to answer each question. Then circle the answer.

1. The small Indian fishing village of Naumkeag was a quiet settlement in Massachusetts. In 1626 a group of adventurous Puritans left Plymouth to establish this new <u>outpost</u>.

   What does the word *outpost* mean?

   A   a frontier settlement

   B   mail delivery

   C   journey

   D   modern urban town

2. At first the Pilgrims lived in temporary dwellings—thatched-roof dugouts, or <u>wigwams</u>.

   What does the word *wigwam* mean?

   F   school

   G   thatched-roof dugouts

   H   fishing village

   J   settlement

3. The Puritans called the village Salem and began building <u>permanent</u> homes in the 1630s. They wanted to create a more stable life.

   What does the word *permanent* mean?

   A   modern

   B   changing

   C   long-lasting

   D   new

4. The community grew, with housing and industries gradually <u>overwhelming</u> the remains of the Native-American village.

   What does the word *overwhelming* mean?

   F   saving

   G   taking over

   H   winning

   J   using

Using Context Clues

Sometimes you can use the **context**, or the words or phrases that surround a word in a passage, to figure out the meaning of the word.

Senator Feldman marched onto the stage, his body stiff with outrage. In a loud voice that was almost a shout, he claimed to be incensed at allegations that his campaign staff had mishandled funds. The senator declared angrily, "This is a plot by my opponent to discredit me because I am ahead in the polls."

The word *incensed* means "furious." What context clues helped you figure out its meaning? His body was "stiff with outrage." He speaks in a very loud voice and speaks "angrily."

Read the passage. Then circle the correct answer.

On August 8, 1974, Richard Nixon left the presidency of the United States. His resignation resulted from controversy over illegal activities that occurred during his presidential campaign. Members of his staff were convicted of breaking into the offices of the Democratic National Party in the Watergate building in Washington, D.C. They were said to have planted electronic surveillance devices in order to obtain information. The president denied any connection with the alleged break-in. Later it became apparent that some of Nixon's aides had been involved. Nixon eventually resigned.

1. Based on information in the passage, what does the word *resignation* mean?

   A understanding   **B** departure   **C** notification

2. Based on other words in the sentence, what does the word *controversy* mean?

   F disagreement   **G** explanation   **H** discussion

3. Based on other words in the passage, what does the word *convicted* mean?

   A found guilty   **B** found not guilty   **C** convinced

4. What does the word *devices* mean?

   F computers   **G** records   **H** machines

5. Using context clues, tell what the word *aides* means.

   A family members   **B** assistants   **C** generals

Practice

Read each passage. Then using context clues, write the word from the passage that matches the given meaning.

During the Renaissance of the 1400s in Italy, people with expertise in many fields were highly respected. The renowned painter Leonardo da Vinci was one such "Renaissance man." In his lifetime he studied constantly and was recognized as an artist, a sculptor, and a scientist, among other things. Da Vinci worked hard to develop his protean talents. He applied himself diligently to each project. More often than not, he succeeded in his goals. Such a multitude of skills in one person is virtually unheard of today.

1. almost entirely   _____

2. famous   _____

3. abundance   _____

4. persistently   _____

5. many and varied   _____

6. knowledge   _____

7. honored   _____

Several kinds of insects have evolved ways of outwitting crafty spiders. One species of fly, when entangled in a web, sprays the spider with a natural toxin and then dissolves the web with its saliva. There is also a kind of moth whose body contains substances poisonous to spiders.

8. poison   _____

9. materials   _____

10. developed   _____

Apply

Use context clues to find out the meanings of the underlined words. Write each definition on the line.

Varied forms of entertainment became available to a wide public in the 1920s. The mass-produced automobile provided much of the middle class with a mobility never before known. This new-found mobility allowed them to enjoy vacations in hitherto remote spots. Moviegoing became a favorite pastime. The advent of movies with soundtracks in the late 1920s made a visit to the cinema even more exciting. Broadcasting began in the United States in 1920, and by the end of the decade the radio was a common fixture in American and European homes.

1. mass-produced   _____

2. mobility   _____

3. hitherto   _____

4. pastime   _____

5. advent   _____

6. cinema   _____

7. fixture   _____

From the first civilizations to those of the late Middle Ages, the possession of a time-tracking device, such as a calendar or clock, was restricted almost exclusively to those of noble birth. Having a calendar to predict the onset of the seasons and to know when to plant crops bestowed power on its owner. For this reason, the secrets of devising an annual calendar were guarded.

8. restricted   _____

9. onset   _____

10. bestowed   _____

Modern architecture can be broadly defined as any building with bold, clean lines not based on a traditional style. The addition of new concepts and contemporary materials creates a uniquely modern form. A variety of schools of architecture has developed in the last 40 years, reflecting such considerations as climate, materials, energy, efficiency, and use of the structure.

11. traditional   _____

12. contemporary   _____

13. considerations   _____

Check Up

Read each passage. Then circle the answer for each question.

Time-release medication is designed to deliver medication over a 12-hour period. That delivery system has proven to be beneficial to patients because they do not need to remember to take additional doses. The release system is predicated on the effectiveness of tiny beads of medication in individual waxy coatings.

1. *Beneficial* means

   A tiring

   B helpful

   C worrisome

   D annoying

2. *Predicated* means

   F predicted

   G based upon

   H dissolved

   J nominated

Before rock and roll, crooners such as Frank Sinatra and Bing Crosby were popular with teenagers and adults. Crooners typically sang ballads—slow, romantic songs. Then, in 1954, Bill Haley and the Comets released two rock 'n' roll numbers that changed teenage music. Teenagers became intent on differentiating themselves from previous generations. Rock 'n' roll became a defiant symbol of youthful rebellion.

3. A *ballad* is

   A rock 'n' roll music

   B a folk song

   C a slow, sentimental song

   D a stanza

4. *Differentiating* means

   F dancing

   G defying all authority

   H being young

   J deliberately making yourself different

5. *Rebellion* means

   A a party

   B rock 'n' roll music

   C an adult group

   D opposition to authority

Read On As you read "Fiddler with a Smile," look for context clues to help you understand unfamiliar words. Then answer the questions.

Spelling Words

Spelling is a skill that you will need throughout your life. Lots of practice can help. So can learning some rules.

Forming Plurals: Words That End in *o*
When a word ends in a vowel followed by *o*, add *-s*.
When a word ends in a consonant followed by *o*, add *-s* or *-es*.

igloo	igloos
auto	autos
hero	heroes

Sounds of *f*
The letters *f*, *ph,* and *gh* often stand for the sound you hear at the beginning of the word *face*.

phone   laugh

Consonant Pairs: *ch* and *tch*
The letters ch and tch usually stand for the sound you hear in **ch**in and ba**tch**. Sometimes the letters ch stand for the *k* sound, as in **ch**aracter. The letters can also stand for the *sh* sound, as in **ch**ef.

chin	batch
character	chef

Follow the rules for forming plurals and write the plural of the word in the correct column. Use a dictionary if you need help

	Add *-s*	Add *-es*
1. solo	_____	_____
2. rodeo	_____	_____
3. radio	_____	_____
4. tomato	_____	_____
5. zero	_____	_____
6. kangaroo	_____	_____
7. potato	_____	_____
8. photo	_____	_____
9. torpedo	_____	_____
10. stereo	_____	_____

Practice

Add *f*, *ph*, or *gh* to make a word. Then use the word to complete the newspaper headline that follows.

1. _____one

   _____ Lines Down for Two Hours During Storm

2. cou_____

   New Strain of Flu Features _____

3. ne_____ew

   _____ of Senator Visits Cuba

4. _____amily

   _____ Farms Fade Away

5. enou_____

   "We've Had _____" Say Union Leaders

6. _____ather

   _____ of Victim Demands New Law

7. grie_____

   _____-Stricken Parents Ask for Help

8. lau_____ter

   _____ Is Good Medicine

9. _____ysics

   Award Given to _____ Teacher

10. gra_____

    _____ Shows Decline in Home Sales

Apply

Circle the *ch* or *tch* in each word in the box. Then write each word next to its definition.

latch	chief	chute	watch	character
mechanic	match	chorus	chimpanzee	chandelier
china	chimney	patch	satchel	chisel

1. leader   _____

2. to go well together   _____

3. door lock   _____

4. medium-sized ape   _____

5. inclined channel or passage   _____

6. skilled worker who repairs machines   _____

7. group of singers   _____

8. decorative hanging light   _____

9. person or animal in a book, movie, etc.   _____

10. to observe or view   _____

11. white ceramic material   _____

12. structure for venting gas or smoke   _____

13. piece put on to mend a hole   _____

14. tool with a sharp edge at one end   _____

15. small bag for carrying things   _____

Check Up

Circle the word that is spelled correctly.

1. Which word names a leader?

   A chief

   B cheef

   C cheif

   D chieph

2. Which word names musical instruments?

   F pianoes

   G pianos

   H pianoss

   J pianoess

3. Which word names a large mammal?

   A eleghant

   B eleffant

   C elefant

   D elephant

4. Which word names dome-shaped dwellings?

   F iglooes

   G igloos

   H iglooss

   J iglooess

5. Which word names people to admire?

   A heroess

   B heros

   C heroes

   D heross

6. Which word names a dairy food?

   F chees

   G chheese

   H ceese

   J cheese

7. Which word names the action of grabbing and holding on to something?

   A cach

   B catch

   C cattch

   D chatch

8. Which word names a reaction to a joke?

   F laugh

   G lauf

   H lauph

   J lagh

9. Which word names a slight mark on a table?

   A skratch

   B scrach

   C scratch

   D scatch

10. Which word names a mammal that swims?

    F dolpin

    G dolfin

    H dolphin

    J dolghin

More Spelling Words

Knowing how to spell correctly will help you to communicate better with other people. Some simple rules can help.

More Than One Suffix
Suffixes are groups of letters that are added to the end of a word.
Some words have more than one suffix.
thank + ful + ly   thank<u>fully</u>

Irregular Plurals
The plurals for some words are formed by changing the spellings of the singular form.
Sometimes the plural form is the same as the singular form.

one man   two men
one sheep   two sheep

Possessive Forms
To make a singular word show ownership,
add an apostrophe and -s ('s).   child   child<u>'s</u>

If a plural word ends in s, add
an apostrophe to show ownership.   dogs   dogs<u>'</u>

Add two suffixes to each word to make a new word. Use the suffixes in the box.

-ly	-ous	-ness	-al	-ful	-less	-ish

1. fool _____

2. thank _____

3. fear _____

4. insight _____

5. danger _____

6. care _____

7. thought _____

8. frantic _____

9. self _____

10. force _____

11. play _____

12. pain _____

13. law _____

14. comic _____

Practice

The plural form of each of these words is irregular. Write the plural form. Then use the plural form in a sentence.

1. tooth _____

_____

2. child _____

_____

3. mouse _____

_____

4. woman _____

_____

5. foot _____

_____

6. goose _____

_____

7. grandchild _____

_____

8. ox _____

_____

9. man _____

_____

10. fish _____

_____

Apply

Write the possessive form of the word in parentheses to complete each sentence.

1. Mary Wollstonecraft was a British leader in the movement for (women)

    _____ rights.

2. (Wollstonecraft) _____ book was titled *Vindication of the Rights of Women*.

3. The (book) _____ impact was a surprise to many people.

4. The (author) _____ views were considered very radical.

5. Her (followers) _____ reactions changed the roles of women.

6. Susan B. (Anthony) _____ work also influenced others.

7. (Susan) _____ father encouraged her to get involved in reform movements.

8. At the time, women were not even allowed to speak at (teachers) _____ union meetings, even though most teachers were women.

9. Susan was concerned about every (woman) _____ right to vote.

10. Inspired by Victoria (Woodhull) _____ speech to Congress, Anthony tried to vote in an election.

11. The (government) _____ response was to arrest Anthony, put her in jail, and fine her $100.

12. Anthony and other (suffragists) _____ struggles are recorded in their book *History of Woman Suffrage*.

13. The (Constitution) _____ 19th Amendment, added in 1920, finally gave women the right to vote.

Check Up

Circle the answer for each question.

1. Which word is spelled correctly?

   A carefuly

   B carefully

   C carfully

   D carefulley

2. Which word is the possessive form of *voters?*

   F voter's

   G voters's

   H voters'

   J voter'es

3. Which word is the plural form of *mouse?*

   A mice

   B mouses

   C mices

   D mouse's

4. Which word is spelled correctly?

   F lawlessnes

   G lawlessness

   H lawlesness

   J lawlesnees

5. Which word is the plural form of *tooth?*

   A teeths

   B tooths

   C toothes

   D teeth

6. Which word is the possessive form of *insect?*

   F insects

   G insect's

   H insects'

   J insects's

7. Which word is the possessive form of *women?*

   A women's

   B womens'

   C womens's

   D womens

8. Which word is spelled correctly?

   F foolisness

   G folishnes

   H foolishness

   J foolishnes

9. Which word is spelled correctly?

   A reasonebleness

   B reasonableness

   C reasonablenes

   D reasonablness

10. Which word is the possessive form of *professor?*

    F professors

    G professors's

    H professor's

    J professors'

Read On Read "The Woman Behind the Lens." Use what you know about spelling words to answer the questions.

Review

Synonyms

Words that have similar meanings are called **synonyms.**

Can you <u>locate</u> Portugal on the map?

A synonym for *locate* is *find*.

Antonyms

Words with opposite meanings are called **antonyms.**

The drum major <u>preceded</u> the band in the Memorial Day parade.

The best antonym for *preceded* is *led*.

Context Clues

You can use words or phrases in a paragraph to figure out the meaning of an unknown word.

The grizzly bear is one of the most dangerous animals in North America. It can run almost as fast as a horse, and it is very strong. In fact, it can crush a buffalo's head with a single <u>blow</u>.

In this context *blow* means *hit*.

Spelling Words

Plurals can be formed by adding *-s* and *-es*. When a word ends in a vowel followed by *o*, add *-s*. When a word ends in a consonant followed by *o*, add *-s* or *-es*.

patios   echoes

The letters *f*, *ph*, and *gh* often stand for the *f* sound.

fantastic   photo   cough

The letters *ch* can stand for different sounds.

church   chauffeur   chemical

Groups of letters added to the end of a word that change its meaning are called **suffixes.**

Some plurals are made by changing the spelling of the singular form, not by adding *-s* or *-es*. Sometimes the plural form is the same as the singular form.

men   deer

Assessment

Circle the answer that is a synonym for each underlined word.

1. The student acknowledged that he had not completed the assignment.
   A contradicted
   B admitted
   C answered
   D questioned

2. There was adequate food for everyone.
   F unsuitable
   G sufficient
   H correct
   J additional

3. The cost to repair the car was approximately $500.
   A exactly
   B roughly
   C similarly
   D close

4. The news story was slanted to make the candidate appear guilty of tax evasion.
   F biased
   G disinterested
   H written
   J memorized

5. The president will clarify his position on the nuclear arms treaty.
   A explain
   B announce
   C confuse
   D change

6. She was modest about winning.
   F proud
   G humble
   H flattered
   J conceited

Circle the answer that is an antonym for each underlined word.

7. She found joy within her family.
   A pleasure
   B misery
   C time
   D solitude

8. Sound conclusions cannot be based on haphazard experiments.
   F systematic
   G sloppy
   H scientific
   J casual

9. Quitting in anger is a rash action.
   A brave
   B foolish
   C understandable
   D careful

10. He made a resolution to exercise regularly.
    F conclusion
    G indecision
    H determination
    J idea

11. There was no excuse for the public official's scandalous behavior.
    A reputable
    B amusing
    C outrageous
    D curious

12. Luis showed genuine regret for his mistake.
    F candid
    G insincere
    H honest
    J flimsy

Choose the correct plural form for each underlined word.

13. an <u>embargo</u> on all foreign ships
    A embargos
    B embargoes
    C embargoies
    D embarges

14. a <u>tuba</u> in the orchestra
    F tubas
    G tubases
    H tubaes
    J tubbas

15. a <u>stereo</u> and two speakers
    A steroies
    B sterreos
    C stereoes
    D stereos

16. a <u>folio</u> number on each page
    F follios
    G folioes
    H folios
    J folioies

Complete each phrase with the word that is spelled correctly.

17. a _____ piece of sandpaper
    A rough
    B rugh
    C rouf
    D ruff

18. _____ a dance for the ballet
    F choreograph
    G coreograph
    H koreograph
    J ckoreograph

19. _____ a message in Morse Code
    A telegraph
    B telegraf
    C telegraff
    D telegrafh

20. an _____ part in planning the project
    F active
    G akteve
    H acktive
    J actev

21. _____ blended in with its surroundings
    A cameleon
    B clameleon
    C kameleon
    D chameleon

22. dried the car with a _____
    F shammee
    G shamois
    H chamois
    J chammy

23. a _____ about snakes
    A fobia
    B phobia
    C fobeah
    D phobea

24. an _____ on defensive driving
    F emfasis
    G emphasys
    H emghasis
    J emphasis

Assessment continued

Read each paragraph and circle the answer for each question.

Mariners caught by storms at sea developed a simple technique years ago to calm the fury of the waves. They carried a can or a bag filled with oil. When a storm threatened their vessel, they pricked holes in the container and allowed the oil to <u>seep</u> slowly into the sea. The oil reduced the power of the waves and gave the ship temporary protection.

25. What is a mariner?

    A a scientist

    B a sailor

    C a geologist

    D a fisherman

26. A synonym for the word *seep* is

    F leak

    G rush

    H smell

    J cover

Bolas spiders, at some time in the distant past, gave up the <u>practice</u> of spinning webs. They developed a <u>unique</u> method of hunting, one that is theirs alone. They make a small blob of sticky silk at the end of a short line and then sling it at any moth or other insect that comes within range. Because this action resembles the hunting technique of South American gauchos (cowboys), the spider has been named after the gauchos' famous weapon, the bolas. The bolas is made of several stones or metallic balls, each fastened to a cord with the cords tied together. When the bolas is thrown at a fleeing animal, the cords wrap around its legs and bring the creature to the ground.

27. In this paragraph *practice* means

    A exercise session

    B usual habit

    C great effort

    D useless repetition

28. The word *unique* means

    F common

    G popular

    H being the only one

    J interesting

Similes and Metaphors

Sometimes an author uses a simile or metaphor to describe something or someone. A **simile** is a figure of speech in which one object or idea is compared with another in order to suggest that they are alike. A simile always uses the word *like* or *as* in its description:

       hands as cold as ice   waddled like a duck

A **metaphor** also compares one thing with another. A metaphor does not use like or as. Instead, it says that one thing *is* something else.

    The moon was a large smooth pearl hanging in the night sky.

Complete each of these similes.

1. as hungry as _____

2. as quiet as _____

3. as soft as _____

4. as blue as _____

5. worked like _____

6. sparkled like _____

7. eyes like _____

8. cheeks like _____

Write a metaphor to describe each of the following.

9. the sun

_____

10. the wind

_____

11. snow

_____

Onomatopoeia

When using details to describe, an author might use **onomatopoetic** words—words that sound like the actual sounds they name.

> The <u>clang</u> of the old school bell echoed across the playground.

A person reading this kind of word can understand its meaning because the word clearly imitates a sound, even if it is not an established English word found in a dictionary.

> The stone fell <u>kerplunk</u> into the pond.

Write a sentence using each of these onomatopoetic words.

1. buzz

_____

_____

2. slurp

_____

_____

3. hiss

_____

_____

4. clatter

_____

_____

5. rustle

_____

_____

6. squeal

_____

_____

Identifying Details

Details are important because they support the main idea of a paragraph or passage. Details are used in many different ways.

Sometimes writers use details to **define a topic.** The details explain more about the topic. They expand the definition.

> In law, a court is the official body charged with administering justice. The term *court* is also applied to the judge or judges who fill the office and the courtroom itself. Courts develop in a society when legal issues are no longer private. However, courts are unnecessary when the state decides all legal matters without debate.

The first sentence is the main idea of the paragraph. The other sentences are details that help to define *court*.

Read this paragraph. Then circle the answer to each question.

> The Pygmies of central Africa are traditionally forest dwellers. The men in the tribe are hunters. The women fish, gather wild vegetables, and cook. The children carry the water. Pygmies make bows and arrows, spears, and baskets, and they build thatched huts. They eat both raw and cooked meat. They wear a short apron of bark or leaves, and they may paint their bodies in geometric designs.

1. The main purpose of the details in this passage is to

   A explain a topic

   B give reasons to support an argument

   C give a sequence of events

2. Male Pygmies of central Africa are

   F warriors   **G** hunters   **H** farmers

3. The Pygmies wear garments made of

   A animal skins   **B** cotton and wood   **C** bark and leaves

4. Underline the sentence that contains the most important details for a reader interested in the role of women in Pygmy society.

Practice

Some details give **examples**, usually as part of an explanation. They can also help a reader understand a broad topic.

Read the passage. Then write the answer to each question.

> Many Indian tribes lived in California. In northwest California, along the coast and around the Klamath River, lived the Yurok, Karok, and Hupa Indians. These were the great salmon fishermen. They built redwood houses. They carved their great river boats with stone. They shaped elk antlers into beautiful spoons. In another area, around the Channel Islands from Santa Barbara south to Los Angeles, lived the Chumash and Gabrielino Indians. They were artistic carvers of soapstone objects. They built massive plank canoes. They looked to the sea for much of their food.

1. Where did the salmon fishermen live?

_____

2. In what type of house did the Yurok, Karok, and Hupa Indians live?

_____

3. What did they use to carve their boats?

_____

4. From what material did they make spoons?

_____

5. Where did the Chumash and Gabrielino Indians live?

_____

6. What material did they carve?

_____

7. What did they build for transportation?

_____

8. Where did they find much of their food?

_____

Apply

Some details give **reasons** that support an argument or opinion. In an argument, the author gives details that are most important from the author's point of view.

Read the passage. Then answer the questions.

Last May, the legislature hiked its base pay 100 percent, making these politicians the second highest paid in the country! Has state government improved 100 percent since then? Particularly outrageous was the "emergency statement" attached to this legislation. The "emergency" allowed legislators to collect a salary increase not only immediately, but also retroactively for several months. Worst of all, future salary hikes are tied to state workers' salary increases. The legislature will receive automatic pay raises without the requirement of a roll-call vote. Please vote NO on Referendum Question 1.

1. Underline the sentence that gives the main topic of the paragraph.

2. What did the legislature vote for in May?

   _____

3. What detail does the author consider most important? What words signal its importance?

   _____

   _____

4. What did the "emergency statement" do?

   _____

   _____

5. How will the legislature now receive pay raises?

   _____

   _____

6. What does the author want the reader to do?

   _____

Check Up

Read the passage. Then circle the answer for each question.

Leadership in a community usually rests in the hands of various types of people. One is the natural leader. This type has personal magnetism and inspires others to follow. A second is the helpful leader. This is the person who organizes and gets practical things done. A third type of leader is the temporary political leader. This is the person who gets out a large neighborhood vote. Finally, there are the professional and business leaders. They have education and respect but feel somewhat apart from most people. In some form or other, these types of leaders may be found in most American communities.

1. The main purpose of the details in the passage is to
   A define a topic and give examples
   B give reasons to support an argument
   C set a tone or mood
   D reveal character

2. Leadership in American communities is exercised by
   F various types of people
   G the business community
   H temporary political leaders
   J an inspiring natural leader

3. The type of leader who gets practical things done is called the
   A natural leader
   B helpful leader
   C temporary political leader
   D professional or business leader

4. The natural leader shows
   F education
   G business sense
   H financial success
   J personal magnetism

5. The leader who organizes a neighborhood to register to vote is probably a
   A natural leader
   B helpful leader
   C temporary political leader
   D professional leader

Recognizing Details

Details support a main idea. Details can have many different purposes.

Some details explain a fact or idea. They use **logical reasoning** to make the fact or idea clear.

Read the passage. Then answer each question.

Not too long ago, some music critics were saying that jazz had lost out to rock and would never be an important part of popular music again. However, with the advent of the compact disc, a new interest in jazz has arisen. The fine quality of sound on compact discs encourages close listening. This factor has increased sales of jazz and classical recordings on CDs. In addition, surveys have shown that unlike previous generations, more of the current generation of twenty somethings is expanding its musical interests, listening to and buying music they didn't listen to as teenagers. They are now buying both the latest recordings and classics by jazz greats of the past.

1. According to this selection,
   A most people prefer classical music to jazz
   B jazz is lost forever
   C the compact disc may have helped encourage interest in jazz

2. Why do people listen closely to music recorded on compact discs?
   F CDs are more expensive than other recordings.
   G The quality of sound on CDs is very good.
   H Sales of these discs have increased.

3. What have surveys about musical preferences shown?
   A Today young people are listening to many different types of music.
   B Jazz has lost out to rock and roll.
   C Jazz compact discs have fine quality of sound.

4. How is the current generation of twenty somethings different from other generations?
   F They buy only the music they listened to as teenagers.
   G They buy music of all different kinds.
   H They buy only rock music.

5. Underline the sentence that contains the most important detail for someone who wants to know what kinds of recordings the new jazz audience is buying.

Practice

Some details reveal **character**. Usually you will find these details in a work of fiction or a biography.

Read the following passage. Then answer the questions.

It was Miss Murdstone who arrived. A gloomy-looking lady she was. She was dark, like her brother, whom she greatly resembled in face and voice. She had very heavy eyebrows, nearly meeting over her large nose. She brought with her two hard black boxes, with her initials on the lids in hard brass nails. When she paid the coachman, she took her money out of a hard steel purse. She kept the purse in a very jail of bag which hung upon her arm by a heavy chain. It shut up like a bite. I had never seen such a metallic lady as Miss Murdstone was.

1. What details help you picture Miss Murdstone?

   _____

   _____

2. Do you find Miss Murdstone appealing? Why or why not?

   _____

   _____

3. What detail provokes the most powerful image to you?

   _____

   _____

4. Think about a person you know. List details about the person. You might describe what the person looks like. Or, you might tell about what the person says, does, or thinks. Then write a short paragraph about the person using your details to describe him or her. Use details that will help the reader understand what the person is like.

   _____

   _____

   _____

   _____

   _____

   _____

Apply

A **fact** is one kind of detail. Facts give information that can be proved about a topic. An **opinion** is what a person thinks or believes. It cannot be proved.

Suppose you have received a request from *Teen World* magazine. They want you to write a description of your school. Use facts and details to complete the questionnaire.

1. Name of school: _____

2. Location: _____

3. How many students attend? _____

4. What do you like best about your school? _____

   _____

   _____

5. Do the teachers at your school do a good job? Tell why or why not.

   _____

   _____

6. Which questions above focus on facts? _____

7. Which questions focus on opinions? _____

Read these statements. Write *fact* or *opinion* to describe each one.

8. The Emerson School is located in Massachusetts. _____

9. The Emerson School is the most respected school in the state. _____

10. There are more than 500 students at the Emerson School. _____

11. All students would like to attend the Emerson School. _____

12. Ms. Alison is the French teacher at the Emerson School. _____

Check Up

Read the passage. Then circle the answer for each question.

Many horse lovers agree that the Kentucky Derby is the most difficult race for horses. That is certainly true, but the race is also potentially dangerous for the horses that run it. The entries have barely turned three years old. Riva Ridge, a winner of the race, was technically even younger. At a time when thoroughbreds are still growing fast and their bones are still soft, they are asked to run a mile and a quarter against fierce competition. They carry 126 pounds for colts or 121 pounds for fillies. The field is usually large, adding more challenges.

1. The main function of the details in this passage is to

   A   give reasons to support an opinion

   B   set a tone or mood

   C   define a topic

   D   give examples

2. The author points out that most of the horses in the Kentucky Derby

   F   have excellent training

   G   are about three years old

   H   are colts

   J   win many races

3. Riva Ridge is mentioned as an example of a

   A   million-dollar money winner

   B   horse injured in a major race

   C   young winner of the Kentucky Derby

   D   late entry in a crowded field

4. The main reason the race can be dangerous is that

   F   the horses are still growing and their bones are soft

   G   the field is always crowded

   H   the horses carry 126 pounds

   J   the race is difficult to train for

5. Colts carry

   A   121 pounds

   B   130 pounds

   C   150 pounds

   D   126 pounds

Read On   Read "Setting the Sky on Fire," and look for main ideas and details. Then answer the questions.

Identifying Sequence

Sequence is the order in which events happen. Understanding sequence is important in both stories and factual articles. One way writers convey sequence is by using words that indicate order, such as *first*, *next*, *then*, *this time*, *before*, *after*, and *finally*.

Read each passage. Write the steps of the process each one describes in order. Then underline the words in each passage that helped you recognize the sequence.

The people of ancient Egypt made mummies because they believed that the dead lived on in the next world. They wanted to preserve the bodies of the dead. It took 70 days to prepare a body. First, the brain and other organs were removed. Next, the stomach was filled with linen pads. Then the body was placed in what we call soda ash until it was dried out. It was finally wrapped in many layers of linen strips and placed in a coffin. Some mummies have been preserved for thousands of years.

1. _____

2. _____

3. _____

4. _____

Hailstones begin as water droplets in clouds. First, water droplets collide with ice pellets and freeze. Then more and more droplets hit the hailstones, adding new layers of ice. The hailstones get bigger and heavier. Finally, they get so big and heavy that they fall to the ground.

5. _____

6. _____

7. _____

8. _____

Practice

Sequence is important when reading and following instructions.

Read the passages. Write the sequence of steps, using words that show order.

> Before you begin to saddle a horse, brush his back lightly to remove any dust, straw, or other source of irritation. Position the saddle pad. Approach your horse from his left side, and gently lay the saddle a few inches in front of the withers. Lightly shake the saddle in place. Buckle the girth, starting with the rear billet.

1. First, _____

2. Next, _____

3. Then _____

4. _____

5. Finally, _____

> You can do the following experiment to observe the properties of water. Cut a coffee filter into a long, narrow strip. Use a water-based marker and draw a line one inch from one end of the strip. Hold the marked tip of the strip in a shallow bowl of water. What happens when the water passes through the ink?

6. _____

7. _____

8. _____

> There is a trick to making a good omelet. Make sure your skillet is hot enough. After you pour in the eggs, slide the skillet back and forth rapidly over the heat. Spread the eggs over the bottom of the skillet and let them cook for a few seconds. Tilt the skillet and run a fork under the edge of the omelet to loosen it. Fold the portion of the omelet nearest to you just to the center and turn the omelet onto a warm plate.

9. _____

10. _____

11. _____

12. _____

13. _____

Apply

Sometimes you will need to use **clue words** and **dates** to determine the order of events.

Read the passage. Circle the answers to the questions.

The practice of dentistry has seen many changes throughout the centuries. In ancient Greece, medical doctors treated tooth problems. The first gold dental bridges date from before 600 B.C. In the Middle Ages, barbers served as both doctors and dentists. It wasn't until 1840 that the first professional dental school was founded in Baltimore, Maryland. Dentists introduced anesthesia for extractions and other operations in 1844. Since then, there have been many advances in dental techniques.

1. When were the first gold dental bridges used?

   A before 600 B.C.

   B 1840

   C 1844

2. Who did the work of dentists in the Middle Ages?

   F teachers

   G doctors

   H barbers

3. When was the first professional dental school founded?

   A before 600 B.C.

   B 1844

   C 1840

4. Which of the following came first?

   F opening of the first dental school

   G use of anesthesia

   H first gold dental bridges

5. Underline words in the passage that helped you understand sequence.

Check Up

The events from the following passage are listed in incorrect order below it. Read the passage. Then write the events in the correct order.

On Thursday, December 1, 1955, an African-American woman named Rosa Parks was asked to give up her seat on a bus to a white man and move to the back of a Montgomery, Alabama, bus. She quietly refused and was subsequently arrested. Her arrest began a 381-day bus boycott that helped launch the civil rights movement in the United States and the career of the civil rights leader Martin Luther King, Jr. Both Rosa Parks's arrest and the bus boycott became vehicles for drawing attention to the rights of African Americans. After Rosa Parks was convicted, her case was appealed to the United States Supreme Court, which ruled that discrimination on buses was a violation of federal law. The bus boycott was also a success, for eventually the bus company went bankrupt without its African-American passengers. The simple protest of one woman helped ignite the battle for equal rights.

Rosa Parks was arrested.
Rosa Parks's case was appealed to the Supreme Court.
A 381-day bus boycott began.
Rosa Parks was asked to give up her seat on a bus to a white man.
Rosa Parks was convicted.
The Supreme Court ruled that discrimination on buses was a violation of federal law.

1. _____

_____

2. _____

_____

3. _____

_____

4. _____

_____

5. _____

_____

6. _____

_____

Recognizing Sequence

Sometimes a writer does not use clue words to indicate **sequence**. Instead, he or she simply presents details about events one after the other in the order they happen.

Read the following passage. Then follow the directions below.

The men were silent. They turned their eyes from the shore to the comber and waited. The boat slid up the incline, leaped at the furious top, bounced over it, and swung down the long back of the wave. Some water had been shipped and the cook bailed it out.

But the next wave crashed also. The tumbling, boiling flood of white water caught the boat and whirled it almost perpendicular. Water swarmed in from all sides. The correspondent had his hands on the gunwale at this time, and when the water entered at that place he swiftly withdrew his fingers, as if he objected to wetting them.

The little boat, drunken with the weight of water, reeled and snuggled deeper into the sea.

Number these events from the passage from 1 to 6 in the order they happened.

_____ The cook bailed water out of the boat.

_____ The boat was whirled almost perpendicular.

_____ The men turned their eyes away from the shore and waited.

_____ Water swarmed in from all sides.

_____ The boat began to sink.

_____ The correspondent pulled his hands away from the gunwale.

Practice

Sometimes a **timeline** is used to show sequence. A timeline is a representation that shows the order of events. It can be useful, especially when the events in a passage are not presented in order.

Read the passage. Write a brief description of an appropriate event for each date on the timeline.

Flowing between England and France, from the Atlantic Ocean to the North Sea, the English Channel is considered by many to be a swimmer's ultimate challenge. The channel's cold water and strong currents can make even crossing by boat dangerous. Nevertheless, in 1981, it was reported that 228 hardy persons had swum the channel. The first recorded swimmer was Englishman Matthew Webb, who swam the 21-mile strait in August 1875. The record for the fastest swim was set by American Penny Dean. In July 1978, she swam the 21 miles in only 7 hours and 40 minutes. It may help nonswimmers to know that in 1964 England and France agreed to build a tunnel under the channel for trains and cars.

Swimming the English Channel

<-->
1875	1964	1978	1981

Answer these questions.

1. Did Penny Dean swim the channel before or after Matthew Webb?

   _____

2. Was the tunnel under the channel planned before or after Penny Dean set her record?

   _____

Apply

Following the sequence in instructions can be critical. Instructions written as a series of steps are often easier to read and follow than those written in paragraphs.

Read the explanation. Write the instructions as a series of steps.

> The Heimlich maneuver is one way to assist someone who is choking. Every year, thousands by people are helped by those who know how to perform it. You need to practice the procedure and act quickly if you are in this situation.
>
> If someone is choking, begin by standing behind him or her. Wrap your arms around the person's waist. Then make a fist and lightly press it against the person's stomach. Place your fist midway between the navel and the rib cage. Next, grab your fist with your other hand. Press your fist in with an upward movement. Continue until the person stops choking.

Step 1: _____

Step 2: _____

Step 3: _____

Step 4: _____

Step 5: _____

Step 6: _____

Write the instructions in order for something you know how to do. Use steps and clear language.

Step 1: _____

Step 2: _____

Step 3: _____

Step 4: _____

Step 5: _____

Step 6: _____

Check Up

Read the following passage. Then answer each question.

Ever since the 13th century, there has been a London Bridge crossing the Thames River in London. However, it has not always been the same bridge. The first London Bridge, built in 1209, lasted 623 years. It saw the bubonic plague come and go, survived the Great London Fire, and suffered through stages of neglect and renovation. When repairing the bridge became impossible, a new bridge was built in 1832. That bridge did not last as long as the first one. It now stands in Lake Havasu City, Arizona. In 1967, the bridge was taken apart in London, shipped, and rebuilt in its new location.

Why did the second London Bridge only last 135 years? The 19th century bridge builders simply couldn't foresee the invention of the automobile and the need for several lanes for traffic. The newest London Bridge, opened in 1973, can handle many cars with its six traffic lanes.

1. When was the first London Bridge built?

   _____

2. How many years did the first bridge last?

   _____

3. When was the second London Bridge built?

   _____

4. Where is the second bridge today?

   _____

5. Why did the second bridge last only 135 years?

   _____

6. When did the third London Bridge open?

   _____

7. How many car lanes does it have?

   _____

8. Which came first—the invention of the automobile or the building of the second London Bridge?

   _____

9. Which came first—the building of the second London Bridge or the Great London Fire?

   _____

 **Read On**   Read "The Birth of the Modern Olympics." Then answer the questions about the sequence of events.

Identifying Stated Concepts

Sometimes the ideas in a passage are clearly stated. Sometimes you need to use other information to figure out the ideas. As you continue to read different kinds of writing, recognizing and **using stated concepts** will help you understand what you read.

Read the following passage. Then underline the answer for each question.

The Pony Express has been romanticized in tales about the early western United States, but it actually played a very practical role. It was begun in 1860 to carry mail between Missouri and California, using the fastest mode of communication available—a man on a horse. A route was a kind of relay race across the country, with relief stations about every 15 miles to give the rider a fresh horse and food and water. After three horses, the messenger handed his mail pouch to the next man in the relay, who continued the route. When the Pony Express had to compete with the telegraph, it became obsolete.

1. What was the purpose of the Pony Express?

   A   to provide a basis for romantic tales about the West

   B   to carry mail

   C   to begin a relay race

2. What did relief stations provide?

   F   mail bags

   G   telegraph messages

   H   food and water

3. About how many miles did a man ride before handing the mail pouch to the next rider?

   A   15 miles

   B   45 miles

   C   60 miles

4. When did the Pony Express stop being used?

   F   when the telegraph became popular

   G   when the relief stations closed

   H   when the telephone became popular

Practice

Read the paragraph. Then read each sentence below it. If the concept is *stated*, circle *stated*. If the concept is *not stated*, circle *not stated*.

In A.D. 79, the city of Pompeii in Italy was a resort for rich Romans. The city had been built next to a dead volcano—Mount Vesuvius. But the volcano was not really dead. It was just sleeping. One day it erupted. It threw hot ash and stone on the city and filled the air with poisonous gas. Pompeii was destroyed, buried under many feet of cinder and ash. Today scientists have uncovered the ruins of Pompeii. They have found the remains of 2,000 people, the shapes of their bodies preserved like shells by hardened ash. The scientists have also restored many of the temples and palaces. Tourists can now walk through the ancient streets of this once great but doomed city.

1. Pompeii was a city in Italy.

   stated   not stated

2. Pompeii was a place where rich Romans liked to go.

   stated   not stated

3. Mount Vesuvius was a volcano that had erupted around A.D. 50.

   stated   not stated

4. Pompeii was buried under cinder and ash.

   stated   not stated

5. The air was filled with poisonous gas from the volcano.

   stated   not stated

6. Hot lava flowed through the streets of Pompeii.

   stated   not stated

7. The remains of about 2,000 people were found.

   stated   not stated

8. The volcano eruption lasted for two days.

   stated   not stated

9. Many homes have been restored.

   stated   not stated

10. Today tourists can visit the remains of Pompeii.

    stated   not stated

Apply

Read each paragraph. Then write the number of the sentence with the stated concept that answers each question.

(1) The first superhighways were built in America long before explorers arrived. (2) A system of roadways was laid out in northwestern New Mexico more than eight centuries ago. (3) The roads were probably built by the Anasazi Indians, who also constructed a number of towns and an astronomical observatory. (4) But scientists have not been able to discover why the Anasazi built the roads, for they used neither vehicles nor pack animals. (5) Their culture seemed to have had no need of roads, yet they built a system of highways that are more than 40 miles long. (6) The Anasazi abandoned the highways when they were less than a century old. (7) The reasons for the building of these ancient roads remain unknown.

1. When were the first roadways in New Mexico laid out? _____

2. What types of structures did the Anasazi Indians build? _____

3. What mystery surrounds the roads? _____

4. When did the Anasazi Indians abandon the highways? _____

5. How long was the system of highways? _____

(1) Dr. James Jensen is known in archaeological circles as "Dinosaur Jim." (2) He is responsible for the discovery of many specimens of fossilized dinosaurs. (3) In 1972 he discovered a shoulder blade and several ribs from a creature he estimates was 90 feet long and weighed 70 tons. (4) He dubbed the dinosaur "Supersaurus."

6. What is Dr. Jensen's nickname? _____

7. What did he discover in 1972? _____

8. What was the discovered dinosaur's nickname? _____

Check Up

Read the selection. Then circle the answer to each question.

Today people can walk into a restaurant at just about any hour of the day and order just about whatever they want. But it hasn't always been that way. Until the late 18th century, restaurants would serve a meal at a set time. Customers would have to arrive at that time and eat whatever meal the manager had decided to serve that day. This system was changed in Paris, where fine cuisine is considered a form of art. As the story goes, in 1765 a restaurant called Boulanger's was the first to give its customers a menu with a choice of several meals. Fifty years later, there were 120 restaurants in Paris using menus.

1. What was different about restaurants before the 18th century?

   A They served one meal at a set time.

   B They opened at 4:00.

   C The meals were free.

   D not stated in selection

2. Where did the system change?

   F London

   G Paris

   H Los Angeles

   J not stated in selection

3. What unusual feature did Boulanger's offer its customers?

   A tablecloths

   B waitresses

   C menus

   D not stated in selection

4. What type of meal did Boulanger's offer?

   F soups

   G beef entrees

   H chicken and fish

   J not stated in selection

5. What change had happened by the early 1800s?

   A Boulanger's closed.

   B Fifty restaurants in Paris offered menus.

   C The number of restaurants offering menus in Paris had risen to 120.

   D not stated in selection

6. Who first suggested creating a menu of meal choices?

   F a customer

   G a manager

   H a restaurant owner

   J not stated in selection

Understanding Stated Concepts

When you read factual material, it is important to understand and remember what you read. Look for main ideas and supporting facts. Be ready to make connections between **stated concepts** and information you have learned elsewhere to understand concepts that are not stated.

Read the passage. Then answer the questions.

Scientists are still not sure why dinosaurs vanished from the earth. One theory is that a change in climate caused their disappearance. Before the great beasts became extinct over 60 million years ago, the earth was a tropical planet. It was much warmer and wetter than it is today. Scientists think that a major mountain-building cycle may have raised the lowlands, destroying the tropical vegetation as temperatures dropped. The plant-eating dinosaurs would then have followed the plants to extinction. In turn, this development would have left the meat-eating dinosaurs without their food source—the plant-eating dinosaurs.

1. How did the earth's climate of 60 million years ago differ from its climate today?

_____

_____

2. According to the theory described in the article, what might have been the effect of the mountain-building cycle on the lowlands?

_____

_____

3. Why did the temperatures fall in the lowlands?

_____

4. If the tropical vegetation died out, what might happen to the plant-eating dinosaurs?

_____

5. What might have happened to the meat-eating dinosaurs?

_____

Practice

Read the passage. Write the main idea and four important facts.

The Red Cross was established more than 120 years ago in Switzerland. The organization was started by Jean-Henri Durant, a Swiss doctor. Durant had been appalled by the horror and bloodshed of the Italian War of Independence in 1859. After the battle of Solferino, an especially violent battle, he wrote a book that deeply affected his readers. The reputation he gained from writing the book enabled Durant to organize the first Red Cross Conference in 1864 in Switzerland. There, 26 nations agreed to respect prisoners and wounded soldiers, to regard hospitals as neutral, and to protect medical personnel. The duties of the Red Cross later expanded to include peacetime work.

Main Idea: _____

Facts: _____

_____

_____

_____

_____

_____

Read the passage. Write the main idea and two important facts.

In recorded history, the earthquake stands out as one of the most destructive forces. The worst single quake occurred in 1556 in Shensi Province, China. That disaster took the lives of 830,000 people. Another severe quake struck in the Kwanto Plain in Japan, doing billions of dollars worth of damage. It leveled 570,000 dwellings in Tokyo and Yokohama.

Main Idea: _____

Facts: _____

_____

_____

_____

Apply

Newspaper stories and magazine articles provide facts and information. Many of these stories focus on the five Ws—*Who, What, Where, When,* and *Why.*

Read the newspaper story. List the five Ws.

One Man Makes a Difference

Chad Pregracke from Quincy, Illinois, is a man with a mission—to clean up the muddy Mississippi. The inventory of junk that he has hauled up includes refrigerators, jugs of pesticide, motorcycles, propane tanks, and jacuzzis. He has converted an old houseboat into his home, and every morning he and his assistants continue to search the river for junk.

"When I started out, a lot of people thought I was nuts. But in America, it's still possible to do something like this," Pregracke said. When he began his work in 1997, without outside funding, he alone removed 45,000 pounds of junk.

Pregracke has big plans—he wants to clean up other major rivers in America. Be on the lookout in your hometown!

Who: _____

What: _____

Where: _____

When: _____

Why: _____

Choose a short article from a local newspaper. List the five Ws.

Who: _____

What: _____

Where: _____

When: _____

Why: _____

Check Up

Read the selection. Then circle the answer for each question.

The seal is a mammal that is in danger of becoming extinct. Its fate has long been an issue of political and social debate. After the United States purchased Alaska in 1867, it claimed control of the seal fisheries in the Bering Sea. But because of a territorial limit that had been in effect since 1793, the jurisdiction of the United States extended only three miles out to sea. English and Canadian seal hunters continued to prey on the seals outside the three-mile limit, and the controversy began. Despite the protests of conservationists, seals were slaughtered in numbers large enough to threaten their existence. Efforts of environmental groups have given the seals a temporary lease on life, but the battle is not over. The animals are still being hunted for their pelts.

1. What is the main idea of the passage?
   - **A** Environmental groups are helping seals.
   - **B** Seals are in danger of becoming extinct.
   - **C** The United States purchased Alaska.
   - **D** Seal hunters continue to prey on seals.

2. When did the United States purchase Alaska?
   - **F** 1793
   - **G** 1867
   - **H** 1899
   - **J** not stated

3. The three-mile limit extends
   - **A** into the air
   - **B** inland in from the coast
   - **C** down into the ground
   - **D** out into the sea

4. The word *extinct* means
   - **F** popular and common
   - **G** existent without limits
   - **H** no longer living anywhere
   - **J** available everywhere

5. Hunters slaughter seals for their
   - **A** bones
   - **B** teeth
   - **C** tails
   - **D** pelts

 **Read On** Read "Habitat for Humanity." Use stated concepts in the article to answer the questions.

Review

Details

Details give information about the **main idea** of a paragraph. Details explain a topic more completely.

Michel de Notredame, known today as Nostradamus, lived in the 16th century. Nostradamus, a French astrologer and physician, seems to have possessed extraordinary powers of prediction. In a book called *Centuries*, he predicted several important events that would later take place, such as the rise of a dictator dictator in Germany in the 1930s. He also predicted the French Revolution, the career of a man very much like Napoleon, and the dates of many royal births and deaths. He gained his greatest renown in Europe when he predicted the futures of the children of Catherine de' Medici, who was queen consort to Henry II of France. Because of Nostradamus's cryptic writing style, his predictions are subject to interpretation and debate. His supporters defend predictions that others cite as being incorrect by pointing out that they could still come true.

Main idea: Nostradamus possessed extraordinary powers of prediction.
Details are underlined in the paragraph.

Sequence

The **sequence** of events tells the order in which events occur. Words that show order include *first*, *next*, *then*, *this time*, *before*, *after*, and *finally*.

Stated Concepts

Sometimes the ideas in a passage are clearly stated. Sometimes you need to use other information and make connections to understand a passage.

Making a usable invisible ink sounds like a child's science project, but an invisible ink was used by adult soldiers as recently as World War II. Fighting on the plains of Palestine, a contingent of English troops was forced to barricade itself in a fort. But although surrounded and vigilantly watched by their enemies, the soldiers managed to send brief letters to their compatriots. The letters looked like simple blank pieces of paper, but each sheet was covered with words written in rice-water instead of ink. When the paper was washed with iodine, the words appeared in bright blue. Iodine turns starch a blue or violet color.

Stated Concept: Soldiers used invisible ink during World War II.
Unstated Concept: Invisible ink had been used previously because soldiers who received the letters knew how to make the writing visible.

Assessment

Read the passages. Then circle the answers to each question.

The anaconda is feared as one of the most dangerous nonvenomous snakes. It kills in a manner similar to that of a boa constrictor, though anacondas are larger (some snakes 30 feet long have been reported). Anacondas inhabit the lush swamps and rivers of South America, where they proliferate, the female bearing as many as 75 young in each litter. With its immensely strong musculature and wide jaws, an anaconda can capture an animal as large as a pig, which it will squeeze until the animal stops breathing. The anaconda's squeezing power is so renowned that during the American Civil War, a Union Army plan that called for the blockade and strangulation of the South was called the Anaconda Plan.

Acupuncture originated in China more than 2,500 years ago. Acupuncture is the practice of inserting brass-handled needles into certain areas of the body to relieve pain or cure illness. The method, which is painless, is based on the idea that illness is caused by an imbalance of the body's forces. It is believed that the insertion of the needles causes the body to redirect those forces. Today, Chinese acupuncturists employ ancient charts that show where the needles are to be inserted. Even modern practitioners are not exactly sure how the technique works, but they recognize that inserting a needle in one place causes a specific reaction in another. Acupuncture is practiced widely in Asia and Europe and is gaining popularity and respect in the United States.

1. The anaconda kills by
   A poisoning
   B strangulation
   C injecting venom
   D biting

2. The Anaconda Plan was named after a
   F Civil War general
   G famous South American snake
   H boa constrictor
   J blockade around a South American river

3. It is believed that acupuncture needles redirect
   A muscle tissue
   B illness
   C body forces
   D reactions

4. The western medical world has long been resistant to acupuncture, but as more studies of the practice have been made, acceptance has
   F increased
   G declined
   H stayed the same
   J not stated

5. Where did acupuncture originate?
   A in Europe
   B no one knows
   C in China
   D in the United States

Summer is the time for picnics in the park, vacations, and sunny days at the beach. Unfortunately it is also the season of heat-related illnesses. Minor ailments include headache and nausea, while a more serious illness caused by too much heat is heatstroke. Evidence shows that heatstroke is caused by the failure of the body to cool itself off by sweating. This condition can happen when a person works or exercises for a prolonged period in hot temperatures, causing the body's heat-regulating mechanisms to become too fatigued to produce sweat. Without the evaporation of sweat to cool it, the body builds up too much heat. People with heat stress, which is a mild version of heatstroke, can find relief by resting in a cool place and drinking liquids. Heatstroke, however, can cause loss of consciousness and, in extreme cases, death.

6. Heat stress is a mild version of

   F   the flu

   G   evaporation

   H   sweating

   J   heatstroke

7. Should heatstroke occur, the afflicted person may be packed in ice

   A   to bring the body temperature up

   B   to bring the body temperature down

   C   to stop the person from sweating

   D   to make the person drowsy

For several decades in the 16th century, Spain was perhaps the most powerful country in the world. The days of Spain's glory began in 1492, when King Ferdinand and Queen Isabella sponsored Christopher Columbus's voyage. After Columbus stumbled upon the Americas, Spanish explorers made huge claims of land for their country. Spain eventually controlled all of South America except for Portuguese Brazil. It also claimed Mexico and the southwestern United States, all of Central America, and some islands. Spain used riches found in the New World to increase its naval power. During the early 1500s, Spain also claimed lands in North America and Italy and all of the Philippines. Spain inherited the Netherlands in 1506 and by 1590 had conquered Portugal, parts of France, and more of Italy. Until the failure of the Spanish Armada to conquer England in 1588, Spain was called the "mistress of the world and the queen of the ocean."

8. In the 16th century, the Spanish navy was funded by

   F   riches from the Americas

   G   Christopher Columbus

   H   tributes from Portugal and Brazil

   J   King Ferdinand and Queen Isabella

9. What was the New World?

   A   North America and South America

   B   the Philippines

   C   Portugal and Mexico

   D   France and Italy

10. How did Christopher Columbus happen to "stumble" upon the Americas?

   F   He got lost while trying to reach the Indies.

   G   A hurricane blew him off course.

   H   He relied on an out-of-date map.

   J   not stated

On September 22, 1862, five days after a Union victory at the Battle of Antietam, President Abraham Lincoln issued a warning. He said that if the rebelling states did not return to the Union by January 1, 1863, he would declare their slaves to be free. The South rejected Lincoln's ultimatum. After time ran out in January and Lincoln signed the Emancipation Proclamation, there remained many Americans who resented his freeing the slaves. Some of them let their wrath be known, even in the White House itself. In fact, an ugly occurrence took place at Lincoln's inaugural ball in 1865. The President had invited his friend Frederick Douglass, a former slave famous for his writings and lectures on slavery, to the celebration. Although Douglass was the President's guest, no one would let the black man enter, not even the police who were guarding the White House. Douglass finally charged through the mob barring his way and managed to attract Lincoln's attention. Seeing how his guest was treated, the President walked away from his other friends and escorted Douglass in by the hand.

11. People at the ball didn't want Frederick Douglass there because he was

   A   an enemy of Lincoln

   B   a black man and a former slave

   C   not invited

   D   a secessionist

12. When did President Lincoln sign the Emancipation Proclamation?

   F   before September 22, 1862

   G   after January 1, 1863

   H   before January 1, 1863

   J   after 1865

Homographs

A dictionary contains thousands of words. Dictionary information is divided into sections called entries. Entry words are always in dark print and arranged on the left side of the columns on dictionary pages. An entry tells about each word—its spelling, pronunciation, meaning, part of speech, and history. Some words called homographs have more than one entry. A **homograph** is a word that is spelled the same as another word but has a different origin and meaning.

arm[1] *(ärm) n.* **1** upper limb of the human body, esp. the part between the shoulder and the wrist **2** forelimb of an vertebrate animal **3** something used to support or cover the human arm: *the arm of a chair* **4** anything branching out from a larger body: *an arm of government* [Old English *earm* upper limb of the human body]

arm[2] *(ärm) n.* **1** weapon, esp. a firearm **2** combat branch of the armed forces —*v.t.* **1** to provide with or as with weapons or tools: *Arm the people* **2** to provide with something that protects or strengthens; fortify: *The porcupine is armed with quills* [Old French *armer* to furnish, from Latin *armoire*, from *arma* weapons]

Use a dictionary to look up these homographs. Write the different meanings below.

1. rare[1] _____

    rare[2] _____

2. cape[1] _____

    cape[2] _____

3. keen[1] _____

    keen[2] _____

4. box[1] _____

    box[2] _____

    box[3] _____

Using an Almanac

An **almanac** is a book, usually published once a year, that contains many kinds of information. An almanac usually contains a calendar, important dates and events, facts about governments, history, geography, and weather. A general index at the beginning of the book is arranged alphabetically by topic. Some almanacs also provide edge marks on the book that can be used as a quick thumb index.

Use an almanac to find the following information. First, list the index entry you would look under to find each fact. Then write the fact.

	Fact	Entry and Answer
1.	Where was the U.S. center of population in 1990?	
2.	How many Marines served in the Persian Gulf War?	
3.	What is the proper form of address for a United States ambassador?	
4.	What team won the national college football championship in 1998?	
5.	How can you find the circumference of a circle?	
6.	What is the average June temperature in Duluth, Minnesota?	
7.	What is the individual income tax rate in Illinois?	
8.	What year was the College of William and Mary founded?	
9.	What U.S. president's portrait is on a $50 bill?	
10.	Who won the decathlon at the 1996 Summer Olympics?	

Using Graphs

Graphs are used to show information and compare data. A **bar graph** uses bars and a grid. Often a bar graph will accompany a newspaper or magazine article.

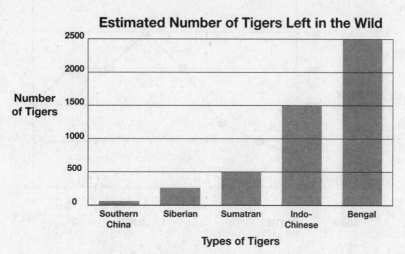

Estimated Number of Tigers Left in the Wild

Source: *Zoo Life Magazine*, 1996

Use the graph to answer the questions.

1. What does the title of the graph explain?

   _____

2. Which type of tiger has the greatest number left in the wild?

   _____

3. Which type of tiger has the least number left in the wild?

   _____

4. Which type of tiger has about twice the number left in the wild as the Siberian tiger?

   _____

5. About how many more Bengal tigers than Indo-Chinese tigers are left?

   _____

Practice

A **line graph** can be used to show changes that happen over time.

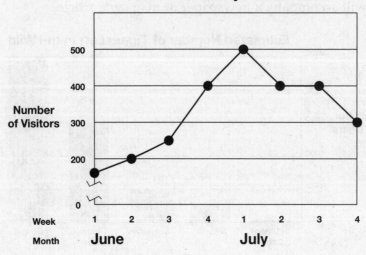

Visitors at Galaxy Planetarium

Use the graph to answer the questions.

1. Which month and week had the greatest number of visitors?

   _____

2. Which month and week had the least number of visitors?

   _____

3. Which weeks had about the same number of visitors?

   _____

4. Which week had 250 visitors?

   _____

5. What can you tell about the numbers of visitors by looking at the graph? Describe the pattern.

   _____

Apply

A **circle graph** is used to show data as parts related to a whole. Each part is given a percentage. All of the percentages added together should equal 100 percent.

Materials in U.S. Landfills

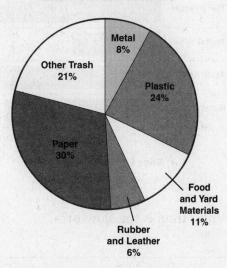

Source: *World Almanac for Kids, 1999*

Use the graph to answer the questions.

1. What percentage of materials in landfills is paper?

   _____

2. Is there more metal or plastic in landfills?

   _____

3. Which type of trash contributes 11 percent of materials to landfills?

   _____

4. Which two categories account for just over half of the materials in landfills?

   _____

5. Which category contributes the least material in landfills?

   _____

Check Up

Answer the questions about the bar graph and circle graph below..

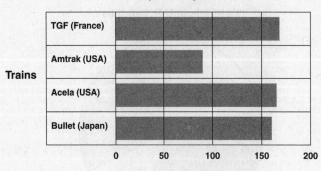

Top Train Speeds

Trains: TGF (France), Amtrak (USA), Acela (USA), Bullet (Japan)

Miles Per Hour (Top Speed)

Source: *Encyclopedia Britannica*

1. Which train is the fastest? Which train is the slowest?

   _____

2. Which three trains travel at about the same speed?

   _____

3. How much faster does the fastest train travel than the slowest train?

   _____

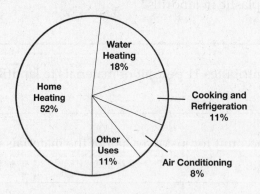

Household (U.S.) Use of Energy

Water Heating 18%

Home Heating 52%

Cooking and Refrigeration 11%

Other Uses 11%

Air Conditioning 8%

Source: *Scholastic Kids' Almanac*

4. Write the order of the uses of energy from least to greatest.

   _____

5. Which two categories account for the same amount of use?

   _____

Reading Maps

A map is a visual representation of an area or location. There are many different kinds of maps. A **physical map** shows features of an area, such as mountains, jungles, grasslands, and deserts.

This map of Africa shows the type of land and the plants that grow there. The **key** lists the types of land. The **compass rose** shows directions.

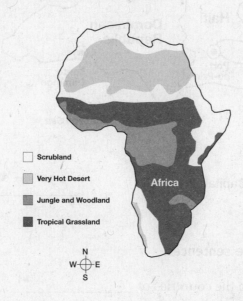

Use the map to answer the questions.

1. According to the key, what type of land is shown by ▢ ?

_____

2. According to the key, what type of land is shown by ▢ ?

_____

3. According to the key, what type of land is shown by ▢ ?

_____

4. Which type of land covers more of Africa, desert or jungle?

_____

5. What kind of land covers the largest area of Africa?

_____

Practice

Political maps show the boundaries of political entities, such as countries and states. The **scale** tells how a map represents distances. You can make a scale ruler for the map below by placing a strip of paper under the scale line and marking the distances. Use your scale ruler on the map to measure distances.

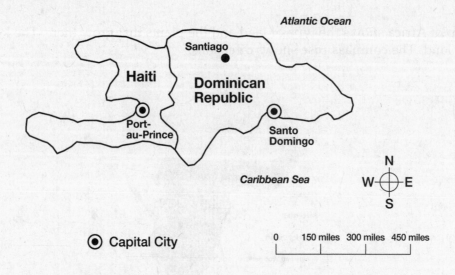

⊙ Capital City

Use the map to complete the sentences.

1. The island is divided into the countries of _____ and

    _____.

2. _____ is a larger country than _____.

3. _____ is the country on the west end of the island; _____

    is the country on the east end.

4. The island is about _____ miles long.

5. The widest part of the island is about _____ miles.

6. Santiago is about _____ miles from Santo Domingo.

7. The capital of the Dominican Republic is _____.

8. If you travel from the capital of the Dominican Republic to the capital of Haiti, you are

    heading _____.

9. Port-au-Prince is located in _____.

10. The body of water north of the island is the _____.

Apply

Many maps of countries or states have an alphabetical list of locations, each labeled with a letter and a number. Use the grid to find the locations by moving across the map to find the letter and then down to find the number. Where these **coordinates** intersect, you will find the location you are seeking.

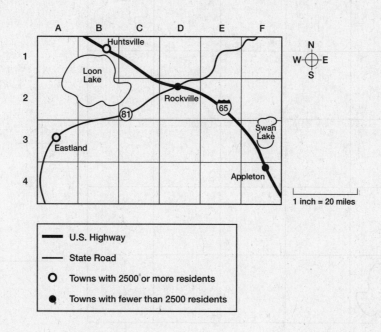

Use the map to answer the questions.

1. Is Rockville east or west of Eastland? _____

2. About how far is Appleton from Huntsville? _____

3. Is Huntsville north or south of Loon Lake? _____

4. Which town has more people, Appleton or Huntsville? _____

5. What coordinates name the location of Swan Lake, F2 or F3? _____

6. What U.S. highway is Rockville located on? _____

7. About how far is Eastland from Rockville? _____

8. Suppose you were giving directions to someone traveling from Eastland to Appleton. What would you say? _____

Check Up

Follow the directions below using the grid to complete the map.

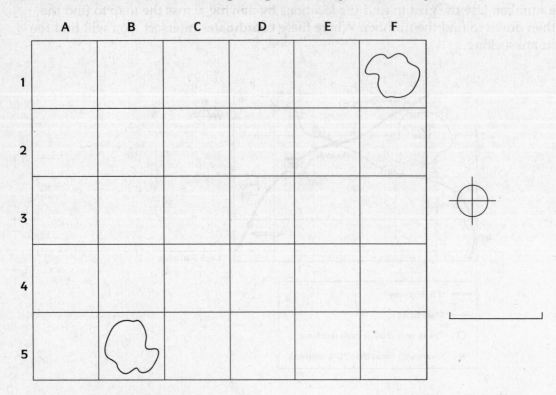

1. Label the compass rose to show the directions.

2. Label the scale to show 1 inch = 10 miles.

3. Draw and label the town of Jackson in A2.

4. Draw and label the town of Portsmouth in D4.

5. Draw a straight highway connecting Jackson and Portsmouth and continuing on in both directions. Label it Highway 43.

6. Label the lake in B5 Green Lake.

7. Label the lake in F1 Mirror Lake.

8. Draw a local road connecting Green Lake and Mirror Lake. Label it Potter Road.

9. Draw a symbol to represent a mountain 10 miles west of Mirror Lake.

10. Draw a symbol to represent an airport 5 miles south of Jackson.

Read On   Read "The World's Longest Railway." Use what you know about maps and graphs to answer the questions.

Using the Dictionary

At the top of each page in the dictionary are two **guide words**. The guide word at the left is the same as the first entry word found on the page. The guide word at the right is the same as the last entry word found on the page. The remaining words on the page are listed in alphabetical order between the guide words.

For example, if the guide words at the top of a dictionary page are *gondolier* and *gooseneck,* then the first entry word on the page is *gondolier* and the last entry word on the page is *gooseneck*. Words such as *gong, good, goof,* and *goose* would appear on the page because they come in alphabetical order between *gondolier* and *gooseneck*.

Guide words are useful because they can help you find words more quickly in the dictionary. If you were looking for the word *gooey,* you would know that it appears on the page between *gondolier* and *gooseneck* because it comes in alphabetical order between those two words.

For each word, write the guide words that would appear on the page in a dictionary where that word would be found.

samba/sample   shone/shore   scoff/score

1. scold   _____

2. shoot   _____

3. same   _____

4. sample   _____

5. sampan   _____

6. scoop   _____

7. shop   _____

8. sconce   _____

9. shook   _____

10. scope   _____

Practice

An **entry word** is the word that you look up in the dictionary. The **entry** shows the spelling of the word, the number of syllables, its part of speech, and its pronunciation. When you look up a word, use the base word.

Choose one of the entry words to complete each sentence. Then write the number of the meaning that makes sense in the sentence.

plate (plāt) *n.* **1** flat or shallow dish from which food is eaten **2** food contents of a plate: *a low-fat plate* **3** collection dish used for money, usually in churches

pledge (plej) *n.* **1** solemn promise or vow **2** something used as security for the keeping of a promise **3** promise to donate money **4** recruit for a fraternity or sorority at a college

po tent (pō′tənt) *adj.* **1** very strong or effective **2** showing persuasion or influence

prime (prīm) *adj.* **1** highest quality **2** a number that can be divided without a remainder only by one and itself

1. The doctor said that the medicine would be _____. _____

2. The salad was served on a decorative _____. _____

3. List the _____ numbers in a separate column. _____

4. My parents made a _____ to community charities. _____

5. Each _____ had to wear a cap for one week when she walked

    on campus. _____

6. The chef demanded that only _____ beef be served. _____

7. The lure of the ad for the tropical vacation was_____. _____

8. I made a _____ to complete my homework before 9:00. _____

9. We passed the _____ during the church service. _____

10. I ordered a low-salt _____ for lunch. _____

Apply

Many words in the English language came from or have roots in other languages. Often dictionaries provide a **word history** for each entry word. The word history explains where the word came from and how it has changed over time.

Read the word history for each entry word. Then answer the questions.

mo cha (mō' kə) *n.* **1** strong, dark brown coffee **2** flavoring made by mixing coffee and cocoa [18th century, named for Mocha, from where related goods were exported]

pi laf (pi läf') *n.* a Middle Eastern dish of spiced rice [17th century via Turkish *pilav*, "cooked rice"]

pre tend (pri tend) *v.* **1** to act if something were true; make believe **2** make insincere claims [14th century via French *pretendre* and from Latin *praetendere*, "to extend in front," from *tendere* "to stretch"]

prince (prins) *n.* **1** man or boy in a royal family **2** male ruler [12th century via French from Latin *princeps*, "one who takes first place"]

rig id (rij' id) *adj.* **1** stiff and firm **2** strictly carried out with no exceptions [15th century, from Latin *rigidus, rigere*, "to be stiff"]

tu na (tü' nə) *n.* large fast-swimming edible fish [19th century, from American Spanish, uncertain origin]

1. Which word is the name of a location that exported the product it names?

   _____

2. From what language does the word *pilaf* come? What does the word mean?

   _____

3. Which word has an uncertain origin? _____

4. How many of the words listed above have Latin roots?_____

5. Which two words began as Latin words, became French words, and then came into English?

   _____

Check Up

Circle the answer for each question.

1. The guide words on a page in the dictionary are *junior* and *just*. Which word would **not** be found on the page?

   A junk

   B jute

   C jury

   D junket

2. The guide words on a page in the dictionary are *cancer* and *candy*. Which word would **not** be found on the page?

   F candid

   G candidate

   H candle

   J cannon

3. The guide words on a page in the dictionary are *telegraph* and *tempt*. Which word would **not** be found on the page?

   A telephone

   B temple

   C ten

   D tempest

Use this entry to answer the questions.

> **force** (fôrs) *n.* **1** power or strength that someone or something possesses **2** physical power used against someone or something **3** condition of being effective **4** group of police officers [13th century from Latin *fortis* "strong"]

4. Which definition makes sense in this sentence?
   The use of force is totally unnecessary.

   F 1

   G 2

   H 3

   J 4

5. Which definition makes sense in this sentence?
   The laws came into force last month.

   A 1

   B 2

   C 3

   D 4

6. The word *force* has roots in what language?

   F French

   G German

   H English

   J Latin

Read On Read "Hong Kong: An Uncertain Future." Use the dictionary to help you answer the questions.

Using Indexes

An **index** of a nonfiction book lists names, terms, and topics that are discussed in the book. Entries are listed alphabetically. Each page where an item appears is listed.

A **subentry** provides more information about a larger topic.

Use the index from the book about Mexico to answer each question.

Index

Caribbean Coast, 612–625
    beaches, 614
    lodging, 620–625
    restaurants, 618–620
    shopping, 618
    sightseeing, 613–617
    sports, 619
    transportation, 612

Caves, 412, 525, 590

Chapala (lake), 79

Chichen Itza (ruins), 275–276

Children
    traveling with, 150–155
    what to do, 155–165

Coba (ruins), 301–302

Dance, 115–118
    festivals of, 21
    flamenco, 313

Dining, 79–120
(See also **Restaurants**)

1. What natural feature would you be likely to see at Chapala?

_____

2. If you are traveling with children, which entries might be helpful?

_____

3. What entries give information about ruins?

_____

4. What entries give information about food?

_____

5. On what page would you find information about flamenco dances?

_____

Practice

Usually textbooks provide an index to help students find needed information. Numbers in **bold type** often show pages where skills are taught.

Use the index from a grammar textbook to answer the following questions.

> **Abbreviations:** business and titles, 424–425; days and months, 419–420; names of places, 422; states, 418–419
>
> **Abstract nouns, 97,** 100, 204–205
>
> **Action verbs, 188,** 192, 212, 290
>
> **Active voice, 193–194,** 230, 255
>
> **Addresses:** abbreviations in, 320–321; business letters, 280–281; on envelopes, 410–411; in friendly letters, 515–516; punctuating, 402–403
>
> **Adjective phrases, 374–375,** 390, 450, 464
>
> **Adjective suffixes, 263–264,** 498, 524

1. On what page could you learn to identify action verbs?

   _____

2. List all of the pages that teach skills and provide practice with adjective suffixes.

   _____

3. On what pages can you learn to write addresses in business letters?

   _____

4. How many subentries are listed under abbreviations?

   _____

5. On what page can you learn about abstract nouns?

   _____

Apply

Some books provide several indexes listed under different topics. The same entry or article may be **cross-referenced** in different places. *Cross-referencing* means sending the user to another entry.

Use the indexes from *Famous People* to decide if each statement is *true* or *false*. If it is false, write the correct information.

Thematic Index	Index
Painters	Gauguin, Paul, 477
da Vinci, Leonardo, 341	Giacometti, Alberto, 551
Monet, Claude, 216	Gilbert and Sullivan, 548
O'Keeffe, Georgia, 330	Gordimer, Nadine, 486
Van Gogh, Vincent, 680	Handel, George Frideric, 492
	Hardy, Thomas, 520
Composers	Hawthorne, Nathaniel, 559
Debussy, Claude, 119	Hemingway, Ernest, 573
Gilbert and Sullivan, 548	Hughes, Langston, 599
Mahler, Gustav, 393	Hugo, Victor, 636
Vaughan Williams, Ralph, 692	Ibsen, Henrik, 654

Writers
Eliot, George, 222
Gordimer, Nadine, 486
Twain, Mark, 502
Woolf, Virginia, 734

1. Nadine Gordimer is a painter.   true   false

   _____

2. You can find information about Gilbert and Sullivan on page 551.   true   false

   _____

3. Georgia O'Keeffe is a painter.   true   false

   _____

4. You can find information about Claude Monet on page 612.   true   false

   _____

5. Ralph Vaughan Williams is a writer.   true   false

   _____

6. Would you prefer to use the thematic index or the alphabetical index? Why?

   _____

Check Up

Use the index from *Animal World* to answer each question.

Index

octopus (mollusk), 192
opossum (mammal), 74
oriole (bird) *picture*, 55
oryx (mammal), baby, 62
ostrich (bird), 195–196
    defense, 313
    nest, *picture*, 454
otter (mammal) *picture*, 370
owl (bird) *picture*, 280
    territory, 302
oyster (mollusk), 242, *with picture*, 243

1. Which entry does **not** have a picture?

   A owl

   B oyster

   C ostrich

   D octopus

2. On what page would you find a picture of an oyster?

   F 242

   G 243

   H 342

   J 454

3. Which animal is a mammal?

   A owl

   B otter

   C ostrich

   D oyster

4. How many subentries are listed under *ostrich*?

   F one

   G two

   H three

   J four

5. What would you find on page 302?

   A information about an ostrich

   B information about an oriole

   C information about the territory of an owl

   D picture of an owl

6. Which entry lists a baby mammal?

   F oyster

   G oriole

   H oryx

   J opossum

Reference Sources

Card catalogs are reference sources found in libraries. Each book in the library is listed in the computerized card catalog. The listings are organized by author, title, and subject. A call number at the left helps you locate the book. Other information about the book is provided as well.

Use the listing to answer the questions.

```
Sn          Alexander, Clarissa
7112        Party Ideas for Every Occasion
.B4         New York: Modern Living Press, 1998
                    398 p.: ill., photos
                    Includes bibliography and index.
                    ISBN 0-21-764377-8

            1. Entertaining 2. Food 3. Title
```

1. What is the title of the book? _____

2. How many pages does the book have? _____

3. What company is the publisher of the book? _____

4. What subjects are related to this book? _____

Card catalog information can be organized in different formats. Use this listing to answer the questions.

Subject	owls	
Author	Hastings, Phillip	
Title	Owls in North America	
Publisher	Boston, MA: Nature Books, c1996	

LOCATION	CALL NO.	STATUS
Jackson Public Library	475.82.H773o	Available

Physical Desc	196 p., color ill., col. maps
Note	Includes index
Subject	Owls
Alt author	Stevenson, Jayne

5. How many pages does the book have? _____

6. What does the Note explain? _____

7. Is the book available at the library? _____

Practice

There are many different reference books that can help you locate information. The list below is an example of some of these books and the type of information they provide.

encyclopedia	provides short articles with facts about almost all topics
thesaurus	lists synonyms, antonyms, and homonyms for words
Books in Print	lists all hardcover and paperback books (if they are still in print) by title, author, and subject
world atlas	provides maps and information about countries
world almanac	provides facts about countries, weather, people, events, and many other topics
The Guinness Book of World Records	provides records that were set by people and events around the world
Bartlett's Familiar Quotations	lists famous quotations and the people who said them

List the reference book you would use to find the following information.

1. an antonym for the word *hardy* _____

2. the author of a book if you know the title _____

3. the population of India _____

4. the locations of the desert regions of Arizona _____

5. the fastest water-skiing speed _____

6. the person who said "I have a dream." _____

7. how clouds are formed _____

8. a synonym for the word *huge* _____

Apply

A **thesaurus** is a special kind of dictionary that lists synonyms, antonyms, and related words. Each entry provides several different listings.

Use this entry to choose a word or phrase to complete each sentence.

CURIOSITY

1. **NOUN** interest, inquisitiveness, desire for knowledge; nosiness, prying, meddling

2. **VERB** want to know, be interested in, ask, question, inquire, seek, snoop around for

3. **ADJ** curious, inquiring, burning with interest, agog; gossipy, meddlesome

1. Since he was young, Alex had had a(n) _____ in space.

2. His _____ was evident to his parents and teachers.

3. He _____ his science teachers about the planets and constellations.

4. His _____ mind led him to study science and mathematics.

5. In high school, he _____ about special courses and colleges.

6. Alex's _____ resulted in a scholarship.

Write three sentences using words that are found in the thesaurus entry for *curiosity*. **Use a noun, a verb, and an adjective.**

7. _____

8. _____

9. _____

Check Up

Use what you know about reference materials to answer the following questions. Then circle each answer.

1. A listing in the card catalog includes
   A   a short passage about the author's life
   B   the name of the author of the book
   C   how much the book costs
   D   a review of the book

2. You could find a synonym for a word in a(an)
   F   thesaurus
   G   encyclopedia
   H   card catalog
   J   atlas

3. You could find out how CD-ROMs are made in
   A   a dictionary
   B   an atlas
   C   an encyclopedia
   D   *Books in Print*

4. If you are having trouble finding a particular book, you could look for publishing information in
   F   *The Guinness Book of World Records*
   G   a biographical index
   H   an encyclopedia
   J   *Books in Print*

5. If you are writing a report about Cuba, it would be helpful to look in all of these sources *except*
   A   an encyclopedia
   B   a thesaurus
   C   a world almanac
   D   an atlas

6. To find information about the most Olympic medals won by a certain individual, you would look in
   F   an atlas
   G   *Bartlett's Familiar Quotations*
   H   *The Guinness Book of World Records*
   J   *Books in Print*

Using Reference Sources

Suppose you are writing a report about Herbert Hoover. There are many different reference sources you could use. For example, you could look in a book about his life.

A **biography** is a factual account of a person's life. Many biographical accounts are found in encyclopedias. The encyclopedia index will help you find information as well as list the volume and page number where the information can be found.

Use the encyclopedia index to answer each question.

Hoover, Allan (uncle of)
  Hoover, Herbert Clark
    (Childhood) H: 352

Hoover, Herbert Clark (U.S. President)
  H: 352–358
  pictures H: 352, 354
  Great Depression (U.S. policies)
    G: 404
  Hoover Commission H: 356
  Roosevelt, Franklin Delano
    (Election) R: 293
  World War I W: 571

Hoover, Herbert Clark, Jr. (U.S. Government official)
  Hoover, Herbert Clark (Hoover's family) H: 353–354

Hoover, Lou Henry (wife of Herbert Hoover)
  First ladies F: 202
  Hoover, Herbert Clark (Hoover's family)
    H: 353–354

1. What does the letter before each page reference represent?

   _____

2. In what volume and on what pages would you find information about Herbert Hoover's family?

   _____

3. In what volume and on what pages would you find information about Lou Henry Hoover?

   _____

4. In what volume and on what page would you find out about Herbert Hoover's connection with World War I?

   _____

5. What can you tell about Herbert Clark Hoover, Jr., from the index?

   _____

Practice

Suppose the first paragraph of your report is about Herbert Hoover's childhood. Read the following section of an encyclopedia entry. Then follow the directions below.

> Herbert Hoover was born in West Branch, Iowa, on August 10, 1874. Herbert's parents, Jesse Clark Hoover and Hulda Randall Minthorn Hoover, had two sons and a daughter. Jesse Hoover was a dealer in farm equipment. He was also a blacksmith. Hulda Hoover was a religious leader among the Quakers.
>
> In 1880 Hoover's father died of heart trouble. He left a $1000 life insurance policy and a little property. Hulda Hoover supported her family through sewing and religious preaching. However, she died when Herbert was 9, and relatives raised the children. Most of the time, Herbert was separated from his brother and sister. For about two years, he lived with his uncle, Allan Hoover, who lived near West Branch.
>
> Herbert enjoyed spending time in the woods, fishing, and swimming. He earned extra money by picking potato bugs. He earned one penny for every 100 bugs that he picked.

1. Write the topic sentence of your paragraph about Hoover's childhood.

_____

_____

2. Write the three supporting details that you would include in your paragraph.

_____

_____

_____

_____

Apply

An **almanac** is a book of information that is published every year. It often lists reference books.

> History
> *The Reader's Companion to American History*, Eric Foner and
>   John A. Garraty
> *The Americans*, Daniel J. Boorstin
> *Album of American History*, James T. Adams
> *Encyclopedia of North American Indians*, Frederick E. Hoxie, Editor
> *The Cambridge Illustrated History of the Islamic World*, Francis
>   Robinson
> *A History of the African American People: The History, Traditions, and
>   Culture of African Americans*, James Horton, Lois Horton

1. Write three sources that you think would be most helpful to you when writing your report about Herbert Hoover. Explain why.

_____

_____

_____

An almanac may also give brief biographies. Read this section from Herbert Hoover's biography.

> HERBERT CLARK HOOVER, the first president to be born west of the Mississippi, was born in West Branch, Iowa, on August 10, 1874. After graduating from Stanford University, he worked as a mining engineer and consultant around the world. In 1899 he married Lou Henry. During World War I, he worked for the American Relief Committee in London, the Commission for Relief in Belgium, and as U.S. Food Administrator.

2. Write two facts that you would choose to include in your report about Herbert Hoover. Explain why.

_____

_____

_____

Check Up

Use what you know about reference sources to answer the following questions. Then circle each answer.

1. A biography is
   A a book about animals
   B a factual account of a person's life
   C a story that includes information about a person
   D a book about plants

2. You could find a detailed report about a person's life in
   F an almanac
   G a thesaurus
   H an encyclopedia
   J *The Guinness Book of World Records*

3. An encyclopedia index is organized
   A alphabetically
   B by volume
   C by page number
   D by topic

4. You might find a list of reference books in
   F *The Guinness Book of World Records*
   G a thesaurus
   H a world atlas
   J an almanac

5. An almanac is published
   A daily
   B monthly
   C yearly
   D every five years

6. You would probably find the most information about Herbert Hoover in
   F an almanac
   G a biography written by a history professor
   H a book about 20th-century U.S. presidents
   J an encyclopedia

Read On Read "Cambodia's Grand Temple." Use reference sources to answer the questions.

Using Forms

A **form** is a document with blank spaces that need to be filled in. When you complete a form, you provide necessary and accurate information in order to obtain services or products.

Suppose you are going on vacation from July 1 to July 7. You want the post office to hold your mail during those dates. On July 8, you want all of the mail delivered and regular delivery to resume.

Complete this form. Then answer the questions.

Authorization to Hold Mail Postmaster: Please hold mail for Name:	Begin Holding Mail *(Date)*
Address: *(Number, Street, Apt., City, State, Zip)*	
A. [ ] I will pick up all accumulated mail when I return and understand that mail delivery will not resume until I do.	
B. [ ] Please deliver all accumulated mail and resume normal delivery on the ending date shown here.	Resume Delivery Date
Customer Signature	
For Post Office Use Only Date Received	

1. Did you fill in the date received? Why or why not?

_____

2. Did you choose option A or B? Why?

_____

3. Why do you think the post office asks for a signature?

_____

Practice

Suppose you want to camp at River Ridge Campground. There will be two adults, two children, and one dog. You will arrive on June 15 and leave on June 21. Your tent size is a four-person, and your license number is BH 2443. The cost for the tent site is $12 per night.

Fill in the form. Then answer the questions.

River Ridge Campground		
Name		In Date
Street		Out Date
City	State	Zip
License #	RV Length	Tent Size
Site Fee x Number of Nights = $_____		
		Total Fee: $_____ (Includes Tax)
Check-out time is 12:00. Signature _____		
No refunds within two weeks of check-in date.		

1. What information did you **not** fill in? Why?

   _____

2. When is the last date that you can cancel your reservation and receive a refund?

   _____

3. Suppose you decide to stay an extra night. What will be the total cost then?

   _____

Apply

You may need to fill out an order form if you want to order merchandise by mail. Suppose you want to order the following items from the *My Way Sports* catalog and pay for them by check:

> 1 stereo carrier, #4228, $19
> 1 black workout bag, #5334, $35
> 2 pairs of blue Snowstopper mittens, size L, #4881, $25

Fill in the form. Then answer the questions.

My Way Sports
3 Circle Drive
West Palm, CA 00033
1-800-MYWAY00

Ship to:
Name: _____
Address: _____
_____
State: _____ Zip: _____
Phone: _____

Item #	Description	Color	Size	Quantity	Price	Total

Payment

[ ] Check   [ ] Credit Card
     #_____

SUBTOTAL: _____
DELIVERY: $5.00
TOTAL: _____

---

1. What would be the total price including the delivery charge?

   _____

2. What is the two-letter abbreviation for your state?

   _____

3. Suppose the company writes to inform you that the workout bag is out of stock. What is the price of your order then?

   _____

Check Up

Suppose you want to send a letter by overnight mail. You are sending the letter to Aaron Gibson, Eagle Book Company, 4433 Lakeside Road, Loon Cove, ME 01122. The phone number is 200-555-1234. You are sending an overnight letter and will bill the recipient, the person who receives the letter.

Fill in the form. Then answer the questions.

Overnight Air Delivery Service	Date _____
FROM:	**Package Service**
Name _____	[ ] letter
Company _____	[ ] package Wgt. _____
Address _____	**Payment**
City State Zip	Bill to:
_____	[ ] Sender
Phone _____	[ ] Recipient
	[ ] Credit Card # _____
TO:	**Service**
Name _____	[ ] overnight
Company _____	[ ] two-day
Address _____	
City State Zip	
_____	
Phone _____	

1. What is the name of the mail service?

   _____

2. How many ways can you pay for the mailing?

   _____

3. What does "Wgt." stand for?

   _____

4. If you mail the letter on Monday, when will it arrive?

   _____

Consumer Materials

The most common way to find out information about a product is through advertisements. However, it is important to analyze the data in an ad carefully. Here are some points to keep in mind.

> Read the product description carefully.
> Investigate the seller's claims.
> Remember, you often get what you pay for! Don't count on unbelievable values.
> Check the company's policy on returns.

Study the ads to see which features each one offers.
Write *Vidcom*, *Smithson*, or *Both* next to each description.

Vidcom
Stereo Sound
Universal Remote
Channel Block-out
12-month warranty
$298

Smithson
Stereo Sound
Universal Remote
Audio Tone Controls
24-month warranty
$350

1. 24-month warranty _____

2. Stereo Sound _____

3. Channel Block-out _____

4. Universal Remote _____

5. Price of $350 _____

6. Audio Tone Controls _____

7. 12-month warranty _____

8. Price of $298 _____

Practice

Sometimes a product or service does not live up to its claims. In that case, you can write a **letter of complaint** to the manufacturer or service provider.

Joan Doe
555 Silver St.
Janesville, AR 22222
July 6, 2005

Acme Appliances
123 Elm St.
Maris, CA 02110

Dear Acme Appliances:

I bought a television set, Model #655, from your store in the Airport Mall on May 20.

[Here the writer states the problem.]

The picture was unclear from the day I bought the set. On May 27, a repairperson from your store came to my apartment to repair the set. He charged me $50 for the visit, and the picture is still unclear. Since my warranty is in effect for one year, the repair visit should have been free. Therefore I ask for two things:

[Here the writer explains what she wants.]

(1) that you remove the $50 charge from my account
(2) that you fix the set or replace it

I enclose copies of the sales receipts and warranties.

Sincerely,

Joan Doe

Joan Doe

cc: Better Business Bureau

Use the model above to write a letter of complaint for a television set (#4433) that you bought from the Hi-Tech Video Store at the Airport Mall on August 15th. The television sound is bad.

Apply

Sometimes a **service form** will accompany mail-order products.

Suppose you bought a swimsuit. The swimsuit is too small, and you also don't like the design. You want to return it.

Complete the form. Then answer the questions.

Sea Glass Swimwear	**CONSUMER SERVICE CARD**
Name _____	Date _____
Address _____	
_____	Phone _____
Do you want to: [ ] return? [ ] exchange?	[ ] credit account [ ] refund money _____
What are the problems with the merchandise? [ ] too big [ ] doesn't look like picture [ ] too small [ ] other (Please explain below.) [ ] wrong color _____ [ ] didn't like fabric _____	

1. Where did you put your comment about the swimsuit's size?

   _____

2. Where did you put your comment about the swimsuit's design?

   _____

3. What are some of the advantages of buying merchandise by mail?

   _____

4. What are some of the disadvantages?

   _____

Check Up

Use the following ads for bikes to answer the questions.

Coyote
Fits riders to 6 feet tall
Climbs easily on steep hills
Wet brakes
Full aluminum frame
33 pounds
$325

Classico
Fits riders to 5'8"
Climbs easily on moderate hills
Wet brakes
Full steel frame
42 pounds
$175

1. If you are 6 feet tall, which bike would you need to buy?

    A Coyote

    B Classico

2. Which bike is lighter?

    F Coyote

    G Classico

3. Which feature is the same on both bikes?

    A price

    B weight

    C wet brakes

    D frame

4. Which bike has a steel frame?

    F Coyote

    G Classico

5. If you are on a tight budget, which bike would you probably buy?

    A Coyote

    B Classico

6. If you bike in areas with steep hills, which bike would you rather buy?

    F Coyote

    G Classico

Using Consumer Materials

There are resources available to help you be a smart shopper. Some magazines and publications rate products and services using different types of rating systems.

Use these ratings of CD players to answer the questions.

CD Players	○ Excellent	● Good	⊖ Fair	● Poor		
Brand/Model	Price	Headphones	Problem Disks	Bumps	Features	
Smith E54	$89	●	⊖	⊖	⊖	
Diskplay 25	$99	⊖	⊖	●	●	
EBT X62	$130	○	●	●	●	
Electra AB30	$125	●	○	●	○	

1. Which CD player is the most expensive? _____

2. Which CD player has the highest rating for headphones? _____

3. Which CD players have problems with bumps? _____

4. Which CD player has the highest overall rating on features? _____

5. If price is the most important consideration, which CD player would you buy? _____

Practice

Some rating systems use a grid to give information and compare products.

Use the ratings chart to answer the questions.

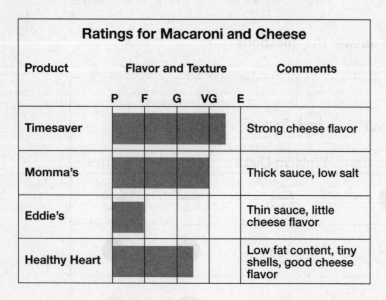

Ratings for Macaroni and Cheese

Product	Flavor and Texture					Comments
	P	F	G	VG	E	
Timesaver						Strong cheese flavor
Momma's						Thick sauce, low salt
Eddie's						Thin sauce, little cheese flavor
Healthy Heart						Low fat content, tiny shells, good cheese flavor

1. What words do the letters in the chart under Flavor and Texture represent?

    _____

2. If you like a thick sauce, which brand would you choose?

    _____

3. If you are on a low-fat diet, which brand would you choose?

    _____

4. Which brand has the highest overall rating?

    _____

5. Which brand has the lowest overall rating?

    _____

6. Do you find these types of ratings helpful? Why or why not?

    _____

Apply

You can find different types of helpful information in consumer magazines and reports.

Circle the correct answer(s) for questions 1–3. Write the answer to question 4.

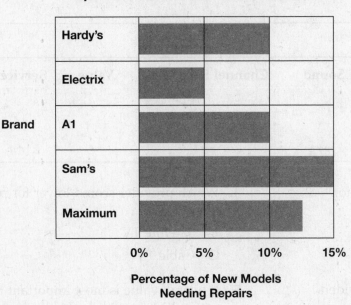

Repairs and Problems of Dishwashers

1. Which brand had the highest percentage of repairs?

   A Sam's   **B** Maximum   **C** Hardy's

2. Which brand had the lowest percentage of repairs?

   F A1   **G** Electrix   **H** Maximum

3. Which two brands had the same percentage of repairs?

   A Hardy's   **B** Sam's   **C** A1

4. Write the names of the brands in order from highest to lowest percentage of repairs.

   _____

Check Up

Look at these TV provider ratings. Then circle the answer for each question.

Estimated Percentage of People Who Rated the Attribute as "Excellent"
+ 25%   ++ 50%   +++ 75%   ++++ 100%

Provider	Picture	Sound	Channel Selection	Value	Service
Satellite TV	++	++	++++	+++	+++
Cable TV	+++	++	++	++	++++

1. Which provider scored higher for Channel Selection?

   A Satellite TV

   B Cable TV

2. In which category did the providers have about the same results?

   F Picture

   G Sound

   H Value

   J Service

3. About what percentage of people were satisfied with Cable TV's service?

   A 25%

   B 50%

   C 75%

   D 100%

4. Which provider scored lower for picture quality?

   F Satellite TV

   G Cable TV

5. If overall value is most important to you, which provider would you choose?

   A Satellite TV

   B Cable TV

Read On   After reading "The Cold Facts," answer the questions about consumer materials.

Review

Graphs

Bar graphs, **line graphs**, and **circle graphs** are used to show information and compare data quickly and easily.

Maps

A **physical map** shows land features. A **political map** shows the boundaries of units of governments, such as countries, states, and counties. The **map scale** explains how the map represents distance.

Dictionary

In addition to defining a word, a **dictionary entry** provides the following information: spelling, syllabication, pronunciation, and the history or origin of a word. The **guide words** at the top of each dictionary page indicate what words will be found on the page.

Index

An **index** lists topics covered in a book and gives the page number where each topic is discussed.

Reference Sources

A **card catalog** contains listings for each book, organized by author's name, title of the book, and subject of the book. The call number tells you the location of the book in the library. Encyclopedias, atlases, thesauruses, and almanacs are **reference sources**.

Forms

A **form** is a document that has blank lines for inserting information. You complete forms for a variety of reasons, including sending a package, applying for a credit card, or filing a tax return.

Consumer Materials

Consumer materials help you become an informed consumer. Some magazines and publications rate products and services.

Assessment

Circle the answer to each question.

Percent of U.S. Foreign Born: 1900 and 1990

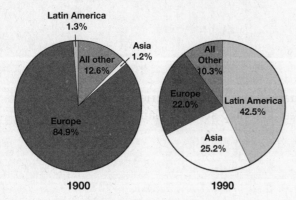

1900   1990

Source: U.S. Census Bureau

Participation in Leisure Activities, 1997

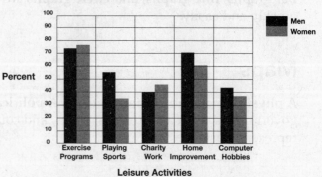

Source: U.S. National Endowment for the Arts

1. In 1900 what percentage of the U.S. foreign-born population was born in Asia?

   A 12.6%

   B 1.2%

   C 84.9%

   D 1.3%

2. Which of the following is the most accurate description of the U.S. population in 1990?

   F The percentage of the foreign-born population from Latin America in 1990 is lower than the percentage of the foreign-born population from Europe.

   G The percentage of the foreign-born population from unspecified areas was about the same in 1990 as it was in 1900.

   H In 1990 the percentage of the foreign-born population from Latin America was greater than the percentages from all other countries combined.

   J In 1990 slightly more than half of the U.S. foreign-born population came from Europe.

3. In general, in which activity do men and women participate equally?

   A Charity Work

   B Computer Hobbies

   C Exercise Programs

   D Home Improvement

4. Which of these could be concluded based on the graph?

   F More women than men pursue computer hobbies as a leisure activity.

   G Significantly more men than women play sports as a leisure activity.

   H The same percentages of women and men do home improvement in their leisure time.

   J More than 50 percent of men and women are active in charity work.

Unemployment Rate in the Civilian Labor Force

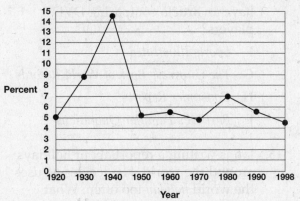

Source: U.S. Department of Labor

5. During which 20-year period did the unemployment rate remain fairly constant?

   A 1920–1940

   B 1930–1950

   C 1940–1960

   D 1950–1970

6. The unemployment rate in 1940 was about double the rate in which year?

   F 1970

   G 1980

   H 1990

   J 1998

7. Which of these cities is farthest west?

   A Little Rock

   B Albuquerque

   C Boise

   D Tucson

8. Which car trip would most likely require crossing a mountain range?

   F Chicago to Houston

   G Bismarck to Omaha

   H Cleveland to Richmond

   J Tallahassee to San Antonio

9. The guide words on a page in the dictionary are *throat* and *thyroid*. Which word would **not** be found on the page?

   A thrift

   B thrush

   C throne

   D throughout

10. Which set of words is in alphabetical order?

   F premier, premise, preoccupy, premium

   G terrier, terry, terrify, testify

   H scratch, scrape, scrawl, scrawny

   J creative, credible, crescent, crest

Assessment continued

Index

11. If you wanted to learn more about the natural resources of Peru, on what page would you look?

    A 913
    B 700
    C 864
    D 915

12. Which page would be most likely to have a picture?

    F 146
    G 900
    H 443
    J 900

13. You are interested in buying a personal computer. Which resource would provide the most objective information and help you make a wise buying decision?

    A newspaper advertisement for a computer
    B clerk in the computer section of a home appliance store
    C magazine article on new computers
    D encyclopedia article on computers

14. Which resource would most likely have an article comparing DVD players?

    F *Sports Illustrated*
    G *The Guinness Book of World Records*
    H *Consumer Reports*
    J *Bartlett's Familiar Quotations*

15. Jan is writing a report about holidays around the world. He decides he uses the world *holiday* too often. What reference source could he consult to find words that he could substitute for *holiday*?

    A an encyclopedia
    B an almanac
    C a book of government publications
    D a thesaurus

16. The buttons came off your new sweater the first time you wore it. You are filling out a form to get a refund on your purchase. Which of the following information would **not** be required?

    F the price of the sweater
    G the date of the purchase
    H your educational background
    J the reason for return

Syllogism

A **syllogism** is a form of reasoning made up of two statements and a conclusion. One statement is the major premise, or general idea considered to be true. One is a minor premise, or specific idea considered to be true. From the premises, a conclusion is drawn.

All infants cry at times.	major premise
Will is an infant.	minor premise
Will cries at times.	conclusion

Complete each of the following syllogisms.

1. People who enjoy surfing enjoy visiting Hawaii.
   Tania likes surfing.

   _____

2. In some states, students must pass a driver's education course to graduate from high school.
   Al graduated from high school in one of these states.

   _____

3. A U.S. citizen who is single and under 65 must file an income tax return if his or her gross income was at least $7,950 in 2004.
   Dolores is a single woman who earned $26,000 in 2004.

   _____

4. All members of the marching band wear red and black uniforms.
   Ted is a member of the marching band.

   _____

5. The only U.S. currency on which George Washington's portrait appears is a $1 bill.
   Ana has nine bills that show Washington's portrait.

   _____

6. Each state of the Union has two members in the Senate.
   Georgia is a state in the Union.

   _____

   _____

Stereotypes

A **stereotype** is a simplified character who conforms to a fixed pattern of behavior or is defined by a single trait. A stereotypical character does not have the complexity and individuality of a real person. Recognizing stereotypes when you read helps you become a more critical reader.

There are many stereotypes portrayed in literature, on television, and in the movies. Think about stereotypes that you have read about or seen. Fill in the chart by identifying the character trait commonly associated with each stereotype.

Stereotype	Character Trait
athlete	
oldest child in a family	
executive	
grandparent	
college professor	
movie star	
politician	
teenager	
American tourist	

Why should you avoid viewing real people as stereotypes?

_____

_____

_____

_____

_____

_____

_____

_____

Identifying Character Traits

Characters are the people who take part in the events of a work of fiction, for example, a short story or a novel.

It is important to think about characters as you read. Ask yourself what traits a character shows. Is he or she cruel or kind? selfish or generous? cheerful or moody? You can figure out a character's traits through what the character says, what the character does, and what other characters say about him or her.

You can practice recognizing character traits in fictional characters by thinking about the character traits of real people whom you meet, hear about, and read about.

Read the passage. Circle the answer to each question.

President John F. Kennedy is one of the most famous leaders in American history. During Kennedy's days in office, however, his wife Jacqueline was easily as well-known as he was. On a tour of France in 1962, Jackie, as she was called, charmed the French. They liked her personality and her ability to speak their language. She was the toast of Paris. She got much favorable newspaper coverage. On the Kennedys' last day in France, the president said perhaps he should introduce himself. He said, "I am the man that accompanied Jackie Kennedy to Paris."

1. Which word best describes the personality trait that caused the French people to admire Jackie Kennedy?

   A wealthy

   B charming

   C curious

   D imaginative

2. The fact that Jackie Kennedy spoke French while visiting France shows that she was

   F rich and conceited

   G interesting and curious

   H humorous and entertaining

   J intelligent and thoughtful

3. President Kennedy's comment about his wife shows that he

   A was jealous of his wife

   B was not as clever as his wife

   C had no sense of humor

   D was proud of his wife

Practice

Read each passage. List three traits shown by the person described in the passage.

First of all I want to introduce myself: My name is Carmen. Some people call me Smiley. I try to act nice, but sometimes I just can't do it. Some people don't help me. In my school not everyone is nice. Some people in my school act tough with me and want to boss me around. I can't always fight because some people have older brothers and sisters who fight for them, and I don't. I have a cousin who is the only one I can count on to help me. But I try not to bother him because I have to learn to stand up for myself to get along in life.

Character Traits:

1. _____

2. _____

3. _____

Movie actor Buster Keaton started his career in vaudeville. He was the youngest member of a family acrobatic act. His parents threw him up in the air and bounced him, literally, off the stage walls. Keaton carried this early training into his movie career. He made movies that demanded stunts and falls. Keaton was the leading character in his pictures. But he also performed his own stunts. Although he frequently filmed while injured, he never complained or slowed down. He worked with sprains, broken bones, and once with a crushed vertebra. After his death, doctors examined Keaton. They reported that nearly every bone in his body had been broken at least once.

Character Traits:

4. _____

5. _____

6. _____

Apply

Read each brief passage about a person. Write the letter of the character trait the person shows most clearly.

A devout   C courageous   E tricky
B determined   D fun-loving

_____ **1.** P. T. Barnum stretched the truth when he was putting on a show. He once claimed that an old woman in his circus was 146 years old.

_____ **2.** Queen Christina became queen of Sweden in 1632 when she was 18 years old. She helped end the Thirty Years War. She reformed the school system and founded several colleges. But she is known best for the fact that she gave up the throne in 1654 because she had become a Catholic, and Catholicism was outlawed in Sweden.

_____ **3.** Before Teddy Roosevelt became president of the United States in 1897, he developed a love for the game of polo. He organized a polo team on Long Island in 1888. In order to make the action in the game more exciting, he organized teams of three players instead of four. The game was so open that injuries were common. Teddy was even knocked unconscious a few times, but he continued to enjoy the game.

_____ **4.** When Elvis Presley was an eighth-grader in Memphis, Tennessee, his teacher said that he had no musical talent. In high school, Elvis worked as a truck driver. After Elvis's first audition at Nashville's Grand Ole Opry, the talent manager told him to "stick to truck driving." But Elvis stuck with his music. In 1956 he released his first Top Ten record. He remained an international star until his death.

_____ **5.** Harriet Tubman was one of the most successful travelers along the Underground Railroad during the American Civil War. An escaped slave herself, she led at least 19 trips through the Underground over a 10-year period. Traveling into the South and back to the North, Tubman brought more than 300 slaves to freedom. She was never captured.

Check Up

Read the passage. Then circle the answer to each question.

Thomas Jefferson was the third U.S. president. He was the chief author of the Declaration of Independence. He was also a noted architect and an accomplished violinist. He had great respect for farmers, saying that "those who labor in the earth are the chosen people of God." As a farmer himself, he became an expert on agricultural techniques. He was also interested in science. He invented some useful devices such as a swivel chair. To find out about the plant and animal life of the American West, Jefferson sent Lewis and Clark on a long expedition to that part of the country.

1. Which of the following words does **not** accurately describe the character of Thomas Jefferson?

   A   bright

   B   curious

   C   narrow

   D   talented

2. Jefferson's words and actions regarding farmers show that he

   F   said one thing and did another

   G   thought farming was a valuable occupation

   H   believed farming was for only uneducated people

   J   did not spend much time thinking about farming

3. Jefferson's actions show that he

   A   considered politics the only worthwhile occupation

   B   was more interested in ideas than in practical knowledge

   C   was highly motivated to discover new things

   D   usually had other people do jobs for him

4. Which of the following character traits is **not** described or implied in the passage about Thomas Jefferson?

   F   honesty

   G   versatility

   H   intelligence

   J   determination

5. In general, how would you describe Jefferson based on this passage?

   A   demanding and temperamental

   B   scholarly and snobbish

   C   shy and isolated

   D   intelligent and well-rounded

Recognizing Character Traits

Authors usually do not tell readers exactly what they should think about their characters. For example, they rarely say a character is funny or angry. Instead, they describe the characters and have him or her saying and doing things that show the character's sense of humor or anger. They show other characters reacting to that sense of humor or anger.

When you read, put the clues—the character's words and actions—together to create a portrait of the character.

> At first the boy, not more than 18 and small, did not impress them. He said simply that he was José, and he wanted to work for the cause. This was all—not a wasted word of introduction. He stood without smiling. He was almost somber. Big, powerful Felipe stepped up to him and felt at once that something was wrong, something frightening. The boy's black eyes were like a snake's, and they burned like cold fire. His eyes searched the room, from one face to another, but the others looked away.

In this passage, the author describes José's actions and appearance to communicate his character: cold, fearless, and rather frightening.

Read the passage. Write at least two traits shown by the character.

> Jean-Paul Marat was one of the leaders of the French Revolution. He wrote many articles that were very violent in tone. He used violent means to silence his enemies. Once in power, he and his fellow revolutionaries put to death all who opposed them.

Character Traits:

_____

_____

_____

Practice

Following are some common character traits. Write one trait after each passage to indicate a character trait shown by the person described.

compassion	ambition	courage
inventiveness	determination	

1. Babe Didrikson won two gold medals and one silver medal for track and field in the 1932 Olympics. Then she turned to golf, once winning 17 straight matches. In 1953 Babe underwent surgery for cancer. She won the Women's Open the next year although she was obviously very ill. She died three years later.

   _____

2. They were perhaps four meters apart when the girl stumbled and fell almost flat on her face. A sharp cry of pain was wrung out of her. . . . A curious emotion stirred in Winston's heart. In front of him was an enemy who was trying to kill him; in front of him, also, was a human creature in pain and perhaps with a broken bone. Already he had instinctively started forward to help her. In the moment when he had seen her fall on the bandaged arm, it had been as though he felt the pain in his own body.

   _____

3. Although he was outwardly modest, Marty had his dreams. He would graduate from middle school and was planning to go to high school in the fall. He was impatient to go to high school and to get into high school track meets. He'd never been coached, and yet look how good he was! Think of how good he would be when he had some coaching! He'd be a streak of lightning, if ever there was one.

   _____

4. In 1870 Alphonse Penaud built a 20-inch "planophore." It had angled wing tips and a tail plane with vertical fins. These features were copied in many later airplanes. Penaud flew his planophore in public. He sold copies of it to other flight enthusiasts.

   _____

5. Mary Cassatt was born in 1845 in Pennsylvania. As a young woman, she studied art at the Pennsylvania Academy of Fine Arts in Philadelphia. She wanted to study art in Europe. However, her wealthy parents did not think studying art in Europe was proper for a young woman. Cassatt finally overcame her parents' objections. She studied in France, Italy, Spain, and Belgium. She became a successful Impressionist artist.

   _____

Apply

Read the passages. Then circle the answer to each question.

Passage 1

People have sometimes escaped death in unusual ways. For example, one man managed to escape having his head cut off by the guillotine during the French Revolution. He was sentenced to death because he was an aristocrat. Just before he was to be killed, the guillotine developed some mechanical problems. The people in charge of the execution tried to fix the machine. In the confusion that followed, the prisoner managed to slip away. He blended into the crowd and escaped from Paris.

Passage 2

Three hundred years ago, an adventurer named Eppelein von Gailing got himself out of a serious scrape. Von Gailing was in prison in a castle in Germany. He was to be hanged. Before he was hanged, he was given a final request. Von Gailing asked for one last chance to mount his beloved horse. The horse was brought into the courtyard. As soon as von Gailing was in the saddle, he and his horse charged through dozens of soldiers. They climbed a staircase to the top of the castle wall. They leaped off the wall into the moat. They escaped unharmed.

1. The man in the first passage could be described as
   A slow to react
   B quick to take advantage of an opportunity
   C fearful
   D hesitant

2. The man in the second passage could be described as
   F stubborn
   G confused
   H clever
   J angry

3. What do the two characters have in common?
   A They both take advantage of opportunity.
   B They both have a philosophical frame of mind.
   C They both tend to be melancholy.
   D They both have a sense of responsibility.

4. Which of the following traits do the two characters **not** have?
   F quickness
   G timidity
   H courage
   J cleverness

Check Up

Read the passage. Then circle the answer to each question.

Then one evening, her husband came home proudly holding out a large envelope.

"Look," he said, "I've got something for you."

She excitedly tore open the envelope and pulled out a printed card bearing these words: "The Minister of Education and Mme. Georges Ramponneau beg M. and Mme. Loisel to do them the honor of attending an evening reception at the Ministerial Mansion on Friday, January 18."

Instead of being delighted, as her husband had hoped, she scornfully tossed the invitation on the table, murmuring "What good is that to me?"

"But, my dear, I thought you'd be thrilled to death. You never get a chance to go out, and this is a real affair, a wonderful one! I had an awful time getting a card. Everybody wants one: it's much sought after, and not many clerks have a chance at one. You'll see all the most important people there."

She gave him an irritated glance and burst out impatiently, "What do you think I have to go in?"

He hadn't given that a thought. He stammered, "Why, the dress you wear when we go to the theater. That looks quite nice, I think."

He stopped talking, dazed and distracted, to see his wife burst out weeping. He gasped, "Why, what's the matter? What's the trouble?"

"Oh, nothing. Only I don't have an evening dress, and therefore I can't go to that affair. Give the card to some friend at the office whose wife can dress better than I can."

1. Based on the conversation, what is a good description of the husband?

   A   happy

   B   fearful

   C   confused

   D   angry

2. What is the best description of the wife's character?

   F   unappreciative

   G   thoughtful

   H   sweet

   J   careless

3. How does the passage provide information about the characters?

   A   through their thoughts

   B   through their words and actions

   C   through what other characters say about them

   D   through the thoughts of other characters

Finding the Main Idea

A paragraph or a longer passage contains many specific details. The details fit together to communicate a **main idea**. When you read a passage, determine its main idea. Sometimes the main idea of a paragraph is stated in the first sentence. Sometimes it is stated in another place in the paragraph. Most often, though, the main idea is *implied*. This means that it is never stated directly. It is communicated indirectly through supporting details. To understand a passage, figure out its main idea: the thought that links all its details.

> We think of the Sahara Desert as one of the driest places on our planet. However, over millions of years it has gone through wet and dry stages. Archaeologists believe that many people lived in the Sahara during one wet period within the past 10 thousand years. In 1933 French explorers in Chad discovered ancient artifacts and rock pictures. They showed that human warriors and hunters and many game animals had lived there. The lush grassland that was once their home has long since vanished in the dry climate of the desert.

The passage above gives some interesting details about what archaeologists have found in the Sahara Desert. It also offers a description of life in the Sahara long ago. However, the passage is not mainly about archaeologists or about the desert thousands of years ago. The main idea that is supported by both these details is that *the Sahara has gone through many changes throughout the ages.*

Read the passage. Circle the answer that states the passage's main idea.

> A lively literary period took place in the Harlem district of New York City in the 1920s. During the Harlem Renaissance, as the period was called, African-American writers showed new confidence and pride in their heritage. Young African-American artists, writers, and musicians gathered in Harlem to share their experiences. A leading figure of the movement was James Weldon Johnson. He wrote the novel *Autobiography of an Ex-Coloured Man*. Poets, playwrights, and novelists enjoyed great creativity in the progressive atmosphere of Harlem until the Great Depression caused them to scatter in search of work and money.

A James Weldon Johnson owes his fame to the Harlem Renaissance.

B During the Harlem Renaissance, African-American artists of all kinds enjoyed a period of energy and creativity.

C The Great Depression caused problems for many Americans.

D Most great African-American writers came from Harlem.

Practice

Read each passage. Then circle the answer that states the passage's main idea.

1.   George Washington and the Continental Army spent the miserable winter of 1777–1778 camped out near Valley Forge, Pennsylvania. The troops that survived were actually strengthened by their ordeal. Washington led his troops there after some serious defeats. He and his soldiers had little food and too little clothing to protect them from the bitter cold. Thousands died from exposure or disease. However, Washington held his position until spring. He drilled the soldiers and created a disciplined army. The troops went on to fight the British successfully in June.

   A   Washington and his troops camped at Valley Forge during the winter of 1777–1778.

   B   The Continental Army's winter at Valley Forge was unbelievably miserable.

   C   The bitter winter at Valley Forge helped prepare the Continental Army for future victories over the British.

   D   Washington was an effective general.

2.   Mound Builders were prehistoric North American Indians. They built many earthen mounds along the valleys of the Mississippi and Ohio Rivers. The mounds seem to have been important to their builders' culture. Archaeologists have learned that the mounds were used as burial places, lodges, or temples. Some mounds were round. Others were square, oval, or flat-topped. The Mound Builders died out in the prehistoric era. But they seem to have been a well-developed society. They used arrowheads and other tools. Archaeologists have not found the exact reason that the Mound Builders died out.

   F   Archaeologists study many prehistoric cultures.

   G   No one knows why the Mound Builders died out.

   H   In prehistoric times, people used mounds for many purposes.

   J   The Mound Builders had an advanced society.

3.   Two thousand years ago, ancient Rome already had one modern utility—running water. The Romans perfected the aqueduct. Under Frontius, the world's first superintendent of waterworks, 85 million gallons of water a day were brought into Rome through the aqueducts. The water came from springs in nearby mountains. Most Romans took their water from public fountains, but wealthy citizens could afford to run pipes to their homes.

   A   Ancient Rome was surprisingly modern in some ways.

   B   With the help of aqueducts, Rome had running water.

   C   Frontius was the first city water superintendent.

   D   Ancient Romans used 85 million gallons of water per day.

Apply

In your own words, state the main idea of each passage.

Mount Rushmore is a granite monument in a cliff in the Black Hills of South Dakota. It is one of the largest sculptures ever created. The faces of George Washington, Thomas Jefferson, Theodore Roosevelt, and Abraham Lincoln adorn the monument. To make the sculpture, workers referred to models made to a scale of one inch to one foot of rocks. They used drills and dynamite to cut the faces out of the granite cliff. The project took 14 years to complete.

1. _____

   _____

Extrasensory perception, or ESP, describes a way of sensing without using sight, hearing, taste, touch, or smell. It involves intuition, which is sometimes called a sixth sense. Scientists continue to debate the existence of ESP. About one tenth of all psychologists believe that ESP is real. Another tenth reject it completely. The rest want further studies to prove or disprove its existence.

2. _____

   _____

Most people know that the Pilgrims landed at Plymouth, Massachusetts, in 1620. But many people do not know that Plymouth was not the first place the *Mayflower* dropped anchor. The *Mayflower* first landed at Provincetown, at the tip of Cape Cod. Some of the Pilgrims stayed there while others scouted for a good place to settle. They found that place at Plymouth.

3. _____

   _____

United States Postal Service mail carriers do not deliver mail only on foot or in a truck. Some mail carriers travel on cross-country skis to deliver mail to hunters and trappers in remote sections of the north and Alaska. Some skiing mail carriers travel more than 30 miles to make their deliveries.

4. _____

   _____

Check Up

Read each passage. If the underlined sentence is the main idea of the passage, write *main idea*. If it is a detail, write *detail*.

Some people believe that the Sydney Opera House in Sydney, Australia, is one of wonders of the modern world. The Opera House contains a concert hall, two theaters, a cinema, and recording and practice studios. It was built on a beautiful site on the harbor. Its walls are distinctive, white, winglike shells. These shells were difficult to construct because they required many more arch supports than originally planned. Four architects and builders worked seven years to complete the building.

1. _____

The La Brea pits in California are one of the world's richest sources of Ice Age fossils. The pits are now part of Hancock Park in Los Angeles. In 1906 the remains of a giant prehistoric bear were found there. Since then, about a million well-preserved skeletons of saber-toothed cats, giant wolves, camels, horses, and other ancient animals have been dug from the layers of oil and tars. Those animals became trapped by the sticky tar when they went to drink from the water that covered the pits.

2. _____

If you ever make rhubarb sauce, be sure to get rid of the rhubarb leaves. Although rhubarb stems are edible, the leaves are poisonous. Rhubarb has large leaves and thick, juicy stalks that are full of vitamin C. But rhubarb leaves contain poisonous acid salts. They will make you sick if you eat them. The acid salts are not present in the stalks.

3. _____

Since the first one appeared in a New York newspaper in 1913, crossword puzzles have been popular all over the world. The puzzle has its roots in the "word square" created in ancient Rome. Three or more words were arranged in a square so that they spelled the same words forward and backward. The puzzles were complete, and readers simply admired them. They remained popular throughout Europe and the United States. In 1913 a puzzle similar to a word square appeared in a newspaper. But some of the letter spaces had been left empty for the reader to complete.

4. _____

Identifying the Main Idea

Identifying the **main idea** of a passage helps you understand and remember what you have read. Finding the main idea helps you paraphrase and summarize a passage. When you state the main idea, you state the general idea that is supported by the details in the passage. Make sure your statement is neither too broad nor too narrow.

Rich people find a variety of ways to exhibit their wealth. They may show off spacious mansions, expensive clothing and jewelry, and fancy vehicles. Chinese aristocrats had a unique way of showing their wealth. As a status symbol, they grew their fingernails, sometimes to as long as two inches. Long fingernails exhibited the fact that they never had to "demean themselves" by doing physical labor.

You might state the main idea of the paragraph above as, "Rich people often show off huge mansions to display their wealth." However, this statement is too narrow. It states a detail, not the main idea, of the passage. Or you might say, "Rich people like to exhibit their wealth." However, this statement is too general. A better statement of the passage's main idea is "Throughout history, rich people have had various ways of exhibiting their wealth."

Read the passage. Circle the answer that states the passage's main idea.

The first dinosaur bones were uncovered in the early 1800s. Scientists figured that the earth had been populated by reptiles as large as 20 to 30 feet long. The experts were amazed! The word *dinosaur*, meaning "fearfully great lizard," was coined for these creatures. But it turns out these scientists didn't know the half of it. In the 20th century, scientists found many more dinosaur skeletons. They learned to judge what the animals looked like and how much they weighed. They realized that the largest dinosaur of all, Brachiosaurus, measured up to 87 feet in length and up to 80 tons in weight.

A Brachiosaurus weighed an incredible 80 tons.

B Not until the 20th century did scientists figure out just how large dinosaurs really were.

C The word *dinosaur* means "fearfully great lizard."

D Dinosaurs were enormous animals.

Practice

Read each passage. Then circle the answer to each question.

Snowmobiling is a popular pastime in the United States. But some people worry that snowmobiles might damage the environment. People who enjoy the sport point out that snowmobiles use less gasoline than any other motor vehicle. So they create less air pollution. But environmentalists reply that other winter sports, such as skiing and ice skating, use no gasoline at all. In addition, snowmobiles travel at high speeds through the habitats of many wild animals, such as deer and rabbits. Many people worry that snowmobiles will threaten the wildlife by ruining their environment.

1. Which sentence best states the main idea of the passage?

   A Snowmobiles create less air pollution than other vehicles.

   B Some sports are healthier for the environment than others.

   C People disagree about whether snowmobiles harm the environment.

   D Snowmobiling is a popular pastime.

The American sport of football was developed from the English game of rugby. A medical student named Walter Camp played rugby when he was at Yale in the 1870s. However, he suggested some rule changes. For example, Camp reduced the number of players on a team from 15 to 11. He created the quarterback position. He devised the system of four downs. Camp is known as the Father of American Football.

2. Which of the following statements is too broad to be considered the main idea of the passage?

   F Football is similar to rugby.

   G Walter Camp was responsible for football's system of four downs.

   H Walter Camp is credited with inventing the American game of football.

   J While rugby had 15 players on a team, football had only 11.

The closest anyone has been able to get to the center of the earth is 36,198 feet below sea level. This depth was reached in Challenger Deep, which is part of the Mariana Trench, located southwest of Guam in the Pacific Ocean. It is the deepest known "ocean deep." An ocean deep is any part of the ocean that is deeper than 18,000 feet. A special diving machine called Trieste descended to the bottom of the Challenger Deep in 1960. It had to withstand water pressures that would have completed flattened an ordinary submarine.

3. Which of the following statements is too narrow to be considered the main idea of the passage?

   A Exploring the ocean is interesting.

   B Any spot deeper than 18,000 feet is called an ocean deep.

   C People are curious about their world.

   D The ocean is very deep in some places.

Apply

In your own words, state the main idea of each passage. Be sure it is not too broad or too narrow.

Kangaroos cannot run, yet even track stars wouldn't be able to keep up with them. A kangaroo's long, powerful hind legs are not mobile enough for running, but they are ideal for jumping. Kangaroos leap across the plains of Australia in jumps 15 to 20 feet long. They go about 20 miles an hour. Their speed allows kangaroos to escape predators.

1. _____

_____

Francis Scott Key would have to been hard-pressed not to see the "star-spangled banner" that flew over Fort McHenry during a famous battle of the War of 1812. That flag is now referred to in the national anthem of the United States. The flag measured 30 by 42 feet. Before the battle, the fort's commander had ordered a "flag so large that the British will have no difficulty seeing it from a distance." Indeed they had no trouble seeing it, for they shot it full of holes. But the next morning, as Key wrote, "our flag was still there." The United States had successfully defended the fort.

2. _____

_____

Baseball players spread a gooey substance called wood tar on their bats. This helps them get a better grip. The medical profession also recognizes the importance of wood tar. For centuries it has been used as an antiseptic. During the 1700s, the Bishop of Cloyne thought he had found a fantastic cure for all human illnesses. He had noticed that North American Indians often used tar in their medical practices. But he had overestimated the value of wood tar. Although it was a valuable antiseptic, it could not cure diseases.

3. _____

_____

Ecology is a branch of science. It is concerned with the relationships among organisms and their environments. Ecology was brought to the attention of the public and the government of the United States in the early 1960s. That is when Rachel Carson published *Silent Spring*. In this book, Carson described how pesticides were destroying plant and animal life. By 1969 many pesticides were banned.

4. _____

_____

Check Up

Read each passage. Then circle the answer that states the passage's main idea.

1.　　A hundred years ago, the job of the schoolteacher was different than it is today. Schoolteachers were expected to provide many services in addition to their teaching duties. They were also expected to behave so that they were a good example for their students. They cared for the oil lamps and tended the fire. They were expected to spend time each evening reading the Bible. Women teachers could not marry. Barber shops were off limits to men teachers because they were places where men gossiped and read sporting magazines.

A Barber shops were different a hundred years ago.

B The life of a teacher was hard a hundred years ago.

C Teachers have always been important influences.

D In the past, the tasks and expected behavior of teachers were different than they are today.

2.　　London had a serious pollution problem in the 1300s. The Thames River stank. The air was filled with a "disease odor" and soot clung to ladies' dresses. London was so polluted that the king had to forbid the use of coal. The government gave fines for a first offense and destroyed furnaces after the second. It seems that at least one lawbreaker was put to death for polluting the air.

F Justice was harsh in England in the 1300s.

G London officials took strong measures to fight pollution in the 1300s.

H Because coal was used for fuel in London, people's clothing got very dirty.

J Air pollution was unheard of until the 20th century.

3.　　The Cherokee Indians built their villages along the streams and rivers of present-day Georgia, Virginia, Kentucky, and North and South Carolina. They built the walls of their houses by planting large, sturdy posts three feet apart. They put smaller posts in between. The posts were held in place by twigs and long grasses woven to provide strength. To protect against wind and cold, the woven walls were plastered with a mixture of grass and clay. Many historians feel that the Cherokee were leaders in early architectural techniques.

A The Cherokee Indians were creative, effective builders.

B The Cherokee used twigs, grasses, and clay for their homes.

C Historians have studied Cherokee houses.

D The Cherokee lived in the southern United States.

Read On　Read "Business Leader: Remedios Diaz-Oliver." Use what you have learned about character and main idea to answer the questions.

Comparing and Contrasting

One way writers organize their writing is by comparing things and ideas. A writer who wants to describe two cities might **compare** them—list the ways in which they are alike. Or he or she might **contrast** them—list the ways in which they differ. Comparison and contrast are often used together. For example, the likenesses and differences of two or more things or ideas may be discussed in one essay.

Read the passage. Then circle the answer to each question.

Japan's capital city has been Tokyo, meaning "eastern capital," for more than 100 years. Kyoto was the great capital for over a thousand years. Today's noisy Tokyo was completely rebuilt after its ruin in World War II. Kyoto was also scheduled to be bombed, but, as one American argued at the time, "It would be like destroying Rome or Jerusalem. It's not just a Japanese treasure, but a world treasure!" Kyoto was spared. Today, mellowed by 12 centuries, it has the grace of old silver. Tokyo is Japan's dynamic today, Kyoto her perfumed yesterday. Tokyo is her brain, Kyoto her soul.

1. What two subjects is the writer comparing and contrasting?
    A Japan and the United States
    B Tokyo's role in World War II and Kyoto's role in World War II
    C the look and smell of Tokyo and the look and smell of Kyoto
    D Tokyo and Kyoto

2. What is the main way in which Tokyo and Kyoto are similar?
    F Both were ruined during World War II.
    G Both served as Japan's capital.
    H Both are beautiful.
    J Both are noisy.

3. What is one way in which the histories of Tokyo and Kyoto differ?
    A Tokyo was always important and Kyoto never was.
    B Tokyo was never rebuilt and Kyoto was.
    C Tokyo was bombed during World War II and Kyoto was not.
    D Kyoto has a history and Tokyo does not.

4. In the last three sentences, the writer compares the two subjects by
    F explaining how the war changed them
    G using a quotation
    H giving sensory descriptions of them
    J telling which one is better

Practice

Read the passage. Then write the answers to the questions.

The Washington Monument, completed in 1884, is in the capital of the United States of America. The Tower of Pisa, completed in the late 1300s, is in an old city in Italy. The two buildings have one thing in common: they are both sinking into the ground. Over several centuries, the 180-foot Tower of Pisa has settled 14 feet on one side. In comparison, the 555-foot, $5\frac{1}{8}$-inch Washington Monument is uniformly settling at the snail's pace of six inches per 100 years. Should the monument continue to settle at its present rate, a visitor in the year 113,984 will find the 55-story obelisk has sunk completely.

1. What two subjects are being compared?

_____

_____

2. Name two major ways in which the two subjects differ.

_____

_____

_____

3. Name one major way in which the two subjects are alike.

_____

_____

4. What transitional phrase indicates a change from one subject to the other?

_____

5. Describe one way in which statistics, or facts using numbers, are used to compare the two subjects.

_____

_____

_____

Apply

Read the passage. Then complete the chart that follows.

    Alligators and crocodiles are alike in many ways. Both are reptiles. This means they are cold-blooded and have dry, scaly skin. Both live in fresh water in tropical climates. However, compared to its wild, aggressive cousin, the crocodile, the American alligator is extremely polite. In captivity, the alligator seems to either ignore humans or calmly tolerate them. A relaxed alligator seen in profile appears to be grinning. In fact, alligators will submit to wrestling matches with humans. Such matches may be put on for tourists at alligator farms in Florida. A strong alligator wrestler will float the reptile on its back and rub its stomach until it is limp. No crocodile would ever take part in such a wrestling match.

ALLIGATORS AND CROCODILES

Likenesses	Differences

Check Up

Read the passage. Then circle the answer to each question.

Muslims share many beliefs with Christians. Muslims are followers of Islam, which was begun in the seventh century by Muhammad. Like Christians, Muslims believe in one God; the Muslims call their God Allah. One difference between the religions is that Muhammad felt that Islam was the true expression of the religion of Abraham and Isaac and that Christianity was a distortion of that religion. Otherwise, there are many similarities. Both faiths believe in an afterlife. Christians believe that Christ is the son of God; Muslims regard Christ as a minor prophet. The Muslim equivalent of the Bible is the Koran, the house of worship is called a mosque, and the most important prophet of Islam is its founder, Muhammad.

1. The biggest difference between Islam and Christianity is that
   A one faith believes in an afterlife and the other does not
   B one follows the teachings of Muhammad and one the teachings of Christ
   C one faith believes in one God and the other does not
   D one has a holy book and the other does not

2. Which of the following is **not** a similarity between the two religions?
   F Both have a house of worship.
   G Both were started in the seventh century.
   H Both believe in one God.
   J Both have a holy book.

3. Which of the following is used as a transition to show contrast in the passage?
   A Both
   B Otherwise
   C similarities
   D One difference

4. What conclusion can you reach from the comparison and contrast of the two religions?
   F All religions worship one God.
   G The world's religions all had the same beginnings.
   H The world's religions have many similarities.
   J All religions have a holy book.

More Comparing and Contrasting

Writers often use **comparison and contrast** to discuss two similar topics. For example, they might discuss the similarities and differences between two types of automobiles or between two restaurants. One way to help readers understand a comparison and contrast is to use specific transitional words and phrases. For example, words and phrases such as *also, likewise,* and *similarly* show likenesses. Words and phrases such as *although, however, in contrast, on the contrary,* and *on the other hand* show differences. Look for transitional expressions like these to help you understand comparisons and contrasts.

Read the passage. Then circle the answer to each question.

> Some comedians are mimics. They imitate the voices and mannerisms of other people. Similarly, some birds can also mimic voices. These birds are called mockingbirds. Mockingbirds have no song of their own, but they can imitate up to a hundred other bird calls. They also mimic other sounds—sounds that the best human impersonator would find difficult. Mockingbirds have been known to imitate locomotives, squeaking pump handles, and police officers' whistles. One bird even learned to imitate a theme song that it heard every morning on the radio.

1. The author describes mockingbirds by comparing them to
   A locomotives
   B whistles
   C comedians
   D people's voices

2. What transitional word is used to show how the two main subjects are alike?
   F Some
   G Similarly
   H also
   J even

Practice

Read the passage. Then circle the answer to each question.

Umpires in American baseball are often yelled at by managers. Umpires in Japanese baseball are treated with much more respect. In America, a dubious call by an ump can cause managers to launch into tirades loaded with unprintable words. Japanese managers, on the other hand, politely inquire as to whether the umpire is quite certain about the call he has made. American managers sometimes become literally hopping mad, and often they are thrown out of the game for their antics. A Japanese manager remains calm even though he may be angry. After the umpire delivers his final decision—which in both countries is almost always the same as his original call—the manager returns to the dugout on his own. Since neither method often results in getting the umpire to change his mind, it seems that American managers might want to consider the Japanese system.

1. What are the two main subjects of the comparison?
    A   Japan and America
    B   Japanese baseball and American baseball
    C   Japanese baseball umpires and American baseball umpires
    D   Japanese baseball managers and American baseball managers

2. What is the main difference between Japanese baseball umpires and American baseball umpires?
    F   Japanese umpires often change their calls, and American umpires do not.
    G   Japanese umpires rarely lose their tempers, and American umpires often do.
    H   Japanese umpires do not get yelled at as often as American umpires do.
    J   Japanese umpires make more wrong calls than American umpires do.

3. What is the main difference between Japanese baseball managers and American baseball managers?
    A   Japanese managers are more polite.
    B   Japanese managers lose their tempers more often.
    C   Japanese managers get thrown out of games more often.
    D   Japanese managers have higher blood pressure.

4. Which transitional word or phrase is used to show contrast between the two main subjects of the passage?
    F   Since
    G   After
    H   on the other hand
    J   even though

Apply

Read the passage. Then complete the chart that follows.

An American watching European football is seeing a different game than he or she is used to. European football is the game that Americans know as soccer. Although American football developed from the European game, it changed a lot when it crossed the ocean. Soccer players kick a round ball into a net goal to score one point. American football players carry a pointed, oval ball over a goal line to score six points for a touchdown. Americans wear heavy padding as part of their uniforms. Europeans protect themselves only with shin pads. American football games last 60 minutes but take longer because of frequent time-outs. European games last 90 minutes, and play rarely stops once the game begins. When Europeans and Americans are playing football, they are not playing the same game.

	European Football	American Football
Ball		
Scoring		
Players' Padding		
Length of Games		
Time-Outs		

Check Up

Read the passage. Then circle the answer to each question.

The Taj Mahal and the Great Pyramid have something in common besides being ancient examples of monumental architecture. They both had been scheduled for destruction. When Arab Muslims took over Egypt centuries ago, they had plans to dismantle the Pyramid for its limestone. But before the plan could be put into effect, they found limestone that was easier to obtain at a nearby quarry, so the pyramid was left alone. Likewise, a British businessperson in India in 1830 expressed interest in taking down the Taj Mahal for its valuable marble. Wrecking crews were hired, and the date for the demolition was set. However, protests from those who pointed out that the temple was a cultural achievement without parallel stopped the destruction in the nick of time.

1. How does the writer organize the discussion of the Taj Mahal and the Great Pyramid?

   A mainly discusses the differences between the two

   B discusses many similarities between the two

   C discusses the differences and similarities between the two

   D mainly discusses one little-known similarity between the two

2. What is one obvious similarity between the Taj Mahal and the Great Pyramid?

   F Both are in Egypt.

   G Both were destroyed.

   H Both are monuments.

   J Both were made entirely of marble.

3. What general idea does the writer communicate by discussing how the Taj Mahal and the Great Pyramid are similar?

   A Building materials should be recycled.

   B Throughout time, some people have been more interested in money than in lasting beauty.

   C It is difficult to destroy very old buildings.

   D Beautiful buildings were more common in the past than they are now.

4. What transitional word is used to show similarity between the two main subjects?

   F however

   G but

   H so

   J Likewise

Drawing Conclusions

Understanding the facts you read is an important step in comprehension. But it is not enough simply to comprehend the facts. You need to figure out what the facts mean. When you put the facts together with your common sense, you are **drawing a conclusion.**

If all the laws that are on the books in the United States were enforced, people would be charged with committing some pretty strange crimes. For example, an ancient statute in Kentucky forbids a man from purchasing a hat in any store unless he is accompanied by his wife. In Washington, D.C., it is illegal to fly a kite, on penalty of a five-dollar fine.

If you concluded from this passage that bizarre laws are enforced in the United States, your conclusion would be faulty. The first sentence states that this is not so. Likewise, you could not conclude that people long ago made crazy laws as a joke. Rather, a reasonable conclusion is that our country has some old, outdated laws on the books that no one has bothered to repeal. When you draw conclusions, make sure they are based on the facts.

Read the passage. Then circle the answer to complete the sentence.

Early people tended to be highly superstitious. Anything out of the ordinary that happened was regarded with fear. Most people throughout history have been right-handed. For that reason, left-handedness was regarded as an evil omen. The Latin word for *left* is *sinister*. Since many people regarded left-handedness as bad, the word *sinister* meaning "evil" entered the English language.

From this passage, you can conclude that superstitions usually grew from

A fear

B left-handedness

C evil omens

D terrifying events

Practice

Read each passage. Then read the conclusion drawn from the facts in the passage. Decide whether the conclusion is a valid one based on the facts. If it is valid, circle it. If it is not, write a conclusion that is reasonable.

1.   In 17th-century French high society, it was considered bad manners to knock on a closed door. At Versailles, the splendid palace of Louis XIV, the practice was to scratch softly on a door with a fingernail. That was the polite way to alert anyone inside the room, without startling the person, that someone wished to enter. For that reason, men at court cultivated one extra-long nail, usually the one on the little finger of the left hand.

Conclusion: Good manners are silly.

_____

2.   Thoroughbred racing is a popular sport. In the United States, the thoroughbred season is highlighted by the Triple Crown. This consists of three races: the Kentucky Derby, the Preakness, and the Belmont Stakes. Thoroughbreds are the fastest runners of all horses. Although many people aren't aware of it, they are a specific breed of horse. A thoroughbred is a type of horse that is descended from one of three Arabian stallions. The three stallions were imported into England between 1690 and 1730.

Conclusion: All thoroughbreds are champion racers.

_____

3.   Scientists recently studied the walking patterns of residents of 15 towns and cities in North America, Europe, and Asia. In each location they measured the pace of pedestrians over a distance of 50 feet. Results showed that the fastest big-city walkers were the residents of Prague, Czech Republic, who zipped along at a brisk four miles per hour. On the other hand, the people of the peaceful Greek village of Itea walked more slowly than anyone: a leisurely two miles per hour.

Conclusion: The speed at which people walk seems to be determined by the size and pace of the city or town in which they live.

_____

Apply

Read each passage. Then answer the question that follows it.

Guglielmo Marconi invented the wireless radio. Unfortunately, he had to work in secret because his father did not like his experiments. Marconi's father destroyed his son's equipment. He called the work with radio waves "childish." Marconi set up a secret lab in the attic of the family home in Bologna. In time, his work paid off. Marconi found that radio waves could be sent across great distances.

1. What can you conclude about Marconi's father's understanding of Marconi's work?

_____

Women's magazines reflect the changing social views of women's role in society. In the 1700s, magazines for women first appeared in Europe. At that time, liberty was an ideal for all people. Women's magazines of the time contained stimulating articles and literary works. Then, during the Victorian Era (late 1800s), women's magazines printed only light verse and fiction. They stressed moral values but had little intellectual content.

2. What can you conclude about attitudes toward women during the Victorian Era?

_____

More than 170 drugs used by Native Americans have been recognized as being effective by medical doctors. For example, powdered skunk cabbage roots were used by the Dakota Indians to relieve asthma attacks. The Kiowas cured dandruff by applying a plant called soaproot. The Cheyennes drank a tonic of boiled mint to settle an upset stomach.

3. What can you conclude about the medical knowledge of Native Americans?

_____

In 1804 Sir George Cayley built the world's first airplane. The plane was only a five-foot glider that was not stable or powerful enough to carry people. But it was a start that preceded the Wright brothers' famous flight in 1903. Cayley correctly predicted some features of today's planes. For example, he said that airplanes would someday be powered by internal-combustion engines.

4. What can you conclude about the origins of complex inventions?

_____

Check Up

Read each passage. Then circle the answer that completes each statement.

All land in North America once belonged to the Native Americans. After the Europeans arrived, the American Indians gradually lost control of their native lands. The Delaware once owned all the land between Ohio and the Atlantic. They signed a treaty with the United States government in 1778. The treaty established an Indian state. Many treaties were signed over the next hundred years. Each new treaty was broken by settlers moving onto Indian lands. The Delawares were pushed west into Indiana, then Missouri, then Kansas, and finally into Oklahoma.

1. We can conclude from this passage that the Delawares

   A were betrayed and pushed off their lands

   B broke all the treaties that were made with them

   C wanted to move farther west

   D were treated worse than any other group of Native Americans

In the late 1400s, the art of papermaking was introduced to Europe. The Chinese had invented decorative papers, but the Europeans were the first to apply decorative paper to walls. The first wallpapers were inexpensive. They were hand-painted or stenciled to imitate tapestry, painted cloth, or wood paneling that were often found in fancy homes. Wallpapers became expensive in the 1600s when flocked paper and painted Chinese papers were used.

2. We can conclude that the first inexpensive wallpapers

   F enabled the middle class to imitate the decor of the wealthy

   G were probably imported from China

   H duplicated formal landscapes

   J were not of very good quality

In ancient history, the kingfisher bird attracted attention because of its fantastic plumage. Ancient Tartar warriors believed that if they brushed a woman's skin with the bird's feathers, the woman would fall in love with them. The Chinese used the shiny blue feathers in their decorative screens.

3. We can conclude that the kingfisher

   A is now extinct

   B excited the imagination of ancient cultures

   C has magical powers

   D is now raised in captivity

More Drawing Conclusions

Sometimes a writer clearly states his or her point or lesson. Often, however, an author *implies* a point or lesson. It is the reader's job to figure out the point that the facts suggest. As you read, practice **drawing conclusions.** Make sure your conclusions are based on the facts presented. Make sure the conclusion you reach is not contradicted by any of the facts.

> Every year thousands of people record songs. Many singers hope their songs will top the charts and bring them fame and fortune. However, trade statistics show that less than 25 percent of all recordings released yearly make money. Also, on average, only 17 new artists a year make it into the Top 40. This is a success rate of less than 1 percent.

If you concluded from this passage that fewer people are trying to make it in show business now than ever before, your conclusion would be faulty. The facts contradict this conclusion. You also cannot conclude that fame brings happiness to successful recording artists. However, the facts of the passage do support the conclusion that many people enter show business despite the odds. This is a valid conclusion. It is supported by the facts in the passage.

Read the passage. Then circle the answer that completes the statement.

> Thomas Edison was one of the greatest inventors in history. He is credited with the invention of the electric lightbulb, the phonograph, and the movie camera and projector. Beginning in his 20s, Edison spent almost all his time in his laboratory. He devoted himself to inventing. Edison had been working since he was 12 years old. By age 22 he was working on Wall Street and had invented a new stock ticker. With the money from that patent, he opened up his laboratory.

From this passage we may conclude that Thomas Edison

A never wanted to be an inventor at all

B didn't care much about money

C was a talented businessperson as well as an inventor

D invented electricity

Practice

Read each passage. Then read the conclusion drawn from the facts in the passage. Decide whether the conclusion is valid based on the facts. If it is valid, circle it. If it is not, write a conclusion that is reasonable.

1.   In 1865 Jules Verne published the novel *From the Earth to the Moon*. In July 1969 Apollo 11 landed on the moon. Verne's fictional launch takes place in Cape Town, Florida, a few miles from the NASA facilities at Cape Canaveral. Verne's fictional rocket was called *Columbiad*. The real one was *Columbia*. The Verne expedition reached the moon in four days and one hour; the real flight lasted four days and six hours. Finally, both Verne and NASA chose an ocean landing for the returning flight.

Conclusion: There are amazing similarities between Jules Verne's novel and the Apollo 11 flight to the moon.

_____

2.   The first typewriter was very different from the machine it became later. Christopher Latham Sholes invented the first practical typewriter in 1868. But it wasn't all *that* practical. It had no lowercase letters, no zeroes, and no punctuation marks except the period and the comma. There was no backspace mechanism. The typists could not see what they were typing. The keys were arranged alphabetically.

Conclusion: The typewriter was a useless invention.

_____

3.   Studies show that certain kinds of noises affect your health. In an experiment at the University of Miami, a group of monkeys was subjected to urban noise for long periods of time. The animals' heart rates and blood pressure suffered adverse effects. Another group of monkeys were exposed to heavy metal rock music. They reacted at first with excitement, then anger, and finally, apathy.

Conclusion: Heavy metal music is better than noise.

_____

Apply

Read each passage. Then answer the question that follows it.

How would you like to look out your window and see a bird with a head four feet long and a wingspan of 18 feet? You won't see one, but you could view the fossil remains of a pterodactyl at a museum. This flying reptile lived with the dinosaurs. It became extinct with them about 65 million years ago. The remains of the largest pterodactyl indicate that it had a wingspan of 51 feet. The pterodactyl was not capable of sustained flight like other birds. In fact, the reptile could stay up in the air only by gliding.

1. What can you conclude by comparing pterodactyls to modern birds?

_____

_____

Susan B. Anthony, born in 1820, was a pioneer of the women's suffrage movement. As a young woman, she worked to abolish drinking and slavery. Eventually she devoted most of her time to gaining voting rights for women. In 1872 she led a group of women to the polls to challenge laws that kept women from voting. She was arrested, tried, and convicted for this act. She continued to work for women's suffrage until her death in 1906. In that year, only four states allowed women to vote. But in 1920, the Nineteenth Amendment to the Constitution granted women equal voting rights.

2. What can you conclude about Susan B. Anthony's effect on women getting the right to vote?

_____

_____

In the 1600s, American colonists made candles by dipping. After bringing back a deer, moose, or bear from a hunting trip, they would boil the animal's fat in water. Then they would dip a piece of twisted cotton into the waxy substance that floated on the water's surface. When one layer hardened on the cotton wick, they dipped it again. The more the wick was dipped, the more wax stuck to it, until it became a useful, tapered candle.

3. What can you conclude about the daily lives of early American colonists?

_____

_____

Check Up

Read each passage. Then circle the answer that completes each statement.

Naming a Native-American baby was an important tribal affair. To the Indians, a name had significant influence on a person's life. A female might be given a name such as Laughing Brook or Smiling Eyes. A male was often named after an animal or a weather condition. Girls kept their names throughout their lives. Often, later in life, a male was given another name that was based on a special deed.

1. We can conclude that the Indians

   A believed that a person's name and personality were closely linked

   B chose only names made up of two words

   C never named girls after animals

   D often chose names that had been in the family for a long time

Twice in the twentieth century, meteorites have slammed into Earth with the power of several H-bombs. A meteorite is a huge stone or metal lump from space. It crashes through Earth's atmosphere and cracks into pieces before it hits the ground. In 1908 and 1947, meteorites crashed in the Siberian wilderness. Both were heard hundreds of miles away. The 1908 crash leveled forests for 20 miles around. The 1947 meteorite exploded into pieces and left more than 200 holes in the earth. Fortunately, no humans were in the area when these meteorites hit.

2. We can conclude that a meteorite

   F would crash right through the earth if it hit the right spot

   G would set off all the H-bombs on Earth if it landed

   H could completely destroy a city if it landed on one

   J destroys by blowing things up with sound waves

In 1984 scientists found the remains of two sailors who had died in 1848. They were buried in the permafrost of Beechey Island in Canada. Remarkably, the bodies were perfectly preserved. The leader of the scientific expedition said that the sailors looked more alive than dead. He said it was like a time machine to see people dressed in the clothing of 136 years before. The English sailors were members of Sir John Franklin's ill-fated search for a water route connecting the Atlantic and Pacific Oceans. Their ship was crushed by Arctic ice, killing the entire crew.

3. We can conclude that

   A Sir John Franklin didn't die on his expedition

   B no other remains of members of Franklin's crew have been found

   C the bodies were preserved by an ancient Arctic culture

   D frigid Arctic temperatures preserved the bodies of the two sailors

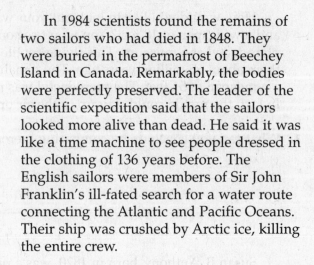

Read On Read "Faith, Family, and Farming." Use your skills in comparing and contrasting and drawing conclusions to answer the questions.

Recognizing Cause and Effect

Sometimes an effective way to explain a topic is to tell *why* something happens. A factor that makes something happen is a **cause.** A result of one or more causes is an **effect.** For example, the change of seasons occurs *because* of the earth's revolving around the sun and the tilt of the earth's axis. The seasonal change is an *effect* of these two factors. Sometimes writers focus on both **cause and effect.** Sometimes writers use the words *cause* and *effect* to discuss the relationship between events. Other words and phrases that indicate cause-and-effect relationships are *so, therefore, since,* and *as a result.* Sometimes writers imply a cause-and-effect relationship.

> If you lived on the planet Mercury, you would have a birthday every 88 days. The reason a Mercury year is shorter than an Earth year is that Mercury is much closer to the sun. Being closer to the sun means that its orbit around the sun is shorter; a single revolution is completed in only 88 Earth days.

In the paragraph above, the word *reason* in the second sentence indicates that a cause-and-effect relationship is being discussed. Reading further, you find that a year is only 88 days on Mercury because its orbit around the sun is shorter. Its orbit is shorter *because* it is closer to the sun than the earth is.

Read the passage. Then circle the answer to each question.

> Over 70 years ago, a fog in Meuse Valley, Belgium, started killing people. No one understood what was happening. The Meuse Valley is 15 miles long and is home to farms, villages, steel mills, and chemical plants. In 1930 a fog descended on the valley. By the end of three days, 60 people had died and thousands were in danger. Officials finally realized that the health crisis was caused by thermal inversion. When warm air trapped a layer of fog in the valley, the fog retained pollutants that were usually released into the upper atmosphere.

1. What **effect** is examined in the passage?

   A   the economy of a region of Belgium

   B   fog

   C   a rash of mysterious deaths and illnesses

   D   pollution

2. What is the **cause** of the effect that is examined?

   F   a health crisis

   G   fog

   H   warm air

   J   thermal inversion

Practice

Read each passage. If the cause is stated below the passage, write the effect. If the effect is stated below the passage, write the cause.

1. The first building to be called a skyscraper was built in Chicago between 1884 and 1885. The Home Insurance Company had the building constructed on La Salle and Adams Streets in the Windy City. It was designed by an architect named William Le Baron Jenny and was made of marble. So that the walls did not have to bear the weight of the building, a steel frame performed that function.

    Cause: A steel frame was constructed for the first skyscraper.

    Effect: _____

2. Julius Caesar had two of his names become common words. The Roman people elected Caesar dictator for life. Because he was such a strong leader, the name Caesar was taken as a title by the rulers who followed him. Because Caesar introduced a calendar reform to correct the Roman calendar, the name of a month changed. After his death, the Romans changed the month known as *Quintilus* to *July*, after the name *Julius*.

    Cause: _____

    Effect: The month known as *Quintilus* was changed to *July*.

3. It has been said that before Europeans arrived in North America, a squirrel could go from the Atlantic to the Pacific and never touch the ground. This statement may have been an exaggeration, but it highlights the fact that large areas of land that were once forested have been cleared of trees. Governor J. Sterling Morton of Nebraska, a concerned tree lover, wanted to make sure that there would always be plenty of trees. So on April 10, 1872, he led the first Arbor Day celebration.

    Cause: _____

    Effect: Governor J. Sterling Morton led the first Arbor Day celebration.

Apply

Read the passages. Then write the answers to the questions.

Whaling in the South Seas was not the romantic adventure that many popular stories might lead us to believe. Life aboard whaling ships had its moments of danger and excitement. But most of the time, the whalers were utterly bored. The thrill of sighting and chasing a whale was often followed by endless periods of waiting. Out of the whalers' boredom emerged the creative genius of the whalers. It was shown in their wonderful tall tales and their intricate whalebone carvings known as scrimshaw.

1. Why was whaling not as exciting as it has appeared to be in legends?

   _____

   _____

2. What was one effect of the boring life of whalers?

   _____

   _____

The *Washington Post* was one of the most powerful newspapers in the United States. During the 1970s, stories that appeared in the *Post* were largely responsible for unseating a U.S. president. And the *Post*'s publication of secret documents called the Pentagon Papers revealed improper behavior on the part of several government agents and caused a nationwide uproar.

3. What reasons does the writer give for asserting that the *Washington Post* was one of the most powerful newspapers in the country?

   _____

   _____

4. Why did the publishing of the Pentagon Papers cause a nationwide uproar?

   _____

   _____

Check Up

Read the passage. Then circle the answer to each question.

Many cultures have used makeup. Ancient Celtic women painted their bodies various shades of blue for festivals and mourning. The American Indians were called redskins not because of their skin color but because of their war paint. The women of some American Indian nations painted their faces black when a warrior died. The use of rouge and blusher today is similar to the way Roman leaders, Indian warriors, and South American women in the past used them. Throughout history, men have used makeup to make themselves look strong and brave. Women have worn it to enhance their beauty.

1. Why did ancient Celtic women paint their bodies various shades of blue?

   A for singing and dancing

   B for eating and sleeping

   C for walking and running

   D for festivals and mourning

2. Why were American Indians called redskins?

   F because some people were prejudiced against them

   G because their skin had a red tone

   H because of their mourning customs

   J because of their war paint

3. Why have men used makeup in the past?

   A to look brave

   B to enhance their beauty

   C for mourning

   D for festivals

4. According to the passage, why do women wear blusher today?

   F to prepare for festivals

   G to enhance their beauty

   H to continue a primitive tradition

   J to improve their health

5. The causes of which main effect are explored in the passage?

   A mourning

   B ancient customs

   C war paint

   D the wearing of makeup

Using Cause and Effect

Explaining the **causes** and **effects** of an event are important for understanding many kinds of information. In scientific fields, you might ask, "Why did the dinosaurs die out?" or "What causes a seed to germinate?" In studying history, you might ask, "What caused the Great Depression?" or "Why was Franklin Roosevelt elected president four times?" Sometimes writers are more concerned with the causes of an event or a phenomenon. Other times they are more concerned with the effects. Sometimes both causes and effects are examined in detail in an article.

> Food allergies are adverse reactions to certain foods. Food allergies cause nausea, rashes, or other symptoms. They are caused by antibodies in the digestive tract that mistakenly attack certain food proteins. There is no drug to cure food allergies; the only way to deal with them is to avoid the foods that cause them.

The passage above discusses both the causes and the effects of food allergies. First it answers the question "What are the effects of a food allergy?" (nausea, rashes, or other symptoms) Then it answers the question "What are the causes of a food allergy?" (antibodies in the digestive tract that mistakenly attack certain food proteins) The repeated use of the word *cause* indicates that the passage deals with cause and effect.

Read the passage. Then circle the answer to each question.

> A sneeze is a relatively violent reaction. The purpose of sneezing is to rid the body's upper respiratory tract of foreign irritants. The irritants may be substances such as pepper, pollen, fragrances, or germs. Sneezing is a reflex action; therefore, a person has little control over a sneeze once it is in progress.

1. What is the main question that the passage answers?

   A What is a reflex action?

   B Why must the body's upper respiratory tract get rid of irritants?

   C How often does the average person sneeze?

   D Why does a person sneeze?

2. Why does a person have little control over sneezing?

   F because it is caused by irritants

   G because it is a violent reaction

   H because it is a reflex action

   J because it is caused by germs

Practice

Read each passage. Decide whether it is mostly concerned with a cause or with an effect. If it is mostly about a cause, write *cause* and summarize the passage. If it is mostly about an effect, write *effect* and summarize the passage.

1.   A phenomenon called a red tide is threatening the world. It appears with increasing frequency along the seacoasts of many countries. With no warning, a portion of the sea begins to turn a dull shade of red. As the color begins to deepen, strange events take place. Fish leap straight up out of the water and fall back dead. Piles of fish slowly collect on the beaches. Dead and dying fish float belly up on the surface of bays and inlets. Waves glow eerily at night. Eventually all marine life touched by the red tide is destroyed.

_____

_____

_____

2.   The disease known as tarantism, which spread through Italy in the 1400s and 1500s, is still a medical mystery. The symptoms included a manic-depressive syndrome, with moods of depression and a lethargy alternating with uncontrolled laughter and weeping. The emotional outbursts were coupled with spinning and dancing, and were followed by a coma and, often, death. Less severe cases resulted in insomnia, vomiting, and overall weakness.

_____

_____

_____

3.   Have you ever wondered why the capital of the United States is not in any of the 50 states? When the 13 original colonies formed a Union after the American Revolution, men and women from every colony wanted to house the capital in their home territory. To solve this problem, the founders decided to put the capital in a location not affiliated with any particular state. In 1791 George Washington picked the site for the capital. He chose the 67-square mile area now known as the District of Columbia.

_____

_____

_____

Apply

Read the passages. Then write answers to the questions.

As people grow older, they need to exercise more. This is because people tend to gain weight with age as their basal metabolic rate, or the rate at which they burn calories, decreases. An older person's appetite may not decrease, but that person no longer needs as many calories as he or she did in earlier years. Many older people exercise less than they did when they were young, so they burn fewer calories. Also, the process of aging tends to convert more food into fat instead of muscle.

1. Why do people gain weight as they age?

_____

_____

2. What is usually the effect on an older person of continuing to eat as many calories as when he or she was younger?

_____

_____

For ostriches, being firstborn is the ideal place in the birth order. Because of the way ostriches care for their young, the firstborn seems to get all the advantages. Female ostriches usually share a common nest during the mating season, often laying several eggs apiece in it. One nest may contain dozens of ostrich eggs. Of course, some hatch before others, leaving the harried mother to feed the hungry chicks. Often she resorts to cracking open the unhatched eggs and feeding the contents to her offspring, since the chicks can't manage the tough foods that the parents eat.

3. Why does one ostrich nest usually contain dozens of ostrich eggs?

_____

_____

4. Why is the firstborn ostrich the most advantaged?

_____

_____

Check Up

Read the passage. Then circle the answer to each question.

In the 1970s many countries experienced high rates of inflation, but none reached the heights of the inflation in Hungary after World War II. Inflation is common after a country has been at war, because the government has spent so much on the war that other goods have become scarce. When supply is low, prices go up. The government often compensates by printing more money to pay its bills. This causes money to be worth less, so prices go up even more. In Hungary this turned into a vicious cycle. The government eventually had to start issuing paper money in higher and higher denominations.

1. Why is inflation common in a country after a war?

   A because prices are low

   B because goods have become scarce

   C because victorious countries have taken the loser's money

   D because the government prints less money

2. Which country faced high inflation after World War II?

   F Germany

   G Japan

   H Hungary

   J Italy

3. Why did the inflation in Hungary become so bad after World War II?

   A because money was worth more

   B because the various cures for high prices became a vicious cycle

   C because the government did not spend enough on the war

   D because the government did nothing to stop it

4. During an inflation, how does a government pay its bills?

   F it borrows money

   G it prints more money

   H it prints less money

   J not stated

5. What is the effect of the supply of goods being low?

   A Less money is printed.

   B Prices go down.

   C Prices go up.

   D The government pays its bills.

Summarizing and Paraphrasing

A good way to understand and remember what you read is to summarize it. When you **summarize,** you state the most important ideas and details in a passage as briefly as possible. A summary is much shorter than the original passage. Sometimes, however, you may feel it is important to recall every detail of a short passage. If so, you might paraphrase the passage. When you **paraphrase,** you include all the details but state them in your own words.

> Benjamin Franklin had unusual views on many subjects. From his own observations and experience, he developed a theory about catching cold that closely matches modern medical facts. He was an avid outdoorsman and swimmer who found that chilly temperatures and cold water had no adverse effects on his body. After ruling out coldness and dampness as causes of colds, Franklin noticed that people often caught cold after being in a crowded space. From that he deduced that colds were somehow passed from person to person when people were close to each other.

A good summary of this passage might be:

> *Benjamin Franklin concluded that colds were not caused by getting cold and wet but by being near many people in a crowded space.*

Notice that the summary is much shorter than the original but states its main ideas.

A good paraphrase of the last two sentences of the passage might be:

> *Franklin had a very modern theory about catching a cold. He observed that being cold and wet did not cause colds and concluded from evidence he observed that people passed colds to one another when they were close together in a crowd.*

Notice that the paraphrase fully explains all the sentences' details but uses different words than the original used.

Write a summary of the following passage. Then write a paraphrase of the direct quote.

> A common complaint of politicians is a sore right arm from too much handshaking. Once President Ulysses S. Grant was asked if he ever got tired of all the handshaking he had to do. "Yes," he said, "I think handshaking is a great nuisance and should be abolished. In 1865 it was awful for me; I thought I would hardly survive the task. It not only makes the right arm sore, but it shocks the whole system and unfits a person for writing or attending to other duties. It demoralizes the entire nervous and muscular systems."

_____

_____

_____

Practice

Write a summary of each of the following passages.

1.   Ancient hunting groups often believed that they were descended from a certain animal. They would, thus, place special importance on the animal, be it a wolf, an owl, or some other species. The animal revered in such a way by a clan is called a *totem*, and the belief in totems is called *totemism*. The totem animal, since it is sacred, is never killed or eaten and is sometimes prayed to as a god or idol.

_____

_____

_____

_____

2.   The cinema has never been more popular than in the years immediately following World War II. In the United States, millions of people flocked to the theater to see the films that poured endlessly out of Hollywood studios. But television soon provided stiff competition for the movie industry. In order to attract audiences, Hollywood started making fewer but more spectacular movies. The 1950s gave birth to a series of epic films, such as *Ben Hur*. Those star-studded movies were shot on location in "living color" and took years to make.

_____

_____

_____

_____

Apply

Write a paraphrase of each of the following passages.

1.   There is evidence that penguins enjoy some types of music. The polar explorer Robert F. Scott noted that penguins would always "come up at a trot" whenever his crew were singing. He said that several of his crew members could frequently be found on the deck of the ship singing before "an admiring group of penguins."

_____

_____

_____

_____

2.   Napoleon Bonaparte was famous for getting by on very little sleep. He would spend many sleepless days and nights preparing for a battle. However, he could fall asleep in the midst of a raging battle. "Nature has her rights," he declared, "and will not be defrauded with impunity. I feel more cool to receive the reports which are brought to me when awaking in this manner from a short slumber."

_____

_____

_____

3.   The short story writer O. Henry's last words were, "Turn up the lights—I don't want to go home in the dark." If he could return to us, he would find that he did not go home in the dark but that an increasing radiance shines around his name and fame. His stories are read today not only in English but in French, Spanish, German, Swedish, and Japanese.

_____

_____

_____

_____

Check Up

Read each passage. Then circle the answer to each question.

It is unclear who invented the windmill. Hero of Alexandria, who wrote in the first century B.C., credits himself with inventing the windmill. Three centuries earlier, however, a Hindu writer described water being raised by "contrivances worked by wind power."

1. Choose the best paraphrase of the passage.

   A At least two different people claimed to have invented the windmill. One was Hero of Alexandria in the first century B.C. A Hindu writer claimed he had invented the windmill three centuries earlier.

   B Nobody knows who invented the windmill. It could have been Hero of Alexandria or a Hindu writer.

   C No one can be sure who invented the windmill. In the first century B.C., Hero of Alexandria claimed to have invented the windmill even though three centuries earlier a Hindu writer had described machines that raised water by wind power.

   D Hindus called windmills "contrivances" while Hero of Alexandria claimed to have invented them in the first century B.C.

Early American settlers and pioneers did not have time for idle play, so when they wanted to enjoy themselves, they would turn their work into fun. They made many of their necessary chores into such group activities as logrollings, cornhuskings, quilting bees, and barn raisings. After the work was finished, everyone would eat, drink, and listen to music.

2. Choose the best summary of the passage.

   F Early American settlers and pioneers rarely played or had fun.

   G Group activities such as logrollings, cornhuskings, quilting bees, and barn raisings were invented by early American settlers and pioneers.

   H Hard-working American settlers often made their work into enjoyable group activities such as a barn raising followed by music and refreshments.

   J Early American settlers did not like to enjoy themselves, so they spent all their time on cornhuskings, quilting bees, and barn raisings.

More Summarizing and Paraphrasing

Summarizing and **paraphrasing** are useful skills when you take notes. When you want to recall the main facts of a passage, summarize it. Write only the main ideas. Combine important details and state them generally. A summary is shorter than the passage on which it is based. Sometimes you may decide it is important to remember more details of a passage. Then you will paraphrase it. A paraphrase may be the same length as the original, but it is written in your own words.

> With varying degrees of success, many women around the world today struggle for equal rights. Historically, women have achieved great equality with men during periods of social adversity. The following three factors initiated the greatest number of improvements for women: violent revolution, world war, and the rigors of pioneering in an undeveloped land. In all three cases, the essential element that improved the status of women was a shortage of men, which required women to perform many of the tasks that had been reserved for men.

A summary of the passage above might read:

> *Throughout history, women have usually obtained equal rights during difficult times such as war, revolution, or when settling undeveloped land.*

A paraphrase of the passage might read:

> *Women today want to achieve equal rights with men. The factors in the past that caused the most improvements for women were violent revolution, world war, and the tasks that came with settling a new territory. In these situations, there weren't enough men available, so women had to perform the tasks men formerly had done.*

Write a summary of the passage below. Then write a paraphrase of the definition of machines in the third and fourth sentences.

> We live in the machine age. We are surrounded by machines. A machine can be thought of as a device that has an arrangement of fixed and moving parts for doing work, each part having some special function. Machines make physical tasks easier by replacing or augmenting the energy that people expend. For instance, when you drive a screw into a piece of wood, you use your own effort to operate the screwdriver, but the screwdriver makes more effective use of that energy.

_____

_____

_____

_____

Practice

Write a summary of each of the following passages.

1.   Sometimes advertisements are hard to spot. They present themselves in many guises. The sign above a supermarket, for example, simply identifies the store, but when the store illuminates the sign to draw attention to itself, it's advertising. In the early days of radio and TV, emcees would often just interrupt programs and launch into commercials. Programming and advertising ran together. Today, regulations try to separate the two, but sometimes it's difficult. For instance, is a music video entertainment or a commercial for a recording?

_____

_____

_____

_____

2.   Many stories have been told of people's hair turning white as a result of terror and fright. But despite the abundance of such tales, medical science has yet to document a case in which the phenomenon has occurred. The majority of the legends are told around campfires or in some other dark and spooky atmosphere, for they are usually "ghost stories" concerning people undergoing horror in a haunted house. Two famous historical figures, however, are said to have undergone a hair color transformation. Some people avow that Mary, Queen of Scots, and Marie Antoinette both turned white-haired just before being executed. But there is no scientific proof of these tales.

_____

_____

_____

_____

Apply

Write a paraphrase of each of the following passages.

1. The first reported deaths from hailstones in the United States occurred in Winnsborough, South Carolina, on May 8, 1784. *The Charleston Gazette*, a South Carolina newspaper, described the storm as "a most extraordinary shower of hail, attended with thunder and lightning" and reported hailstones nine inches in circumference. The storm killed several people and animals.

_____

_____

_____

_____

2. People have always been interested in improving their memories. In the words of Thomas Dequincy, "It is notorious that the memory strengthens as you lay burdens upon it."

_____

_____

_____

_____

3. The ultimate form of communication, one that offers exciting possibilities, is telepathy. By means other than sensory perception, some people claim to be able to communicate using mind waves. Tests of people who are said to possess telepathic powers have been inconclusive, but some reputable experts are convinced that telepathy is not beyond the reach of the average person and can be developed through practice.

_____

_____

_____

_____

Check Up

Read each passage. Then circle the answer to each question.

In the 19th century, some doctors thought that a person's personality, morals, and talents could be judged from the contours of his or her skull. The analysis of the skull for such purposes is called phrenology.

1. Choose the best summary of the passage.

   A You can tell how moral a person is by feeling his or her skull.

   B Phrenology was a bogus science in which a person's character was based on the bumps on his or her head.

   C Some 19th-century doctors practiced phrenology, supposedly learning all about a person from the contours of his or her skull.

   D Each person's skull contours are highly individual.

Rarely did the early government of the United States negotiate fairly with the American Indians, and justice often occurred only when the government was forced to be fair.

2. Choose the best paraphrase of the passage.

   F The early American government treated the Indians well because the Indians forced it to be fair.

   G Laws supporting the American Indians forced the U.S. government to treat them fairly.

   H The U.S. government usually did not deal with American Indians fairly unless it was forced to.

   J The American Indians were forced to negotiate fairly with the U.S. government.

Billiards is a game with a varied reputation. Unlike many other well-known games, billiards has been most popular at the two extremes of the social scale. Fine billiard tables are frequently found in the most elegant homes. At the same time, billiards is considered, in many places, to be a lower-class game played mainly by persons of ill repute.

3. Choose the best summary of the passage.

   A Both poor and wealthy people have always liked billiards.

   B It is hard to tell which group of people plays billiards the most.

   C Even though most billiard players are poor, many wealthy people have beautiful billiard tables.

   D Billiards has an unusual reputation because it has been popular with both extremely wealthy people and with people considered to have poor reputations.

Read On Read "Battle of the Ballot." Use story clues to help find cause and effect. Then answer the questions.

Finding Supporting Evidence

When writers make a generalization or present a viewpoint, they must offer **supporting evidence**. Evidence to support a general statement may be in the form of **details or examples**. Evidence to support an opinion may be in the form of **facts and statistics**.

> Birds will go to great extremes to protect their young. They will attack intruders they would normally try to avoid. A mother hen will flail at a charging cat to defend her chicks. Adult robins, both male and female, issue piercing cries of alarm and fly frantically about, sometimes "dive bombing" an invader. The usually peaceful swan may attack suddenly. It will strike out viciously with its beak and wings if its nest is threatened.

The first sentence of this paragraph is a general statement. The writer supports this statement with examples that describe the behavior of three specific birds: hens, robins, and swans.

Read the passage. Then circle the answer to each question.

> Moscow, the capital of Russia, owes a lot to foreigners. The city's founder was Prince Yuri Dolguruki, the son of an English woman. The Kremlin was designed by three Italian architects. In the Kremlin are buried four Americans who were famed communists. Even the Russian name for the Soviet capital, Moskva, is derived from a word in the Finnish language.

1. Which sentence states the main idea of the passage?
   A Moscow was founded by an English person.
   B Italian architects are better than Russian ones.
   C People from many nations have influenced the city of Moscow.
   D People from all over the world have lived in Russia.

2. What kind of evidence does the writer use to support the main idea?
   F statistics about the number of foreigners in Moscow
   G details about buildings in Moscow created by foreign architects
   H details about people who have betrayed their country for Russia
   J examples of people from other countries who have affected Moscow

Practice

Read each passage. Then underline its main idea. Write one detail, example, fact, or statistic from the passage that supports the main idea.

1.   Mary Pickford was the first Hollywood film star. She began acting in 1909 when she was sixteen. She became known as America's sweetheart. But Mary was also a skilled businesswoman. In less than two years, she got her bosses to raise her salary from 40 dollars a week to ten thousand. In 1916 she formed the Pickford Corporation and started producing her own movies. In 1918 she joined with three male actors to form United Artists. Today, United Artists is one of the film industry's most successful studios.

Supporting Evidence: _____

_____

2.   College days in colonial times could be difficult, especially for first-year students. A college freshman could never wear his hat on campus unless it was raining or snowing, or unless he had both hands full. And why might both hands be full? A freshman had to act as an errand boy for all upperclassmen who demanded his services. At their command, he carried food and notes, delivered wigs to the curler, and took clothes to be pressed. What's more, all errands had to be performed with respect.

Supporting Evidence: _____

_____

3.   Some of the world's greatest art has resulted from the suffering of its creators. For example, Leo Tolstoy wrote *War and Peace* while considering suicide. Romantic poet Lord Byron had a club foot. Dutch painter Vincent van Gogh created colorful masterpieces while suffering from mental illness. Chopin wrote 24 preludes while he had tuberculosis.

Supporting Evidence: _____

_____

Apply

Read each passage. Then answer the questions.

The hardships faced by early European settlers in North America were many. They first endured a long, uncomfortable, and dangerous sea journey. Upon their arrival in America, they faced hunger, disease, and Native Americans trying to protect their lands. Consequently, persuading people to leave a relatively safe European life for the adventure of colonization often required a little public relations work. One of the first to engage in public relations on behalf of America was George Weymouth, who had explored the coast of Maine in 1605. He returned to England with five American Indian women. The women learned English and dressed in English clothes. They made public relations appearances through which they promoted the New World as an unclaimed Utopia.

1. Name two examples that support the first sentence, which states the main idea.

   _____

   _____

2. Summarize the evidence that supports the view of George Weymouth as one of America's first public relations person.

   _____

   _____

A city located near the equator isn't necessarily a tropical paradise. True, some equatorial cities do have some warm climates. In Singapore, Malaysia, and Nairobi, Kenya, for instance, the temperature rarely drops below 60° Fahrenheit. But Quito, a city in Ecuador, is a very different case. There the weather is crisp year-round; sometimes the temperature dips below freezing. That's because Quito is located in the mountains, and its great elevation keeps it cool.

3. What city is used as an example to support the first sentence?

   _____

4. Why does the author mention Singapore and Nairobi?

   _____

   _____

Check Up

Read the passage. Then circle the answer to each question.

The 1920s produced writers, painters, and musicians who were part of a revolution in the arts. Novelists such as Marcel Proust and Virginia Woolf did not focus on story and action. They wrote about emotion and the subconscious. Others, such as D. H. Lawrence and James Joyce, tried to free the novel from restrictions on the use of coarse language and descriptions of sex. Erich Maria Remarque and Ernest Hemingway wanted to write realistically about war's tragedy. They wrote novels that showed the impact of World War I on individuals.

1. The "revolution" mentioned in the first sentence refers to

   A fighting in World War I

   B using coarse language

   C rebelling against current standards in art

   D giving up the arts

2. What kind of artists does the writer use as examples to support the main idea?

   F poets

   G novelists

   H painters

   J musicians

3. In what different ways did the artists participate in the revolution?

   A by focusing on action

   B by ignoring emotion

   C by focusing on emotion, rejecting restrictions, and writing realistically

   D by rejecting the subconscious

4. How did Marcel Proust participate in an artistic revolution?

   F by writing about emotion instead of action

   G by writing about wars

   H by writing like D. H. Lawrence

   J by not writing about the subconscious

5. Which author wanted to write about war's tragedy?

   A Virginia Woolf

   B Ernest Hemingway

   C D. H. Lawrence

   D James Joyce

Using Supporting Evidence

Good writers do not simply state a generalization or an opinion. They support the general statement or opinion with **examples, facts, and statistics**. Good readers pay close attention to these kinds of **supporting evidence**. Evaluating the evidence helps them decide whether the writer's opinion or generalization is valid.

> There are strange stories about what several famous composers did to stimulate their creativity. Some say that Ludwig van Beethoven liked to pour ice water over his head to shock himself into creativity. Wolfgang Amadeus Mozart supposedly composed his greatest works while playing billiards. And Richard Wagner would get into the spirit of his operas by wearing costumes while he composed.

In the passage above, the writer begins with a general statement. A reader's natural response to such a generalization is to look for examples that prove it. The sentences that follow the generalization provide these examples. The examples are the passage's supporting evidence.

Read the passage. Circle the answer to each question.

> Some famous explorers were not very popular with the people on their expeditions. They probably inspired the anger of the people they managed because the nature of their job was to lead people into dangerous, uncomfortable places and situations. Henry Hudson, for example, was set adrift in the bay that bears his name by a disgruntled, hungry crew. It was Hudson's last voyage. The explorer La Salle was killed by a band of 20 explorers on the Gulf Coast in 1687, and his body was left to the buzzards. This dreadful act may be explained by the fact that the band of 20 was all that remained of the original force of 400.

1. What function does the second sentence of the passage serve?
   A It states a generalization.
   B It provides supporting evidence for a generalization.
   C It states a fact.
   D It further explains a generalization.

2. Why, apparently, did La Salle's crew kill him?
   F They were outlaws.
   G They were hungry.
   H They blamed him for the hardship they had endured.
   J They wanted credit for the expedition.

Practice

Read each passage. Then underline its main idea. Write one example, fact, or statistic that supports its main idea.

1.   The Celtic culture arose in southwestern Germany around 500 years before the birth of Christ and spread all over Europe. The Celtic culture is notable for its emphasis on the importance of women. All elected judges were women, and the wife in any marriage had the final say in all business matters. The Celtic husband needed his wife's permission before he could enter into any transaction. The Celtic gods were females, and their paradise, or heaven, was called "the land of women."

Supporting Evidence: _____

_____

2.   Since dogs were first domesticated about ten thousand years ago, people have adopted hundreds of kinds of animals into the human environment. The most common domesticated animal in the world is the chicken. Currently, there are about four billion domesticated chickens all over the world. No other domesticated animal, with the possible exception of sheep, comes close to that number. Other animals, such as goats and horses, were domesticated in prehistoric times, and even cats go back as far as ancient Egypt.

Supporting Evidence: _____

_____

3.   The most powerful strongman of the ancient world was Milo of Croton. Born in a Greek colony in Italy around 560 B.C., Milo was the greatest wrestler of his time. He won the wrestling event in six separate Olympic Games between 540 and 516 B.C. His other feats of strength included carrying a full-grown ox across the stadium at Olympia. He challenged athletes from miles around to bend one of the fingers on his hand—no one could do it.

Supporting Evidence: _____

_____

Apply

Read each passage. Then write the answers to the questions.

The Tarahumare Indians of the Sierra Madre are known as runners of extraordinary stamina. The territory they live in is too rugged for wheeled vehicles or even mules. So they have highly developed walking and running skills. Through the centuries, various customs have grown to test the endurance of the Tarahumares' best runners. One custom that still survives is a kickball race that covers 100 miles or more. Teammates rotate in the position of kicker. While one person kicks the ball ahead, the other participants jog along behind. The race sometimes lasts as long as three days and nights without pause.

1. Why have the Tarahumare Indians become especially good runners?

   _____

   _____

2. What aspects of the Tarahumare kickball race prove that the participants have excellent endurance?

   _____

   _____

   Not too long ago, illnesses that are hardly heard of today raged across the U.S. Cholera first hit in 1832, killing over 100 people. Polio, which was at one time a crippling disease with no cure, claimed 123 victims in Vermont in 1894. Smallpox, which is no longer in existence, swept across the Northeast in 1616, nearly wiping out whole Native-American nations. It is said that English Indian fighters gave Chief Pontiac and his followers smallpox-infested blankets during the French and Indian War. That tactic of using an epidemic as a weapon of war caused the disease to move through the Great Lakes region, killing many Native Americans.

3. Name the diseases used as examples to support the first sentence of the passage.

   _____

   _____

4. What statistic supports the statement that polio was one of the illnesses that raged across the United States?

   _____

   _____

Check Up

Read the passage. Then circle the answer to each question.

Television was not really invented; it was developed over many years through the work of numerous scientists and engineers. The history of television began with the first experiments with electricity. In 1817 a Swedish chemist found and named the element *selenium*. It conducts electricity strongly when it is exposed to light. Work with selenium led to the photoelectric cell, which converts light into electrical impulses. A German engineer built a practical mechanical television in 1884. In the 1920s scientists combined radio-broadcasting techniques with the mechanical television. An American and an Englishman separately developed picture transmission by combining photography, optics, and radio. More efficient systems, based on the work of these early scientists, were soon built.

1. The first step in the development of television was

   A the discovery of selenium

   B the invention of the photoelectric cell

   C experiments with electricity

   D the invention of radio

2. The element selenium conducts electricity most when it is exposed to

   F light

   G heat

   H cold

   J darkness

3. In what year was a practical mechanical television built?

   A 1884

   B 1848

   C 1817

   D 1921

4. In what way was the invention of the radio related to the invention of the television?

   F Its technology was important in developing television.

   G It was invented after television was invented.

   H Both were based on the photoelectric cell.

   J There was no relationship.

5. What general technique does the writer use to prove the generalization on which the passage is based?

   A using several unrelated examples

   B using statistics

   C describing the lives and works of several scientists

   D tracing historical developments

Read On As you read "Ready for High Speeds," use your skills in summarizing, paraphrasing, and finding supporting evidence to answer the questions.

Review

Characters

When you read, you analyze a **character's traits**. You put a character's words, thoughts, and actions together to understand what the character is like. You also can learn about a character from what other characters think or say about him or her.

Main Idea

The **main idea** is the most important idea in a paragraph. Sometimes the main idea of a paragraph is stated in the first sentence. Sometimes it is stated in another place in the paragraph. Often, though, the main idea is **implied**. It is not actually stated. It is communicated indirectly through **supporting details**.

Comparing and Contrasting

An author who wants to describe two people or things might **compare** them—list the ways in which they are alike. He or she might also **contrast** them—list the ways in which they differ.

Drawing Conclusions

When you decide how the facts in an article or story add up, you are **drawing a conclusion**. You draw a conclusion based on things that are stated directly, things that are implied, and things that you already know.

Cause and Effect

Authors use **cause and effect** to explain how one event causes another. A factor that makes something happen is a **cause**. A result of one or more causes is an **effect**.

Summarizing and Paraphrasing

When you **summarize**, you state the most important ideas and details in a passage as briefly as possible. When you **paraphrase**, you restate a passage, including details, in your own words.

Supporting Evidence

Authors use **supporting evidence** to tell about the main idea of a passage. Supporting evidence can be facts, statistics, examples, or reasons.

Assessment

Read each paragraph and circle the answer to each question.

He snapped off the bedside light and dropped the magazine to the floor. He heard the rain, the hiss, and swish of the traffic in the street. He felt almost too lonely for words. Again he thought of his father, of the failing body that had once been tireless and strong. He thought of the many failures, of the jobs that never quite worked out, the schemes that never quite paid off. Thinking of this and remembering when they had been a family and when his mother had been alive to hold them together, he cried.

1. What is revealed about the main character?

   A He is angry because he is an orphan.

   B He is sad because he misses his family.

   C He is afraid to be alone.

   D He is proud to be self-sufficient.

2. The author reveals information about the character

   F through the character's actions

   G through the character's thoughts

   H through a description of the character

   J through other people's opinion of the character

Because of the damage that mice do, people have made clever traps to catch them. Early people built a simple trap. When the mouse touched the bait, a heavy rock fell on it. Since then, people have invented all kinds of traps. Most of them work, even though the mice are quite clever. One trap looked like a small prison with bars at the side of a small door. When the mouse walked in, its weight would cause the door to spring shut. This trap, like many others, did not kill the mouse. It put the mouse in "jail." Another kind of trap has a door held shut by a weak spring. Once inside, the mouse could not come out. The most common trap today is a small piece of wood with a spring in the center that snaps a wire across the mouse's neck.

3. What sentence states the main idea of the passage?

   A Since then, many people have invented all kinds of traps.

   B Once inside, the mouse could not come out.

   C Most of them work, even though the mice are quite clever.

   D Because of the damage that mice do, people have made traps to catch them.

4. Which of the following is the best title for this passage?

   F Trapping Wild Animals

   G Mice and Disease

   H Mice, Beware!

   J Cruelty to Animals

Few people realize that concrete and cement are the not the same material. Cement is a chemical powder that forms a paste when mixed with water. It is used mainly to make concrete. Concrete is a mixture of cement, water, sand, gravel, and crushed stone. The cement and water in the mixture hold the other materials together. Concrete can be molded into any shape and hardens very quickly. This extremely strong material is mainly used for buildings, roadways, dams, and other structures.

5. What is being contrasted in this paragraph?

    A roadways and dams

    B powdered materials and molded materials

    C concrete and cement

    D buildings built with concrete and buildings built with cement

6. What is the best summary of this paragraph?

    F Cement is a chemical powder that is mixed with other materials to form concrete. Concrete is a strong material that is used to build large buildings and other structures.

    G Cement is a powder that is mixed with water, sand, gravel, and crushed stone to make concrete. Most large structures in a city are made of concrete.

    H Concrete is made of cement. It is a used in molds and is very strong.

    J Builders use concrete to make many structures because it can be molded into many shapes. Concrete hardens quickly into an extremely strong material. It is made from cement, water, stone, and other materials.

To protect against fire or shock, every electrical system in your home includes one of two types of safety devices: fuse or circuit breaker. They operate differently but serve the same purpose—to stop the flow of electric current. Too much current can flow through a circuit when a single outlet is used for too many appliances. A burned-out, or blown, fuse must be replaced before the current can flow through a circuit again. Circuit breakers trip, or break, the circuit by automatically snapping open to stop the flow of electric current. The circuit breaker is then reset by hand.

7. What might cause a fuse to blow or a circuit breaker to trip?

    A plugging 20 appliances into a single outlet

    B leaving an appliance plugged in too long

    C having too many circuits in your home

    D failing to pay your electric bill

8. You can conclude from reading this paragraph that before replacing a fuse or resetting a circuit you should

    F purchase new appliances

    G determine which appliances are no longer needed

    H determine the cause of the trouble and correct it

    J understand that circuit breakers and fuses are more trouble than they are worth

Gemstones are identified according to their color, crystal form, luster, and hardness. Color is the first quality noticed in a gemstone, but people should not identify gems by their color alone. The colors of some gemstones do not change. Many gems, however, have a wide range of colors. Iron and copper may slightly change the color of some of them. A better method of identifying gems is through crystal shapes. These shapes form within a certain range of temperatures and pressures. The luster, or shine, of a gemstone may be described as glassy, pearly, waxy, silky, or brilliant. Hardness is measured by a scratch test. The tester tries to scratch the gem with another mineral or a steel knife blade. The diamond, with a hardness rating of 10, is the hardest gemstone known.

9. According to the information given, you can conclude that
   A the whitest diamonds are the hardest and most expensive
   B a perfect stone has several outstanding qualities
   C a ruby is a gem
   D most gems have the same crystal shape

10. Using the information in the passage, you can conclude that
    F no other gemstone is harder than a diamond
    G a diamond has a brilliant luster
    H gems with a high luster are never found in nature
    J most gems can scratch steel

Biased Language

An important skill in critical reading is the ability to recognize **biased language**. Authors often express their own particular bias that is, positive or negative slant, about a subject by using **euphemisms**. A euphemism is the substitution of an inoffensive term for one considered offensive or politically incorrect.

> An industrial park is a euphemism for a factory.

Write your own euphemisms for the following terms:

1. used car _____
2. cheap _____
3. expensive _____
4. old-fashioned _____

5. In what parts of a newspaper would euphemisms most likely be found?

_____

Read each paragraph. Underline the phrases that are examples of biased language. Write _positive_ or _negative_ to identify the bias the author conveys.

6.   As the mayor of Oak Creek, I recommend hiring Rehab Restoration to repair our historic city hall. I have seen evidence of their quality work as I have traveled throughout the state. They do fast, clean, quality work. Their bid is competitive with those of all other repair companies, and I have recommendations from other municipalities. I feel sure that hiring them for the job would be a mutually beneficial arrangement.

_____

7.   How could you have fallen for that advertisement? Even though the flyer promised up to $1500 a week selling products over the phone, you have absolutely no guarantee that you will earn that much. What kind of reputable company advertises for a "first-rate" sales force by blanketing every car in the city with gaudy yellow flyers? Did you even know what kind of junk you would be selling? If selling this product were as easy as the advertisement promises, everyone would have snapped up these jobs long ago.

_____

8.   The Bonanza is the best new car on the market. In addition to getting 32 miles to the gallon, the Bonanza provides the smoothest ride on the road. Its classic styling and elegant color selections make it _the_ automobile for the discriminating driver. Interior temperature control, sport wheels, CD player, and leather seats are standard equipment on this affordable but upscale car. This car is one you will be proud to drive for years to come.

_____

Personification

An element of style is the use of figures of speech. A **figure of speech** is an expression in which words are used in ways not usually associated with them. **Personification** is a figure of speech in which a living or nonliving thing is given human characteristics.

> The North Wind was a fierce warrior as it invaded the level prairie.

The North Wind is given human qualities like those of a warrior.

> The shadow crept along the floor, signaling that night was fast approaching.

The shadow creeps as a person or an animal might.

Write a sentence personifying each of the following living or nonliving things, without naming it. Remember to describe the thing as if it were human. Read your personifications aloud and have others identify what you have described.

1. the wind _____

_____

_____

2. a flower _____

_____

_____

3. a bicycle _____

_____

_____

4. a mouse _____

_____

_____

Predicting Outcomes

One way to better understand what you read is to **predict** how events will turn out. To do this, pause at critical points and ask, "What will happen next?" You can use all the elements of a story or an article, including character, plot, style, and theme to help in your predictions. Writers often offer hints, called **foreshadowing**, about how situations will turn out. Practice taking note of foreshadowing to help you predict outcomes.

> Have you ever found a valuable jewel in your backyard? How about in a horseradish field? In 1928 a lucky "miner" from West Virginia named William Hones found an interesting stone in a field. Hones didn't realize what he had found, but he took the stone home. Fifteen years later, after a visitor told Hones that the stone looked valuable, he showed it to a stonecutter.

In reading the passage above, you might pause at this point, just before the final outcome, and ask, "What will happen next?" Many clues indicate that the story will have an interesting twist. The words and phrases "valuable jewel" and "lucky" are just some of the clues that foreshadow that Hones's find will turn out to be extremely valuable. Now read the end of the story:

> The stonecutter informed Hones that it was a 32 carat diamond. It was one of the largest diamonds ever found in the United States.

If you read the passage attentively, you probably guessed the general outcome of the story. Work on **predicting outcomes** to improve your comprehension.

Read the passage. Circle the answer with the most likely ending to the story.

> Bargain shoppers should beware of a popular underhanded sales tactic. Consider what happened to one shopper who read the following ad: "Color TV, only $79. Two day sale. Hurry!" When she got to the store ready to buy, she discovered that the advertised sets were sold out. What happened next?

A The salesman said he would order a $79 set for her.

B The salesman lowered the price of a better TV to $79.

C The salesman drew her attention to a better TV that cost $359.

D The salesman angrily told her that she should have come to the store earlier.

Practice

Read each passage. Circle the answer with the most likely outcome to each story.

1.   Every year since 1949, an unknown admirer has visited Edgar Allan Poe's grave, leaving three fresh-cut roses and a bottle of brandy. The mysterious stranger arrives after dark on the mystery writer's birthday. Several Poe scholars who knew about this annual event once tried to find out who the unknown admirer was. The night of January 19, 1983, they kept watch over Poe's grave in Baltimore, Maryland.

   A Around 1:30 A.M., a dark figure in a long coat approached the grave, only to flee after seeing the people waiting.

   B They played music and read excerpts from Poe's works.

   C The next day they reported they had seen the ghost of Poe at the grave.

   D Unfortunately, they got frightened and soon went home.

2.   The rules of tennis changed in 1971. In 1969 Pancho Gonzales and Charles Pasarell played the longest match ever played at Wimbledon. Gonzales won the match, but not until one set that was decided by a score of 24 games to 22 and another that stretched to 16 games for Gonzales and 14 games for Pasarell. The entire match consisted of 112 games and took 5 hours and 20 minutes to complete. After this match,

   F officials decided that Gonzales and Pasarell could not play any more matches at Wimbledon

   G officials instituted a tiebreaker if a set is tied after six games

   H officials said no matches at Wimbledon could be shorter than 5 hours and 20 minutes

   J Gonzales and Pasarell realized they were the best players in the world

3.   Many people say they don't understand abstract art, but those people are not usually museum curators. In October of 1961, the Museum of Modern Art in New York City hung a painting by Henri Matisse, one of France's most respected 20th-century artists. For the next month and a half, over 100,000 people visited the museum, and most of them looked at the Matisse painting. Art critics also toured the museum on a regular basis, and none of them reported anything out of the ordinary after viewing Matisse's work.

   A The painting was returned to France after a successful showing.

   B Finally, the museum's curator admitted that he did not like Matisse's work.

   C Finally, a visitor notified embarrassed officials that the painting had been hung upside down.

   D Later, the painting was stolen.

Apply

Read each passage. Write the letter of the most likely ending to each passage.

A Migrating gray whales play offshore during their journey north to the Bering Sea.

B The ship rammed the white, silent giant of nature and sank in less than three hours.

C Soon, however, older citizens began to study the sky toward the southeast, toward the Caribbean where hurricanes are born.

_____ 1.   During the first week of September 1900, everybody in Galveston Beach, Texas, went swimming. There had never been such fine surf—great rolling combers that swept in from the Gulf. Yet, there was hardly a breath of wind. A blanket of humid heat lay over the city. Storm warnings had gone out to the Gulf shipping companies. The barometer was falling. Those signs should have been of concern to the people of a town on a sandbar only nine feet above the sea at its highest point, but nobody seemed worried.

_____ 2.   Spring, with all its stirrings and green renewals, is a splendid season to sample the riches of Point Lobos State Reserve. This bit of land on the Monterey County coast in California is a glorious living museum of wild things. There are things that swim in the sea or sail in the ocean winds or scamper along the forest floor or blossom in the meadows. Sea lions bellow from the offshore rocks. Otters float in the blue coves, cracking mussels and grooming their whiskers.

_____ 3.   In 1912 a luxury liner was making its first Atlantic voyage from England to New York. Early in the night the captain of the ship had been warned that there were icebergs in the area. The warning was apparently ignored as the big liner sped on through the darkness, heading swiftly toward its destiny.

Check Up

Read the passage. Then circle the answer to each question.

There's usually no harm in a little extravagance, but in 1905 some wealthy American socialites learned a hard lesson about overdoing it. As guests at the stylish Savoy Hotel in London, these people decided to throw a lavish birthday party for one of their friends. The theme was "Venice," and with the help of the hotel, the entire front courtyard was flooded with water that was dyed blue. An authentic gondola was shipped in, and doves were imported. Swans were brought in to paddle around the "canal." Finally, after a baby elephant towed in the giant birthday cake and the guests were at the height of merriment, . . .

1. The first sentence of the passage foreshadows what kind of ending for the story?

    A happy

    B frightening

    C optimistic

    D unfortunate

2. Which phase foreshadows the story's ending?

    F learned a hard lesson

    G the stylish Savoy Hotel

    H a baby elephant

    J an authentic gondola

3. Which is the most probable outcome of the story?

    A Italians protested the imitation of Venice for a party.

    B The socialites invited many poor people in to enjoy the party with them.

    C The swans suddenly died from the cobalt-based blue dye in the water.

    D The elephant ate the doves and the swans.

More Predicting Outcomes

When you watch a movie, you probably try to figure out how it will end. You use many clues, such as remarks made by the characters and outstanding details, to make your predictions. You should do the same thing when you read. Authors often give hints, called **foreshadowing**, about how a story will end. They also insert and emphasize important details.

> Jim hesitated. He didn't like the man's looks or the way he talked. Any other time he would have said, "No thanks," but his leg hurt, and it was a long walk home.

This short passage gives several clues as to what Jim will do. The phrase "any other time," the transition "but," and the statement that "it was a long walk home" help you figure out what Jim will do:

> He got in. The big car started off in a burst of speed.

Read the passage. Circle the answer with the most likely ending to the story.

> Eric Liddell was scheduled to run the 100-meter dash in the 1924 Paris Olympics. The runner from Scotland was a devout Christian. Then he discovered that the qualifying heats were to be held on a Sunday. For most Christians, Sunday is the Sabbath. Some have tried to dedicate their Sabbath to prayer. They avoid activity that is not essential.

A Liddell did not hesitate to participate in the heats.

B Liddell refused to participate.

C Liddell won his qualifying heat.

D Liddell had the Olympic officials change the day of the heats.

Practice

Read each passage. Circle the answer with the most likely ending to the story.

1.   All armies are constantly trying to improve their battle strategies. But one important element they have no control over is luck. For instance, in the 1660s, a British general Sir Henry Morgan and his troops were laying siege to a Spanish fortress in Panama. Inside were most of the Spanish troops in the region. The defenders were strong; Morgan was thrust back each time he made an assault on the fortress. But according to one story, something happened that would change the outcome of the battle. One of Morgan's troops took an arrow in the shoulder. The soldier yanked the arrow out, loaded it into his musket, and fired it back into the fortress.

   A Then the soldier died from the arrow wound.

   B The arrow fell at the Spanish general's feet.

   C It landed on the enemy's gunpowder, burst into flames, and the fortress exploded.

   D It killed a Spanish soldier.

2.   Most people have never heard of one of the worst maritime disasters in United States history. In April of 1865, the Civil War was drawing to a close. Hundreds of Union prisoners of war as well as other passengers boarded the steamboat *Sultana*. The ex-prisoners were anxious to return home. The ship would take them north via the Mississippi River. The boat's normal capacity was 376 passengers; over 1,400 soldiers boarded the boat. Early in the morning, the *Sultana's* boilers exploded. Then the boat collapsed and caught fire.

   F Most of the men on board were killed.

   G Most of the men on board suffered no injuries.

   H The Confederate army came to the men's rescue.

   J The men were recaptured by the Confederate army.

Apply

Read each passage. Then answer the questions.

Once a lion was asleep and a little mouse began running up and down upon him. The lion woke up. He placed his paw upon the mouse and opened his jaws to swallow it. "Pardon, O King," cried the little mouse. "Forgive me this time. I shall never forget it. Who knows but perhaps I may be able to do you a favor one of these days? After all, I have very sharp teeth." The lion was so amused at the idea of the mouse being able to help him that he lifted up his paw and let the mouse go. Some time later, the lion was caught in a trap. The hunters tied him to a tree with a thick rope while they looked for a wagon to carry him on.

1. How will this story end?

_____

_____

_____

So far our trip through the African countryside had been uneventful. Feeling secure and quite pleased with my skills as a wilderness traveler, I dipped my oar into the water and began to paddle down the jungle river. Suddenly something moved beneath the water. I screamed as a hippopotamus surfaced and our canoe listed to one side. Just as we were about to capsize, I saw a vine hanging from a branch. "Grab it!" I yelled. Ann and I clung to the vine for dear life and began to climb the steep cliff that lined the river bank. We were almost at the top when we heard a sound like distant thunder. Boulders began to bounce past us.

2. What do you think will happen next?

_____

_____

3. Write two hints from the paragraph that help you guess what the narrator might do next.

_____

_____

Check Up

Read the passage. Then circle the answer to each question.

Thirty-five yards into the grass the big lion lay flattened out along the ground. His ears were back, and his only movement was a slight twitching of his long black-tufted tail. His stomach and lung wounds were gradually robbing him of his strength and brought a thin foamy red to his mouth each time he breathed. His flanks were wet and hot, and flies covered the openings the solid bullets had made in his tawny hide. His yellow, hate-filled eyes looked straight ahead. They blinked with pain, and his claws dug into the soft baked earth. All of him, pain, sickness, hatred, and all of his remaining strength, was tightening into an absolute concentration for a rush. He could hear the men talking and he waited, ready to charge as soon as they entered the tall grass.

1. What will happen next?
   A   The lion will turn away from the men.
   B   The lion will charge the men.
   C   The lion will recover from its injuries.
   D   The lion will become calmer.

2. What is the narrator's attitude toward the lion?
   F   hatred
   G   sympathy
   H   fear
   J   apathy

3. Which of the following is **not** helpful in predicting the outcome of the story?
   A   general knowledge of lions
   B   the narrator's attitude toward the lion
   C   the description of the lion's pain and hatred
   D   the description of the landscape

Identifying Fact and Opinion

Brightly colored trees and pleasant weather characterize autumn in New England.
Autumn is the best season of all in New England.

Which of the above statements is a fact and which is an opinion? The first sentence is a **fact,** a statement that can be proved. The second sentence is an **opinion**, a statement that expresses someone's ideas or thoughts. It cannot be proved.

Many articles that you read in magazines and newspapers are entirely factual. The writer uses statements that can be checked for accuracy, like the first statement above. Other times, writers may hope to convince their readers to agree with a particular opinion, as in the second statement above. This kind of writing appears in editorials and letters to magazines and newspapers. A good writer backs up his or her opinion with strong facts and examples. Then readers may decide whether this evidence persuades them to agree with the writer's opinion.

It is important for readers to distinguish between facts and opinions. When you read an opinion, check to see whether it is supported by valid facts.

Read the passage. Then answer the questions.

Nathaniel Hawthorne lived in the 19th century. He wrote *The Scarlet Letter* and other novels. But you probably wouldn't have liked him. He was usually dissatisfied and became troubled over the slightest incidents. A windy day could upset him. Brief separations from his wife and children caused him severe anxiety. He is said to have once suffered a deep depression because his wife served the same breakfast two days in a row.

1. Which sentence in the passage states an opinion?

   _____

   _____

2. What evidence, if any, supports the opinion?

   _____

   _____

   _____

   _____

Practice

Tell whether each statement is a fact or an opinion. Write *fact* on the line if the statement is a fact and write *opinion* on the line if the statement is an opinion.

_____ 1. Coffee is a universal beverage that is served in different ways around the world.

_____ 2. No one wrote poems that described life in the country better than Robert Frost.

_____ 3. The bow is the oldest projectile-throwing weapon still in use.

_____ 4. The Louvre in Paris is the most exciting art museum in the world.

_____ 5. New York's Empire State Building is one of the most marvelous buildings in the world.

_____ 6. The most beautiful characteristic of Japanese haiku poetry is its delicate brevity.

_____ 7. People who talk and sing to plants are crazy.

_____ 8. The blue whale is the largest creature on Earth.

_____ 9. Most doctors think that most people cannot live beyond 100 years.

_____ 10. Some people live in strange places, but about the strangest of all is a town of 1500 high up in the crater of an extinct volcano on the island of Saba in the West Indies.

Apply

Read each passage. Write the opinion stated in the passage, and list or summarize the facts that support it.

1.   One of the most amazing sea voyages on record was made by the Arctic exploring ship *Resolute* between 1854 and 1855. *Resolute* was one of five British ships that became locked in the polar ice in the Arctic Ocean. The ship was abandoned on May 15, 1854. Her captain and crew reached England safely before the end of the year. On September 15, 1855, another ship was sailing around a southern tip of Baffin Island. Suddenly the captain and crew came upon a ship of unusual appearance. When they boarded her, no crew was visible. This was the *Resolute*, as sound as ever. In 474 days, the *Resolute* had sailed 2,000 miles by itself.

Opinion: _____

_____

Supporting Facts: _____

_____

_____

_____

2.   The pyramids are some of the most impressive human creations. They are remnants of the culture that thrived in Egypt 4,500 years ago. The Great Pyramid is built from over two million stone blocks. Each block weighs on average over two tons. The ancient Egyptians cut the blocks with manual saws and copper chisels. These huge pharaohs' tombs have become a symbol of Egypt.

Opinion: _____

_____

Supporting Facts: _____

_____

_____

_____

Check Up

Read the passage. Then circle the answer to each question.

Americans are wasteful people, not used to saving. The people who settled the frontier began this pattern, for nature's resources were so plentiful that no one ever imagined a shortage. Just a few years after the first Virginia settlement was founded, for example, pioneers burned their houses when they were ready to move west because they wanted to have the nails for future use. No one gave a thought for the priceless hardwoods that went up in smoke.

Americans destroy many things that other people save. I noticed this when I was living in England. I received a letter from one of England's largest banks. It was enclosed in a used envelope that had been readdressed to me. Such a practice would be unthinkable in the United States. American banks, even the smallest, use expensive stationery for all their mailings.

1. The first sentence of the passage is

   A a fact

   B a statistic

   C an example

   D an opinion

2. The writer uses a story about the pioneers to prove that they began a wasteful pattern in what is now the United States. What other conclusion might be drawn from the story?

   F The colonists came from countries that did not believe in using resources wisely.

   G Metal objects such as nails were easy to obtain.

   H Objects made of metal were much scarcer than wood.

   J The pioneers wanted to make sure they could not return to their old homes.

3. "Just a few years after the first Virginia settlement was founded, for example, pioneers burned their houses when they were ready to move west. . . ." This is an example of a(an)

   A opinion

   B exaggeration

   C fact

   D conclusion

Read On Predict outcomes as you read "The Trade-Off." Make predictions and express your opinions supported by facts when you answer the questions.

Using Fact and Opinion

One reason for writing is to persuade readers to accept an opinion. An **opinion** is a personal viewpoint. Often an opinion includes words such as *all, every, should,* and *best.* A writer may want to convince the audience that a particular candidate is best, a certain law should be passed, or even that all families should eat dinner together. Each of these opinions must be backed up by evidence. Writers may use facts, statistics, examples, or a detailed anecdote to back up an opinion. A **fact** is a statement that can be proven to be true.

As a reader, you need to be able to distinguish between a writer's opinion and factual evidence. You also need to evaluate whether the evidence provided adequately supports the opinion.

> Every kid should have an older brother or sister to look up to. A kid requires understanding, protection, and a strong sense of belonging and identity. I guess Kevin, my older brother, was my security blanket. It wasn't that he allowed me to follow him around puppy-style. But he was always there when I needed him. If you don't have an older brother or sister, you're missing one of the great pleasures of growing up.

This passage begins with an opinion. Then the writer supports the opinion with facts.

Read the passage. Circle the answer to the question.

> The Great Wall of China was one of the most ambitious engineering projects ever undertaken. The barrier, which was intended to protect central China from attacking Huns, was begun around 403 B.C. It stretches from the Gulf of Chihli of the Huang He to a point 1,500 miles inland. In some areas the Wall is no more than a mound of stones and dirt, but much of it is well constructed and solid.

Which of the following is an opinion?

A   The Great Wall of China was one of the most ambitious engineering projects ever.

B   The Great Wall was started around 403 B.C.

C   The Great Wall extends for 1,500 miles.

D   The Great Wall is well constructed.

Practice

Decide whether each statement is a fact or an opinion. Write *fact* on the line if the statement is a fact and write *opinion* on the line if the statement is an opinion.

_____ 1. A healthful diet is good for the heart.

_____ 2. One of the best ways to understand people is to know what makes them laugh.

_____ 3. Our country's worst health problem is overeating.

_____ 4. Television programs are too violent.

_____ 5. Changing citizens' attitudes toward conservation is the most important factor in improving our environment.

_____ 6. The demand for fuels in the United States is growing steadily.

_____ 7. Men tend to be more argumentative than women, making them less desirable as public speakers, newscasters, or political candidates.

_____ 8. Choosing a dog is an important decision, but some "dog lovers" don't give it the thought it deserves.

_____ 9. Only people who don't care about personal safety would ever parachute from a plane.

_____ 10. In ancient times, people believed that salamanders were born in the flames of fire.

Apply

Read each passage. Summarize the opinion and supporting facts in each.

1.   Most Americans will not walk anywhere either for practical purposes or for pleasure if they can help it. You can do your banking from your car without dragging yourself out of the driver's seat. You can mail your letters in mailboxes that reach the level of your car window without even troubling yourself to open the door. At countless fast-food restaurants, you can "drive-thru" to order, purchase, and eat a meal without ever using your legs for more than braking and accelerating.

Opinion: _____

_____

Supporting Facts: _____

_____

2.   The discovery of polio vaccine is one of the most thrilling stories in the history of medicine. In the ten years following the development of polio vaccine, the reported cases of polio in the United States were cut by 80 percent. In New York City alone, it dropped by 93 percent. One of the most dreaded of diseases was brought under control by a simple vaccination.

Opinion: _____

_____

Supporting Facts: _____

_____

3.   One of the most important tasks a factory manager can do is to improve working conditions in their factories. Cleaner working areas have been shown to improve the workers' attitudes and their output. In some factories, management has taken steps to make the work itself more interesting. Interesting work, more than any other single factor, enables workers to take pride in what they do and obtain satisfaction from their jobs.

Opinion: _____

_____

Supporting Facts: _____

_____

Check Up

Read the passage. Then circle the answer to each question.

Back in Thomas Jefferson's day, the United States was a nation of farmers and merchants, and the boss of each farm or store was the owner. Some worked hard, were cruel, and enjoyed prosperity. Some worked hard, were fair, and prospered even more because they attracted loyal workers who didn't need as much expensive supervision. Some were lazy, and they failed. In any event, it was their business, and they were entitled to run their business any way they saw fit, free from the meddlesome government with which businesses today must deal.

1. The first sentence of the passage is

   A a fact

   B an opinion

   C an anecdote

   D a statistic

2. What opinion is expressed explicitly in the passage?

   F Bosses in Jefferson's day were cruel.

   G Our country has improved since Jefferson's day.

   H Everyone was a farmer or a merchant during Jefferson's day.

   J The government meddles too much in private business today.

3. What is the main evidence used to support the writer's opinion?

   A Businesses were more prosperous in Jefferson's day.

   B Farmers and merchants owned their own businesses in Jefferson's day.

   C Business owners were in charge of their own destinies in Jefferson's day.

   D Lazy business owners failed in Jefferson's day.

4. What opinion is **not** directly stated but is implied in the passage?

   F Farms and businesses should not be run by their owners.

   G Farms and businesses should not be too large.

   H Laws should protect employees from cruel bosses.

   J The government should let owners run businesses as they choose.

Recognizing Author's Purpose

Each paragraph, story, or article is written for a particular reason. The writer may want **to entertain** his or her audience with a story, poem, play, or article. He or she may want **to inform** the audience about what has occurred, how to do something, or why something happens. Finally, an author may want **to persuade** the audience to accept his or her opinion on an issue. Identifying an **author's purpose** helps readers understand and evaluate an article or piece of literature.

> Parakeets, small, brightly colored birds of the parrot family, have been favorite pets since the days of ancient Rome. The colors of parakeet feathers are combinations of red, green, blue, orange, yellow, and purple. Many different species of parakeets used to live in warm climates all over the world in places such as Australia, India, Thailand, and even the southeastern United States. Many of these have been captured for pets.

In this passage, the author describes parakeets. If the author had wished to entertain the audience, he or she might have written a poem or story about parakeets that used many specific details and figurative language. If the author wanted to persuade the audience that parakeets were the best pet, he or she would have stated this opinion and proven it with supporting facts. However, in this passage the author chose to simply inform the reader about parakeets by using a combination of descriptive details and facts.

Many pieces of writing serve more than one purpose. For example, an informative article may also be an entertaining one. However, most writers have a primary purpose when writing about a particular subject.

Read the passage. Tell whether its main purpose is to entertain, inform, or persuade.

> The high gray-flannel fog of winter closed off the Salinas Valley from the sky and from all the rest of the world. On every side it sat like a lid on the mountains and made of the great valley a closed pot. On the foothill ranches across the Salinas River, the yellow fields seemed to be bathed in pale gold sunshine.

Purpose: _____

Practice

Read each passage. Tell whether its main purpose is to entertain, inform, or persuade.

1. It was a British Boy Scout's good deed that was the foundation of the Boy Scouts of America. In 1909 an American businessman named William C. Boyce became lost in one of London's famous heavy fogs and was helped by a British Boy Scout. Boyce was impressed by the boy's cooperation, and in 1910 Boyce founded the Boy Scouts of America.

    Purpose: _____

2. Only the scrape of our boots against rock and loose pebbles broke the silence as we moved deeper into the cave. Breathing had become an effort. The air, long stagnant from being kept in this tomblike cave, burned our throats and left a rancid taste. Foul-smelling and heavy, it seemed to stick in our lungs after each intake of breath. The miner's lamps on our helmets cut a thin slice out of the thick, black gloom around us.

    Purpose: _____

3. The visitor to New York City who decides that "It's a nice place to visit, but I wouldn't want to live there" has failed to find the city's open sesame. Don't give up on New York until you have tried it. The jade expert can find an emperor's collection of carvings in the Jade Room of the Metropolitan Museum of Art. The artist can study at leisure a rare volume of William Blake's etchings in one of the specialized rooms of the main library or walk for years through the endless public and private galleries. But New York's magic door will open only if the visitor arrives with a key and a willingness to learn.

    Purpose: _____

4. Where is the world's largest university? That depends on how you look at it. The State University of New York has colleges in 20 cities. The combined total of students is about 300,000. But the world's largest college *building* is part of Moscow State University. That complex holds all the science departments, the offices, the Museum of Earth Science, and dormitories for thousands of students.

    Purpose: _____

Apply

Read each passage. Circle the phrase that indicates the author's purpose as shown in the passage.

1. The adjective *American* causes confusion and resentment. That is because many people have come to associate *American* exclusively with the United States. There are millions of Americans who are not citizens of the United States, and many of them take offense at being automatically linked with that country. Canadians and Mexicans in North America and the people of Central and South America are all "Americans." Therefore, people should say "United States" when they are talking about that specific part of the Americas.

   A to entertain   **B** to persuade

2. The first textbook printed in the United States was *A New Guide to the English Tongue* by Thomas Dilworth. The book dealt with reading, spelling, and grammar. It was originally published in England in 1740. In 1747, the text was reprinted in Philadelphia, Pennsylvania, making it the first textbook in the colonies. One significant fact about Dilworth's *New Guide* was that the author provided spelling word lists. Before that time, spelling had not been taught as a separate skill.

   A to entertain   **B** to inform

3. Thanks to irresponsible polluters, Lake Erie, the recreational front yard of Buffalo, Cleveland, Toledo, and Detroit, is almost gone. Though it supplies water for 10 million people, even the heart of it has none of the dissolved oxygen necessary for the fish, plants, and insects on which lakes thrive. Lake Erie now supports little aquatic life, except for trash fish, sludge worms, and bloodsuckers. A monstrous cancerlike growth of algae, nourished by phosphates from industrial wastes, has taken over this body of water. A river often washes and restores itself, but a lake is a bathtub that can be defiled to the point of becoming an open sewer. I urge all concerned citizens to take action to save Lake Erie before it is too late.

   A to persuade   **B** to entertain

Check Up

Read the passage. Then circle the answer to each question.

The planting of a new nation in North America was no holiday undertaking. It meant grim, dirty, toilsome, dangerous work. Here was a great shaggy continent, its eastern third covered with pathless forests; its mountains, rivers, lakes, and rolling plains all upon a huge scale. Its northern stretches were fiercely cold in winter, its southern areas burning hot in summer. The land was filled with wild beasts. It was a forbidding land. It could be reached only by a voyage so dangerous that some ships buried as many as they landed. But despite all its drawbacks, it was admirably fitted to become the home of an energetic, thriving people.

1. What is the main subject of the passage?
   A the landscape of America
   B the sea voyage to America
   C the difficulties of settling America
   D the animals native to America

2. What is the best description of the nature of the passage?
   F a descriptive discussion
   G a persuasive description
   H a series of opinions
   J an entertaining argument

3. What was the author's main purpose in the passage?
   A to entertain
   B to describe
   C to convince readers to take action
   D to inform

Identifying Author's Purpose

Good writing always has a purpose. The writer may want to entertain the audience with an amusing, scary, or touching story. The writer may want to inform the audience by describing or analyzing a subject or by explaining how or why something occurs. The writer may want to persuade the audience to accept an opinion. The writer decides what kinds of details to use and how to arrange the details based on his or her purpose. Readers need to identify the **author's purpose** in order to respond appropriately to the writing.

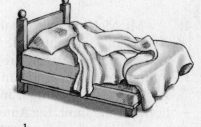

> Every child should hear a story before being put to bed. While an adult reads a bedtime story to a child, the child has a chance to quiet down and get ready for sleep. Being close to the adult he or she loves most gives the child a sense of contentment. Finally, bedtime stories can begin a lifelong love of literature.

The primary purpose of this paragraph is to persuade. The word *should* in the first sentence is a signal that the statement is an opinion. The details are provided to support this opinion.

Read the passage. Circle the answer to the question.

> Cartoonist Al Hirschfield had hidden his daughter's name in his famous caricatures for over 30 years. Finding the "Ninas" had become something of a sport for Hirschfield fans. Next to the artist's signature is a number that tells how many times he had skillfully woven Nina's name into the cartoon.

What is the best description for the passage?

    A an opinion and facts meant to persuade the audience

    B a colorful description to inform readers

    C an interesting story to entertain readers

    D facts and statistics used to inform readers

Practice

Read each passage. Tell whether the author's purpose is to inform, persuade, or entertain.

1.   Mt. McKinley's eternal snowcap, towering 20,320 feet, is the highest point on the North American continent. Wide valleys, worn by such meandering streams as the Kuskokwim and the mighty Yukon, are filled with unique and colorful plants and animals. Big game hunting and fishing are unparalleled. Moose, bear, Dall sheep, and caribou are plentiful. Arctic grayling, salmon, and spectacular trout abound in lakes and rivers. This is Alaska, home of the Inuit, the American Indian, and the Aleut.

Purpose: _____

2.   You need your lungs to breathe in oxygen and breathe out carbon dioxide. Taking care of your lungs is important. Air pollution and smoking both can affect how your lungs work. Smoking can cause diseases that make breathing difficult. It can also cause lung cancer. These are just two reasons why you should never smoke. Although there are many other reasons not to smoke, the health risk is the most important.

Purpose: _____

3.   From childhood, my sister and I have had a well-grounded dislike for our friends the birds. We came to hate them when she was ten and I was eleven. We had been sent to one of those horrible girls' camps where we were given names like bluebirds and redbirds, and the owners put up little signs telling everyone to be good sports. From the moment Eileen and I arrived at dismal old Camp Hi-Wah, we were bad sports, and we liked it.

Purpose: _____

Apply

Read the passages. Then circle the answer to each question.

Passage 1

The approaching jungle night was, in itself, a threat. As it deepened, an eerie silence enveloped the thatched village. People were silent. Tethered cattle stood quietly. Roosting chickens did not stir and wise goats made no noise. Thus it had been for countless centuries and thus it would continue to be. The people of the village knew the jungle. They had trodden its dim paths, forded its sulky rivers, borne its steaming heat, and were familiar with its deer, tapir, crocodiles, screaming green parrots, and countless other creatures.

Passage 2

The Portuguese explorer Ferdinand Magellan should be known as the greatest navigator of all time. The fleet under his command discovered the Strait of Magellan, a passageway at the tip of South America that connects the Atlantic and Pacific oceans. Although he died before his voyage was completed, his navigational planning helped his crew finish their trip around the world. Magellan's discovery of the Strait of Magellan helped other explorers learn more about the Pacific Ocean. But most important, his long voyage proved that the world is actually round.

Passage 3

Over the centuries, church bells did more than just beckon people to services. During the Middle Ages, for instance, they had several practical civic uses and were also believed to have supernatural powers. Bells were rung in towns to announce the evening curfew, to warn people of fire, and to remind citizens of tax deadlines.

1. Which passage uses facts to persuade the audience?

   A Passage 1

   B Passage 2

   C Passage 3

   D none of the above

2. Which passage's main purpose is to inform?

   F Passage 1

   G Passage 2

   H Passage 3

   J all of the above

3. Which passage uses vivid detail for the main purpose of entertaining?

   A Passage 1

   B Passage 2

   C Passage 3

   D none of the above

Check Up

Read the passage. Then circle the answer to each question.

> You have probably been warned not to stand under a tree during an electrical storm. That is excellent advice, because one lightning bolt can send millions of volts of electricity through the layer of the tree that is directly underneath the bark. When that happens, the sap immediately heats to the boiling point, which causes a violent expulsion of steam to rip through the bark. Large chunks of the trees are often catapulted outward. This is one of the most dangerous possible consequences of using a tree for shelter: a flying chunk of wood can be deadly. If you are caught by a storm while hiking in the woods and are surrounded by trees, stand under the shortest tree available. The taller the tree, the more likely it is to be struck.

1. Which device is **not** used in the passage?

   A   vivid specific details

   B   cause-and-effect explanation

   C   facts

   D   summary

2. What is the best description of the subject of the passage?

   F   the story of a person getting struck by lightning

   G   why lightning is dangerous and how to avoid the danger

   H   how lightning affects a forest

   J   how lightning is formed

3. What is the author's main purpose in the passage?

   A   to persuade people not to stand under tall trees during an electrical storm

   B   to entertain with vivid description

   C   to share feelings with the reader

   D   to inform and entertain

Recognizing Author's Point of View

Some factual writing is neutral: the author does not express or imply an opinion on the subject. The author does not express a **point of view**. However, in some factual writing and in persuasive writing, writers express and/or imply their attitudes toward the subject matter.

> Alcohol is one of our country's main health problems. The results of alcohol abuse are well-known. The social drinker turned alcoholic, the drunken driver's contribution to highway death, the broken homes, and so on all point to the dangers of alcohol abuse.

In the above passage, the writer's attitude toward alcohol is clearly negative.

> Telephone Crisis Intervention Services, better known as hotlines, provide counseling to anyone in need. Found in many cities across the country, hotlines lend a kind ear to people who need help. Young people favor hotline services because they sense a real concern in the listener.

In this passage, the author has a positive attitude toward the subject. The phrases "kind ear" and "real concern" **explicitly** communicate this attitude. Sometimes a writer uses subtle word choices to imply a positive or negative attitude. Then the attitude is **implicitly** communicated.

Read the passage. Circle the answer to the question.

> The best way to begin a National Forest adventure is to stop at an Information Station or a Visitors' Center. The former provides maps, brochures, and directions. The latter offers talks, films, and exhibits. Both provide the advice of a knowledgeable, highly trained staff. These professional services are free, contribute to the public's safe enjoyment of the forests, and play an important role in the development of our forest resources.

What is the author's point of view toward the subject of the passage?

  A neutral

  B A positive attitude is expressed.

  C A positive attitude is only implied.

  D A negative attitude is expressed.

Practice

Read each passage. Then circle the answer to each question.

David R. Scott and James B. Irwin, the pilots of *Falcon*, began history's first drive on the moon after unfolding the Lunar Roving Vehicle (LRV) from *Falcon* and setting it up. The ability of the *Apollo 15* astronauts to explore the moon's surface was aided by the use of the LRV. During three separate motor trips, they explored the rim of Hadley Rille, the edges of deep craters, and the slopes of the Apennine Mountains.

1. What is the author's attitude toward the LRV?

   A neutral

   B explicitly positive

   C explicitly negative

   D implicitly negative

Demand for fuels in the United States is growing steadily, but domestic supply is lagging. Our oil production has peaked and is declining, and natural gas is already scarce in some sections of the country. Coal is in severe trouble, thanks to the efforts of environmental fanatics, and protests by nervous Nellies and crackpots of all stripes have put construction of nuclear power plants off the energy agenda.

2. What is the author's attitude toward environmentalists?

   F implicitly positive

   G explicitly positive

   H implicitly negative

   J explicitly negative

The world watched in awe for nearly half a century as an island nation in the Far East rose from the ashes of defeat in World War II to become one of the world's most powerful industrial nations. That nation, Japan, currently boasts a booming economy. It also has one of the world's strongest currencies, the yen, and industry that, in terms of sophistication, is second to none.

3. What is the author's attitude toward Japan?

   A neutral

   B positive

   C explicitly negative

   D implicitly negative

Apply

Read each passage. Circle the word that indicates the author's point of view.

1.   Present U.S. transportation problems began with changes after World War II. Suburbs were booming, and suburbanites drove cars. Tax money went to build expressways and interstate highways, not to maintain public transportation. The quality of mass transit declined, so fewer people used it. As less money was collected, transit systems raised fares and cut back services. This ill-advised policy encouraged a dissatisfied public to turn even more to the automobile. The result of these mistakes is visible in any city today: endless traffic jams and a public transportation system that is a disgrace.

        A neutral   **B** positive   **C** negative

2.   Next to ordinary grass, clover is the most useful plant a farmer can feed his cattle. Its scientific name means "three-leafed meadow dweller," which is certainly an accurate description. Clover is usually mixed with other kinds of grasses, but whole meadows can be blanketed by the three-leafed dweller. Farmers have discovered that it is advantageous to grow and store clover separately as cattle enjoy a little variety in their diets.

        A neutral   **B** positive   **C** negative

3.   If you know anyone who thinks he or she is too old to accomplish anything, you might mention Grandma Moses. Anna Mary Robertson Moses didn't begin to paint until she was in her 70s. She had embroidered since childhood, but when she got older she had arthritis. This made her unable to hold needles. She turned to painting and became one of the finest folk painters in the United States. After a one-person show in New York City, her fame spread. The nickname "Grandma Moses" was coined. Her most famous paintings show people in lovely settings doing pleasant things. For example, she showed people bringing Christmas trees home in a sleigh through a New England snowfall. Grandma Moses died in 1961 at the age of 101. She has taken a place next to Norman Rockwell as one of America's truly "American" artists.

        A neutral   **B** positive   **C** negative

Check Up

Read the passage. Then circle the answer to each question.

Humorists tell a story gravely, concealing the fact that they even dimly suspect that there is anything funny about it. They let the humor work its magic unassisted. Comic storytellers, however, announce beforehand that a story is one of the funniest they have ever heard. They blurt it out with impatient delight and are the first to laugh when they get through. Sometimes, if they get a laugh, they are so happy that they will repeat the point of the story and glance around from face to face, hoping to collect a second laugh. It is a pathetic thing to see.

1. What is the author's attitude toward humorists?

   A neutral

   B implicitly positive

   C explicitly positive

   D negative

2. What is the author's attitude toward comic storytellers?

   F implicitly positive

   G explicitly positive

   H implicitly negative

   J explicitly negative

3. What attitude is communicated by the word *blurt*?

   A neutral

   B positive

   C negative

   D angry

4. How would you describe the point of view suggested by the sentence "It is a pathetic thing to see"?

   F implicitly positive

   G explicitly positive

   H implicitly negative

   J explicitly negative

Identifying Author's Point of View

When you read an informative or persuasive article, note the attitudes that the author communicates. In the ideas communicated and the words chosen, a writer may express a negative or positive **point of view.** If so, be aware that the author is expressing a personal opinion. Writers sometimes do not express their attitudes but instead imply them.

> For most people, public TV is the spinach of the video diet—something they think they should like, even though the junk-food channels are more appealing. It is the station of earnest dissertations on birds, planets, economics, and science.

In this passage, a negative attitude toward public TV is implied with words like *spinach* and *earnest*. It is important for readers to recognize **implicit attitudes** such as this one so they are aware that the author is expressing a personal point of view and not a fact.

Read the passage. Circle the answer to the question.

> In 1793 the war between France and Great Britain increased the hazards of the American sailor's life. Both sides preyed on American shipping for the supplies and ships they so badly needed. Great Britain also began stopping American ships on the high seas and kidnapping sailors. The British sorely needed sailors for their navy. Claiming that those removed from American ships were lawful subjects of the Crown, the English were not fussy about credentials. Although American sailors took to carrying identification papers, these papers failed to impress the captors of American sailors.

What is the author's attitude toward Great Britain?

A   neutral

B   positive

C   implicitly negative

D   explicitly negative

Practice

Read each passage. Then circle the answer to each question.

1.   Arabella A. Mansfield was the first woman lawyer in the United States. She began practicing in Mount Pleasant, Iowa, in 1853. Until then, the Iowa Code had kept women from practicing law through a statute that provided admission to the bar to "any white male person." In 1853 it was demonstrated that admitting white males did not necessarily exclude white females, and the door was opened for Mansfield. She was admitted to the bar in June 1869.

What attitude does the author express toward Arabella A. Mansfield?

A   neutral

B   explicitly positive

C   implicitly negative

D   explicitly negative

2.   A collector of antiques rarely finds a deck of early American playing cards. To the prim-and-proper Puritans, cards were "the devil's picture book." Cards were not seen in respectable American homes until the 1840s. Those early cards were not much fun; they had pious verses on the face and the usual designs on the back. Until then, the moral ban on cards was strict since they were considered gamblers' tools. This holier-than-thou attitude still persists in some areas, even in our more enlightened times.

What attitude does the author express toward Puritans?

F   implicitly positive

G   explicitly positive

H   implicitly negative

J   explicitly negative

3.   In almost every line of work today, from journalism and publishing to business, education, and manufacturing, computers have become indispensable tools. In recent years, computers have become cheaper, more powerful, and smaller; consequently, they have found their way into more and more occupations. All this computerization has created many jobs that did not exist before.

What attitude does the author express toward computers?

A   neutral

B   implicitly positive

C   explicitly positive

D   negative

Apply

Read each passage. Identify the author's point of view by writing *neutral, positive,* or *negative.* If the attitude is positive or negative, list at least two words or phrases that help communicate this attitude.

1.   Recently, studies have been undertaken to determine whether a relationship exists between violence on television and mounting violence in the schools of the United States. More and better research is needed to assess fully the effects of exposure to violence on human behavior. However, early results seem to indicate that some people are influenced negatively by what they see on television.

Attitude: _____

Words and phrases: _____

_____

2.   Farmers and hunters often regard birds such as hawks with disapproval; however, we know that these birds of prey feed upon rats, mice, and other pests. They sometimes do kill poultry and game, but even then they may perform another service by eliminating birds that are feeble or sick. In a recent experiment involving many flights by homing pigeons, the pigeons were frequently attacked by hawks, but the only pigeon caught was a runt—the weakest member of the flock.

Attitude: _____

Words and phrases: _____

_____

3.   Here can be seen some of the most fascinating exhibits anywhere in the world. The Wright Brothers' plane is in one small corner of the huge museum. Nearby is astronaut John Glenn's *Friendship 7.* The world's largest elephant stands in lifelike splendor for all to view. A visitor may ponder over dinosaur bones, Lincoln's hat, and realistic wax figures. An extraordinary blend of the realistic and the unusual, the Smithsonian Institution in Washington, D.C., offers something for everyone.

Attitude: _____

Words and phrases: _____

_____

Check Up

Read the passage. Then circle the answer to each question.

Surely no one writes lovelier stories, yielding a purer pleasure, than John Steinbeck. Here are tragedy and suffering and violence, to be sure, but with all that is sharp and harsh distilled to a golden honey, ripe and mellow. Even cruelty and murder grow somehow pastoral and idyllic, seen through this amber light, as one might watch the struggles of fish and water snakes in the depth of a mountain pool. Beyond question, Steinbeck has a magic to take the sting out of reality and yet leave it all there except the sting. Perhaps it is partly the carefulness of his art, with endless pains devising and arranging every detail until all fits perfectly and smoothly as polished ivory. But probably it is more the enchantment of his style, of that liquid melody that flows on and on.

1. How many sentences of the passage convey a neutral point of view?

    A   none

    B   one

    C   three

    D   all

2. Which of the following does the author **not** use to describe Steinbeck's work?

    F   explicit praise

    G   words communicating a positive viewpoint

    H   words communicating a negative viewpoint

    J   comparisons

3. This passage is probably part of

    A   an encyclopedia article on Steinbeck

    B   a book review

    C   a textbook introduction

    D   a short story

Recognizing Generalizations

Suppose you were watching a movie set in Paris during the spring. If the movie showed trees in bloom, sunny weather, and people enjoying life in a park, you could generalize that Paris is pleasant in the spring. When you make a **generalization,** you come to a general conclusion based on specific pieces of evidence.

Chimpanzees have been taught sign language. They have also been taught to operate computers, draw, converse with each other, organize wars, manipulate tools, and solve problems.

This passage provides specific details about chimpanzees. From these details, a reader could make the following generalization: Chimpanzees are intelligent animals.

Read the passage. Circle the most valid generalization based on the facts in the passage.

The Ganges River flows through India from the Himalayas to the Bay of Bengal. The river is held sacred by 350 million Hindus, who believe it has special powers. For this reason, bathing in the river is a holy rite. Members of the Hindu religion also cast their dead into the river, believing that their souls will be sent straight to heaven. Side by side with these ancient beliefs exists the need for industrial development to feed India's vast population. The Ganges is considered the key to this development. It has an untapped hydroelectric potential estimated at 25 billion kilowatt hours per year.

What generalization can you make based on these specific facts?

   A   Indians are building hydroelectric plants on the Ganges.

   B   India's vast population is starving.

   C   The Ganges is an important river for more than spiritual reasons.

   D   The Ganges is the largest river in Asia.

Practice

Read each passage. Circle the most valid generalization based on the facts in each passage.

1. The power of glaciers is evident in the mountains and canyons shaped by the ages of glacial movement. The North American ice sheet, for example, gouged an average of 30 feet of rock from the surface of over two million square miles of territory. Hundreds of mountains around the world were fashioned by glaciers, and the Great Lakes are also a product of their handiwork.

    A Ice is destructive.

    B Mountains were formed by many different forces.

    C Glaciers were active in North America for thousands of years.

    D Glaciers were both a destructive and a creative force.

2. Early Middle Eastern countries had virtually all of the face creams, tonics, lotions, and powders that people use today. One ancient recipe, which was for a face treatment that guaranteed smooth, wrinkle-free skin, was made with powdered ostrich eggshells and wheat germ. A cream used for getting rid of dandruff was a combination of hippopotamus fat, fish oil, and animal grease.

    F Ancient cosmetic science was more advanced than our own.

    G Old recipes for beauty treatments were dangerous to people's health.

    H People have used cosmetics for thousands of years.

    J In ancient times, animals were more often used for cosmetics than for food.

3. Seaweed is high in minerals. It has been part of the daily diet in Japan for thousands of years. In other countries, such as France, Norway, and Scotland, where seaweed is gathered by machines that can reap up to 25 tons an hour, it is used as a fertilizer for other food crops. In the United States, seaweed is used as the source of the chemical iodine and of additives used in foods such as ice cream and gelatin.

    A Ocean plants are useless.

    B Seaweed cannot be eaten.

    C Some poor countries must use seaweed in food production.

    D Seaweed is a valuable, versatile plant.

Apply

Read each passage. Write a generalization based on the details in the passage.

1.   Although morphine is frequently prescribed to relieve pain and relax the nervous system, in large amounts morphine can cause unconsciousness and eventually death. Copper, a necessary mineral found in the body, can stop the heart if taken in large doses. Fluoride, when added to toothpaste and drinking water, hardens tooth enamel and reduces tooth decay, but too much taken all at once can quickly kill a person.

Generalization: _____

_____

_____

2.   Umbrellas were first used as sunshades. Sculptured images of them have been found on the monuments of Egypt and the ruins of Ninevah, an ancient Assyrian city. Their use by Chinese and Indian royalty also dates back to ancient times. Today, in certain parts of Asia and Africa, the umbrella is still used as a symbol of royalty. From the paintings found on ancient Greek vases, there is no doubt that umbrellas similar to those used today existed years before the Christian period. They were also used by the Romans, but as with many other cultures, only by Roman women.

Generalization: _____

_____

_____

3.   The Dead Sea has water six times saltier than ocean water and enormous quantities of various other minerals besides. The Dead Sea can support life only in bacterial form. At 1,300 feet below sea level, the Dead Sea is the lowest point on Earth, and it is one of the hottest locations on the planet as well. Few birds inhabit the region. The birds avoid the sea because there are no fish or insects for them to eat.

Generalization: _____

_____

_____

Check Up

Read the passage. Then circle the answer to each question.

The ancient Greeks used many shapes for coffins, including a triangular coffin that allowed the corpse to be buried in a sitting position. Chaldean coffins were clay urns that were formed around the body, encasing it closely. The Seri Indians of Mexico buried their dead between the upper and lower shells of a turtle. Other North American Indians disposed of their dead by laying them in canoes that they mounted on scaffolds. Or they placed them in wicker baskets that they floated downstream or out to sea.

1. What would be the most appropriate title be for the passage?

   A Burial Customs of Ancient Greeks

   B Coffins Through the Ages

   C Indian Funerals

   D Life After Death

2. What was the author's purpose in the passage?

   F to startle the audience with strange customs

   G to persuade the audience that American burial customs are best

   H to inform the audience of unusual burial customs

   J to entertain the audience with bizarre folklore

3. Which generalization can you make based on the evidence in the passage?

   A Coffins have not always been rectangular wooden boxes.

   B Chaldean coffins were difficult to make.

   C North American Indians did not treat their dead with respect.

   D People have not paid much attention to burying their dead.

Read On   Read "The Art of Acupuncture" and apply the author's purpose towards answering the questions.

Making Generalizations

Whether you are summarizing a passage or simply reading to understand its main ideas, making generalizations is a useful skill. When you make a **generalization,** you look for a general idea suggested by specific details.

> Reykjavik, the coastal capital of Iceland, is located just below the Arctic Circle. However, the city's average winter temperature is 29 degrees Fahrenheit higher than that of Chicago, Detroit, or Boston, which are much further south. Reykjavik is warmer because Iceland lies directly in the path of the Gulf Stream, an ocean current that begins in the warm waters of the eastern part of the Gulf of Mexico and flows northeastward across the Atlantic Ocean toward the coast of Europe.

This passage gives detailed information about the climate of a particular city. From this information, a more general fact can be stated: *The average temperature of a city can depend on more than how far north or south the city is located.*

Read the passage. Circle the most valid generalization based on the facts in the passage.

> The bird species with the greatest population is the feathered locust, also called the redbilled quela. Experts estimate that there are 10 billion redbilled quelas living on the African continent. Historically, the only other bird whose population compares to the redbilled quela has been the passenger pigeon. In 1840 the passenger pigeon numbered nine billion. It is sobering to think that due to human hunting the passenger pigeon is now extinct.

What generalization can you make based on the facts in the passage?

   A Birds are more common in Africa than on other continents.

   B Birds have become extinct more than any other kind of animal.

   C Redbilled quelas are pests.

   D Even the most populous animal species can become extinct due to human actions.

Practice

Read each passage. Circle the most valid generalization based on the information in each passage.

1.   People have been wearing wedding rings for thousands of years. Ancient Eurasian tribes used jewelry of all types to demonstrate possession. A potential suitor could look to a woman's neck, wrist, or finger to find out if she was "taken." The ancient Egyptians attached a deeper spiritual significance to wedding jewelry. They believed that the ring represented eternity and the lasting qualities of true love. Today, a wedding ring symbolizes love and devotion; it also serves as a visual sign to unmarried people to look elsewhere.

A   People have always experienced jealousy in regard to their spouses.

B   Wedding rings have always had both personal and societal meanings.

C   People of ancient cultures wore large quantities of jewelry.

D   Ancient Eurasians invented wedding rings.

2.   No one knows exactly how the first American flag came to be. Tradition says that Betsy Ross sewed the first flag, but many historians doubt this story. Her husband, Colonel George Ross, did have a hand in designing the flag along with Robert Morris and George Washington. The stars and the stripes were intended to symbolize the original 13 colonies. The reasons for the choice of colors, however, are not so well known. George Washington offered this explanation: "The stars are set against the blue of the heavens. The red represents England, our mother country, and the white represents our separation from her—our liberty."

F   Historians usually don't know the truth about the past.

G   The American flag has a colorful but mysterious history.

H   George Washington created the first American flag.

J   The legend that Betsy Ross made the first American flag is untrue.

3.   Many of the commonly accepted hints for distinguishing a poisonous mushroom from an edible one are false. For instance, there are no consistent markings that can be used to tell the two apart. A safe mushroom growing in one area might look just like a poisonous one found elsewhere. Many people believe that brightly colored mushrooms are poisonous, but some of the most brilliant ones are edible.

A   Experienced mushroom hunters can tell the difference between poisonous and edible mushrooms.

B   People should not pick and eat mushrooms that grow wild because they may be poisonous.

C   Poisonous mushrooms look much different than edible mushrooms.

D   The safest policy is to avoid eating wild mushrooms altogether.

Apply

Read each passage. Write a generalization that can be made from the facts.

1.   Anise is a member of the parsley family. It tastes like licorice and is used to flavor everything from cake to coffee to alcoholic spirits. The ancient Romans hung the plant by their beds at night in the belief that it would prevent nightmares. Similarly, it was thought that holding a small bunch of anise flowers in one hand would prevent attacks of epilepsy. Those traditions are long gone, but anise is still used for medicinal purposes. A special anise tea is said to cure stomach disorders and to help insomniacs sleep.

Generalization: _____

_____

_____

2.   Have you ever observed young animals? Young birds and young bats must be taught to fly. Thousands of young seals drown every year. They never learn to swim "naturally." The mother has to take the baby seal out under her flipper and show it how. Birds sing without instruction; however, they do not sing well unless they are able to hear older members of their species. The young elephant does not seem to know at first what its trunk is for. It gets in the way until the baby's parents show it what to do.

Generalization: _____

_____

_____

3.   The discovery of gold in California in 1848 brought an intense demand for a transportation link across Panama to connect the Atlantic and Pacific Oceans. A railroad line was completed after six years of hard labor in the swamps and jungles. During its construction, more than 2,000 workers died from yellow fever and malaria. In 1881 a French organization tried to build a canal across the isthmus. Again workers struggled mightily against heat and disease. At least 15,000 died before the French gave up their attempts to build the canal.

Generalization: _____

_____

_____

Check Up

Read the passage. Then circle the answer to each question.

The American Pony Express was a mail route that went from Missouri to California. It lasted only 18 months before the telegraph made it obsolete. And it wasn't even an original idea. Both Persia and China had overland mail routes long before the Pony Express came along in 1860. Marco Polo told of a similar system in China during the 13th century. Pony Express riders did have it easier than their predecessors—stopping at a rest station every 15 miles and having only a 75 mile workday. In Persia, some riders went 100 miles without a break. And Chinese couriers often didn't even have the luxury of horses.

1. What is the general subject of the passage?

   A the American Pony Express

   B the history of overland mail routes

   C the schedules of Pony Express riders

   D China's remarkable culture

2. What generalization can you make about the history of the Pony Express?

   F The Pony Express was never very effective.

   G It took hundreds of years to perfect the American Pony Express.

   H The American Pony Express was exactly like that of the Chinese.

   J The idea of a pony express had roots in other cultures of long ago.

3. What generalization can you make about the importance of the American Pony Express?

   A The Pony Express was a crucial means of communication for a long time in the western United States.

   B The importance and originality of the American Pony Express have perhaps been exaggerated.

   C American Pony Express riders did a job that had never been accomplished before.

   D If it had not been for the Pony Express, the western United States may not have developed as successfully as it did.

Identifying Genre

Writing takes many forms. However, almost all written material fits into a recognized **genre,** or class, of writing. Literary genres include fiction, poetry, and drama. Nonfiction genres include essays, biography, and autobiography. Understanding individual genres can help you appreciate specific pieces of writing.

The following brief definitions will help you recognize the various genres.

Literature

Poetry	Explores feelings and experiences in verse form, using language that is rich in imagery and figures of speech
Fiction	Tells of events that happen to imaginary characters, using narration and dialogue
Drama	Tells of events occurring to characters in dialogue form; performed on stage

Nonfiction

Essay	Deals with real people or events to inform or persuade the audience
Biography	Tells the story of a real person's life
Autobiography	Tells the story of a real person's life and is written by that person

Read the passage. Circle the answer to each question.

The wind rose higher, and the waves came faster. The swells uncoiled like green snakes and burst into white at the top, then fell apart with an angry roar. They rolled beneath the light raft and raised us up until we looked into a sickening depth. We clutched the sides of the raft as it would spin downward, sometimes missing the break, sometimes whirling in the wild white froth. We shipped water, gallons at a time, and bailed frantically with our hands. We watched the waves like surf riders, rolling our weight from side to side as the raft was tossed like a toy. We learned to shift ourselves skillfully when the crest hit, to keep the raft in balance.

1. What are the main features of the passage?

    A   verse form

    B   imaginary characters and plot

    C   events involving characters in dialogue form, to be performed on stage

    D   description of real events to persuade readers

2. Judging from the way the incidents in this paragraph are presented, it is most likely from

    F   a review

    G   an editorial

    H   a novel

    J   a poem

Practice

Read each passage. Identify its genre by writing *poetry*, *fiction*, *drama*, *essay*, *biography*, or *autobiography*.

1.   Until I was 13 and left Arkansas for good, the Store was my favorite place to be. Alone and empty in the mornings, it looked like an unopened present from a stranger. Opening the front doors was pulling the ribbon off the unexpected gift. The light would come in softly (we faced north), easing itself over the shelves of mackerel, salmon, tobacco, and thread.

_____

2.   Religious freedom has been a political issue around the world for many centuries. The Edict of Nantes, a decree issued in 1598 by the Catholic King Henry IV of France, was a milestone in the development of religious freedom. The edict was the first official document evidencing religious toleration in a large European country. It granted religious freedom to Henry's Protestant subjects, the Huguenots.

_____

3.   Giuseppe Garibaldi was the hero of the Italian Risorgimento, the 19th-century movement to unify Italy. He was one of the great masters of guerrilla warfare, and he led most of the military victories of the movement. Garibaldi was also an expert propagandist.

_____

4.   The man stepped out of the house and stood quite still, listening. Behind him, lights glowed in the cheerful room, the books were neat and orderly in their cases, the radio talked importantly to itself. In front of him, the bay stretched dark and silent, one of the countless lagoons that border the coast where Florida thrusts its great green thumb deep into the tropics.

_____

Apply

Read each passage. Circle the genre to which the passage belongs.

1. Cities have been smothered with volcanic ash, leveled by hurricanes, and shaken apart by earthquakes. But no disaster quite matches the one that struck Port Royal, Jamaica, at 11:43 A.M. on June 7, 1692. In less than 10 minutes, the thriving pirate port sank into the Caribbean.

    A biography

    B fiction

    C essay

    D drama

2. Benjamin Franklin was a famous American, but he was admired by people of other nations as well. During the Revolutionary War, Congress appointed Franklin as minister to France. Franklin was warmly welcomed by the French people. They were charmed by his kindness, wisdom, and tact.

    F fiction

    G poetry

    H autobiography

    J biography

3. It had been raining for a long time, a slow, cold rain falling from iron-colored clouds. They had been driving since morning, and they still had 130 miles to go. It was about three o'clock in the afternoon.
       "I'm getting hungry," Laura said.

    A autobiography

    B essay

    C fiction

    D drama

4. As a child, I was a science fan. My education was scientific. I even wrote a short article for a scientific magazine. Science, to my mind, was, and still is, the one reliable means we have to discover the truth.

    F fiction

    G biography

    H autobiography

    J poetry

Check Up

Read the passage. Then circle the answer to complete each statement.

When the first light went out at 6:45, the Texas sun had just poked its nose over the horizon and the hundreds of Navy training planes nestling on the ramp looked like gray ghosts in the dim morning light. Mounting the steps to the squadron control tower a few minutes earlier, I had noticed, far off to the north in the dew-infested haze, a scowling bank of black clouds. I remember feeling relieved that I wasn't flying that day. I had, instead, drawn the assignment as tower duty officer. Later, I would have been happy to trade places with almost anyone in the squadron.

In the glass-encased tower atop the hanger, all the disconnected threads of the complex operations of a warm naval-air-training squadron were fathered and loosely held. Here, we were in direct radio contact with hundreds of practicing pilots. This day one would survive an experience that dozens of others would never forget.

1. The language of the passage consists mostly of
   A   imagery and figures of speech
   B   narration and dialogue
   C   dialogue
   D   persuasive language

2. The passage is written by
   F   a narrator about imaginary characters
   G   a writer about a real person's life
   H   a writer about her own life
   I   a poet about his or her own experiences

3. The genre of the passage is
   A   poetry
   B   fiction
   C   drama
   D   essay

Read On   Read "NAFTA: Boon or Bust?" Apply passage elements to help answer the questions.

Identifying Style Techniques

One enjoyable aspect of reading all kinds of writing is appreciating the writer's use of language, or **style.**

- One element of style is **word choice**. Good writers choose specific words to communicate moods or to make readers feel sad, angry, or amused. Some words are useful for persuading readers while others simply provide information.

- Another element of style is the use of **imagery**. An image can appeal to any of the five senses. It makes readers imagine that they can see, hear, touch, taste, or smell what the writer is describing.

- A final element of style is **figurative language**.

    - One form of figurative language is the figure of speech called a **simile.** A simile is a comparison using the word *like* or *as*: "The new sports car looked like a spaceship."

    - The figure of speech may be a **metaphor**, in which a comparison is stated: "The new sports car was a sleek spaceship."

    - Another kind of figurative language is **personification**, in which an animal or an inanimate object is compared to a human being: "The building was a friendly soldier, guarding the neighborhood." Often personification is implied: "We moor beneath towering smokestacks whose fierce breath once blackened the city." The "breath" of the smokestacks implies that they are alive.

Read the passage. Circle the answer to each question.

Only the scrape of our boots against rock and loose pebbles broke the silence as we moved deeper into the cave. Breathing had become an effort. The air, long stagnant from being kept in this tomblike cave, burned our throats and left a rancid taste. Foul-smelling and heavy, it seemed to stick in our lungs after each intake of breath.

1. To which sense does the image in the first sentence appeal?

    A sight

    B sound

    C taste

    D smell

2. What main technique does the writer use to create the gloomy mood of the cave?

    F personification

    G similes and metaphors

    H word choice

    J sight imagery

Practice

Read each passage. Then circle the answer to each question.

Snow fell against the high school all day, wet big-flaked snow that did not stick well. Sharpening two pencils, William looked down on a parking lot that was a blackboard in reverse. Car tires had cut smooth arcs of black into its white.

1. What figure of speech is used in the second sentence?
   A simile
   B metaphor
   C personification
   D image

The asteroids were like tiny unnamed islands lost in the vast sea of space.

2. What figure of speech is used in this sentence?
   F simile
   G metaphor
   H personification
   J image

The noises made it so lonely in that swamp you just wanted to cry. A bittern roared. A heron squawked. A kingfisher rattled. A deer snorted and barked. A bird screeched. A crow cawed.

3. What main style technique is used in this passage?
   A personification
   B imagery
   C vivid word choice
   D metaphor

When the first light went out at 6:45, the Texas sun had just poked its nose over the horizon.

4. Of what figure of speech is this an example?
   F simile
   G metaphor
   H personification
   J image

Apply

Read each passage. Write the name of the sense or senses to which the imagery mainly appeals: *sight, sound, touch, taste,* or *smell*.

1. In the distance I saw a lighthouse silhouetted against the gray dawn.

   _____

2. From the shore bluffs you can hear the cry of the oyster catcher and the hiss and rumble of surf over pebbles.

   _____

3. The air was full of the sweet smell of fruit from the packing plants.

   _____

4. Almost everything used to taste better when I was a kid. Now everything looks great but tastes like cardboard.

   _____

5. The boy's black eyes were like a snake's, and they burned like cold fire.

   _____

6. The odor coming from the swamp water reminded her of the smell of decayed leaves in the late fall.

   _____

7. The cedar-wood smell of pencil shavings mingled with the musty odor of the wet windowsill.

   _____

8. The days came in, cool and crisp, warmed to a pleasant slowness, and chilled again.

   _____

Check Up

Read the passage. Then circle the answer to each question.

The coal dust, suspended in the air of the hold, had glowed dull-red at the moment of the explosion. In the twinkling of an eye, in a fraction of a second, I was sprawling full length on the cargo. I picked myself up and scrambled out. It was quick like a rebound. The deck was a wilderness of smashed timber, lying crosswise like trees in a wood after a hurricane.

1. To which sense does the image in the first sentence appeal?

   A sight

   B sound

   C touch

   D smell

2. "The deck was a wilderness . . ." is an example of what figure of speech?

   F simile

   G personification

   H metaphor

   J image

3. The figure of speech, "smashed timber, lying crosswise like trees in a wood after a hurricane," is a

   A simile

   B personification

   C metaphor

   D image

4. Words chosen to create a sense of emergency include

   F suspended, glowed

   G sprawling, scrambled

   H deck, cargo

   J dust, air

Recognizing Author's Effect and Intention

A writer begins writing with a **purpose:** to entertain, to inform, or to persuade. In accomplishing this purpose, the writer must decide on an attitude toward his or her material and audience. For example, a writer may want to persuade readers that reality-based television shows are ridiculous and decide that a humorous approach will be most effective in achieving the goal. **Style techniques** such as word choice, imagery, and figurative language help the writer communicate **tone,** or attitude toward his or her subject. These elements help readers determine the **author's effect.** An author's tone may be sarcastic, humorous, angry, frightened, or cheerful. The author communicates this attitude through the style techniques listed above.

> A dog howling in the night . . . is enough to scare the sense right out of me. It's a primitive sound, a wail right out of the wilderness. I lay and listened and hoped it wouldn't waken my wife. Then I heard a sharp intake of breath and she asked in a tense whisper, "What's that?"

In this passage, the writer uses the words *howling, primitive, wail,* and *wilderness* to create a sense of fright and suspense. He also uses words that indicate fear on the part of his wife and himself. So the effect of the passage is suspense. The author's tone could be described as frightening or suspenseful.

Read the passage. Circle the answer to each question.

> Astronomy was the first of my lasting loves. It overtook me during the total eclipse of 1925. I was staggered by the "diamond ring" effect, caused by the last bit of the sun's face blazing between mountain peaks on the moon's edge. Then the total eclipse began, the stars came out, and I was thrilled.

1. What is the author's tone in the passage?

   A sarcastic

   B depressed

   C amused

   D excited

2. Which words best communicate the author's tone?

   F peaks, total

   G eclipse, stars

   H staggered, thrilled

   J overtook, began

Practice

Read each passage. Circle the word that best expresses the author's tone in the passage.

1.   I am a person who bears grudges, and I have a lot against three of my children, Manuel, Roberto, and Consuelo. My body is becoming half-paralyzed from being so angry with these children of mine.

    A bitter

    B enthusiastic

    C cheerful

    D frightened

2.   I never meant to say anything about this, but the fact is that I have never met a dog that didn't have it in for me. You take Kelly, for instance. He's a wirehaired fox terrier, and he's had us for three years now. I wouldn't say that he is terribly handsome, but he does have a very nice smile. Kelly spends his whole day, every day, chasing swans on the millpond. I don't actually worry because he will never catch one.

    F grieving

    G humorous

    H realistic

    J sentimental

3.   When work has accumulated to the point where you feel overwhelmed, you can help matters by getting organized. First, list all the tasks that must be done and decide which ones require immediate attention.

    A hopeless

    B depressed

    C helpful and practical

    D condescending

4.   On our first visit to Rome, we took a great bus tour. The guide showed us sights I had only dreamed about. I could hardly wait to return to a few of them on my own.

    F humorous

    G sarcastic

    H sorrowful

    J enthusiastic

Apply

Read each passage. Write a word that describes the author's tone in the passage.

1.   Mother met me with a white, strained face. "Your father is suffering terribly. Go for the doctor at once." I could hear my father groan as I moved about the kitchen, putting on my coat and lighting the lantern. It was about one o'clock in the morning, and the wind was cold as I picked my way through the mud to the barn. The thought of the long miles to town made me shiver, but as the son of a soldier, I could not falter in my duty.

_____

2.   The lion lay still in the grass, watching. She scanned the horizon for any sign of movement. She had left her newborn cubs and began her search for food. Nothing escaped her. Every sound, every movement was the source of a potential meal. She was hungry, and she would wait patiently. Before long a herd was sure to come to the water hole, and when it did, she would be there—waiting. She would choose a target and pounce.

_____

3.   My sister, Betts, loves word play and acts on it. Once when we were young, I asked if she would dust for me. She tossed a silky powder in the air and said, "There, I've dusted." What could I say? I had asked her to dust, but, of course, I had meant to wipe up the dust, not to throw more down! Then there was the time I said that I wished I had a peaches-and-cream complexion. I don't need to tell you what she did, do I?

_____

4.   True!—nervous—very, very dreadfully nervous I had been and am; but why WILL you say that I am mad? The disease had sharpened my senses—not destroyed—not dulled them. Above all was the sense of hearing acute. I heard all things in the heaven and in the earth. I heard many things in hell. How, then, am I mad?

_____

Check Up

Read the passage. Then circle the answer to each question.

In a small town in lower Burma, I was hated by large numbers of people. It was the only time in my life that I have been important enough for this to happen to me. I was a deputy police officer of the town. In an aimless, petty way, anti-European feeling was very bitter. As an English police officer I was an obvious target and was baited whenever it seemed safe to do so. When a nimble Burman tripped me up on the football field and the referee (another Burman) looked the other way, the crowd yelled with hideous laughter. This happened more than once. In the end, the sneering faces of young men that met me everywhere and the insults hooted after me when I was at a safe distance got badly on my nerves.

1. The feelings and attitudes of the writer result in a tone of

   A humor

   B bitterness

   C pride

   D hopefulness

2. The attitudes of the Burmese toward the author were

   F affectionate

   G tolerant

   H sympathetic

   J contemptuous

3. Words that help communicate the author's tone include

   A hideous, sneering

   B nimble, laughter

   C important, deputy

   D obvious, yelled

4. The author's intention as communicated in the passage is

   F to share an unpleasant memory

   G to humorously relate an upsetting experience

   H to warn readers to stay away from Burma

   J to explain why people from Burma disliked Europeans

Applying Passage Elements

When you read, build on your knowledge of all the elements of good writing to analyze, understand, and appreciate what you read.

Read the passage. Circle the answer to the first question. Then write an answer to the second question.

Some unique signs were posted in an English hostel. The hostel (which is like a hotel, but provides no services aside from a sleeping room) issued instructions to its guests through signs bearing pointed messages. One sign, for instance, says, "Americans are requested to retire before 2:00 A.M." Another notice asks that German visitors stay in bed until at least six o'clock in the morning. "Italians," one last sign reads, "are requested to refrain from singing after 10:00 P.M."

> Americans
> are requested to
> retire before
> 2:00 A.M.

1. What generalization can be made from this passage?

   A Most hostel guests are inconsiderate.

   B The hostel owners had some amusing stereotypes about various nationalities.

   C Hotels are much more expensive than hostels.

   D All English hostels display signs about specific nationalities.

2. Write three generalizations about specific nationalities upon which the hostel owners based their signs.

   _____

   _____

   _____

   _____

   _____

Practice

Read each passage. Circle the phrase or clause to complete each sentence. Then write an answer to the second question.

Everything from clothing to food has been subject to trends over the years. But have you ever heard of a fashionable disease? Tuberculosis, or consumption, as it was called in the 1800s, was *the* disease for poets and intellectuals. John Keats wrote his verse while suffering from the illness. Lord Byron claimed that he would rather die of consumption than of old age. Some aspiring artists avoided the sun to acquire the sick pallor of consumption. Unfortunately, the state of medicine in the 1800s made it quite easy to actually have the disease. Keats, for one, eventually died of consumption.

1. Lord Byron's personality was probably

   A   calm and reasonable

   B   strict and straitlaced

   C   emotional and high-strung

   D   unimaginative

2. Write a different kind of example as supporting evidence for the first sentence of the passage.

   _____

   _____

In the 1600s, a woman used a fan to get messages to a prospective suitor. A whole array of signals was developed. By making a small, seemingly innocent movement with her fan, a woman could relay to a gentleman when and where she could rendezvous with him, who might be with her, and whether or not she was in love with him. All of the signs were designed to escape the watchful notice of the woman's chaperone.

3. From the passage we can conclude that

   F   women of the 17th century often got too warm

   G   17th-century men understood women's fan signals

   H   women of the 17th century were too shy to let men know of their interest

   J   women and men of the 17th century were often left alone together

4. What more general conclusion can you reach about courtship in the 1600s?

   _____

   _____

Apply

Read each passage. Circle the phrase or clause to complete each sentence. Then write an answer to the second question.

William Henry Harrison served the shortest term of any president of the United States. He caught a cold on his inaugural day in 1871 and died 30 days later. John Tyler was vice president at the time, but no one could find him directly after the president's death. He was finally tracked down in Williamsburg, Virginia. Upon hearing the news, he immediately set out for the capital and arrived there 53 hours after Harrison had died. Tyler proceeded to upset the Whig Party backers of the Harrison-Tyler ticket by undoing much of the party platform he had supported as a candidate. By the end of his term, he had destroyed the Whigs by killing all the bills they introduced in Congress. Harrison's death also proved to be the death of the Whig party.

1. The main cause-and-effect relationship examined in the passage is

    A   the cause of President Harrison's death

    B   the cause of the Whig Party's getting upset with President Tyler

    C   the cause of the Whig Party's demise

    D   the cause of Tyler's delay in getting to Washington

2. What communication and travel conditions probably caused a gap of 53 hours between Harrison dying and Tyler taking office?

    _____

    _____

Union leaders are right when they complain of society's indifference toward the skilled blue-collar worker. The blame rests with the opinion molders: television, movies, and the press. From their air-conditioned offices high atop ivory towers, the image makers glorify the glamorous professions. They look down their noses at the more than 10 million unsung workers who aren't afraid to get their hands dirty. Without the skills and services of these workers, the United States would come to a grinding halt.

3. Which of the following statements from the passage is a fact that could be verified?

    F   Society is indifferent toward blue-collar workers.

    G   The blame rests with the opinion molders.

    H   Image makers look down their noses at blue-collar workers.

    J   none of the above

4. Write an opinion opposed to the opinion stated in the passage. Write at least one fact that supports the opinion you state.

    _____

    _____

Check Up

Read each passage. Circle the answer to the first question. Then write an answer to the second question.

After the drab, utilitarian clothing made necessary by the lean economy during World War II, the fashions of the late 1940s and 1950s provided a welcome contrast. Bright colors and new materials such as nylon were used, and women's styles became more feminine. The trend in the 1950s was to dress casually, with sweaters and cardigans gaining popularity. The jeans and duffle coat popularized by students were adopted by many young people, who were attracted to both the cheapness and the simplicity of the style.

1. What was the major difference between fashions of the 1940s and fashions of the 1950s?

   A Clothing in the 1940s was practical and serious; clothing in the 1950s was casual and fun.

   B Clothing in the 1940s was bright; clothing in the 1950s was drab.

   C Clothing in the 1940s was made of synthetic fabrics; clothing in the 1950s was made of natural fabrics.

   D Clothing in the 1940s was cheap; clothing in the 1950s was expensive.

2. Write a sentence or two comparing and/or contrasting clothing of the 1950s to the clothing of today.

   _____

   _____

   _____

When it was first settled in the 1850s, Seattle, Washington, seemed to have everything going for it: timber, fishing, and the perfect location for a port to allow trade with East Asia. But male workers who flocked there, tempted by the promise of riches, found that Seattle was lacking one important thing: women. Enter Asa Mercer, entrepreneur. Mercer promised that for each deposit of $300 he would bring a young, attractive woman from back east to live in Seattle.

3. What is the probable outcome of the story?

   F The male workers in Seattle were not interested in Mercer's offer.

   G Mercer brought back hundreds of women, and they were soon married.

   H A few male workers accepted Mercer's offer.

   J Mercer accepted many orders but was unable to find women who wanted to move to Seattle.

4. How do you think men and women today would react to an offer like Mercer's?

   _____

   _____

Read On As you read "A Tarantula—Big Hairy Deal," think of what genre this would best represent. Then answer the questions.

Review

Predicting Outcomes

You can better understand what you read by predicting how events will turn out.

Fact and Opinion

It is important for readers to distinguish between fact and opinion. A **fact** is a statement that can be proved. An **opinion** is a personal viewpoint, a statement that cannot be proved.

Author's Purpose

The most common purposes for writing are to entertain, to inform, to persuade or express an opinion, to describe, and to explain or instruct.

Author's Point of View

An author's **point of view** is how he or she feels about the subject.

Making Generalizations

When you make a **generalization**, you come to a general conclusion based on specific pieces of evidence.

Genre

Literary genres include fiction, poetry, and drama. **Nonfiction genres** include essay, biography, and autobiography.

Style Techniques

Word choice, **imagery**, and **figurative language** are style techniques authors use to communicate moods and feelings.

Author's Effect and Intention

An author's **tone**, or **attitude** toward his or her subject, helps readers determine the author's effect.

Applying Passage Elements

You can use elements in the passage to extend meaning.

Assessment

Read each passage. Then circle the answer for each question.

The theory of ESP contains many mysteries. For doubting scientists, the biggest mystery is whether ESP exists at all. Other scientists think that they have proven that ESP is real. The doubters disagree. They claim that the power of ESP can be explained in other ways. Perhaps, they say, some people have stronger natural senses than others. This attitude is nonsense. The senses of sight, hearing, smell, taste, and touch can't do the work of ESP. ESP uses invisible brain waves that are produced by one person and received by another. If researchers would just look at the facts and make the effort to discover the center in the brain that sends and receives brain waves, the mystery would be solved for once and for all. Then we could get on with developing our ESP.

1. The writer uses words that suggest

   A   bad things about ESP itself

   B   good things about doubting scientists

   C   bad things about doubting scientists

   D   bad things about ESP believers

2. The author seems to think that

   F   ESP is really nothing more than strong natural senses

   G   ESP has not been proved

   H   scientists aren't investigating ESP enough

   J   ESP has been proved false

People who give permission for doctors to use parts of their bodies when they die are called organ donors. Some of the donated organs are studied by medical researchers who are trying to find cures for diseases. Some donated organs are used for transplants. There is no reason for any healthy person not to become an organ donor. Many states have a provision on a driver's license to indicate that the driver has chosen to become an organ donor.

3. From this paragraph you can generalize that

   A   organ donations may help save lives

   B   medical researchers believe there is a greater need for organ donors

   C   transplanted organs are often the treatment of last resort

   D   everyone should have access to organ donations

4. Which of the following statements is **not** a fact?

   F   People who give permission for doctors to use parts of their bodies when they die are called organ donors.

   G   Some donated organs are used for transplants.

   H   There is no reason for any healthy person not to become an organ donor.

   J   Many states have a provision on a person's driver's license to indicate that the driver has chosen to become an organ donor.

During the early days of the United States, coins were desperately needed. A new mint was authorized. The need for it was so great that one of the federal government's first acts was to build a mint building. But much more than a building was needed before coins could be made. First the mint needed a supply of precious metal. And that was not easy to come by. Citizens were asked to turn in gold, silver, and copper to be melted down into coins. But people wanted to keep their precious metal and were slow to send it in.

5. Why was precious metal for coins in short supply?

   A There was no metal in the United States.

   B People sent all their metal to Europe.

   C Banks had closed.

   D People hoarded metal, so there was little available.

6. What is the author's purpose?

   F to persuade readers to collect coins

   G to explain why there were few coins in the early days of the United States

   H to tell readers how coins were made

   J to convince readers that coins are important currency

   Tennis was first introduced to North America in 1874 by Mary Ewing Outerbridge, who brought rackets, balls, and nets from Bermuda. According to a popular story, custom officials could not figure out which section of the Tariff Act the equipment came under, so after a week of hesitation they let it into the country duty free. The first tennis court was laid out on grass at the Staten Island Cricket and Baseball Club, of which the Outerbridge family were members. The Outerbridges became the first tennis family in the United States. Within seven years, the sport had become so popular that the United States Lawn Tennis Association was formed, and competitions began to be held. Since that time, tennis has become a big business and an extremely lucrative profession for the better players.

7. Which style technique does the author use?

   A dialogue

   B figurative language

   C historical description

   D exaggeration

8. This paragraph would most likely be found in a

   F textbook

   G newsmagazine

   H athlete's diary

   J company's annual report

When he thought about the incident later, Ben wished he had paid more attention to his gut feelings. As he and Jon laced up their skates, Ben had second thoughts. Jon was always one to take chances.

Ben looked suspiciously at the frozen pond. "I don't think it's thick enough to skate on," he muttered. "Remember when those kids fell through the ice last winter?"

"Relax, Ben," scoffed Jon. "You always think of something to worry about. Just try to have a good time."

"I know that there have been too many accidents on this pond. Hey, Wait!" Ben called frantically as he watched Jon skate off blithely out to the middle of the pond.

9. What do you predict will happen next?

A   Ben will decide to go home.

B   Jon will convince Ben that the pond is not safe to skate on.

C   Ben will put his worries aside and have a good time skating.

D   Jon will fall through the ice.

10. What sentence gives the reader a hint about the outcome?

F   When he thought about the incident later, Ben wished he had paid more attention to his gut feelings.

G   Ben looked suspiciously at the frozen pond.

H   "Relax, Ben," scoffed Jon.

J   "Just try to have a good time."

Posttest

Posttest continued

Circle the word that is spelled correctly and completes each sentence.

1. Women with the highest singing voices are called _____.

   A sopraneos

   B sopranoes

   C sopranos

   D sopranose

2. Our office has _____ electronic equipment.

   F sophisticated

   G sofisticated

   H sofistickated

   J sophistikated

3. The room was filled with the sounds of _____.

   A laffter

   B laughter

   C lafter

   D laphter

4. The gown is made of silk and _____.

   F shiffon

   G shifon

   H chifon

   J chiffon

Circle the answer that is a synonym for the underlined word.

5. <u>bear</u> the pain of a broken leg

   A endure

   B relinquish

   C submit

   D conquer

6. a <u>feeble</u> cry for help

   F loud

   G energetic

   H frail

   J sturdy

7. remained <u>calm</u> in a crisis

   A frantic

   B tranquil

   C nervous

   D vague

8. a daily household <u>chore</u>

   F task

   G hobby

   H option

   J rotation

9. a campaign <u>speech</u>

   A promise

   B duet

   C conversation

   D address

10. <u>displays</u> his athletic abilities

    F conceals

    G curtains

    H attracts

    J shows

Posttest continued

Circle the answer that is an antonym for the underlined word.

11. sentimental reasons
    A realistic
    B romantic
    C personal
    D mushy

12. convict the offender
    F sentence
    G condemn
    H liberate
    J forget

13. hasten our departure
    A accelerate
    B delay
    C rush
    D denounce

14. definite answer
    F vague
    G explicit
    H incorrect
    J specific

15. daring escape
    A surprising
    B reckless
    C bold
    D timid

16. contradicted her claim
    F affirmed
    G completed
    H denied
    J frustrated

Circle the answer to each question.

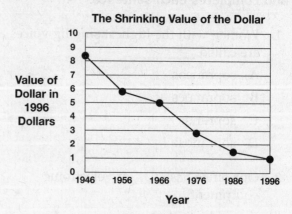

The Shrinking Value of the Dollar

Source: *Time Almanac, 1999*

17. During which decade did the value of a dollar shrink the least?
    A 1946–1956
    B 1956–1966
    C 1976–1986
    D 1986–1996

18. About how much would you need to earn in 1996 to equal the purchasing power of a weekly salary of $100 in 1956?
    F $300
    G $900
    H $600
    J $150

19. If you look in a card catalog for *The Longest Winter*, which information would **not** be found?
    A author
    B call number
    C publisher
    D times checked out

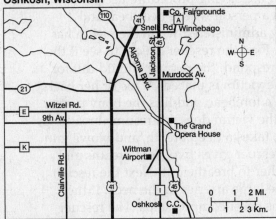

Oshkosh, Wisconsin

(41) U.S. Highway
(21) State Highway
[E] County Highway
■ Points of Interest

20. Lee lives at Clairville Road and 9th Avenue. If he drives to Winnebago, which way should he drive?

   F north on U.S. Highway 41

   G west on State Highway 21

   H south on County Highway I

   J west on Witzel Road

21. About how far is it from the Oshkosh Country Club (Oshkosh C. C.) to the County Fairgrounds?

   A 8 miles

   B 2 miles

   C 16 miles

   D 20 miles

22. Which information would likely **not** be needed when you fill out a form to order clothes?

   F credit card number

   G your address

   H shipping costs

   J your employer

23. Which words are **not** in alphabetical order?

   A petulant, pharmacy, philosophy, physics

   B rhapsody, rhinoceros, rhythm, ribbon

   C scholarly, scissors, shrimp, shareholder

   D wharf, whirl, whisper, whistle

24. Which word matches this pronunciation: eks trakt'?

   F extra

   G extract

   H extort

   J exert

25. Which book would tell what states border North Carolina?

   A an atlas

   B a book about North Dakota

   C a thesaurus

   D a dictionary

26. Which is the best place to find unbiased information about a DVD player you are thinking about buying?

   F consumer magazine

   G store ad in the newspaper

   H ask your friend who has one

   J television

Cardiopulmonary resuscitation (CPR) is a life-saving procedure used to maintain respiration and blood circulation in a person whose heartbeat and breathing have stopped. It is most commonly administered when the victim has had a severe heart attack or serious accident. First the rescuer checks to see if the victim is unconscious. If the victim does not respond, the rescuer should call for help before beginning to administer CPR. The victim is placed on his or her back. Then the rescuer presses down on the victim's forehead and lifts the bony part of the chin to clear the victim's air passages. If the victim does not resume breathing, the rescuer pinches the victim's nostrils shut, takes a deep breath, and blows into the victim's mouth to inflate the lungs. The rescuer gives two slow breaths and releases the victim's nostrils to allow him or her to breathe out. Next the rescuer checks the victim's pulse by feeling one of the large arteries in the neck. If the rescuer cannot detect a pulse, he or she begins chest compressions. The rescuer places both hands—one on top of the other—on the lower part of the victim's breastbone. The rescuer compresses the chest 15 times, followed by giving the victim two full breaths. The procedure should be performed continuously until the victim's heartbeat and breathing resume. When help arrives, the victim must be taken to the hospital for further care.

27. What is the first thing a rescuer does to the victim?

    A pinch the victim's nostrils

    B establish an open air passage

    C determine if he or she is unconscious

    D compress the chest 15 times

28. CPR is most commonly administered

    F when the victim is choking

    G when the victim has had a severe heart attack or serious accident

    H when the victim has been burned

    J when the victim has high blood pressure

29. What pattern does the rescuer follow when administering CPR?

    A 1 breath, 15 compressions, 1 breath

    B 2 breaths, 15 compressions, 2 breaths

    C 1 breath, 15 compressions, 2 breaths

    D 15 breaths, 2 compressions, 15 breaths

30. This paragraph would most likely be found in

    F a collection of stories

    G a first-aid manual

    H a third-grade health book

    J an almanac

Early people found fire in natural forms, and it became a central part of life long before they learned how to make it themselves. We know that many of today's forest fires are set by lightning. These fires were just as common in the ancient past. There were also fires that came from the hot lava of volcanoes. And there were fires that came from stones crashing together. What people saw taught them how to use fire. But when they first used fire, they had to carry it with them from place to place.

31. Why do you suppose fire was so important to early people?

    A Fire was dangerous.

    B It was a mysterious element.

    C Fire provided warmth and a way to cook.

    D Fire gave them an advantage in war against people who did not have it.

32. Why did early people carry fire with them from place to place?

    F They did not know how to make it themselves.

    G They used fire to light the way as they traveled.

    H They traded fire for food and clothing.

    J They used fire to announce their arrival.

    Civil War Index

    Fair Oaks, battle of, *photo* 78
    Farragut, David, 76, 177–178
    Ford's Theatre, 217–219; *photo* 233
    Fort Sumter, 28, 217; *photo* 28
    Fredericksburg, battle of, 87–89

33. Which index entry includes a picture as well as a page reference?

    A Fair Oaks, battle of

    B Farragut, David

    C Ford's Theatre

    D Fredricksburg, battle of

The
Human Difference

John Allan

A LION BOOK

Oxford · Batavia · Sydney

Contents

Special Features

Part I

Introducing Human Life

BIRTH, LIFE AND DEATH

A baby is lying in its pram, eyes bright but impassive. Its hands and feet are tiny and delicate; its skin soft and flawless. Another human life, just begun.

How does it feel to be a baby? And how will it develop?

What does the future hold for this eight-and-a-half-pound packet of human life?

Obviously, no one can tell exactly. There are over five billion of us on this planet, and many new human beings arrive every minute. Human lives take a tremendous variety of courses, dictated by family circumstances, accidental occurrences, culture, health and intelligence. But some things are fairly standard. Let's assume that our baby survives infancy and lives through a generally typical lifetime (typical, that is, for that part of the world's population which isn't facing daily starvation and health risks). Which phases will this human being pass through? What will the landmarks be?

Birth and babyhood

There is no definite answer to the question, 'When does human life begin?' But it is clear that even before the moment of birth, a child already has a well-developed existence inside its mother's body.

In fact, as soon as the egg cell of the mother is penetrated by the sperm cell of the father, the child-to-be already has its distinct identity

determined. Sex, intelligence, size and shape, colouring and temperament—all these details are already firmly decided. Four weeks later, still only a quarter of an inch long, its heart will be beating, eyes and mouth will have started to appear, and ears will have begun to form. Before the pregnancy is two-thirds complete, the new human will be able to cry, to use its hands to grasp and hit, and to kick its legs.

What is it like to be inside the womb? Brain activity begins early, at six or seven weeks, but there can only be a very rudimentary kind of

awareness. There can be no real understanding of space or sense of time. The new life is completely insulated from the many different stimuli it will encounter in the world outside. Its needs for nourishment, warmth and shelter are automatically met. Life couldn't be simpler.

And so the moment of birth must come as a tremendous shock! Suddenly we come into contact with all sorts of things we have never encountered before: pain, for example, and cold. The brightness of daylight must seem terrifyingly dazzling. And hunger becomes a reality: our food needs are no longer auto-matically supplied, and even if our mother hurries to feed us as soon as she realizes we are hungry, there is still a slight delay between the need and the fulfilment. No wonder we cry. This has never happened before!

The change in our mother is bewildering, too. Up until birth, she had been the whole of our world. We lived inside her. Now, after one traumatic upheaval, she shrinks to just one part of that world, outside us and operating independently. She can even leave us and walk away!

(Perhaps we never quite forget the first view we have of our mother. Some psychologists claim that many men are attracted to women with pale faces and dark eyes because that is how a baby first glimpses its mother: a blurred white oval in which only the dark shadow of the eyes is discernible. Perhaps this is true; certainly women in many different civilizations have tried to increase their sex appeal by whitening their faces and darkening their eyebrows.)

As brand new babies, we have difficulty at first in deciding what is 'me' and what is 'something else'. For example, a baby can watch with great curiosity its own hand moving and waving while not really appreciating that the hand is actually connected to its own body, or that baby itself is causing the birth movements. But gradually we begin to settle down in our new world. We start to learn how to use our eyes, to follow objects visually as they move away from us, rather than just registering blankly those sights which happen to drift in front of us. Our hands start to grasp objects firmly. Our ears start to distinguish between sounds.

Now the world is becoming less terrifying. Our mother may have changed her position in relation to us, but she does not appear to be abandoning us, she is still meeting our needs and feeding us; we start to develop a sense of trust in our new environment. (Obviously, if our needs are not met sufficiently at this critical stage, it can cause problems in our development later on. The more stroking and caressing a baby receives, for example, the greater its chances of adjusting naturally to sexual activity when it grows up.)

We begin to develop the first faint stirrings of memory. This gives us a growing sense that there is a continuity in the things which are

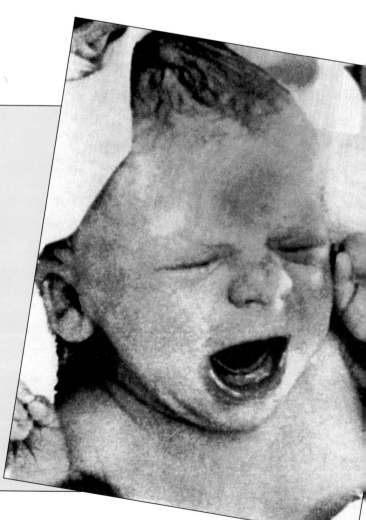

CAN LIFE START IN TEST-TUBES?

When Louise Brown was born in Oldham, Lancashire, in July 1978, she was a perfectly normal, very attractive human baby. Yet she made history. For no human being had ever come to life in the same way that she had.

Louise was born through 'in-vitro' fertilization. This means that the egg cell from her mother's body and the sperm cell from her father's had not come together in the normal way—within the body of the mother, after sexual intercourse—but that the egg cell had been removed from the mother, cultured in a laboratory until it reached ripeness and then artificially fertilized with sperm. After a period of growth outside the mother's body it was re-implanted inside the womb, where it grew and developed like any other normal growing foetus.

On 25 July 1978, at Oldham General Hospital, England, Louise Joy Brown was born by caesarian section. Louise was the world's first test-tube fertilization baby. She is a perfectly normal child, and lives with her mother Lesley and father John.

happening to us; life is not all just a parade of inexplicable events. Around now we start to become aware for the first time that we have an individual identity. 'Myself' has started to arrive.

Being a toddler

We start to leave the baby stage when we gain some control over our bodies. We discover that we can stand upright and learn to walk. And our excretions—until now quite involuntary, leaving an endless procession of nappies on the line—we suddenly find to be susceptible to our own control. This gives us a lot of satisfaction. Psychologist Sigmund Freud wrote that we gain two different kinds of pleasure from this new achievement: first from co-operating with our parents and doing it when they want us to; but then also from refusing to do it, so as to defy their authority and enjoy the power this gives us. Independence is beginning to develop. . .

It is often when children are two years old that their parents suddenly find, to their horror, that what was once a sweet, compliant baby has all at once developed a determined mind of its own! Screaming matches, stubborn disobedience and deliberately naughty behaviour start to develop. The child is beginning to realize its own independent identity, and test out how much it can afford to defy the wishes of others.

This was a tremendous breakthrough, which had been forecast for over a decade—ever since in 1966 Dr Robert Edwards had shown that it was possible to extract oocytes (undeveloped cells) and develop them artificially. It doesn't exactly happen in test-tubes, but certainly in a laboratory, under the direction of scientists.

Since then, many other 'test-tube babies' have been born, and extravagant claims are being made for the future. It is said that some time soon scientists will be able to manufacture eggs—rather than taking them from the mother—and so create a living baby from scratch, without using already existing human material. A geneticist in San Marcos, California, has founded a 'Repository for Germinal Choice', a sperm bank where the donors are distinguished scientists,

Nobel Prize-winners, and similar high achievers. The aim is to allow women who would otherwise be unable to have a family to choose a father for their children from among the most talented, intelligent people in the world.

There are many difficulties with the new discoveries. One is that 'IVF' (in-vitro fertilization) is not a sure-fire guarantee of successful birth. The highest level of success which can be expected is likely to be around 30–35 per cent.

Another problem is that projects like the 'Repository for Germinal Choice' assume that intelligence and creativity are all that matter in creating a 'successful' child. The importance of close, natural, loving family relationships can be forgotten, and the technique can be misused to produce children without a normal family and social network to

support them in their growing up.

Even more controversial, the technique used for extracting eggs usually leaves a few 'spare embryos', fertilized but unwanted, at the end of the process. Should these be destroyed? Or should they be used (as has often happened) for further research? If so, are you annihilating or experimenting with a potential human being?

There are many problems to be solved. But it cannot be denied that 'IVF' has brought new hope to many childless couples, and can be a tremendous force for good if used responsibly.

There is a story (probably apocryphal) that Albert Einstein did not utter a word until he was four years old. Then at dinner one day he suddenly remarked, 'This soup is too cold'. His parents were delighted and relieved to find their child talking at last, and asked him why he had said nothing before. He replied, 'Everything has always been all right until now.'

Another stubborn non-talker was poet Alfred Lord Tennyson, who remained silent until one day a maid spilled some boiling water over his foot. As she tried to clear up the mess and bandage his foot, the infant Tennyson is supposed to have said coldly, 'You may desist from your applications. The pain is now considerably abated.'

It sounds too good a story to be true—and perhaps it is. But it serves to remind us that children grow up at different speeds and in different ways. And certainly a toddler can understand a lot more than it can say. For most children, however, talking will begin somewhere between eight and twenty months. This provides another source of power, a new medium through which to assert our will. Which is why the first words each of us learned included 'No!', 'Don't!', and 'Mine!'.

Becoming aware of ourselves means becoming aware of others, too. We start to find that other people have wishes and desires which sometimes conflict with our own; the toddler's big problem is how to assert his or her new sense of individuality and autonomy without conflicting too much with the wishes of others, and so ending up with a smacked bottom. Until the age of two, most children play alone. After that, they begin to let other children into their games, although cautiously at first, and only one at a time. Not until they are five will most children play with several others. Social relationships are tricky; they need to be built slowly.

Developing into childhood

From the age of five onwards, play becomes much more important. The child's imagination suddenly starts to develop in a wild, fantastic way. Children at this stage often make up

Digging like dad, wearing dad's jumper — children model themselves on parents in their play, for good or ill!

stories about fictional things they have done, invent imaginary playmates, devour fairy tales and story books of all sorts. The boundaries of fantasy and reality often seem quite blurred in the child's mind, but the imaginative expansion which is going on is just another way of trying out our newly-found identity against the real world. Play has been described as 'moving from the known to the untried and unknown'. The little girl who pretends to be running a sweet shop is trying out social skills she may need in future. The boy who pretends to be doing woodwork like his daddy is imaginatively putting himself into an adult situation and 'trying it on for size'.

Relationships with other children become more complex. Likes and dislikes begin to emerge; children begin to feel some responsibility for those younger than themselves, and often enjoy looking after little brothers and

sisters. Most importantly, the increased knowledge of other people and their reactions is making the child aware of 'what will happen to me if. . .' *If* I make a mess of my bedroom, Mummy will shout at me. *If* I eat up all my dinner without making a fuss, she will be pleased. Instead of just acting on impulse and then waiting to be praised or smacked, the child starts to realize that it can prevent the smackings by choosing to behave in a certain kind of way!

In other words, the child has now begun to appreciate what the value systems of others are, and how to apply them to its own conduct. Instead of others being in control she or he realizes the possibility of controlling his or her own conduct. This child has begun to have a conscience.

The age of learning

Beginning school is a milestone in a child's life. Suddenly a new source of authority comes into being—the teacher. And now, with a whole class of other children to relate to, the child's social circle all at once becomes much broader. Life changes dramatically.

School helps to satisfy two major needs which emerge in a child's development between the ages of six and twelve.

■ One is to learn practical skills: children soon become bored with purposeless play, and start wanting to do something useful and productive. The ability to complete an activity with a purpose—adding up a sum, weighing flour for cakes, or making Christmas decorations for the classroom—gives a sense of participating in the real world.

■ The other is to adapt to other people socially. Children need to leave the cosy, restricted circle of their own family and closest playmates, and start to meet a variety of new people in a wider group. School provides the place where all the social experiments—gangs, best friends, rivalries and jealousies—can be worked out. Children at this stage are often extremely cruel to those who are different: those who look unusual, talk with a different accent, are too slow at lessons (or too good at lessons). It is all

part of the social experimentation which is going on.

And children can be marked for the rest of their lives by the impact of injuries received at this stage. Philosopher Søren Kierkegaard had a lonely, gloomy childhood with little love and friendship. Later in life, he was distrustful of relationships and constantly hurt by the attacks of others; he backed away from marriage to a girl whom he sincerely loved, afraid that intimacy would destroy them both. And on his deathbed he refused communion from a minister who was his oldest friend.

J.M. Barrie, author of *Peter Pan*, grew up desperately trying to please his mother, knowing that he was just a poor substitute for the son she had really loved—his brother David, killed in an accident when Barrie was six. And so Barrie's adult personality was marked by fantastic gestures of generosity in the quest to win friends, by pathological possessiveness and crippling jealousy. In his books he idealized childhood in an unreal, sentimental way, and he was incapable of adult sexual relations.

But these are exceptional cases. Most children get through the later years of their childhood pretty much unscathed. John J. Mitchell has written:

For many children the year which produces the least difficulty, whether it be psychological or social, internal or external, is the tenth year. On the whole, Ten is rather well-adjusted to himself, his family, and his limited community. . . His personal and social harmony are much more conspicuous trademarks in his daily life than are their opposites.

And then everything changes.

On into teenage

By the age of eleven or so, we have more or less settled down in our world. We have a fairly clear idea of who we are, how we are supposed to behave, and how we fit in with other people. Then begins an epic upheaval.

Most noticeable are the physical changes. Girls begin to menstruate, boys to have broken voices. In both sexes there are rapid alterations in size and shape. A boy's muscles double in size between his twelfth birthday and his sixteenth birthday.

There is some evidence that as the years go by these physical changes are taking place earlier and earlier in life. Between 1830 and 1960 the average age of puberty crept forward by four months every decade. But there can be wide differences between individuals, and this causes even more bewilderment and insecurity. It is no fun to be the last boy in the class to develop adult sexual organs, or to be a prematurely full-breasted girl.

There are other changes in teenagers, too. The sex drive becomes a much more prominent part of life. Freud showed that our sexual drive is already there from birth, but it is not until our genitals begin to develop fully that sexual impulses become a strongly-felt part of our experience. It has been claimed that the average nineteen-year-old thinks about sex once every twenty-five seconds, though it is hard to see how this could be tested! But certainly sex occupies much more of his thoughts than it did when he was eleven!

Adolescent friendships often go through four phases of development:

- At first young people will make friends with other members of the same sex only, and hang around in single-sex groups.
- Then one special friend of the same sex will emerge as more important than the rest of the group, and an especially close relationship will form.
- In the next phase boys and girls start to mix socially in groups of friends.
- Eventually one boy and one girl will single each other out for a close relationship. It is as if the single-sex friendship of the second phase is a 'trial run' for the life partnership which will take place later on.

This pattern is often obscured in our society by the attention which is focused on love and romance, the prestige attached to having a romantic relationship, and the pressure on boys and girls in some groups to 'pair off' earlier and earlier. But the basic pattern of the four phases remains the same.

The changes taking place in a teenager's life leave a deep uncertainty about questions such as 'Who am I really?' and 'What am I supposed to do with my life?' In our mid-teens we develop our intellectual skills: now we are able

IS THERE REALLY A 'GENERATION GAP'?

Mark Twain once commented that when he was seventeen he was amazed at how little his father knew. When he was twenty-one, he realized how much the old man had learnt in four years.

Young people and older people have always been prone to write one another off. 'The young people of today think of nothing except themselves,' wrote Peter the Hermit. 'They have no reverence for parents or old age. They are impatient of all restraint. They talk as if they know everything, and what passes for wisdom with us is foolishness to them.' It may have an oddly contemporary ring, but this statement was made in 1274.

Even further back, three hundred years before Christ, Aristotle wrote, 'When I look at the younger generation, I despair of the future of civilization.'

The natural misunderstandings which can exist between the generations have never been so much talked about as in the years since the Second World War, when the phrase 'generation gap' became popular to describe the gulf between adolescents and parents. The reason for this is really commercial. In the lean years of austerity which followed 1945, not many adults had a great deal of cash to spare; but manufacturers and advertisers soon realized that unmarried young people were a ready and lucrative market, if only they could be made to feel important. And so 'teen culture' came about. Whereas in 1948 a BBC radio discussion programme found that most young men aimed to dress like their fathers, five years later there were distinctive teen fashions, teen music, teenage meeting places and leisure activities. Youngsters started to pride themselves on having created a private world into which adults were not invited, a Teenage Heaven which reflected *their* individuality and *their* sense of self-worth. Most importantly, there was rock'n'roll, a new music which upset adults and offered a way of expressing adolescent feelings vividly:

*Take out the papers and
   the trash
Or you don't get no
   spending cash.
If you don't scrub that
   kitchen floor
You ain't gonna rock'n'roll
   no more.
Yakety yak. Don't talk back.*

Since those early days there have been many changes in 'youth culture', following a pattern which George Melly has described as 'revolt into style'. A new movement comes along (punk, Merseybeat, heavy metal) which sparks off a fresh revolt against the status quo; this trend is captured by the business entrepreneurs, marketed commercially and turned into a slick product; then it continues to exist merely as a meaningless style, but a fresh revolt is called for. And so on.

It might have been expected that 'youth culture' would widen the gap between adults and teenagers more than ever before, but that does not seem to be happening. Some of the latest studies by sociologists show that today's generation of teenagers feel closer to their parents than their parents did to their mothers and fathers. Parents still constitute one of the most important sources of advice and strength in the life of most teenagers, and it has been shown that while teenagers are enormously influenced by their peer group on minor issues—fashion, spending patterns, and so on—for the big decisions in life they are liable to follow their parents' lead.

There is a 'generation gap'. But it is not as wide as commercial propaganda would like to make us think.

to think systematically about ideas, hypothesize, conjecture. We become aware of all sorts of possibilities we never considered before.

And so teenagers can spend a lot of time thinking and even worrying about themselves. They are especially sensitive to criticism from their own peer group, and in an attempt to find their own identity are often prone to identify themselves closely with various 'images', or people they admire. Some wear outlandish clothes in imitation of rock heroes; some try to be like a deeply-admired teacher or youth leader; some fervently espouse causes ranging from Animal Liberation to the legalization of cannabis. In each case, a certain style is being 'tried on', so that the teenager can examine how well it fits and decide how much of it reflects what he or she is really about.

It is all complicated by the fact that our emotional awareness reaches its lifetime peak during adolescence. We feel things more keenly than we ever will again. The heights of exultation, the depths of misery—no one experiences them more dramatically (or savours them more curiously!) than a teenager. This is why a book about teenage emotions, such as *The Growing Pains of Adrian Mole*, can be so comic:

*3 a.m I have used a whole Andrex toilet roll to mop up my tears. I haven't cried so much since the wind blew my candy floss away at Cleethorpes.
5 a.m. I slept fitfully, then got out of bed to watch the dawn break. The world is no longer exciting and colourful. It is grey and full of heartbreak. I thought of doing myself in, but it's not really fair on the people you leave behind.*

It is not surprising that the majority of us make our basic decisions about what we will believe for the rest of our lives during the time we are teenagers. Religious conversion, adherence to Marxism, despair of ever making sense of it all—whatever we end up believing, the mid-teenage years are likely to fix it in place for us.

Young adulthood

One of the problems of being a teenager in our society is that there is no indicator to mark exactly when someone becomes an adult. Many primitive societies have 'rites of passage' which take individuals from childhood to adulthood in one clearly-definable step, but 'developed' societies allow teenagers admission to different aspects of adult society at different ages. When are you *really* grown up? When they let you get married? Or vote? Or drive a car? Or drink and smoke legally? Or join the army and kill people? Young people exist in an uncertain borderline area on the fringes of adult life.

Round about twenty, however, we are indisputably through the border at last and on to the next stage: young adulthood. Robert Wrenn and Reed Mencke have described it:

This may be a lonely stage. Young adults are usually 'between families' during part of this time. They are often on their own for the first time or living with someone who may or may not be particularly supportive. A number of events take place in this stage and major decisions are made for which little or no training has been given—for example, buying a house, deciding on marriage, or having a child.

Developmental psychologist Robert Havighurst comments that at this time we are moving from an 'age-graded' society to a 'status-graded' one. In other words, where throughout school and college our place in society tended to be fixed by the year group we belonged to, now in the wider world we find that our job throws us into contact with people widely different from us in age. And that gives us the problem of working out where we slot in and what behaviour is appropriate to which relationship (you don't talk to the boss's wife as you would to the cleaning lady).

Indeed, the main problem for a young adult is to work out the patterns of relationships and responsibilities on which the rest of life will be founded. Work relationships, social ties, marriage and parental responsibilities—now there is a much more complex web of duties and obligations than at any stage of life so far.

Many people find, in the course of sorting all this out, that their tastes, likes and dislikes become more firmly fixed than ever before. Suddenly they become aware that the music they really like best is not the latest hit records, but much more their old favourites from their mid-teens. They find less and less time for keeping up with each twist and turn of fashion.

The ground is being prepared for the day when their teenage offspring will start complaining, 'Oh, Mum, you're so dated. . .'

Other interests may start to loom larger than before. Many young adults discover an increasing interest in politics and a greater awareness of world issues. Suddenly the world no longer belongs to the previous generation: we wake up to the fact that responsibility for it belongs to us as well.

One man studied by a group of American psychologists reflected, 'At twenty to thirty I think I learned to get along with my wife. From thirty to forty I learned how to be a success at the job. And at forty to fifty I worried less about myself and more about the children.' He had followed a typical pattern.

Often young adults go through a time of re-evaluation around the age of thirty. Suddenly, it seems, we realize that three decades of life are now behind us, and the word 'young' doesn't fit us quite as well as it used to. And so we ask ourselves some questions. What have I achieved so far? Where am I going from here?

And we try to sort out the contribution we want our life to make in the public world of jobs and achievements.

It is interesting to trace how many great people took a vital step in their careers not long after their thirtieth birthday. Marx wrote the *Communist Manifesto* at thirty. De Gaulle founded the Free French movement. Werner von Braun built the first true missile in history. Augustine of Hippo embarked on a spiritual journey which was not to end for another three years; Martin Luther did the same thing, but did not resolve his thinking until he was thirty-six. At thirty-two William Blake wrote his first great collection, *Songs of Innocence*, Fidel Castro attained power in Cuba, Herman Melville wrote *Moby Dick*.

'The various decisions that were made in one's twenties do take their toll.' remarks Robert Wrenn. 'During the thirties divorces are high, careers are derailed, and accidents and suicides occur with great frequency.' Many couples who married in their twenties experience a 'seven-year itch', when they feel a sudden impulse to break free. But the most significant crisis—especially for men—usually comes ten years later.

Middle age

Somewhere between forty and forty-five, many people—especially men—begin to question the effectiveness and purpose of their lives. Many realize that they are at the pivotal point of their careers; they have not many years left; from here on it will be up, or down, all the way. H.C. Lehman's work on creativity reveals that we are at our most creative between thirty and thirty-four, then fall to only 47 per cent of maximum rate by our late forties, and reach nearly zero after seventy. Men in the mid-life

A face pack — one weapon in the war against wrinkles. As the years pass by some people become disturbingly conscious of good things being lost. But are other good things being gained?

crisis often sense the downward curve of their powers of creativity, and start to worry.

Energy diminishes, too. After years of vigorously establishing ourselves in society and working to bring up a family, it is easy to suddenly feel overwhelmingly tired. Some people have not achieved much by their forties, and so have to push themselves harder. Others have made their mark, but find that now they have to work more strenuously to maintain their position.

The dissatisfaction with oneself, and the determination to make a mark in the world, can lead to some remarkable achievements. It was in the forties that Marie Curie isolated pure radium. Marcel Proust wrote *A la Recherche du Temps Perdu*, Scott reached the South Pole and Nelson won Trafalgar. All George Eliot's great novels were written between forty and fifty-three, while Sir Walter Scott had not written any prose fiction before he was forty-three. Einstein finally produced his general theory of relativity at the end of his forties.

For both sexes, during this period, there are unmistakable signals of the passage of time. Children grow up and leave home—and the unaccustomed silence brings many couples to a sudden bleak feeling of emptiness in their married life. Parents become old and infirm, and often depend on their children for attention and help. And every glance at the mirror reveals more evidence of advancing years.

'Middle-age spread' develops as body fat increases to form 20 per cent of total body weight (during adolescence it was only 10 per cent).

To some people, these things are the cause of grave discontent. It is not uncommon for men who have been married, seemingly happily, for years, suddenly to leave their wives for someone much younger, in a subconscious

effort to deny the reality of advancing age. Or for a woman to try with increasing desperation to prolong her youth artificially by her choice of clothes and hairstyle. The reason for such uncharacteristic behaviour lies in the mid-forties feeling that something vital has been missed out of life and could easily slip away for ever.

Psychologist Carl Gustav Jung said, 'We overlook the essential fact that the achievements which society rewards are won at the cost of a diminution of personality. Many aspects of life which should have been experienced lie in the lumber room of dusty memories.' Quoting these sentences, Rabbi Harold Kushner commented:

I looked at that sentence when I had read it and had the feeling of confronting a truth I had always known and had worked hard at not admitting to myself. Only now, in my late forties, was I prepared

HOW LONG DO PEOPLE LIVE?

Today in the Western world human beings can expect to live—barring accidents—for about seventy years. But it hasn't always been that way; nor is it like that in many other parts of the world.

Our ancestors seem to have lived much shorter lives than we do. The life expectancy of people in the Bronze Age is estimated to have been around eighteen years. By medieval times it had risen to only thirty-seven, and even in the year 1900 life lasted on average for about fifty years.

It has to be remembered, however, that these figures are influenced by a very high rate of infant mortality. Professor Carlo Cipolla

describes an agricultural society of the past:

Of 1,000 newborn children, 200 to 500 usually died within a year. Many of the remaining ones died before reaching the age of seven. A famous sixteenth-century physician, Jerome Cardano of Pavia, used to maintain that he could cure anyone on condition that the patient was not younger than seven or older than seventy.

The high life expectancy we now enjoy is not shared by poorer countries. In 'middle-income' countries such as Kenya, Morocco and Peru, health spending is only an average $15 per person per year—compared to $235

to face it. Like so many people, I had become very good at certain aspects of my work, but at the cost of distorting my personality. My family, my own sense of wholeness had paid the price, but society at large was so appreciative of the imbalance that I managed not to notice what I was doing.

Psychologist Erik Erikson says that the challenge of the middle years is to choose between 'generativity' and 'stagnation', between continuing to make an impact and nervously filling in time until death. One of the most creative and fulfilling ways in which middle-aged people can make an impact is by passing on some of their experience and skills to other, younger, people. Daniel Levinson highlights the potential:

Being a mentor with young adults is one of the most significant relationships available to a man in middle adulthood. The distinctive satisfaction of the mentor lies in furthering the development of young men and women, facilitating their efforts to form and live out their dreams. . . More than altruism is involved: the mentor is doing something for himself. He is making productive use of his own knowledge

Developed world: more old people ❯❯

Developing world: more young people ❯❯

in industrialized countries. Not surprisingly, life expectancy is only sixty years. And in low-income countries, with an average health spending of only $1 per year, average life expectancy is forty-eight.

The fact that people now live longer in Western society has produced several new social problems. For one thing, it means that our population is increasingly dominated by older people, and this increases the

burden upon medical services. Also, marriage now lasts much longer. In Shakespeare's day a couple who married could expect thirty or so years together; today a lifelong marriage could last for twice that time. This is probably one reason why divorce has become much more common.

and skill in middle age. He is learning in ways not otherwise possible.

Middle age can be rewarding and satisfying. It all depends on our attitude. Do we become excessively preoccupied with ourselves, the extent of our own achievements, the time still remaining to us, our health, popularity and capacity for enjoyment? Or do we set out to make a difference to others instead?

The final stages

In the United States, 50 per cent of all suicides are committed by people over forty-five—and 25 per cent by those over sixty-five. Our society has placed a high premium on the attractiveness of youth and the importance of looking young. When people just cannot manage to appear youthful any more, many decide they have nothing left to live for.

This is sad. Certainly old people have reached a stage in life where there are many problems. Friends and acquaintances begin to die, and the social circle shrinks. Loss of energy and reduced mobility make it hard to find new friends. Physically, illnesses become a more persistent problem, and mentally, slower reactions and failing memory can cause great frustration. It is easy to lose sympathy with a brash young world in which one seems not to fit any longer, and shrink back into constant daydreaming about 'the good old days'. Financially, too, life can be hard, since expenses can rise but retirement from work and a fixed income reduce the money available.

The death of a spouse can be traumatic. Men tend to die a little younger than women. But whichever partner goes first, facing a life bereft of one's 'other half', deciding whether to continue living alone or to move in with someone else, involves a colossal emotional upheaval. No wonder that many elderly people die soon after their partners.

Bernice Neugarten has studied the personality attributes of over 2,000 elderly people. She

IS THE HUMAN RACE COSMICALLY SIGNIFICANT?

Suppose you had a spaceship which could travel from London to New York in three seconds. And suppose you wanted to travel right across the solar system in it. The journey would take three-and-a-half monotonous weeks.

Then suppose you decided to travel to the next closest star to earth after the sun. How long would it take? The answer is staggering: 430 years!

Just how big is the galaxy we live in? Two American astronomers put it like this.

Let the sun be the size of an orange; on that scale the earth is a grain of sand circling in orbit around the sun at a distance of thirty feet. Jupiter, eleven times larger than the earth, is a cherry pit revolving at a distance of 200 feet or one city block from the sun. The galaxy on this scale is 100 billion oranges, each orange separated from its neighbours by an average distance of 1,000 miles.

And if this were not humbling enough, our galaxy is only one of innumerable galaxies which exist in the immensity of the universe. The most distant one that we know about

(but there could be others) is no less than 5,000 million light years away from us. And the diameter of the entire universe—as far as we can calculate it—could be 26,000 million light years.

This means that for our spaceship to cross the entire universe would take a full 2,600,000 *million* years. And, remember, it is travelling constantly at 3,600 times the speed of Concorde!

In the vastness of the universe, human beings are very small indeed. We are just the inhabitants of a tiny planet circling around a medium-sized star in a fairly ordinary galaxy. (Some of the larger stars are 1,220 times the size of the sun in diameter.) Does it really make sense to believe that human life has any significance?

Again, if scientists are correct in their guesses about the age of the earth, human beings have been here for a very short time indeed in the history of this planet. Nobel Prize-winning biologist Francis Crick claims that if the age of the earth were only a week. . .

. . .on such a scale the age of the universe, since the Big Bang, would be about two

or three weeks. The oldest macroscopic fossils (those from the start of the Cambrian) would have been alive just one day ago. Modern man would have appeared in the last ten seconds and agriculture in the last one or two. Odysseus would have lived only half a second before the present time.

And the future of the earth? Unless we succeed in blowing it up, say the scientists, it could last for another 10,000 million years. We live on quite a young planet.

When we are confronted with facts like these, can we still maintain that humanity is significant? And is it still possible to believe in a God who has a special concern for human beings? Many scientists who are Christians maintain that all they have discovered has only strengthened their faith. Says Dr Donald Carr, a specialist in geological-age determination:

Speaking of my own particular branch of science, the study of geochemistry teaches one to look at things on a vast scale; to think of time in units of billions of years of earth history, of space in terms

claims to have found four major personality types:

- The integrated, who manage to continue in sturdy psychological health;
- The defended, who face life with determination, shopping obsessively for just the right foods, and being ultra-careful of their health;
- The passive dependent, who make themselves depend on the care and attention of other people;
- And the disintegrated, a final small group, unable to cope alone, who are disorganized and psychologically unwell.

Neugarten points out that 75 per cent of those studied claimed to be satisfied with their lives since retirement. And this points to the fact that there can be tremendous compensations in old age, alongside the difficulties. The physical slowing-down can provide the first chance in years to reflect on the varied experiences of life, and grow in wisdom. If the short-term memory does not function so well as formerly, the long-term memory is often improved. And sexuality does not come to an end. Physical relationships may be less frequent and more gentle, but the expression of love and

that encompass the universe, of processes that involve world-wide cycles. The vastness of it all leads one inevitably to a new appreciation of the majesty of God.

It is sometimes thought that people in earlier ages managed to believe in God only because they saw the universe as a very small, cosy affair with the earth at the centre of everything. But C.S. Lewis pointed out that this was not the case at all.

People usually think the problem is how to reconcile what we now know about the size of the universe with our traditional ideas of religion. That turns out not to be the problem at all. The real problem is this. The enormous size of the universe and the insignificance of the earth were known for centuries, and no one ever dreamed that they had any bearing on the religious question. Then, less than a hundred years ago, they are suddenly trotted out as an argument against Christianity. And the people who trot them out carefully hush up the fact that they were known long ago. Don't you think that all you atheists are strangely unsuspicious people?

companionship between older couples can remain an important part of life.

Death is closer. But oddly enough the terror of it does not necessarily increase. It is the middle aged who are more likely to be scared by the prospect of their own end. Older people, living constantly with the possibility of death, are often more objective about it. Said the philosopher Lao-Tze, 'Who dies and, dying, does not protest his death—he has known a true old age.'

What it was all about

You may, of course, be a visiting astronaut from another planet who has picked this book up out of curiosity. But I suspect that like most readers you are a human being yourself—and so can place yourself somewhere on the journey we have sketched out over the last few pages.

Human life is the richest, most complex phenomenon we know about anywhere. But we are all part of it, and moving through it rapidly—more rapidly than often we would like. What is it really all about? When the end comes, and the notice of our funeral appears in the local paper—what will it have been for? Harold Kushner again:

I am convinced that it is not the fear of death, of our lives ending, that haunts our sleep so much as the fear that our lives will not have mattered, that as far as the world is concerned, we might as well never have lived. What we miss in our lives, no matter how much we have, is that sense of meaning.

I believe Kushner is right. And the rest of this book is designed to help you look at these questions. Who am I? Does it matter?

WHAT MAKES EACH INDIVIDUAL UNIQUE?

When two baby boys were born in an Irish hospital, the nursing staff made a terrible mistake. They mixed them up. And so two mothers were each presented with the wrong child—an error which took ten days to sort out. Eventually blood tests proved conclusively which baby was which. But the case made headline news in the newspapers of several countries, and one of the mothers was most reluctant to give up the baby to which she had already grown attached.

Why was this a 'terrible mistake'? Why were the newspapers so interested? Why was it so important to sort out which baby was which, and why did it matter to the aggrieved mother which baby she had? After all, both mothers ended up with exactly what they had to begin with: a healthy baby boy.

The answer, obviously, is that human beings are not transferable. Any baby wouldn't do. We treat human beings as having a worth and a unique identity of their own; you can't switch them around like packets of sausages, or even like pet gerbils.

This is why we are so shocked by mass brutality, such as the extermination of Jews in the Second World War, or the horrific genocide in Kampuchea in the 1970s. Every person who dies is an individual, with a specific history, a unique personality, his unique personal importance. We resent being treated as statistics or code numbers by government departments because we believe in our own individual

significance. I am not just a specimen of a certain biological phenomenon, *homo sapiens*; I am *me*.

This is all obvious. We think like this from our earliest years. But *why* do we assume human beings are unique and valuable? Is our claim of 'uniqueness' real, or is it just a delusion? And if we are 'unique'—does it matter? Is this special value something which gives meaning to life, or does our uniqueness perish with us when we die?

Our sense of personal identity is one of our strongest natural instincts. We may go through all sorts of changes in our lives—violent swings in our opinions and attitudes, startling new discoveries which transform the way we see life, physical alterations even to the extent of changing our sex—and yet, despite everything which happens to us, we retain a stubborn sense of being the same person. The physical materials of our body are constantly changing, and will alter completely ten times or so in the course of an average life span; but we are convinced that 'the real me' hasn't changed, that there is some sort of continuity between what I was at age five and what I will be at age eighty.

'Although we cannot understand this mystery of identity,' comments Professor M.V.C. Jeffreys, 'we accept it, we expect it and count upon it. Indeed, if the tough cord of continuity is broken, we immediately assume some mental disorder.' Every so often a person suffering from amnesia will wander into a police station and plead for help, explaining shamefacedly that all memory of who he or she is has been lost. Yet such people are not in any doubt that they are somebody, even if they have no memories of past experiences to back up the feeling.

The philosopher David Hume thought at one stage that our sense of 'ourselves' was composed of nothing more than our jumble of past experiences:

When I enter most intimately into what I call myself I always stumble on some particular perception or other, of heat or cold, light or shade, love or hatred, pain or pleasure. I can never catch myself at any time without a perception, and never can observe anything but the perception.

But this is too neat (and Hume later changed his mind). It doesn't help us much with the amnesiac in the police station. And other questions arise. Can thoughts exist without someone to think them? And if we define 'ourselves' simply as a jumble of thoughts and experiences, what differentiates my thoughts from your thoughts? Our thoughts and experiences are certainly intimately associated with our sense of being unique, but they do not constitute the whole story.

How it all begins

Psychologists have explored the tricky question of how our sense of uniqueness and identity develops. When a child is born, it has no clear idea of where 'myself' ends and 'the external world' begins. It takes a while before the limits are established. And not until the age of two will a child begin to lose its preoccupation with itself, and start to become interested in other people. It is at this time that pronouns begin to appear in its vocabulary—'my', 'me', 'you', 'I', usually in that order. And while the child is two it goes through a stage of rebelliousness and wilfulness in which it suddenly becomes domineering, endlessly inquisitive, and impatient when its wishes are not gratified straightaway. The child seems to be waking up to the fact that it has an identity of its own which needs to

HOW MUCH DO WE INHERIT FROM OUR PARENTS?

Are you overweight? If you are, and you marry another overweight person, your poor children stand three chances in four of being fairly portly themselves. On the other hand, if neither Mother nor Dad are too heavy, there is less than one chance in ten that the children will be.

We all inherit all sorts of characteristics from our parents. How does it happen?

The answer is: through our genes. These are the small units inside a cell which determine what a new human being is going to be like. It is difficult to tell how many we have; one estimate is that each parent contributes 10,000 or so. At fertilization each of the genes 'pairs up' with another from the other parent, and it is these pairings which decide the size, weight, colouring, and much else, of the future person. Some genes are 'dominant' and some 'recessive'. In other words, some have more power to express themselves than others. For example, if a blue-eye gene from the father

pairs up with a brown-eye gene from the mother, brown is dominant to blue, and so the baby will have brown eyes. Its only chance of blue eyes should be if two blue-eye genes come together.

I have just written 'should be', because in reality things are a little more complicated! Many of our features are caused not by one gene, but by several. And so, in just one case in fifty, two blue-eyed parents will in fact produce brown-eyed children— because as many as three pairs of genes can be involved. The same complex situation is true of qualities such as height, colour and physical build. For a complicated organ such as the eye, there may be hundreds of genes all playing a part.

The number of genes, and the interplay between them, means that we are all truly individuals. No one quite the same as you has ever been born before—and if

someone exactly like you should emerge in the future, it will be a fantastic fluke. You are not a carbon copy of either of your parents, but an incredible, haphazard mixture of genetic material from both of them.

Another factor that has to be remembered is 'regression towards the mean'. When two sets of super-intelligent parents each have super-intelligent children, and these children marry one another, it does not follow that their children will be even more intelligent yet, and so on for ever. In fact, in a family where the level of intelligence has steadily been increasing for a few generations, there will sooner or later be a down-swing again—in the direction of the average intelligence level of the population. The same thing happens with height. Two tall parents will have tall children, but probably their children will be not quite as tall as Mother and Father. Similarly, short parents will have diminutive children who are nonetheless just a bit taller than themselves. . .

Inheritance is an intricate business. And it doesn't *determine* us, by locking us in to one inescapable future: we are still responsible for the kind of people we become. As the geneticist Theodosius Dobhzhansky put it, 'The genes do not determine "characters". . . the genes determine the reactions of the organism to its environment.' We cannot blame our behaviour on our genes.

Parents struggling to cope in poor conditions can become tense and violent. Their children sometimes pick up similar ways of reacting and repeat the process in the next generation. Can anything break the cycle?

fit in alongside the identities of other people, and is simply testing out the limits of its powers and freedoms.

When this subsides, the child goes into a phase in which it gradually picks up the attitudes and responses of its parents, and starts to copy them. Imitating adults is one way of finding out about oneself. But gradually the imitation becomes less necessary. The child scraps the imitation but keeps the character which results, and this now becomes a part of his own personality. No longer does he say, 'I'm a brave boy *like Daddy'*, but, having incorporated his father's standards of behaviour, says, 'I'm a brave boy.' He has now established within himself a guiding principle of life by which he can control and direct all his native impulses, and so harmonize his personality. The centre of gravity of his behaviour has shifted from the other person to within himself.

This transition brings a lot of changes to the child's personality. A little girl who at two years old would chatter away quite happily to strangers who had come to tea, becomes shy and tongue-tied at age four, and hangs her head when addressed by someone she does not know. She has become 'self-conscious'—aware of herself as a person. There is now a part of her mind which is observing the other part of her mind, watching critically how she behaves and responds, and throwing her into embarrassment and confusion.

It is at this stage, too, that we become conscious of a gap between the way we behave and the way we would like to behave! We start to realize that sometimes our instinctive impulses are not good ones. We may feel like attacking the child who has just wandered off with one of our favourite toys—and at two years old we would have bashed him quite cheerfully without thinking twice about it. But by now we have made the discovery that hitting other children has social consequences—we do not want our own bottom smacked—and we have taken on board enough of our parents' attitudes to feel, 'This is something I shouldn't do.' Thus we start experiencing the tug-of-war between 'what I want to do' and 'what I ought to do' which will continue for the rest of our lives.

And so at around the age of three or four we start to take responsibility for our own moral choices, to look at ourselves and criticize our own conduct, to gain a view of ourselves as individual, unique beings. This is what happens. But *why* does it happen? There is no logical necessity for it, says Gordon Rattray Taylor:

It is so surprising. If the mind is machinery, merely, one would not expect it. Robots are not seen as having an identity. Machinery does sometimes acquire a certain identity with the passage of time, as seen by its users (one thinks particularly of cars and boats). But it does not demand identity as a condition of its own effective functioning.

Does our identity have a purpose? Or is it just an illusory psychological by-product?

The mystery of identity

Over the last century, several things have happened to make this a vitally important question for human beings to answer. For example, there has been a massive growth in personal freedom to choose—at least in the Western world. Centuries ago the inhabitants of a village in Central Europe would have had the main contours of their lives already determined before they were born: their occupation, their diet, their clothes, their religious understanding, their spare-time occupations. They would not have been able to travel very far, and so their choices of marriage partner would have been very limited. Their understanding of other cultures and other possible ways of life would have been minimal. They would have lived a life very like that of their parents, their grandparents, and their great-grandparents. And they would have had very little say in the matter.

But nowadays our culture presents us with a bewildering variety of choices to make—ranging from our career ambitions to our favourite brand of toothpaste. We can change our religious views and political affiliations as often as we like. We can move house frequently or

WHERE DO OUR IDEAS OF RIGHT AND WRONG COME FROM?

It is a curious fact that widely different human societies have all tended to come up with the same basic code of morality. C.S. Lewis once wrote about 'the triumphant monotony of the same indispensable platitudes which meet us in culture after culture'. Why is this?

Obviously, some of our moral ideas come from **sheer common sense.** It is not difficult for human beings, wherever they live, to see that they cannot have a stable society unless they can trust one another, and respect property that belongs to others. So lying and stealing are obviously bad things to encourage.

But morality is not just a matter of logic. There is a kind of inbuilt **moral intuition** in all of us too, which makes us take certain

directions. We fume when we hear of injustices. We automatically feel pity for the underdog. And this instinct-ive reaction exists quite apart from our rational calcula-tions, or our religious beliefs.

Where did it all begin? One famous suggestion is that morality developed from an act of prehistoric parricide. One of our pre-human ancestors killed his father and felt guilty about it, and so started to evolve an idea that there were things one should do and things one shouldn't. But as C.S. Lewis pointed out, 'If the parricide produced a sense of guilt, that was because men felt they ought not to have committed it.' And if they felt they 'ought not', clearly they already *had* some sort of moral framework.

More recently Konrad

Lorenz has suggested that our adherence to moral codes is 'caused by creature habit and by animal fear at their infraction'. In other words, we developed morals as inhibitory mechanisms which helped the species to survive, and now we cannot shake them off. E.O. Wilson says much the same, except that he sees morality as something which derives from our genetic conditioning: 'Beliefs are really enabling mechan-isms for survival. . . thus does ideology bow to its hidden masters the genes.'

Ideas like this have an inbuilt contradiction. On the one hand, they are saying, 'We're stuck; we're con-ditioned. This is how we have to be.' And then on the other hand they are adding, 'So let's realize it and become different.' (Wilson, for

stay in the same town for the whole of our lives. And all of this, say the sociologists, makes the question 'Who am I?' much more important than ever before.

It is possible for an individual to picture himself or herself as having different biographies, each carrying its own separate identity. And the more one can choose one's 'biography' for oneself, the more anxious one is likely to become. 'Am I doing this right? Have I taken the best decisions? Did I take a wrong turning two years ago? Have I got the right job, and the right marriage partner, to fulfil the needs of my personality? What is my personality anyway? What is unique about being me? Who am I?'

But there is another side to this question of individual identity. We have become much more conscious of our own insignificance this century, as we have realized how many people actually live on this planet, and how many different civilizations there have been. We have also come to appreciate how humblingly small we are in such an immense universe. Does the

example, says, 'The time has come for ethics to be removed temporarily from the hands of the philosopher and biologicized.') But if morality is not a rational, purposive phenomenon at all—if it is simply a survival mechanism—what point is there in continuing to speak of a 'reasonable' or 'fair' morality?

Religion has always been closely connected with morality, so can Christianity suggest anything better than the 'survival' mechanism theory? Christians say that God is the origin of human moral ideas, and that humans have a natural moral sense because they bear the image of their Creator. Paul wrote that even those who have never read the Bible can still show evidence that the law of God is 'written on their hearts'.

And so all human beings have an instinctive moral sense which, in culture after culture, tends in the same direction. Christians do not follow their particular faith because they feel that they

have a moral code which is completely different and superior to everyone else's. Their motive is rather that they see in Jesus Christ a possibility of gaining the power to live up to the moral

aspirations which human beings have always had, but could never realize on their own.

Amin, Hitler, Himmler... Millions have suffered and died because of the peculiarly evil men thrown up by this century, and every previous one. Are we all capable of similar evil, given the same circumstances? Or can we choose to go another way?

Which one is Marilyn Monroe? Two people may share identical physical appearance, but never the same identity. We are all uniquely ourselves.

individual really matter?

To make this question even tougher, some of the most important developments in the realm of thought have chipped away at our sense of uniqueness and importance. Charles Darwin caused a revolution in biology by demonstrating links between human life and the rest of creation. How many of the decisions I take are really an expression of my own free, unique mind, and how many are really just a pre-programmed survival of animal behaviour?

Karl Marx, whose theories now influence the political destiny of almost half the world, based his view of human life on the claim that our behaviour is dictated by our economic circumstances. In Marx's teaching, humans are not free agents, as they like to think, but are the puppets of the forces at work on them in society. If this is true, what does it mean for human dignity? Is there any point in treating individual human beings as if they matter? It was within a year of the Russian Revolution that Lenin began the Gulag Archipelago—the cynical, dehumanizing system of slave labour in

Russia which Alexander Solzhenitsyn claims has killed millions more than Hitler ever destroyed.

And when psychology became a respected discipline at the start of the twentieth century, human self-confidence had to take another knock. Sigmund Freud showed that a lot of human behaviour was related, not to free choices by unique individual minds, but to murky drives and compulsions buried deep in the subconscious. Behaviourist psychologists such as J.B. Watson went even further and denied that human ideas, intentions and perceptions had any real value. Human beings were just predictable machines. Change their environment, and the machines would function differently. Choice and purpose had nothing to do with it; as one behaviourist put it, there was no difference between a man training for a race and a man racing for a train.

And yet, despite all this evidence against individuality, we still cling to our own uniqueness. What *is* personal identity? To answer this question, we need to look at several other questions first.

The body and the self

The first (and most mysterious) question is: what exactly is the relationship between 'myself' and my body? Because obviously there is a very close link indeed.

If I have an accident in which my brain is damaged, my whole personality may alter. A well-known case of this kind of personality change is the Russian sub-lieutenant Zasetsky, who was hit in the head by a German bullet at the Battle of Smolensk, and suffered irreversible damage to part of his brain. He described his condition like this:

Again and again I tell people I've become a totally different person since my injury, that I was killed on 2 March 1943, but because of some vital power of my organism, I miraculously remained alive. . . I always feel as if I'm living out a hideous, fiendish nightmare— that I'm not a man but a shadow, some creature that's fit for nothing.

Antidepressant drugs and electroconvulsive therapy can have an equally radical effect. And

brain surgery such as lobotomy (an operation to sever the frontal lobes from the rest of the brain, popular in the 1940s and 50s but now less commonly practised) has led to dramatic changes of personality. This means that the brain surgeon has awesome responsibilities— and terrifying moral problems to solve. It has often been asked whether such operations are equivalent to terminating the life of one individual and introducing another, quite alien personality.

In the light of this, another question arises. Our sense of identity seems to be perilously dependent on the healthy working of the brain. Does that mean that identity is just a chance by-product of the brain, with no independent existence of its own? That my sense of being 'me' is just a psychological trick which my own brain has foisted on me? That really I *am* just a machine?

Obviously, if this were true, there would be no such thing as immortality. If my brain is totally responsible for generating my sense of identity, then I will stop when my brain stops—at death. Any ideas about heaven, the spirit world or reincarnation are all equally impossible scientifically.

But in fact there is no need to be so gloomy about our potential. There is plenty of evidence to suggest that our personalities are not simply a casual spin-off from the workings of the human machine. One of the most bizarre pieces of evidence is the odd phenomenon known as 'multiple personality'.

Very occasionally a human being suddenly loses all recollection of the past and takes on a completely different personality. The new personality will often do things which are out of character with the former 'self'. One celebrated case this century was a lady named Chris Sizemore, who alternated between being a demure, teetotal, churchgoing housewife, and a malevolent, whisky-drinking party-goer prone to rush into completely unsuitable liaisons with strange men. The physical characteristics of the two personalities (which would switch themselves on and off with bewildering unpredictability) were different too. The 'bad girl' was allergic to nylon, which brought her legs out in blotches; the 'good girl' had no such problems, and the blotches faded when she took over. If a doctor anaesthetized one of the personalities, and 'she' started to fall asleep, the other personality might take over—and show no signs of being affected by the anaesthetic.

Flora Rheta Schreiber has reported that in one case of multiple personality, each of four 'selves' demonstrated different brainwave patterns and responded differently to word-association tests. Colin Wilson comments:

If the personalities are really just chips off one original block, then they ought to have the same brainwave patterns and the same word-association responses. In fact, such cases look far more like the medieval concept of possession. It is just as if the same body is literally taken over by a series of different people, each with their own personality.

And this, he says, suggests that whatever the 'self' turns out to be, it cannot simply be explained away as the by-product of the brain. 'We shall have to replace the old mechanical models,' he argues, 'with a model in which the brain and body are the puppet, and the "ego" is the puppet master.'

Wilson mentions 'possession' as a 'medieval concept', but in fact there are still plenty of cases today where one personality seems to be invaded by another—something which is extremely difficult to explain in terms of 'mechanical models'.

The studies of the subject are all clear: what is being spoken about is not just changing behaviour. The 'possessed' condition is a radical change for the worse from normal, of which the best available analogy is of an invasion by something previously external, and which has to be made external again to restore normality.

Perhaps, then, we need to ask a different sort of question. How *independent* is our personality of our body? Is it possible for our sense of identity to exist outside of a body? Is the self permanently tied to the workings of the brain—or could it express itself in some other form? Professor Paul Davies sees no reason why this could not be the case:

The essential ingredient of mind is information. *It is the pattern inside the brain, not the brain itself, that makes us what we are. Just as Beethoven's Fifth Symphony does not cease to exist when the orchestra has finished playing, so the mind may*

endure by transfer of the information elsewhere. . . Rather than 'ghosts in machines', we are more like 'messages in circuitry', and the message itself transcends the means of its expression.

If the brain and the self do have this kind of relationship—a bit like the difference between 'hardware' and 'software' in the world of

INTELLIGENCE AND HOW TO MEASURE IT

'The whole theory of learning and intelligence is in confusion,' wrote psychologist Harold Lashley. 'We know at present nothing of the organic basis of these functions.' Lashley was writing some sixty years ago, but still today many researchers would agree with his analysis of the situation. We all like to think we are 'intelligent'. Yet there is no generally agreed definition of what 'intelligence' is. . . or how it is caused.

The problem is that intelligence is actually a mixture of different kinds of skills, including the sorting of new information in the brain, the ability to discern relationships between the new information and what is already stored there, and the power of making good decisions quickly on the basis of all this. Canadian neurologist D.O. Hebb also distinguishes between 'Intelligence A'—the mental capacity we are born with—and 'Intelligence B'—the mental capacity which develops within us as we respond to the stimulus of our surroundings and grow up from babyhood.

computers—there is no reason to suppose that the 'programme' (myself) could not be run on a different machine (for example, a different kind of body after death—what the apostle Paul described as the 'resurrection body') without the loss of anything vital. And just as a defective computer will sometimes make a mess of a programme which is run through it,

we could expect a defective brain (after brain damage, or contamination with drugs) to distort the personality which it expresses. Computer users soon learn to keep a back-up copy of any important programme, just in case of accidents, because the fouling up of one copy doesn't necessarily mean the end of the programme. Similarly, the distortion or even death of human personality through brain damage does not necessarily mean the end of that human being; if there is a Creator who possesses the master copy of the programme, perhaps it can be run again in a different form.

It is hard to measure 'Intelligence A', since by the time a child is old enough to take some form of intelligence test, 'Intelligence B' has had a good length of time to develop! So is it the case that intelligence testing actually measures a combination of Intelligence A and Intelligence B? Perhaps. But some scientists claim that such tests are actually a measure of 'Intelligence C'—our ability to respond appropriately to the kind of behaviour our society expects from us. In other words, problem-solving, logic-based challenges are highly valued in our Western society, and so people with a lot of 'Intelligence C' can cope with them well. But it would be possible for someone to have a lot of natural intelligence (A) and to be developing impressively (B), yet still do very badly in an intelligence test! Whether this is true or not, it shows how complicated the whole subject can become.

It seems likely that Intelligence A accounts for 80 per cent of our total intelligence. What we inherit from our parents is more important than the circumstances of our upbringing and education. Identical twins show little difference in intelligence, even when one is brought up in a cultured family and the other grows

up in a slum. The intelligence of adopted children is closer to their real mother's than to that of their adoptive mother. This is not to say that upbringing doesn't matter; 20 per cent is still quite a chunk of the total, and a supportive, stimulating environment which encourages Intelligence B can be enormously important to a child's development.

Yet it must be remembered that intelligence is not all that matters in life. Tests can measure our logical and mathematical skills; they cannot measure artistic sensitivity, maturity in relationships or practical wisdom. Philip Mason points out, 'We do not automatically make the man with the highest IQ the Prime Minister or the President: we wait to see what other qualities he will develop. We judge him by his total response to the situation in which he finds himself.'

Schoolgirls grapple with a computer. The new information technology requires a mental ability rather different from the traditional academic mind.

Four views of our identity

Philosophers who have wrestled with the problem of human identity have developed four main theories about it. Some are **materialists,** believing that ideas such as 'mind' and 'self' and 'identity' are really illusory. Ultimately the human brain works in a mechanical way, which determines our actions and choices in advance, and so we have no genuine freedom. As we have just seen, this view does not seem to cover all the evidence.

Further, it involves us in insisting that the most memorable experiences of life—love, beauty, creativity, ambition—are totally without meaning. It may just be possible to believe this. But it is certainly not possible to live in such a way. We have to act *as if* our opinions matter, *as if* we are free to choose, *as if* other people are responsible individuals with a say in their own destiny. To be a materialist we have to disregard the most basic data that our minds receive from the world around us.

We do not *seem* to be 'just machines'. Gordon Rattray Taylor has written about the difference between our mental processes and the workings of a computer:

Within our skulls there are complex circuits. . .The equipment analyzes input from the world around and then selects and executes some behavioural response. Nothing odd in that; a computer, in its crude way, can do much the same. But in our case there is a seemingly superfluous miracle: we see a brilliantly coloured scene. . . we have the sensation

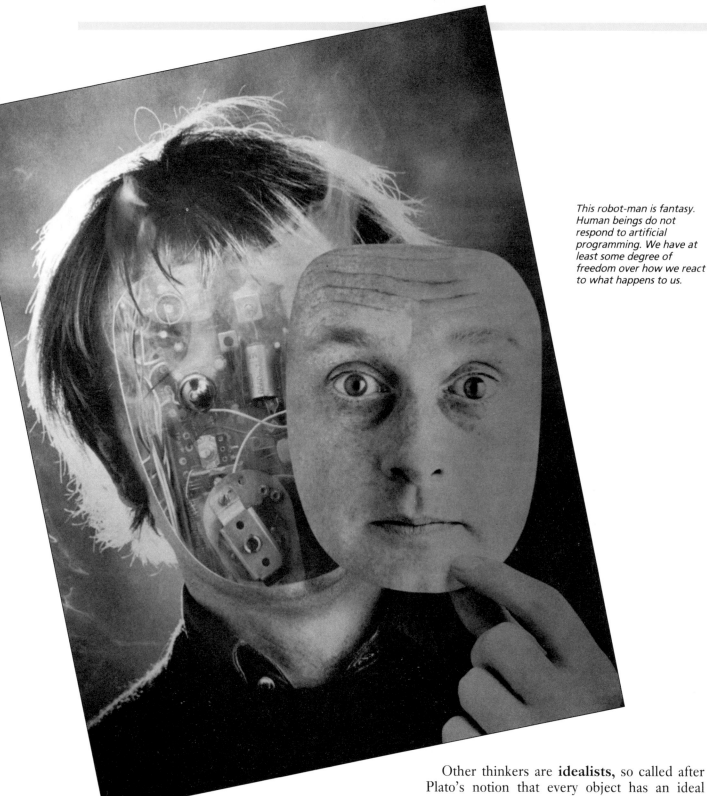

This robot-man is fantasy. Human beings do not respond to artificial programming. We have at least some degree of freedom over how we react to what happens to us.

of falling in love. . . we recall events from the past and even, as some would claim, from the future. The humble electrochemistry has given rise to a vivid personal experience.

If we are just machines, something inside us is trying very hard to deceive us about it.

Other thinkers are **idealists,** so called after Plato's notion that every object has an ideal form. They theorize that since our knowledge of the world comes only from the impressions we receive mentally, our *perceptions* must be real, but we cannot be sure about the physical world! This philosophy is just as hard to live by. It hits the same problem: we have to behave *as if* the physical world is real. And idealism logically leads to doubting the existence of everything—and everybody—outside ourselves. How can we be sure of anything, if what constantly presents itself to us as real actually isn't?

Both materialism and idealism are attempting to get rid of half of the evidence—the physical reality of the brain, or the mental reality of our perceptions—in order to maintain that the *other* half is real. It seems more true to our experience to say, 'Both are real.' This has led to the other two theories: 'dualism' and 'holism'.

Dualism is often thought to be the Christian view, and in fact many Christians have maintained it. But it is not the Bible's teaching and really came into Christian thinking only when some well-meaning church leaders tried to incorporate the best insights of Greek philosophy into Christianity. So ultimately dualism comes from a Greek view of reality.

The philosophers of ancient Greece tended to see 'the soul' as an intangible, spiritual part of humanity which was unhappily imprisoned inside the body. The most important aim of life was to cultivate the soul and allow it to grow in importance, so that one day it could fly from its prison to freedom and fulfilment. Thus human beings were composed of two parts: a physical component and a spiritual one.

Following this idea, Christians have often talked about 'the soul' as an intangible essence which somehow lived undetected inside the body, the 'ghost in the machine'. The philosopher Descartes suggested that the soul and body were joined to one another through the 'pineal gland'. The idea was that soul and body were two distinct substances, which could be sharply differentiated.

This war cemetery at Verdun, France, reminds us that death awaits us all. But is death the end? If not, what comes after?

But this is not the Bible's view at all. In the Bible the 'soul' is not a special bit of human life, which can be separated from the rest. The term stands for the *whole* of a human life, seen from the point of view of its meaning and uniqueness. And when we humans die, it is not merely our 'souls' which drift off, disembodied, to sit on a cloud somewhere playing harps. The Bible talks of a day when all the dimensions of human life—the body as well as the soul—will be brought together again. In the Christian view, every part of a human being has its own importance—not just a ghostly substance called 'soul'.

And so the Christian view is a *holistic* one. Holism means recognizing that the final truth about something cannot be known until it is considered *as a whole*, with every bit of evidence brought into consideration. To say that human beings are 'nothing but machines', or 'nothing but perceptions', is to miss out most of the truth; and even to say that we consist of two 'kinds of stuff' is to divide up what should be held together. Seen from one point of view, human beings are sophisticated computers; seen from another, they are biologically efficient forms of animal life; seen from another, they are unique individuals, with personalities and life histories of their own, and an importance in God's plans. And *all* of these different descriptions are complementary parts of the same truth.

The meaning of people

This brings us to the most important question of all. If people really are individuals, and there is something uniquely personal about them—does it matter? What is the meaning of our individual identity?

Many writers this century have argued that there *is* no ultimate meaning—that identity is

Does the yuppie matter more than the drop-out? Do people's value and importance depend at all on their position in society?

something we must merely accept and respect. Professor Morton Hunt ends his book about the human mind with these words:

Now that we know so much about our minds, we have reason to appreciate and value ourselves after all. And if we truly value ourselves, if we appraise the human difference at its real worth, how can we then, except in self-defence or the defence of others, treat any other person or people as less than precious?

On the face of it, this seems perfectly reasonable. It gives us a reason for taking care of one another and honouring human life, without bothering too much about questions of ultimate

value and meaning. But some worrying questions arise.

First, if the 'human difference' came about simply as some kind of cosmic accident, have we really any reason to be so proud of ourselves? Why should we exalt our own species above others which just didn't have the evolutionary luck to develop quite so advantageously? Is it fair to treat humans as more valuable than dogs and cats just because we had all the breaks?

Second, if what we value in human beings is our stunning mental performance, how does that mean we grade people? As less or more worthy, depending on their ability to perform? If we come across examples of humanity which are no better than lower forms of life—people who are 'human vegetables', for example—are we free to take away respect from them and dispose of them? And if the answer is no—why ever not?

Most crucially, we may agree that the 'human difference' demands that we treat one another as 'precious'. But how far does that mean we should go for one another? Does it make sense to die for someone else? If a situation arises in which the rights of one individual are at stake, do we defend that person's rights even if it means the community has to suffer? Or do we allow that one to be deprived so that the majority can benefit? If you apply this policy consistently, you may well end up by bringing about another Gulag Archipelago!

Obviously we need something more. We need to know that individual human beings have a value and a meaning which does not depend simply upon their ability to perform more feats than the rest of the animal creation. And one of the most agonizing problems for many twentieth-century thinkers has been that they could not see any genuine source of value for human life.

If death ends all, what am I here for? What can justify me in adopting this or that value or scale of values?

Thus a great deal of twentieth-century thinking ends up by going round and round in despairing circles. There has to be a value in the individual human life, to make the business of living sensible. But where can we get it from?

People in the mass can seem to lose their individual identity. But each of these Korean schoolboys has his own sense of being himself, and his own way of understanding what is going on.

Discussions of 'human rights' tend as a result to be imprecise and unsatisfactory, for how can you define the rights of human beings without first defining what human beings are? In an attempt to give a fuller account of the non-mechanical side of human life, some psychologists devised 'humanistic psychology' to replace the older schools of Freudian psychoanalysis and behaviourist materialism. But its great weakness proved to be that none of its exponents could define very clearly what a human being really meant. As a result a fourth school, 'transpersonal psychology', has been formed to seek for the true meaning of humanity in some kind of spiritual or mystical experience.

The 'human difference', then, consists in something much more far-reaching than an advantageous evolutionary development. And this is where Christian teaching has an important dimension to add. Christians insist that human identity and human uniqueness make sense only if we see people as the deliberate creations of a God who loves them and has a purpose for their lives. Without this dimension of reality, the others are incomplete.

Without a God, the miracle of human consciousness, the inbuilt sense of identity which we all possess, has no explanation and no value. But if God exists, our uniqueness ceases to be an unanswerable puzzle. It becomes a pointer to the source of life itself.

The Potential of Human Beings

3

PEOPLE: LIKE AND UNLIKE THE ANIMAL KINGDOM

Human beings are animals. That's why we flock to zoos: it isn't just that we are fascinated with the variety of other species in the world, but that they tell us something about ourselves. It's always the animals which are most human in appearance that draw the biggest crowds of spectators—the monkeys and apes, the penguins walking upright. And shows which feature animals doing human-like things (menageries, dolphinariums, circuses) have fascinated *homo sapiens* for centuries. We are like them. We are animals too. And yet—there is a difference.

It would be obvious to any casual visitor to earth that human beings are quite unlike any other life form here. For one thing, there are more of us, and we live in many more kinds of environment than any other animal. We are the only creatures who can travel so easily around the world—and even out of it to other planets. The marks of human domination can be seen all over the planet. We're the most aggressive of animals, too (as we shall see in another chapter), and that makes it serious that we are the only animals capable of destroying the entire earth.

What is the one essential difference between

humans and other animals? Many attempts have been made to answer this question. It used to be said, for instance, that only human beings use tools. But this is incorrect; we know now of some animals who employ sticks and stones for certain tasks. Perhaps humans are the only tool-*making* animals, then? No; some chimpanzees in the wild make crude tools. Are we the only ones to communicate by language? The only ones to cook our food? Peter Farb comments:

The search for such a single unique trait is futile. Scientists now know that the chasm separating humans from animals is not so wide as it once appeared. Some animal species have evolved a rich communication system, while others make and use tools, solve difficult problems, educate their young, live in complex social organizations, and apparently possess an aesthetic sense. On the other hand, no other species even approaches the human one in the scope and intensity of these behaviours... So any definition of human uniqueness obviously would have to be based on differences in degree. Humans exhibit more of certain behaviours than other animals.

Most of the physical abilities of human beings are not as impressive as those of other species. A man can run at 27 miles (43.5 kilometers) per hour on an even surface, but even ponderous creatures like rhinos and hippos can better that time. A man who is really good at high jump can clear well over two metres; but that's nothing to a kangaroo, or even a tiny

bushbaby. And what gymnast or trapeze artist can equal the feats of a monkey in the tree-tops?

Part of the flexibility comes from the fact that we walk upright. We pay quite a price for this accomplishment: humans wouldn't suffer so many back problems and hernias if we walked on all fours, and the narrowing of the pelvic outlet means that childbirth is much more painful for a woman than for the female of any similar species. We would be cleaner, too, if we didn't walk upright: our buttocks are designed (like those of other primates) so that waste matter drops away quite cleanly when we move on all fours. Obviously walking upright is not the most obvious way for human beings to behave. Why did we do it?

One obvious answer is that walking upright leaves us free to use our hands for other purposes. With our hands we can touch, probe, manipulate, gesture, signal, manufacture. We can start to shape our environment, communicate with one another, experiment with technology. None of the most important human activities would be possible if it were not for the fact that we have freed our hands of the responsibility for propelling us around.

It also helps that human beings have a longer period of infancy and childhood than other species. The young of some animals are able to function like their parents almost from the day of birth. But it takes years to become a

fully-fledged member of adult human society. At birth a rhesus monkey has a brain which is 65 per cent of the maximum size it will finally grow to. A new-born chimp's brain is 40.5 per cent of its normal size. But a human being has only 23 per cent of the brain size he or she will one day achieve.

Human teeth come later. Sexual maturity arrives later. The skeleton develops to its final form later than in any monkey or ape. W.M. Krogman, an expert in child growth, claims, 'Man has absolutely the most protracted period of infancy, childhood and juvenility of all forms of life... nearly 30 per cent of his entire life-span is devoted to growing.'

And all of this helps us become the clever animal we are, argues evolutionary theorist Stephen Jay Gould:

But what is the adaptive significance of retarded development itself? The answer to this question probably lies in our social evolution. We are pre-eminently a learning animal. We are not particularly strong, swift, or well designed; we do not reproduce rapidly. Our advantage lies in our brain, with its remarkable capacity for learning by experience. To enhance our learning, we have lengthened our childhood by delaying sexual maturation with its adolescent yearning for independence. Our children are tied for longer periods to their parents, thus increasing their own time of learning and strengthening family ties as well.

WHAT DOES STRESS DO TO US?

Why is it that company directors are seven times more likely to die from coronary disease than miners? Why do they have twenty times as many fatal strokes as clergymen? Why do so many elderly married men die very soon after the death of their wives, and why is it often a bad idea for retired couples to move to a dream bungalow in an unfamiliar area?

The answer to all of these questions is one word: stress. This is the name we give to the way the body reacts to change—especially worrying change. Stress can have profound effects on our health and even on the length of our lives.

'Stress is not defined by what causes it,' explains Dr Peter Tyrer, 'but by a person's reaction to the cause, technically called the stressor.' Some of the things which I would find incredibly stressful (for example, free-fall parachute jumping, or working for the Inland Revenue) may not bother you at all. The similarity is not in the cause, but in the effects.

But some events do tend

Just how important are 'family ties'? Does a human being need other humans in order to develop properly? All infant animals need

Sometimes the body's formation goes wrong, for genetic reasons, through damage before or during birth, sometimes as infants develop. Modern technology can come to the help of the handicapped.

to be more stressful than others, for all of us; and in 1967 the *Journal of Psychosomatic Research* published a league table of the most common causes of stress. Top of the list was 'Death of spouse', followed by 'Divorce', then 'Marital separation', 'Imprisonment', 'Death of close relative', 'Personal injury or illness', and 'Marriage'. This last item demonstrates one very important fact: that *all* change can be a cause of stress—not just unpleasant, unwanted changes. That is why the retirement bungalow may prove to be too much for the health of people who go to live there.

What are the effects of stress? When we feel threatened by change, the 'autonomic nervous system' gets to work straightaway. It makes our lungs breathe more quickly, our heart pump blood faster, our muscles tense up and our mouth go dry. This is so that more blood can be diverted to the muscles immediately —in case the 'emergency' we have encountered requires us to fight, or run away. All of this happens without our even thinking about it.

When the crisis is over, the 'parasympathetic system' of the body—responsible for rest, sleep, digestion, and overall regulation of the body's processes—will get to work to restore the balance. Stress begins to *harm* us when the parasympathetic system is not given enough time to repair the damage: for example, when we go on working long hours without taking adequate rest, or when we keep exposing ourselves to anxiety-producing situations. A study of the blood samples of racing drivers showed that their blood was almost milky in consistency— because their breakneck driving resulted in quantities of cholesterol being pumped into their bloodstreams, ready for a burst of violent physical energy. But there was no burst of energy (none is needed in driving), and the cholesterol remained suspended in their blood.

The autonomic nervous system works with amazing efficiency. But we misuse it at our peril!

Racing drivers work under great stress, but cannot undertake the physical activity which stress demands.

stimulation to develop properly. In an experiment on white rats, one group was given extensive handling, another was subjected to mild electric shocks, and a third group was simply left alone. The group that fared worst was the ignored one.

Throughout history there have been just one or two cases of children deprived of any normal social development. For instance, in 1938 a ten-year-old girl was discovered in a loft of an American farmhouse. She had been imprisoned there since birth, with no human interaction whatsoever; she had no idea how to talk, no concept of normal human behaviour; she was the child of an incestuous relationship, and the family had been so ashamed of her that they had kept her alive but simply pushed her out of sight. Studies of such children as these show that association with other human beings is vitally necessary if infants are to become fully human. We are born with human physical equipment and a few reflexes, such as sucking, grasping, and so on; but unlike some other animals we do not inherit many of our patterns of behaviour. Human behaviour needs to be learned.

Culture and symbols

This means that humans are much more social beings than most animals. Not many mammals form organized, long-lasting societies; but human beings invariably do. And societies develop another uniquely human product, 'culture': a store of values, ideas, information, viewpoints and customs which can be transmitted from generation to generation. Culture means that human babies do not have to re-learn everything about life by painful experience. Their ancestors have heaped up a collection of facts and rules to get them started. In turn, when they die, they will leave the store behind for those who come after them—slightly increased and altered by the discoveries that have been made during their own lifetime.

Cultures vary from society to society, but human culture in general is one of the most important advantages we have over the rest of the animal kingdom. We are not restricted to following the patterns remorselessly dictated by our instincts. We can learn new and more effective ways of behaving. We can try out different forms of organization in society. We can assert our individuality by making our behaviour a little different from what our culture expects from us. The rich variety of human life, the colour and imaginative abundance which characterizes no other species—all of this comes from culture.

And culture depends, in turn, on the ability humans have to construct 'symbols'. A symbol is something which we experience which reminds us of something else we have experienced. Thus when I look at the *Mona Lisa*, I experience a vision of bits of paint on a canvas background; but I hardly even notice the paint. Instead it makes me think about a beautiful woman. When you say the word 'Laura' to me, I experience your voice making certain noises; but it makes me think about my daughter. This ability to make symbols—to produce objects, sounds and marks that remind us of something else—has extended human behaviour and made it more complex than the most intelligent animal could understand. No other animal could make sense of a football match, a religious service, a comedy programme. No dolphin or gorilla could appreciate the importance of queuing at a bus stop or saluting a flag.

The most widespread and valuable way of making symbols, awesomely simple and effective, is human language. Again, this is something that other animals cannot copy. Or so think most scientists, though Carl Sagan, for one, disagrees. In a book about human and animal

intelligence, he wrote:

Although a few years ago it would have seemed the most implausible science fiction, it does not appear to me out of the question that, after a few generations in such a verbal chimpanzee community, i.e. where chimps have learned a vocabulary of around 100 words as some have been trained to do, there might emerge the memoirs of the natural history and mental life of a chimpanzee, published in English or Japanese. . .

42

Of what value are our bodies? Of great value, because they express our selves. The solemn funeral rites of different cultures show this connection, as in a funeral pyre at Varanasi, a procession in Rajasthan, and a Mayan-influenced Christian cemetery on Yucatan peninsula.

What are the facts? In 1966 two American psychologists, Beatrice and Robert Gardner, embarked on an experiment to teach Ameslan (American sign language) to two chimpanzees, Washoe and Lucy. Their pupils proved able to learn an impressive number of gestural signs— Washoe managed 200 in the first four years— and to employ them in sentences. They even created new expressions for phenomena they had not seen before: 'water bird' for duck; 'drink fruit' for watermelon; 'cry hurt food' for radish (after Lucy had burned her mouth on one).

Lana, a chimpanzee in Georgia, has been taught to type out sentences using a specially-designed computer language, and to monitor the results on a display screen. One day her trainer, using a separate computer console in the same room, began spoiling her sentences by interposing a nonsense word in the middle of them. Lana suddenly realized what was happening, and composed a new sentence: 'Please, Tim, leave room.'

When chimps can understand complex sentences ('If red on green then Sarah take red'; 'Sarah insert banana in pail, apple in dish'), invent new terms, and even swear at their trainers, can we really say that human abilities are that much different? Isn't it simply a matter of time until they catch up with us?

No, says psychologist Herbert Terrace. 'Apes can learn many isolated symbols (as can dogs, horses, and other non-human species), but they show no unequivocal evidence of mastering the conversational, semantic, or syntactic organization of language.' A trained adult chimp and a child of two may have roughly the same vocabulary size, but children will develop a grasp of more and more complex structures, enabling them to express finer and finer shades of meaning. Chimps will stay exactly where they are.

Another problem for chimpanzees is their physical construction. To quote Peter Farb again:

It is impossible for apes to speak because their vocal tracts are so constructed as to prevent them from sounding important vowels. This lack is not so trivial as it might seem... Humans can count rapid pulses of sound made by certain electronic machines at rates up to ten per second. Beyond that the pulses fuse and are heard as one continuous tone. Humans, though, speak at a rate of about twenty pulses per second—and these do not fuse. It is the vowels attached to consonants that allow us to decode the sounds as speech signals; these vowel sounds are the very ones that the vocal tracts of the apes are unable to produce.

Society, culture and language make it possible for human beings to enjoy more complicated relationships with one another than the rest of the animal kingdom. Human sexual development has helped here too.

Most animals follow the rule of the oestrous cycle—they have a mating season. Humans are one of the few species where mating can continue throughout the entire year (and usually does, according to all the surveys of human sexual behaviour). With other animals the sexual act is often very brief (a few seconds for a bull or ram, under ten seconds for a chimpanzee; less than thirty for an elephant). Human beings can vary the length of it, and usually take at least a few minutes. Human females can experience orgasm, too, which is unknown among other animals. And humans are the only mammals who prefer making love in a face-to-face position (although they are capable of wild experimentation, also unlike other species).

All of these factors combine to make sex among humans a much more intense, personal, emotion-laden kind of thing than it is among other animals. It is not just a physical function but a means of communicating with another human. And it is capable of becoming a rich language, with infinite subtleties and variations of expression, between two partners who learn to use it in lasting commitment to one another—another human trait which doesn't appear very often in other species.

Humankind, then, is much more than 'the naked ape'—as the title of Desmond Morris' popular book once suggested. (We aren't descended from apes anyway, as zoologists are constantly pointing out. We represent a different branch of the *Hominoidea* superfamily.) By any standard there is an awesome gulf between even the most advanced of other animals and ourselves. It prompts a question. Is this simply chance, a random development? Or, to quote Sir Bernard Lovell, a well-known astronomer, 'Is the universe the way it is, because it was necessary for the existence of man?'

The apostle Paul, at least, had no doubt:

The God who made the world and everything in it is the Lord of heaven and earth... From one man he made every nation of men, that they should inhabit the whole earth; and he determined the times set for them and the exact places where they should live. God did this so that men would seek him and perhaps reach out for him and find him, though he is not far from each one of us.

The human body

What are humans made of? Let's assume you weigh around ten stone (70 kilograms). If we could separate you out into your constituent elements, this is what we would find: 100lb (45.4kg) of oxygen; 28lb (12.7kg) of carbon; 15lb (6.8kg) of hydrogen; 4.6lb (2kg) of nitrogen; 2.3lb (1kg) of calcium; 1.6lb (0.7kg) of phosphorus; a few grams of potassium, sulphur, sodium, chlorine, magnesium, iron and zinc; and traces of copper, manganese molybdenum, cobalt, selenium.

Clearly this is not the whole story (it is often commented that a chemist would give you one pound sterling for the lot). The importance of the human body is not in the rare and precious things it is made of, but in the intricate way in which it uses these building materials. And as we shall see, there are few things in nature more awesome than the efficient complexity of the human body.

Very little in the human body seems to be superfluous. Biologists have often been puzzled by seemingly meaningless parts of the body, only to find later that they do serve an important function. Take the thymus, for example. Until quite recently it was dismissed as a useless survival of an earlier stage of development, but now it is known to be the control centre of the body's defence system against germs. Tonsils and adenoids were often removed from children, because they were thought to serve no function. Now we realize they help to protect the throat and nose against infection.

We all have a strange organ known as an appendix, the cause of a lot of sudden operations when it becomes inflamed; in England and Wales, says Anthony Smith, 'at any time, one in fifty of the general hospital beds is occupied by someone who has every reason to wonder what on earth the human appendix is all about'. However, we may be about to discover the answer. The appendix may be part of our lymphatic system.

Before looking at the various 'bits' of the body—the bones, muscles, organs and so on—we ought to look at the building-blocks of which they are all constructed. These are the cells. A human body contains about sixty billion cells, shaped slightly differently depending on the job they have to do. (Red blood cells are saucer-shaped, and liver cells square-shaped, for example; while nerve cells have long extensions on the end.) All of these cells trace their origin back to one original cell—the one that was formed when an ovum from the mother was penetrated by a sperm cell from the father. Every one of the sixty billion cells is potentially capable of forming a complete human on its own; it contains all the information necessary (except for the red blood cells, that is, which have no nucleus).

In the human body cells are grouped together to form specialized units. Each unit is called a 'tissue'. Tissues are grouped into organs, and encased in a watery substance known as tissue fluid. Actually, water is a very large component of the human body: it accounts for about 60 per cent of a man's body weight, and 50 per cent of a woman's. The average male body contains about nine gallons of water.

Inside a cell, among a quite complex set of components, is the nucleus, which contains twenty-three pairs of chromosomes. These chromosomes contain the blueprints for a human being's life: whether that person will be male or female, have blue eyes, grow tall or

short. And, remember, there are 60 billion production plants like this in your body.

Cells produce proteins. And this is important because proteins (amounting to 12 per cent of your body weight) are the agents that act on the orders of the chromosomes. They work to shape the characteristics of the individual cells, fitting them for the job they have to do in the body, and control the changes that take place within them. They form 'hormones' (the chemical messengers inside us which direct our growth, our 'biological clock', our basic drives and emotions) and 'enzymes', which help to precipitate biochemical reactions in the body.

The body's framework

'As a chassis,' claim Christian Barnard and John Illman, 'the skeleton is unique. It twists and bends to permit a wide range of movement

TWINS

In June 1979 James Lewis, a security guard in Lima, Ohio, finally succeeded in tracing his twin, James Springer. He had not seen his brother for thirty-nine years; both boys had been adopted at the age of five by different families.

The two found they had the same sleeping problems, migraines and haemor-rhoids; they had both had two confirmed or suspected heart attacks; both liked

maths but had trouble with spelling. But there was more.

Each twin had married a wife called Linda. Each had divorced his Linda and married a girl called Betty instead. Each had owned a dog called Toy, had worked as a deputy sherriff and had also been employed by Macdonalds. Each had had a spell as a petrol-pump attendant. Lewis's eldest son was called James Alan; Springer's was James Allan!

These coincidences are quite unusual, even for identical twins. But they show that, even when brought up quite differently, identical twins will exhibit a significant amount of behavioural similarity. If one twin is alcoholic, for example, there is a 65 per cent chance that the other will be. For male homosexuality, there is a 98 per cent correlation; for schizophrenia 86 per cent. Why is this?

'Identical' twins and 'similar' twins come to birth in quite different ways. When an egg cell is fertilized by a sperm cell, it usually starts multiplying into a cluster of cells and developing into one new human being. But just occasionally it will split into two eggs, which then start growing side by side in the womb. (Sometimes the splitting process doesn't happen quite in this way, but takes place after the egg has already become implanted in the uterus; however, the process is very similar.) This phenomenon produces two children (of the same sex, except in very unusual circumstances) who share the closest possible genetic matching. It happens about twice or three times in every thousand human births. It does not run in families.

The ability to have 'dissimilar' twins does run in families, however. This is because the female hormones which release eggs at the time of ovulation each month are controlled by genes—and some people inherit genes which in some months permit two eggs to be released, instead of the usual one. And so two eggs can be fertilized by quite separate sperm cells. (In fact, if the woman has been sleeping with more than one man, it is just possible that the sperm cells will come from different donors, with the result that twins are born who have different fathers!) Obviously, with this type of twin, there will not be nearly so much close matching, because the twins are quite separate individuals with slightly different genetic mixes, who just happen to be inhabiting the same womb at the same time.

The number of 'dissimilar' twins born tends to vary from society to society. Food, health, age of parenthood and genetic inheritance all have something to do with whether the rate is low or high. Much less common, however, are triplets, quadruplets and quintuplets; in fact, it almost never happens that more than four babies are born simultaneously, unless the mother has been receiving hormonal treatment.

The strangest case of multiple birth is 'Siamese twins', when a single egg divides to form twins, but never quite completes the job. The result is that two individuals are born whose bodies are fused together at one or more particular points. The phrase 'Siamese twins' comes from a celebrated pair, Chang and Eng, who were born in 1811 (but weren't actually Siamese!) and were exhibited as a circus curiosity by P.T. Barnum. Later they became farmers in North Carolina, married two sisters and had over twenty normal children. No other pair has ever lived so long. But at least this century scientists have become able occasionally to separate some 'Siamese twins', so that the two can lead independent lives.

---

unequalled by any man-made machine.' Part of the supremacy of human beings over other animals has got to be due to the tremendous range of things their bone structure allows them to do.

There are just over 200 bones in the adult body. They account for only 14 per cent of our total weight; steel bars of the same size would weigh more than four times as much. But they are very strong, because of their structural design. The thigh bone, which is really a hollow cylinder, is capable of withstanding a pressure of 1,200 pounds per square inch whenever we walk. Bones contain a tough protein fibre called 'collagen' on which calcium and mineral salts are deposited, creating hardness and strength. The total effect is to supply all the strength of reinforced concrete.

We do not have the same number of bones throughout our lives. A new-born baby has 300 bones, but some of them fuse together after a while. There can also be differences between individuals: something like one person in twenty is born with a thirteenth pair of ribs.

Can bones lose their size and density through under-use? That seems to be the experience of Apollo and Gemini astronauts. Weightless floating was producing a loss of bone structure of four grams of calcium per month. At that rate, twelve years of weightlessness would have removed half the calcium from their bodies. If humans are to exist for long periods in space, this is one of the unexpected problems they will have to face.

Different bones have widely divergent functions. The skull is the most important protective device in the body. It contains twenty-nine bones, including the six smallest ones we possess: three in each middle ear, which are crucial to our sense of hearing. They convey sound vibrations from a membrane in the outer ear, which receives them, to an organ further inside which turns them into nerve impulses and then transfers them to the brain for decoding.

Moving further down, the skull is supported by the spine—twenty-six bones called vertebrae, separated by flat discs of cartilage, which is a flexible white tissue. The discs are extremely important. They act as shock absorbers (so that our spine is protected when, for instance, we jump off a wall) and allow movement so that the spine can bend and rotate. It is curious how similar the skeletons of mammals can be. A long-necked giraffe has the same number of cervical vertebrae as a man—seven; and so does the whale, which has no neck at all.

More than half of our bones are in our arms and legs (thirty-two in each arm, thirty-one in each leg). Of this collection of 126 bones, 112 are in our extremities—hands and feet, wrists and ankles. This arrangement allows us a degree of flexibility in the use of our hands and feet which is vital for the tasks we have chosen to perform.

Similarly, the ears and nose tip are flexible because they are not made of bone, but of cartilage. In fact, the skeleton of a foetus is initially made of cartilage too, but bone cells start to appear in the seventh week after conception.

So much for the bones. But how do we move them? This is where the muscles come in—collections of strong fibres which can contract forcibly to manoeuvre the body into different positions. Muscles are tied to the bones by tendons. They account for just over one-third of the body's total weight. And they fall into three groups: skeletal or 'voluntary' muscles, which we use to move ourselves around; cardiac or 'heart' muscles, which keep our heartbeat going regularly; and smooth or 'involuntary' muscles, which operate automatically to run our internal systems, such as breathing and digesting food.

How efficient is the human muscular system?

Our bodies are capable of remarkable feats of strength and elasticity when we exercise and train with enough determination.

48

At first sight, it doesn't appear very impressive: the average human body is only 25 per cent efficient, which means that three-quarters of the energy it generates is simply squandered. But then most machines are even less efficient. A finely-tuned car can achieve 30 per cent efficiency, but a human body in top physical condition can soar as high as 50 per cent.

Muscles work by contracting—suddenly tensing themselves to become much shorter than usual (some muscles will contract by as much as two-fifths). This means that every movement they introduce is a pull, not a push, even when the body itself is pushing something. You can easily see how this works by pushing your arms against a hard surface, such as a wall, and feeling how your arm muscles tense up. When muscles are repeatedly used, without being given enough chance to rest, they will eventually lose their power to contract at all. On the other hand, if muscles are not used enough, they will atrophy, and again lose their power.

There are some muscles over which we have complete control. Thirty muscles, for example, supply the amazing range of expressions and contortions a human face can achieve. But others aren't under our direct conscious command. What is it, for instance, that makes our heart muscles speed up, during strenuous exercise, from the steady rhythm of forty-five beats a minute to something maybe four or five times as fast? And what slows it down again afterwards?

The accelerator for all of our involuntary muscles is the 'sympathetic nervous system', and the brake is the 'parasympathetic nervous system'. By working regularly in opposing motion to one another, they produce strong waves of muscular contraction throughout the body that help to keep the body's processes going. It is this process, for instance, which pushes food along the twenty-five-foot channel of our digestive tract.

Is it ever possible for us to control these processes directly? Not much is known. But Dr Elmer Green of the Menninger Foundation, Topeka, Kansas, has carried out some tests which at least indicate a possibility. In 1970 he tested an Indian yogi, Swami Rama, who claimed to be able to stop his heartbeat altogether. Although this did not happen, the

Swami did manage to achieve 'atrial flutter'—an amazingly high heart rate of 300 beats a minute, which should have left him unconscious, but didn't. Clearly concentrating the mind can have *some* effect on physical processes.

The workings of the body

So much for the body's framework. But what of the processes that go on within it? Here we have space to look at only two of the most important: breathing, and the role of our blood.

Breathing is something we do most of the time without thinking about it. But we do an enormous amount of it, getting through something like 3,300 gallons (15,000 litres) of air each day, which means anything between 10,000 and 20,000 breaths per week. The purpose of all this activity is to bring quantities of oxygen into the body, and get rid of the carbon dioxide and other substances left behind when the oxygen has been used. Human beings cannot cope with much carbon dioxide: if we breathe in air which contains more than 5 per cent of it, we will probably

faint. (We can, however, put up with a lot of impurities in the air we breathe: it has been estimated that the average city dweller breathes in 20,000 million particles of foreign matter every day.)

We draw breath in by expanding the lungs. This happens when we do two things simultaneously: the diaphragm pulls itself downwards and the rib muscles contract. This expands the chest wall and thus creates a slight vacuum, which air from the outside rushes in to fill up. Breathing out simply reverses the action, and as the lungs are forced inwards again, the pressure drives the air out. But not all of it. Only about one-sixth of the air which is already in the lungs will be changed over in any one breath. So it's possible that some molecules of the first breath you take as a baby will still be there in your lungs at the end of your life!

Once the air is in the lungs, the oxygen needs to be distributed throughout the body. For this purpose, the lungs have a vast surface area—somewhere between 800 and 1,000 square feet (90 square metres); books about the human body often compare this to the size of a tennis court. This colossal area is necessary so that the blood cells can be charged with oxygen regularly and quickly enough to keep the body surviving. We will examine this more closely in a moment.

Our breathing can sometimes produce strange side effects. Why do we yawn, for instance? Nobody really knows. Anthony Smith suggests that it 'may be a physiological attempt to get more blood to lungs and brain; but blood flow is frequently boosted on many other occasions without the bewildering grimace of a jaw-cracking, ear-popping yawn.

Hiccups are another mystery. Probably the nerves controlling the diaphragm are responsible for it, but why does it happen? And what is the best way of stopping it? There are hundreds of folk remedies, but sometimes they all fail, and a victim can be hiccuping for months or even years.

Laughing, crying, sighing—the ways in which we vary our breathing patterns are strange indeed. One of the strangest is called 'hyperventilation'. This is an extremely rapid breathing process which often occurs in unusual states of consciousness, and during mediumship. Perhaps the unusually fast arrival of oxygen in the brain

alters perception in some way. Yoga meditation, too, uses a special breathing technique, pranayama, which reduces the body to stillness very quickly.

The blood system is the body's distribution network. Blood carries all sorts of things from one part of the body to another: oxygen and carbon dioxide, as we have already mentioned, but also hormones, various nutrients, antibodies which prevent infection, and water.

The average body contains 10.5 imperial pints (6 litres) of blood. It causes no harm to the system for a blood donor to give away a pint or so in blood transfusion and even as much as a third of the body's blood can be lost without serious trouble. But if more than half goes missing, life will no longer be possible.

Our blood supply is constantly engaged in an endless journey round and round the body. By the end of your life, your heart may have

A giraffe's is a prince among necks. A whale doesn't have one. Yet both have the same number of vertebrae — seven. And human beings have seven as well.

pumped the equivalent of 50 million gallons (227 million litres); at its maximum rate, it can push through 5.5 gallons (25 litres) a minute, which means sending the entire blood supply right round the body several times in sixty seconds!

What happens to all this blood on its journey?

The trip starts in the right side of the heart. From there the blood is pumped to the lungs, where it is squeezed through 'blood capillaries', tiny channels so narrow that only one red blood cell can pass through at a time. Each cell will have only three-quarters of a second in the capillary before it is pushed out by the next ones following it, but that is long enough for it to jettison the cargo of carbon dioxide it is carrying, and pick up fresh oxygen atoms instead.

From there the blood goes back into the left side of the heart, and is pumped on again—this time through a 60,000-mile system of arteries, capillaries and veins, giving up its load of oxygen where it is needed and taking on board carbon dioxide to dispose of as refuse.

Why do we feel dizzy sometimes when we leap out of bed? Because when we are lying down it is not so difficult for the heart to pump blood lengthways to the brain. When we stand up, the increased gravitational pull means that the heart has to work faster to get the oxygen up to the head; and so momentarily we have a reduced supply, which makes us feel faint.

But blood does other things, besides acting as the transport system. As well as red cells, the blood contains 3,000 million white cells which are the body's main line of defence against invading bacteria or viruses.

Once a germ has managed to slip into a vulnerable area of the body, the white blood cells start to multiply at the point of attack. Here they kill off the enemy by eating it and digesting it. (For this reason, they are also called 'phagocytes', literally, 'eating vessels'.) The germs release poisonous toxins in their own defence, and these wake into life another sort of white cell, an 'antibody', which produces defence chemicals to counteract the poison. After the germs have been destroyed, the antibodies stay around. They remain in the bloodstream for some time, ready to repel the invader should it come again. That is why you are unlikely to catch measles or chickenpox more than once!

The body's defence system is highly versatile. In a lifetime it may come up against 100,000 different poisonous forces—and produce antibodies to deal with every one. One of the few things to outwit it, unfortunately, is the common cold! So many different viruses can cause it that the body never has a chance to build up a resistance to them all. That's why cold cures make so much money for pharmacists. And why none of them can be guaranteed to work!

The body's information systems

How many kinds of signals do we receive from our senses? We know the difference between seeing a pretty girl, hearing a brass band, tasting a mouth-watering meal and touching wet paint. How many sensations does our body receive?

Earlier this century a distinguished American psychologist, Edward Titchener, started counting. Eventually he proclaimed that we have 46,709 elementary sensations, not counting an indeterminate number of smells. He counted 11,000 tones that our ears can recognize, but only four basic tastes.

Nobody would place much reliance on Titchener's work today, but it does show what an immensely complicated job the human senses do. Take the sense of sight, for example. The human eye is such a complex instrument that Charles Darwin, when first he formulated his theory of natural selection, was at a loss to explain how the eye could have developed simply by chance. 'When I think of the eye,' he wrote, 'I shudder.'

What happens when a light wave strikes your **eye?** First it passes through a layer known as the 'cornea', which begins to focus it; then it penetrates through the 'pupil' gap. (The pupils of our eyes dilate or contract depending on how much light they are receiving, but they are also affected by fear, interest in a subject which is being discussed, sexual excitement, and other emotional states.) Then the 'lens' of the eye picks up the partially-focused beam and sharpens the focus fully. The light travels on to the 'retina', the part of the eye which decodes the signals and sends the proper message about it to the brain.

The retina contains an enormous number of receptor cells to do the 'decoding' job. 125 million of them are called 'rods', and enable us to detect different shades of grey, thus making it possible to see at night. The other 7 million are

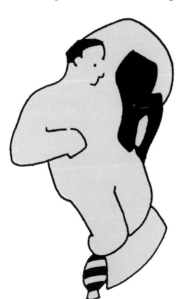

What do you see in this picture? Just one image, or more?

'cones' (the name comes from their shape); they help us distinguish colours, essential for day vision.

The combined messages of the receptor cells are put together in receiving stations known as 'ganglion cells'. This explains why one can actually see and distinguish objects whose image on the retina is narrower than a single cell across. A telegraph wire is visible against a bright sky at a distance of a quarter of a mile. Its image may cover no more than one twenty-fifth of the receptor, yet it is seen sharply.

From the ganglion cells, the optic nerve transfers the information to the brain, and recognition takes place.

What we 'see', however, does not simply depend on the information which the retina passes on to the brain. The information coming in is checked against our previous knowledge of patterns, shapes and appearances, and we classify the new experience in terms of what we already know. (For instance: I have hardly noticed what my wife is wearing today. I am so used to seeing her that I do not need to look at her very closely to identify the fact that she is there; and so I do not 'see' her directly; I 'see' my mental image of her instead. When psychologists ran a test in which various men were dressed up to look as if they had lost a limb, wives of the volunteers were less likely to notice anything wrong with their husbands than with strangers.)

And so our eyes can be deceived. But nevertheless they give us a vast fund of information about the world around. And they have tremendous adaptive ability: when we are thrown into a darkened prison cell, our eyes will rapidly grow accustomed to the light—in the first hour sensitivity increases by 75,000 times.

Eyes are never still. Apart from the fact that our head is always moving slightly the eyes also dart about, constantly changing the pattern of light which is being directed on to the retina. Otherwise fatigue, and perhaps blindness, would inevitably follow. And we need to blink: although we're rarely conscious of doing it, we take this automatic step of caring for our eyes from six times to thirty times a minute. Few people can last a full minute without needing to blink.

Our other senses are just as intricate. The

human **ear** can distinguish about 1,600 frequencies of sound, at 300 different intensities in volume, between twenty cycles per second and 20,000. This is a startlingly wide range, although dogs can hear higher frequencies and grasshoppers lower. (Just for comparison, a male voice is around 100 cycles per second, a female voice 150, and middle C on a piano 256.)

What is it in our **nose** that makes us able to smell? Tiny cells with long hair-like 'cilia', embedded in a layer of mucus. There aren't nearly so many sense receptors for the sense of smell as for sight (only fourteen), yet since they operate in different combinations in a flexible

pattern, we can still, with a little practice, detect over 10,000 different odours. (All of which seems quite pathetic to a dog, whose nose is a million times more acute even than that!)

For the sense of **taste,** we have receptors located in our 3,000 taste buds, which can be found on the front, back and sides of the upper surface of our tongue. (There are some in our palate, pharynx and tonsils, too.) It used to be thought that there were different receptors for the four 'primary sensations'—sweet, bitter, sour and salt—but research has shown that the pattern is much more complicated. It is still true, however, that we sense most sweet and

IS THERE A BIOLOGICAL CLOCK INSIDE US?

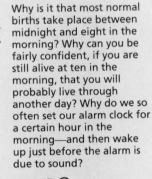

Why is it that most normal births take place between midnight and eight in the morning? Why can you be fairly confident, if you are still alive at ten in the morning, that you will probably live through another day? Why do we so often set our alarm clock for a certain hour in the morning—and then wake up just before the alarm is due to sound?

All of these strange facts are explained by the discovery that there are a number of 'clocks' inside us, regulating our lives by different rhythms, ensuring that physical changes take place at the appropriate moment.

The most obviously recognizable rhythm is the daily one: every night, our life processes slow down, as we go to sleep. If we try to disrupt this rhythm, we are in trouble—like a nurse friend of mine who found when she was on night duty that she was waking up to go to the toilet at all the wrong times. 'Jet lag' happens when we cross quickly from one time zone into another. Our bodies keep on working according to the time schedule of the zone we have left, and the

'clock' will not be 'reset' for three or four days after our arrival. This is why long-distance jet pilots are less healthy than average, and have a shorter life expectancy, while pilots who operate within just one time zone have a normal expectation of life.

If we adjust our clocks permanently—for example, by staying on the night shift for several years—we suffer no ill effects: the body adjusts. Night workers actually tend to be slightly healthier than those on a day shift. All the same, there are some humans who operate best at night, and others who work best in the morning. This has a physiological basis: 'night birds' really do take longer to get going in the morning, with a slightly subnormal temperature and heart-rate for the first hour or two after waking up. This tendency seems to be inherited.

The daily rhythm is not the only one. There is a twice-daily one too: our heart-muscle rate slows at around 1 p.m. and 9 p.m., inducing less efficiency and alertness. Just before lunchtime is not a good time to be doing work which requires care. This seems to have something to do with the regeneration of cells in our bodies: just at the times when our active energy level is lowest, cell regeneration

reaches its highest point.

Then there are rhythms which are longer-term. Patients in mental hospitals, for instance, can show behaviour which changes from day to day according to a certain cycle—altering from 'almost normal' to 'extremely disturbed'. And there are the once-for-all changes which take place when (for example) a boy who has shown no interest in the opposite sex suddenly starts to feel a desire for a girlfriend, or a married woman who has never really wanted children becomes desperately keen to have a baby. The clock's hands have moved on one more minute —and there is no reversing the process!

salt tastes with the tip of the tongue, sourness at the sides, and bitterness at the back.

Is **touch** one sense, or several? Again, the picture is complicated. There are some parts of the body where one set of nerve endings seems to have the job of reporting *all* the touch sensations to the brain, and other parts where there are specialized endings for touch, pressure, pain, heat and cold. We have four million receptors in all; pain receptors far outnumber the others. And it is a good thing that this should be so!

Pain is the body's early-warning system of impending danger; a woman without pain can break her ankle and not notice, or suffer severe internal injuries and not discover them until it is too late for her life to be saved.

We suffer two kinds of pain. There is the sharp, stabbing pain which warns you instantly that you have done something wrong (cut your hand with a knife, for instance); and there is the dull, settled, aching pain which will continue until you have treated your hand and healing has begun.

These two types of pain each have their own separate nerve system—A-Delta fibres and C fibres—because they have separate messages to deliver. One is saying, 'Quick! Get out of trouble *now*!'; the other is insisting, 'I'd just like to remind you of a matter which requires some attention. . .'

Pain messages are oddly unpredictable, however. Sometimes there is *no* warning when trouble is on the way (such as, for instance, a sudden heart attack or appendicitis); sometimes the message is too shrill (the raging pain of toothache when there is really very little wrong); and sometimes, curiously, we may feel no pain when we are shocked—after a road

WHAT IS PAIN FOR?

Anyone who has suffered appendicitis—or an ingrown toe-nail, or protracted dental treatment—knows about pain. It isn't a pleasant experience. Why do our bodies allow it to happen?

Confusingly, pain and pleasure sometimes com very close together. Sinking into a hot bath at the end of a busy day, experiencing the enjoyable aching of the limbs and the stinging heat of the water—this has an obvious link to pain, but it isn't like the dentist's chair. The *Kama Sutra*, a famous Oriental 'love manual', recommends scratching and biting to heighten sexual pleasure, and sexologist Alfred Kinsey noticed that the movements and facial expressions of people at the point of sexual climax are virtually identical to those of people suffering agonizing torture!

Approximately one child in 400,000 is born with a total inability to feel pain. This is caused by a rare genetic disease called 'familial dysautonomia'. In a short life this child may suffer deep cuts, severe burns, broken bones and internal injuries without knowing anything about it. Such children may not realize there is anything wrong with them until it is too late for medical care.

Pain is nature's early-warning system, telling us that something is wrong before we damage ourselves too severely. Without it, we are in serious trouble. It may at times be inconvenient, but it can prevent many worse things happening.

The body even grades the kind of pain messages it sends through, in order to tell us how bad the problem is. The three layers of the skin, for example, send out different pain messages: an itchy feeling from the top layer, when it is disturbed (for example, by something we are allergic to); a stabbing pain from the layer underneath, when a pin is stuck through it; and a deep settled ache from the lower layer when the trouble has gone further (such as when the pin has gone right through). The system is not foolproof, of course; Manchester City goalkeeper Bert Trautmann played right through a Wembley Cup Final without realizing his neck was broken, and excitement often blunts the edge of pain. But it is nonetheless a very useful system.

And, says Rabbi Harold Kushner, 'Only human beings can find meaning in their pain.' He points out that two of the most painful things we can suffer are giving birth and passing a kidney stone. From a purely physical point of view—the way in which animals experience pain—these events are equal. But the difference in purpose between the two—simple malfunction and creative, productive pain—can make them an entirely different experience. And so, Kushner says, 'When we understand that, our question will change from, "Why do we have to feel pain?" to "What do we do with our pain so that it becomes meaningful and not just pointless empty suffering?"'

Lepers feel no pain. As a result their feet and hands often get damaged by burns or cuts from which the rest of us, taught by pain, would instantly withdraw.

accident, say—or engrossed in what we are doing. Rugby players and warriors in battle can sustain fearsome wounds without really noticing until later.

Some years ago, at Harvard University Medical School, 162 people who were recovering from operations were given injections by doctors. Supposedly these were of a pain-killing drug, but in fact it was nothing but salt and water. Yet half of them reported relief from pain as a result of the injection.

Perhaps, as scientist Ronald Melzack has concluded, 'Pain is a function of the whole individual.' What we actually feel is a combination of what our senses tell us, *together with* the convictions our brain already has on the subject. But we will look more closely at the workings of the brain in another chapter.

The wrapper round it all

It has been said that if you asked a good tailor to create a close-fitting garment to cover the whole of your body, he would need six yards of material thirteen inches wide (or 5.5 metres, 30 centimetres wide). Yet every few weeks our own bodies supply us with a new covering of twenty square feet (two square metres) which completely replaces the old one and fits us perfectly.

The reason why our body needs to replace it so frequently is that we are always wearing it away. The friction involved in washing and normal movement grinds away the surface of the skin, and it needs to be constantly renewed. Skin does a lot of things for us (apart from preventing our insides from falling out!). It keeps moisture out of the body; it forms a barrier against germs and dirt; it keeps moisture *in*, too, so that we don't start drying out; and, together with the fatty layers underneath, it helps to cushion us against all the bumps and knocks we encounter.

Skin consists of two main layers. The upper layer is called the 'epidermis', and its surface is made up of dead cells (living cells cannot survive when exposed to air). Because these cells are soon flaked away, others are constantly pushing up from below to take their place in the front line. The epidermis is as thin as a sheet of paper.

Colour of skin has become the great symbol for humanity's racial variety.

The lower layer is the 'dermis', which contains fat cells, hair roots, sweat glands and capillaries to conduct blood (which is why even a small cut will always draw blood). The dermis is responsible for the pattern of our fingerprints. As almost everyone now knows, your fingerprints are one of the most distinctive features of your body; no two individuals seem to have an identical set, even though there are only four basic patterns (whorls, loops, arches and composites) producing the endless variations. It is humbling, though, to realize that the Chinese were using fingerprints as a means of identification in AD700, over a thousand years before Western police departments 'discovered' them!

The sweat glands in the skin (700 to the square inch; about 270 per square centimetre) release salty water which then evaporates and keeps the body cool. Even in a temperate climate, we sweat about half a pint a day; in the tropics, this can rise to about six pints.

The skin also contains oil-producing 'sebaceous glands' (the amount of oil they produce determines whether you need shampoo formulated for 'greasy hair' or 'dry hair'), and their product lubricates the skin, making it waterproof. Also found in the skin are bulb-like hair follicles. It is a fallacy that men have more than women. The hair is less obvious on the female body, but the quantity is exactly the same.

Sometimes our skin does funny things. What produces 'goose pimples', for example? The answer is the tiny muscles in the hair follicles; in cold conditions they contract, and this produces the unusual pimply, hair-standing-on-end condition. In some animals this manoeuvre is an effective device in warding off cold; humans have less hair, and so it does not work particularly efficiently. But it does remind us to put a coat on.

Skin also contains a pigment called 'melanin', which guards us from the heat of the sun.

This Good Friday penitential procession in the Philipines shows people will go to great lengths to master their bodies. But does such humiliation reveal a wrong view of what our bodies are for?

Melanin explains the difference in colour between races, and also why fair skins tan when exposed to sunlight. Sometimes the melanin in a body groups itself together in clumps and then we have what we call 'freckles'.

Eventually, later in life, our skin will start to wrinkle. It no longer fits the body quite so well. This is because in old age the fatty tissues which lie beneath the skin gradually disappear; the body shrinks in size, but the skin does not shrink with it. Young mothers have a similar problem when they try to get rid of stretch marks after pregnancy.

Skin, like many other features of the body, is something we take for granted most of the time. But in reality it is an indispensable marvel—just one of many in the amazing human body.

The real value of the human body

In the week in which this chapter was written, a helicopter pilot lost his life when his craft crashed into a Scottish mountainside. He was trying to rescue the body of a woman climber who had died in an accident on that mountain.

Why take such risks for something which is inert and useless? Yet within the Christian tradition, the body has always been highly regarded—even after death. People spend vast sums to have the bodies of relatives flown home, after they have died abroad. Elaborate funerals treat corpses with great respect. In more warlike days, a way of inflicting the ultimate degradation on an enemy was to assault his body after death—hanging, drawing and quartering, perhaps, or cutting off the head and displaying it on a pike. Rotting bodies were left on gibbets as a warning to other criminals.

There is some evidence that traditions of respect for bodies go a long way back. Archaeologists working in Northern Iraq have uncovered the remains of a grave from thousands of years ago, where flowers had obviously been solemnly collected and arranged around the body. 'It is difficult to dismiss the conviction,' writes David Hay, 'that at that Neanderthal funeral 60,000 years ago there was a religious

ARE THERE STRANGE POWERS OF HEALING?

Oskar Estebany is a retired Hungarian Army colonel who claims the power to heal people by laying his hands on them. Just a bizarre claim—or the truth? In 1972 he was put to the test when researchers in Montreal took forty-eight female mice and removed an oval piece of skin from their backs. They kept them in groups in separate cages, then called in Estebany to see if he could heal one group.

For fifteen minutes at a time, twice a day, Estebany held the 'treatment cage' on his left hand and poised his right hand over it—without touching. He concentrated his mind on attempting to heal the wounds of the mice. After fourteen days, the treated mice had wounds which were only two-thirds as large as those of the untreated mice. Somehow, the 'radiation energy' of Estebany had helped. A second test confirmed the results.

Do some people have special healing abilities? The claim goes back to the earliest days of humanity. And today, there are thousands of unorthodox healers all over the world, using a colourful variety of techniques. In Britain the General Medical Council has now given permission to doctors to refer their patients to healers, provided they maintain overall control of each case. A Christian movement concerned for spiritual renewal, the 'charismatic movement', has since the 1960s brought a new interest in the 'gifts of healing' mentioned in the New Testament. Many baffling cures have been reported.

Doctors emphasize that we need to be exceptionally cautious. Many so-called healers are frauds. A number of the 'psychic surgeons' who plunge their hands into patients' bodies without even cutting them open, and somehow magically pull out diseased organs, cancerous growths, and the like, have been shown to be impostors. Also, it is possible for a disease to be wrongly diagnosed; in which case it may clear up with dramatic speed and surprise everyone into thinking that a 'miracle' has occurred. Or 'spontaneous remissions' can take place, when a patient suffering from an illness will suddenly, quite unaccountably, feel much better and stop showing signs of disease. This is not a cure, though, and the disease may later return in strength.

For all this, there seems to be plenty of evidence to suggest that some people do have a natural ability to bring health improvement to others. It is not always necessary for the person being treated to have much faith in the cure; often children and animals are cured, and sometimes total sceptics. Healing seems to be confined to certain kinds of problem. Some types of disability seem more amenable to such healing than others. Says Christian healer Canon Jim Glennon, 'I do not consider it reasonable to believe that an amputee can grow a new limb.'

Many Christians believe that there is a special gift of healing given by God. Non-Christian healers may therefore have a genuine ability, but until it is surrendered to God and brought under his control, it will not operate as it should. And none of this in any way replaces the work of doctors and hospitals; medicine is a vital gift from God as part of his care for humanity's needs.

New Age thinking believes the mind to be just as important as the body in illness and healing.

tenderness for the departed person which would be perfectly recognizable to modern man.'

Other traditions have had a different view of the body's importance. In some Greek philosophical thinking, the human body was just the prison house which incarcerated the really valuable part—the human spirit (we saw this in the last chapter). Plato's *Phaedrus* talks about four kinds of 'divine madness' (including inspired prophecy, divine love and artistic inspiration) which take us beyond the physical level into true 'spiritual' reality.

Influenced by these ideas, Christians have sometimes thought that it is extremely spiritual to think of the body as dirty, worthless and untrustworthy. When the third-century church leader Origen was an enthusiastic young extremist, he voluntarily castrated himself in an attempt to become more spiritual—an act which he later regretted. But this is not how the Bible approaches the subject. Old and New Testaments show a healthy respect for the body as part of God's creation. When the apostle Paul uses the word 'flesh', he does not imply distaste for the body and its functions; many modern translations render this word as 'sinful nature'.

The old Platonic view survives today in various psychic movements who try to explore out-of-the-body experiences, such as astral travel, or ecstatic experiences, such as the higher grades of Transcendental Meditation, as routes to spiritual power or awareness. We will say more about these attempts in chapter five. In the days of the early church, something quite similar was going on in the city of Colossae, and Paul wrote scathingly to Christians there about the 'hollow and deceptive philosophy', 'idle notions' and 'harsh treatment of the body' which was involved.

The great Eastern religious traditions, such as Hinduism and Buddhism, also have fairly dismissive views of the body. The real 'you', in Hindu thought, is not to be identified with your body, or even with what seems to be your personality, because these things will pass. When your body wears out, you will simply reincarnate in a different one, and so the more honour and attention we pay to our body, the more confused we will become about our real identity. This is why the spiritual tradition of Hinduism is such an ascetic one: denying the body's wishes, ignoring its demands and rising above physical processes, are ways of achieving spiritual understanding. Yogis who hold their breath for exceptionally long periods, or sit on beds of nails, or exist on a handful of food daily, are not just performing party tricks. They are trying to conquer their body, which is a hindrance to finding God.

This same view has been taken into many modern religious fringe groups. Scientology, for example, propounds an elaborate mythology according to which we are all several trillion years old, and have existed in this galaxy or others for lifetime after lifetime in a bewildering succession of different bodies—sometimes made of different substances. And so Ron Hubbard, founder of the group, talks contemptuously of our 'Meat Bodies'. 'In Scientology,' comments

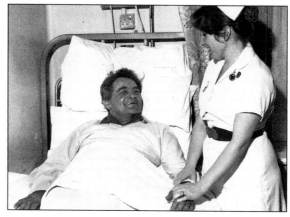

Modern hospitals are in direct line of descent from Christian foundations in previous centuries. Right

from the days of Christ the healer, Christians have been concerned to cure people's illnesses.

ex-follower Cyril Vosper, 'there is a revulsion and contempt for bodies and indeed, all materiality.'

One indicator of how we think of our bodies is the way we try to heal them. Holistic medicine has become very important to 'New Age' thinkers (those who believe the world is starting to undergo a transformation of consciousness which will radically alter our view of life, society, politics, sex and spirituality). In her best-seller *The Aquarian Conspiracy* Marilyn Ferguson announces the death of 'the old paradigm of medicine', which treated the body as a 'machine in good or bad repair'; under the new paradigm, the body becomes a 'dynamic system, context, field of energy within other fields'. The body is important because it is inextricably linked with the mind and spirit (indeed, the mind is the 'primary or co-equal factor in *all* illness'). This isn't far from the Christian view, but it goes beyond Christian claims in assuming that the body and mind together can introduce us to the realm of spiritual reality. Christians would claim that a spiritual rebirth has to happen first, and that without it, explorations into 'natural' spirituality are an exotic wild goose chase. But more of this later.

Buddhist thought is close to Hindu ideas when it comes to the body. And so in Tibet funerals can be rather different, as one Western teacher discovered:

The sky burial is a part of Tibetan Buddhism. . . When a person dies, they chop the body to small pieces—or burn it, like that one over there. They chop the body ritualistically, starting with the feet and working up. They break the bones. They smash the skull in. Then they feed it to the vultures. So they commit the person to the sky.

When the Buddha died, say the sacred scriptures, it was 'with that utter passing away which leaves nothing behind'. The dead body is just a souvenir of a previous existence, a reminder of a life which is no more. It has no intrinsic importance in itself.

On the other hand, some writers who have no belief in a religious dimension see the body as very important indeed, because it is one of the few solid realities of life. Perhaps our bodies contain the real key to why we act as we do, what life is really for, even what the future holds? Transplant surgeon Christian Barnard has written, in a book with John Illman:

We live but to create a new machine of a little later model than our own, a new life machine that in some ineffable way can help along the great process of evolution of the species somehow more efficiently than we could do if we were immortal.

Later they add, 'It is as if the world is a laboratory and we are the experiments.'

Nobody has taken this kind of thinking further than Richard Dawkins, author of *The Selfish Gene*, whose book caused a sensation by advancing claims like these:

The argument of this book is that we, and all other animals, are machines created by our genes. Like successful Chicago gangsters, our genes have survived, in some cases for millions of years, in a highly competitive world. This entitles us to expect certain qualities in our genes. I shall argue that a predominant quality to be expected in our genes is a ruthless selfishness.

And so human bodies are just 'survival machines —robot vehicles blindly programmed to preserve the selfish molecules known as genes'. But if we amounted only to this, there wouldn't be much point in our knowing about it—as the philosopher Anthony Flew observed in a stinging retort to Dawkins:

If any of this were true, then it would not be a bit of use to go on, as Dawkins does, to preach: 'Let us try to teach generosity and altruism, because we are born selfish.' No eloquence could move programmed

According to a popular view of human nature, our behaviour is rooted in animal instincts; we are really 'naked apes'. But aren't the differences between people and animals more fundamental than this?

robots. But in fact it is none of it either true or even faintly sensible. Genes... do not and cannot necessitate our conduct. Nor are they capable of the calculation and understanding required to plot a course of either ruthless selfishness or sacrificial compassion.

A more sophisticated writer of the same sort as Dawkins is Harvard biologist Edward O. Wilson. His book *Sociobiology* suggests that 'in a Darwinist sense the organism does not live for itself... the organism is only DNA's way of making more DNA'. All human behaviour therefore has a genetic base: 'Altruism is conceived as the mechanism by which DNA multiplies itself... spirituality becomes just one more Darwinian enabling device'. And 'beliefs are really enabling mechanisms for survival'; we behave in certain ways because these give our genes the best possible chances of survival into another generation.

But, as Flew points out, this does not say anything about whether or not the beliefs we hold are *true*. 'The questions whether and in what way it is rational to support the norms which we do support are... not biological questions.' And, Keith Ward objects, sociobiology is attempting to reconstruct our experience of the world according to an artificial scientific model—which means leaving out the things which are most immediate and most undeniable in our experience:

Genetic theories are, after all, abstract, generalized and mathematically specified models of the real world, using certain very precisely defined technical concepts. The aim of these abstract models is to help us to understand organic and human life better. Something has gone drastically and fundamentally wrong when we begin to talk about the model as though it was the reality, and about the real world it should be helping us to understand as though it did not even exist. Sociobiology... is one modern equivalent of those pure theoreticians who refused to look through Galileo's telescope to see the facts, in case the sight spoiled their theory.

An even more popular author (whose work has encouraged several imitators) is Desmond Morris, to whom the human being is just *The Naked Ape*. As we have already seen, that description is zoologically incorrect, but Morris uses the arresting phrase to sum up his view of humanity: as carrying round with us conditioning traits and ways of behaviour which we have inherited from our animal past. Morris believes that if we explore our biological links to the animal kingdom, we can discover the truth about why humans act as they do.

A human being is just 'a primitive tribal hunter, masquerading as a civilized, super-tribal citizen'. Our learned behaviour, which we pick up from society around us, ultimately doesn't count for nearly as much as the old, deeply-buried animal instincts which are still there inside us, and will not be denied. 'The fundamental patterns of behaviour laid down in our early days as hunting apes still shine through all our affairs, no matter how lofty they may be.'

But this is just to ignore the very real differences between human beings and other species—the chief one being, as we saw at the start of the chapter, the human discovery of ways of storing and passing on knowledge, so that each new member of the race no longer has to learn everything from scratch. The triumph of learning and education over inherited instincts has been the major factor in human dominance. To deny its importance is to turn everything we know about the world upside down.

It would be more plausible if Morris founded his theory on unassailable data. But in the estimation of scientific writer Denis Alexander, 'there is little real evidence for some of these speculative ideas... the attempt to extrapolate from theories about animals to theories about man... takes us far beyond the evidence that is in fact available'. In the final analysis, Morris is making a subjective, loosely documented statement of personal belief—not a scientific argument at all.

Not our own

The body as a loathsome prison house; the body as a temporary transit vehicle; the body as the undiscovered director of all our behaviour. Does Christian teaching follow any of these lines? What do Christians believe about the body? Does it tally with what we know about the complexity and wonder of our physical being—and yet not claim too much for the body's importance, as Morris, Dawkins and others seem to do?

The basic Christian claim about the body is that it is part of God's creation, in fact a crowning part. In the creation story of Genesis, human bodies are formed 'from the dust of the ground'—of the same basic stuff as every other living creature—but they are made on the climactic 'sixth' day of creation, as one of the most important things God put together.

And so Christians believe in treating the body with respect. 'You are not your own,' writes the apostle Paul to some early Christians. 'You were bought at a price. Therefore honour God with your body.' A Christian's body, Paul writes, is a 'temple of the Holy Spirit'—spiritual life and physical life are not opposed to one

Human bodies are
wonderful mechanisms, of
which robots are fumbling
imitations. But people are
more than machines.

components, but as inextricably bound up with one another. Consequently, the Christian vision of the future is that some day whole human beings—body as well as spirit—will be permanently in God's presence, enjoying the totality and fulness of his plan for human life.

Our bodies then will be somewhat different. Paul writes, for instance, about the difference between the 'natural body' which goes into the grave and the transformed 'spiritual body' which comes out. But it will be the same basic body. How can this work? C.S. Lewis pointed out that our bodies are a bit like waterfalls—constantly changing their contents. Any one droplet of water is part of the waterfall only for as long as it takes to shoot from the top to the bottom; it is immediately replaced by thousands of others. In the same way, the cells of our bodies are constantly being renewed; you do not consist of the same 'materials' that you did seven years ago! But there is continuity in the waterfall because of its overall shape and structure; and so, perhaps, it would be possible for the molecules of a human body to be arranged in a different way, with different abilities, while that body would still continue to be, recognizably and genuinely, the same entity as before.

Certainly the Bible emphasizes that our body will be part of us for ever. The marvellous machine which is the vehicle for your life is not just a disposable wrapping, but an integral part of God's purposes for you.

another, but go hand in hand.

And so right down through the history of the church Christians have always been concerned about meeting the needs of people's bodies as well as doing something to their souls. It has been estimated that 85 per cent of all hospitals in the world have been founded by Christians. By contrast with other religions, which have often adopted a passive attitude to physical misfortunes, Christians have been in the forefront of attempts to feed the hungry, care for lepers, relieve the needs of prisoners, reform the medical system.

As we saw in the previous chapter, Christians do not see 'body' and 'soul' as two detachable

4

HOW THE BRAIN WORKS

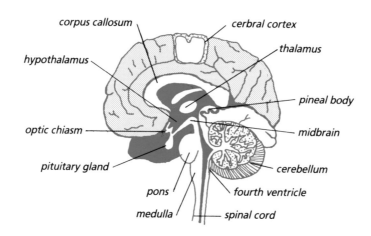

At first sight it looks rather unpromising. Two handfuls of pinkish-grey, crinkled tissue, looking a little like an elderly walnut and feeling as floppy as jelly. Yet the human brain has something like sixty times the informational complexity of the entire United States telephone system.

Our brains are not even as big as the brains of some animals. But in the average human life, the brain's owner will stow away 500 times as much information as there is in the *Encyclopaedia Britannica* (or 500,000 times as much, if you count items that are stored more than once). And some people have been able to do amazing things with their brains.

Take for example Karl Friedrich Gauss, a mathematician. When he was six years old his teacher asked the class to add up all the numbers from one to ten. Gauss raised his hand and gave the answer immediately. He had spotted right away that the ten numbers included five pairs each of which added up to eleven. Not surprisingly, when he reached the age of thirteen Gauss was told by his teacher not to come to school any more: there was nothing else he could learn there.

Or take Shereshevskii, a failed Russian musician and journalist. He was able to memorize poetry in languages he did not know, long strings of numbers, complicated mathematical formulae—and repeat them all without error several years later. Bruno Furst was just as unusual. He memorized the entire German Civil Code, comprising 2,385 paragraphs of tortuous legal statements, and could quote any paragraph on request. He also committed to memory hundreds of poems, dozens of plays, about twenty novels, and literally thousands of addresses and telephone numbers. One of his favourite tricks was to fan out a deck of cards after shuffling it, examine it for a few seconds, and then repeat the sequence of cards purely from memory. Two decks took him just over a minute. (And this man had still not learnt his multiplication tables by the age of ten. But then Albert Einstein, too, learnt to speak very late and was once refused a place at a polytechnic.)

People like this are quite obviously exceptional. Yet, says psychologist Morton Hunt, *every* human brain is special.

It is just because most of our thought processes are so ordinary that we rarely realize how remarkable, how unlike anything else in the known world, they are. When we watch a bird building a nest, we marvel at the skill and complexity of its performance. Yet we take for granted the vastly more skilled and complex mental acts we ourselves routinely perform every day, and even every waking hour.

For example, look at this sentence:
The brain is a wonderful thing.
What took place in your mind as you read it? You had to recognize the shapes of the letters, compare them with those in your memory, perceive the complete words they made up, identify the meanings of the words, and make sense of their relationship in the whole sentence. And how long did it take you? Less than a second?

Or try another example. Answer this question:
What is the best route from your house to the Post Office?
This time, you probably conjured up a picture in your mind, a sort of internal map; and then found words to express what you were viewing on your internal screen. Once again, the process was amazingly quick. How did you manage to select the correct picture so fast, from all the thousands of images stored in your head?

Just one more demonstration. Read these words:
The rear controls on this set have been factory adjusted and should need no further attention. If however your picture is moving upwards or downwards, adjust to the vertical hold control he is marked V. HOLD until the picture is correctly locked and steady position.

As soon as you begin to read this paragraph, your brain starts to work out what is happening, not just from the information contained in the words themselves but also from your mental reserves of knowledge and experience. You probably saw immediately that this was an excerpt from the instructions for some electrical equipment. After the second sentence you knew it was a television set, although nothing there says so. And you probably realized quickly that it was of foreign manufacture, because your brain instantly spotted something wrong with the English. Not a bad performance for a few seconds' work.

Hippocrates, a great Greek physician who lived centuries before Christ, wrote:

Men ought to know that from the brain and the brain only arise our pleasures, joys, laughter and jests as well as our sorrows, pains, griefs and tears... It is the same thing which makes us mad or delirious, inspires us with dread and fear, whether by night or by day, brings sleeplessness, inopportune mistakes, aimless anxieties, absent-mindedness and acts that are contrary to habit...

Nothing but...

What is the brain, and how does it work? And does the brain relate to the 'mind'? Is there such a thing as the mind, or are our thoughts, dreams and emotions simply the by-products of chemical reactions? Some scientists have thought so; psychologist B.A. Farrell announced bluntly, 'A human being is a modulator of pulse frequencies, and nothing more.' That makes us simply complex machines, relatively advanced computers. Is there anything more to human beings than this?

Earlier this century, a Russian experimenter, Ivan Pavlov, insisted that all our behaviour could be explained in terms of automatic reflexes. Pavlov proved that it was possible to 'condition' dogs to do things that they would not do naturally, to alter the pattern of their responses so that they behaved in certain predetermined ways; and he argued that the

Nobel Prize-winner Ivan Pavlov used his famous dog in experiments to demonstrate the 'conditioned reflex'. He showed that behaviour can be controlled by conditioning. But is this all there is to psychology?

same thing ought to be true of human behaviour. The machine could be tampered with.

Shortly afterwards, the influential psychologist J.B. Watson launched in America the new ideas of 'behaviourism'. This is a school of psychology which refuses to admit anything real about human consciousness. As Watson wrote:

The time has come when psychology must discard all reference to consciousness. . . its sole task is the prediction and control of behaviour; and introspection can play no part in its method.

Watson claimed that, given twelve healthy infants, he could pick any one at random and bring him up successfully to become 'any type of specialist I may select'. Human personality was unimportant; anybody could be conditioned into anything.

Are the behaviourists right? Today a growing amount of evidence suggests that they have got it wrong. For one thing, it makes the study of psychology very narrow and restricted; behaviourists are cut off, by their principles, from examining the kinds of experience which people find most interesting: dreams, moods, hallucinations, fears, desires. These mental events are the ones which we experience most acutely, and seem most real to us as individuals. Suddenly to declare them all insubstantial is to box oneself in to a very unnatural universe indeed.

And when behaviourist therapies were tried out on human beings, in an attempt to change their 'conditioning', they failed to work very well. Behavioural sex therapies and marriage therapies have to be combined with other approaches if they are to achieve lasting results. 'Aversive' therapies, which attempt to destroy alcoholism, gluttony or homosexual behaviour, tend to work for a while and then wear off. And the reason is not hard to work out: dogs or rats do not know that an electric shock is being deliberately given to them for a purpose; but human beings do. And they know that after the treatment they can go back to their former ways without fear that any further unpleasant shocks will be administered.

Even simpler animals than ourselves refused to behave in a 'behaviourist' way. Rats, for instance, were supposed (according to the theory) to learn a certain route through a maze towards food, and then for ever afterwards to choose that route automatically in order to arrive at the desired reward. They would memorize their way through the maze by learning a pattern of muscle movements to take them round all the right corners. But rats are curious; after learning the route, they would often wander round the rest of the maze, just to see what was there, rather than streaking straight to the reward. And even when a rat had been through a maze several times before, he would still often stop at a corner, look around himself, and perhaps even take a few steps backwards before going on. Clearly he was considering various alternative paths in his mind, and choosing between them.

The 'pattern of muscle movements' theory was torpedoed when someone had the rather cruel idea of cutting off the rats' back legs, or (less drastically) turning the maze upside down. The rats still managed to get to the food, whether or not they had legs, whether or not the right turns had suddenly become left turns.

Obviously, brains work in a rather more complicated fashion than the stimulus-and-response way envisaged by behaviourists. One problem is memory. The behaviourist theory stated that a series of trials and reinforcements would build up a conditioned response in us; in other words, the harder we worked at memorizing something, the more likely it would be to stick in our minds.

Now some memorizing does happen in that way (I spent three years learning French irregular verbs by constant repetition!). But not all. For instance, someone told me her telephone number yesterday, and I managed to hold it in my memory for five minutes until I could write it down, but now I have no clue what it was. Yet the most inconsequential things, which I have made no attempt to learn, will remain effortlessly in my mind: the

WHY DO WE DREAM?

Everybody has dreams. If you meet people who claim they don't, they are simply mistaken. Some of us cannot remember our dreams afterwards, but everybody dreams. And if we did not, the results would be catastrophic.

We know this because scientists have discovered that sometimes, when we are asleep, our eyes dart back and forth as if they were watching some action, even though our eyelids remain closed all the time. These movements are called REMs (Rapid Eye Movements), and they signal that a dream is going on. From observing them, we know that dreams can last quite a while: only two to ten minutes in the early part of the night, but up to an hour as morning draws near. The old idea that dreams last only a split second has no basis in fact.

What happens if we are not allowed to dream? Scientists explored this by monitoring people for evidence of REMs—then waking them up as soon as the REMs began. Before long, these hapless subjects

were suffering hallucinations and daydreams. It became obvious that prolonging the experiment would put their mental health at risk. Now it has been calculated that the longest any human being can survive without REM sleep is about ten days. After that, mental breakdown is inevitable.

In the 1920s in America there was a craze for 'dance marathons'. This cruel type of contest (outlawed in 1933) offered cash prizes to the couple who could dance the longest—after everyone else had literally dropped down with exhaustion. The effort of staying awake for long periods led to all sorts of problems, and one young man fell down dead in 1932 after forty-eight days of dancing. Obviously, not much REM sleep was possible under these conditions, and contestants often suffered mentally. A similar victim was New York disc jockey Peter Tripp, who kept himself awake for eight days in aid of charity. Sitting in the window of a Times Square store, he went visibly to pieces before the end of

the week, and suffered a three-month depression as a result.

Why is dreaming so vital to our health? Sigmund Freud, the father of psychoanalysis, was the first person to suggest a convincing answer. He believed that in the depths of our subconscious lie buried thoughts, wishes and emotions which are so unacceptable to our conscious minds that we never let them rise to the level of consciousness. But they must find expression somehow. And so a dream is 'a disguised fulfilment of repressed wishes'.

Experiences of the previous day form the starting-point of a dream, Freud taught, and these trigger off the 'latent dream thoughts' which cry out for expression. Because these thoughts are so unacceptable to us, we dress them up in symbols and pictures—a process called the 'dreamwork'—and the true meaning of the dream becomes distorted into the strange jumble of fantasies which we remember when we wake up. But a skilled

psychoanalyst can undo the 'dream-work' and give us a clue about what we have in our minds that triggers off a certain dream.

Freud's theories have undoubtedly helped us understand much better what goes on when we dream. It is a curious fact, though, that many of the symbols, ideas and situations which crop up in dreams are the same from person to person. And so other psychologists—notably Carl Gustav Jung—have suggested another explanation. The imagery of dreams may be related to ancient myths and symbols which control the human imagination—Jung called this the 'collective unconscious'. This provides us with a ready-made way of evoking the thoughts and wishes we want to express. Probably both ideas are partly true.

registration number of an old Bedford van my parents owned thirty years ago; the details of my seventh birthday party; the stray fact that since 1904 forty-nine dead mice have been found in unopened bottles of Coca Cola; and so on. Behaviourism has no explanation for this.

In his book *Battle for the Mind*, psychiatrist William Sergeant tried to show that religious conversion was based on behaviourist principles: when the correct stimulus is presented to our brain, we give the appropriate response and become 'converted'. Sergeant drew direct parallels between the work of evangelists such as Billy Graham and Pavlov's experiments with his dogs. Yet some of the cases he examines destroy his own argument: John Wesley was not converted in the heat of great excitement (which is how Sergeant says it should have happened), but in a quiet, unemotional Bible reading. The apostle Paul became a Christian despite having strong beliefs that should have 'inoculated' him against conversion.

It is not so much that behaviourism is wrong. Some of its tenets are true: we *do* sometimes learn things by mechanical stimulus -response means, especially when we are young (or mentally retarded); but there are other, more complex ways of learning, choosing and thinking. Behaviourism is incomplete; it describes a tiny part of the experience of being human.

And that is just as well. Brain researcher Steven Rose writes of the danger of so concentrating on what he calls 'lower-order', purely chemical explanations of behaviour, and ignoring 'higher-order' explanations such as our social experience. 'From here to social control by the use of chemicals and to an argument that one must change humans to fit reality rather than change reality to fit people, is but a step.'

Rose criticizes other kinds of thinkers who make the same mistake as the behaviourists—beginning their statements with the words 'Human beings are "nothing but. . ."' He calls one group 'machinomorphs'. These are the thinkers who claim that the human brain is 'nothing but' a computer, and that sooner or later we will develop computers which will be more powerful and intelligent than ourselves.

Is this a realistic idea? It has furnished the

THE POWER OF THE MIND?

The First Church of Satan may sound like something out of a Dennis Wheatley novel. But it exists, both in America and in Europe. Actually, it is less interested in worshipping Satan than in exploiting unusual sources of power. It holds 'hate rituals' in which people concentrate their minds on one person to whom they wish to do harm; and 'lust rituals' in which members focus on an individual whom one of the membership wishes to seduce. They say it works.

A group of researchers in Toronto once decided to 'invent' a ghost. Having created an imaginary historical figure and decided on the details of his life story, they tried to make contact with him by concentrating hard. 'Philip', their ghost, eventually obliged—producing strange rapping noises and making tables move. 'He' even did it for the television cameras.

In her book *The Autobiography of a Witch*, Lois Bourne tells how a coven of white witches trained her in supernatural abilities. 'They confirmed that what I felt inside me was the incipient witch power. They taught me how to release it, to utilize it and how to harness all the forces of nature which were all around me, and by the development of my mind and will, to project this power into a specific objective.'

All of these are examples of how the concentration of a human mind, or several minds together, can sometimes produce unusual effects. This is a major part of the technique of magic. Occultist Peter Underwood calls it 'the means whereby can be discovered unknown forces of nature, and the

harnessing and employment of those forces'. Spells, rituals and elaborate equipment are all aids in focusing the mind in the desired way. 'To be an effective practitioner,' claims magician Gareth Knight, 'one needs to be skilled in the techniques of visualization, to be capable of long, sustained concentration, to possess controlled psychic sensitivity, and to have that depth of intuitional understanding that comes only from long practice of meditation.'

Are the results of magic purely imaginary, or are they genuine? Sometimes it is hard to tell. Certainly many of the great magicians of the last hundred years—Eliphas Levi, Sar Peladan, S.L. MacGregor Mathers, Aleister Crowley—have been unusually vain and self-important people with a colourful and inaccurate imagination. On the other hand, successes such as the 'Philip' story take some explanation. And it is likely that poltergeists (those strange 'spirits' who sometimes move tables and chairs at night, cause objects to fly around the room, induce malfunctions in electrical apparatus, and generally cause a lot of household mischief) are not really 'spirits' at all, but have their origin in the subconscious mental processes of someone living in the affected house, who is 'having a nervous breakdown outside his own head'.

If it is true that the mind can affect physical circumstances in this way, it seems possible that fierce concentration really can produce results. There are only two problems. First, the results are not always what was hoped for. The 'Philip' researchers wanted him to

120,000 soldiers form up before Hitler at Nuremberg during the 1930s. The Nazi propaganda machine cajoled millions of people into acting against conscience.

materialize, not make rapping noises; I have known people who have concentrated on a ouija board, hoping to receive messages, who have accidentally levitated chairs instead! Second, if the Bible is correct, God has not invited us to tamper with the inner workings of the universe this way. Real power is found, not in trying to 'play God' with nature, but in allowing the real living God to inform and empower our lives.

HOW DOES BRAINWASHING WORK?

The colourful term 'brainwashing' was coined by an American journalist, Edward Hunter, to describe techniques used in China after the Communist take-over. The same phrase—*hsi nao* ('wash brain')—was used by his Chinese sources to describe the methods which led to dramatic changes of political opinions, vivid confessions of unexpected crimes and odd personality changes in people who had experienced the treatment. Since then, 'brainwashing' has been associated with all kinds of repressive governments, anti-spy agencies and extreme religious cults. But what is it? And how does it operate?

Obviously, the idea of literally washing someone's brain clean of all past memories is quite impractical. The memories that cause our key beliefs are caused, not by a single impulse, but by experiences recorded over years, and it seems unlikely that any memory which was really important to our belief system could ever be totally eradicated—except by damaging the brain physi-

cally, and even that would not achieve reliable results. But it is possible to destroy people's sense of their own individuality so completely that they gratefully accept a new identity, ready-made, from the people who have removed their former personalities.

This, says psychiatrist Joel Kovel, is what goes on in 'est training': a very expensive form of mind-conditioning course popular among career people. 'From one side, haranguing and privation are battering resistance, while from the other the group experience leads a person to dissolve his or her individuality, and its stubborn resistance, and to psychologically merge with the others in the room. . . The result for the individual is a state of openness, receptivity: and weakened discrimination. Into the gap steps the 'est' philosophy. . .'

Robert Lifton analyzed the way in which brainwashing was practised on prisoners in the hands of the Chinese. The first stage, he said, was **the assault upon identity**: the prisoner was given a number, not a name, and continually surrounded by

other prisoners exhorting him to confess. He began to become extremely disoriented, and the poor diet and sudden bursts of interrogation confused him further. The next stage was **the establishment of guilt**: all of us have guilt feelings, real or imaginary, which can be played on, and constant appeals for a confession make the prisoner start to feel he must really have done something wrong. Next comes **self-betrayal** when a confession is actually given, falsifying what the prisoner once knew to be reality; but the captors do not appear satisfied. They want more. At this point the prisoner reaches the stage of **total conflict and basic fear**, when his personality seems to be disintegrating completely, and he can no longer hold on to any sense of individuality at all. When they see that this is happening, his captors move to **leniency and opportunity**, suddenly becoming kindly and offering a new kind of hope for the future. There are five more stages after this, but they are just the mopping-up operation. The job has been done.

These principles have been adopted by some religious cults who specialize in intensive indoctrination courses in remote centres in the countryside. But the claim made by some psychologists (such as William Sergeant in his book *Battle for the Mind*), that such manipulation explains *all* conversions, is far too sweeping. Professor Donald Mackay, who has studied the subject, points out that the experience of God's forgiveness 'can be received only at the personal level by a man in full possession of all his faculties. There is no substitute for personal reconciliation in mechanical manipulation. The mass evangelist ought to know about brainwashing techniques for the same reason that a dietician ought to know about poisons—not in order to use them, but in order to avoid damaging those towards whom he has responsibility.'

plot for a thousand science-fiction stories. But will we ever have machines which rival human brains? It might not be worth our while to try to build one. For computers have far more parts than human brains (as we shall see later in this chapter). Assembling a hundred billion transistors might take rather a long time...

And there are more important differences. In a computer, the input goes through a central processor which carries out some operations on it and then reports the result. The whole process is a chain of events, in sequence, each one depending on the last in the line. If you feed in rubbish at the start, that's what emerges at the end.

By contrast, the operations of the brain are interdependent. Any one cell is in constant communication with thousands of others, and decisions are taken by a kind of 'majority vote' rather than in a blind sequence of events. And so even if we could build a computer with 100 billion mini-computers inside it, we would still have to link the mini-computers so that every one affected nearly every other one. Not a job for a Saturday afternoon.

Furthermore, thinking processes do not take place in just one part of the brain at a time. Studies of brain-damaged patients show that for normal thinking to take place, many different brain centres need to be working in harness with one another. This was confirmed by a Danish group of physiologists who injected radioisotopes into the bloodstream of volunteers in order to see how blood flowed through the brain. (The levels of radioactivity they could then detect at different points in the brain showed them where the work of the brain was being concentrated.) They concluded that the brain's thinking system involves a complex interplay of different 'sub-routines'.

All of this means that computers are much more predictable than human beings. The output can be foretold from the input (assuming the computer is working properly). But the interconnections in the brain make it virtually impossible to predict with any accuracy what conclusions it will produce. Human beings do not function like Mr Spock in *Star Trek*.

Steven Rose adds:

And this says nothing yet about the programme. In general, computers are doing one or a few specific jobs at any time, corresponding to individual

programmes fed into them. The brain, by contrast, is performing a vast number of separate tasks at any one time. As I write this my brain is not only concerned in the organization of the thoughts which will enable me to compose coherent grammatical sentences and a (hopefully!) powerful argument, and the direction of my hand, holding the pen, across the page, but also continuously monitoring random visual input, the noise of someone whistling elsewhere in the house and the pressure of the chair on my back, while my hypothalamus, limbic and reticular systems are regulating drives, homeostasis and attention...

All of this means that computers have no 'real-world knowledge' which is anything like ours in complexity. We can understand what is going on behind a conversation like this:

Boy: You doing anything tonight? *Girl:* I'm washing my hair. *Boy:* How about Thursday? There's a good film on. *Girl:* Why don't you drop dead?

We understand all sorts of things about this exchange on the basis of just a few verbal clues, because we have a lifetime of experiences in the world to draw on. A computer's experiences are artificially given to it. And the array of equipment needed for it to harbour the same amount of information as we store is absolutely unthinkable.

That is why the most clever computers still have problems with human symbols and their meanings. Asked to translate a sentence into Russian—'The spirit is willing but the flesh is weak'—one computer came up with words which meant 'The vodka is fine, but the meat is tasteless'.

Finally (although there is much more that could be said), what is the real purpose of computer operations? A computer works towards a 'known-end state': a goal defined by its

Painter Salvador Dali, athlete Carl Lewis, Nobel Prize-winning medical scientist Sir James Black — the particular abilities of individual brains can bring excellence in totally different areas.

creator. A machine can learn to improve on its own programme, but not to alter it radically. Yet human beings change their minds about the most fundamental things all the time. They are much more creative than machines could ever be—because of the intuitive, non-logical processes that spark off ideas and discoveries, and the creative work of the 'unconscious'. A computer is bound by logic. It has no 'unconscious'.

And so 'machinomorphs' are wrong to say 'Human brains are nothing but computers'. And Steven Rose goes on to attack another group of thinkers whom he calls 'chimpomorphs'. They are the people who claim, 'Human beings are "nothing but" sophisticated animals.'

There are many similarities between the brains of some animals and our own. Many scientists believe that this is because our brains were once the same as theirs, but we have now evolved further. If so, the old animal brain is still there inside us. And some popular writers have claimed that this is the ultimate key to human behaviour.

Writers such as Desmond Morris (whom we mentioned in chapter three) and Konrad Lorenz and Robert Ardrey (whom we shall meet in chapter six) make detailed parallels between aspects of human behaviour—such as sexuality, aggression and competitiveness—and the social behaviour of animals, especially apes. And so marriage is just an example of the 'pair-bonding' practised by some species; war and territorial disputes are just an echo of the instinct animals have to defend their own private space. Robert Ardrey says that we will not be able to build a just society until we accept that we are animals, with certain undeniable, built-in drives and behaviours, and stop trying to pretend that we are anything more:

When we renounce our hubris; when we see ourselves as a portion of something far older, far larger than are we; when we discover nature as our partner, not our slave, and laws applying to us as applying to us all: then we shall find our faith returning. We have rational faculties of enormous order. We have powers granted never before to living beings. But we shall free those powers to effect human solutions of justice and permanence only when we renounce our arrogance over nature and accept the philosophy of the possible.

Is this truly what we are? Would we be fooling ourselves to claim that we are free, choosing beings—because we are actually puppets manipulated by the strings of our own evolution?

If so, we are condemned to hold a pessimistic, even reactionary view of human life: change is not to be expected; nothing will get any better; human beings are treacherous animals who need to be carefully watched and forcefully controlled. But human society has in fact made staggering advances over the last 5,000 years (chapter eight details the story), and this marks it off sharply from the unchanging, static world of apes and chimps. Human society is ever changing from century to century; it is transformed by humans themselves as they think great thoughts, try out temporary fashions, make technological advances, overthrow governments. To compare this with the rigid arrangements of the animal kingdom is to oversimplify dreadfully. Human beings are different.

One reason that we are so different is that we can talk to one another. Language (as we saw earlier) is something which no other species commands, and it creates a traffic of relationships between us which is entirely unknown in any other animal society. If we didn't communicate verbally, our social life would be terribly impoverished. It is foolish to ignore the tremendous difference between the rich culture of language-users and the monochrome interactions of less fortunate species.

In fact, our brains contain only a very small remnant of what may be 'animal brain', and an outstandingly large area of 'uncommitted cortex'. We will look at what the 'cortex' is in a moment, but the phrase means that a large area of our brains—larger than in any other species —is unassigned to any particular task or function. It is available for complicated processes of thought, rather than having all of its time taken up monitoring basic bodily functions. And as a result we can control whatever 'evolutionary remnant' of instincts we still have left, by bringing into play other parts of the brain which liberate us from having to follow the drives of our primitive instincts.

Mapping the brain

What is our brain, and how does it work? Even the first anatomists who took apart human brains realized quickly that to talk of 'the brain' is slightly inaccurate. There are several components in there—in fact, four separate brains, each with its own function.

As we travel up the human body from the neck to the top of the head, we find that the brain starts at the top of the spinal cord, with a couple of swellings known as the 'old brain'. At the back of these swellings is a wrinkled structure the size of a fist, the 'little brain' or 'cerebellum'. Further up, as the brain stem broadens out into the skull cavity, it blends into a number of odd-shaped structures which are linked to it by smaller stems; these structures make up the 'mid-brain'. Finally, wrapped over the whole structure is a crumpled sheet of tissue between three and four millimetres thick, called the 'cortex' or 'roof brain'. It is crumpled because of our level of intelligence; the rabbit's cortex fits quite smoothly into its skull, but ours is a tight fit. Strangely, the same wrinkles appear in almost exactly the same places in different human brains. And although the cortex is divided in the middle, producing two hemispheres, each side is virtually a mirror

image of the other.

The 'old brain' is in charge of our automatic systems (heart-beat, respiration and the like). The central nervous system is organized from here, too, and it is the 'old brain' which gives the warning to the cortex when there is cause for alarm or attention. The cerebellum controls fine muscular movements and careful co-ordination; a snooker player's reputation depends heavily on the quality of his cerebellum. And it is the cerebellum which enables us to perform complicated tasks 'without thinking': driving a car, shooting a pistol, playing jazz chords on a guitar. At first, the effort of learning means that our cortex has to be involved. But as soon as a skill becomes 'second nature', the cerebellum takes charge.

These two brains are obviously important and basic, but it is the other two that are responsible for our conscious thought processes. The mid-brain is the centre of our emotional life, the cortex the analyzing and clarifying counterpart to it. A living animal without a cortex will still move around, see dimly, accept food and shun pain. But its sensations will be vague and imprecise: the mid-brain is collecting the necessary information, but the cortex is not there to explain it all.

The mid-brain is impulsive and impatient, prompting us to act suddenly and emotionally. The cortex tells us to wait, and calculates what the results of our actions will be. When we are in the grip of powerful emotions—fear, amazement, ecstasy—we often find it difficult to think clearly; and this is because the mid-brain is taking charge, refusing for a while to allow the cortex to tell us anything.

The cortex is made up of two kinds of substance. On the surface is a layer of 'grey matter' (actually white with a tinge of yellow), and underneath it is 'white matter' (which in fact looks pink). The 'grey matter' contains billions of minute specks with thin hairs sprouting from them. Each of these specks is a 'neuron' or nerve cell. There are about thirty-five thousand cells for each square millimetre of surface, and the whole brain contains something like a hundred thousand million of them. (Gordon Rattray Taylor observes, 'If your brain cells were people, they would populate twenty-five planets like the earth.')

Staggering enough. But it is the tiny hairs

that really explain the brain's complexity. They are called 'dendrites', and they ensure that each neuron is in contact with about six hundred other neurons. The inter-relationships are impossibly intricate: trillions of pathways constantly exchanging information. No wonder we can perform some functions with different parts of our brains, so that if one area is damaged, another will take over cheerfully and perform the same tasks; no wonder it doesn't matter that ageing people are said to lose 100,000 brain cells each day (they can spare them); no wonder we can recall information from memory much faster than any computer system could locate it.

The dendrites receive incoming signals, but outgoing messages travel from cell to dendrite via the 'axons'—long threads running from the neuron (in some cases for several feet), acting as channels along which electrical impulses can be sent to contact the dendrites of other cells.

The axons make up the white matter in an intricate interlacing network. They do not connect directly with the dendrites which receive their messages: at the end of the axon there is a tiny space called the 'synaptic gap', and when an electrical impulse is sent down the axon, it fires into the gap a volley of molecules (of norepinephrine, dopamine, or some other appropriate chemical). The molecules jump the gap, and try to influence the behaviour of a second neuron—either to persuade it to fire, or to deter it from doing so. But because similar messages will have arrived at exactly the same moment from hundreds of other neurons, our molecules will have only one vote among hundreds.

All of this is happening as you read these words, in billions of neurons in your brain simultaneously, and at a rate of several hundred cycles per second. Enough to make a computer manufacturer give up in despair.

If you were to stretch out the axons of your brain in a single straight line (which is not recommended), they would stretch three times as far as to the moon and back. Such is the length of inner cabling which you carry around in your head, and it is the secret of the power and flexibility of the human brain.

Sometimes it is suggested that, because we now know a lot about how the brain works, we should be able to find surgical techniques that

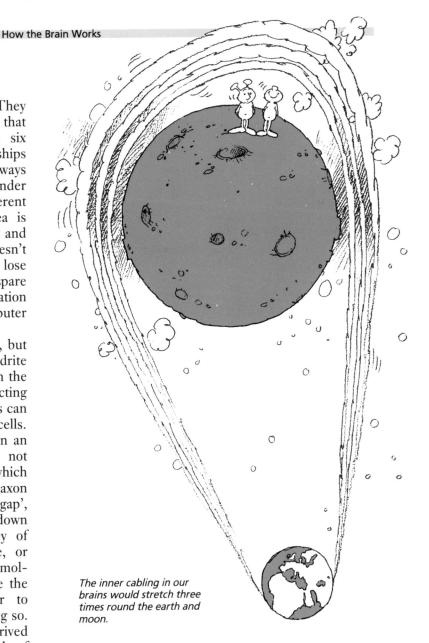

The inner cabling in our brains would stretch three times round the earth and moon.

will control human impulses, cure depression, remove a tendency to evil. But because of the complexity of the brain, things are not so simple. Psychosurgery certainly can achieve some results. But, as we have seen, particular jobs can be distributed in different parts of the brain: it isn't the case that one area produces aggression, another fear, another violence, and so on. It is not sufficient to find the offending bit of tissue and pull it out.

Furthermore, there exists a sophisticated relationship between the brain and the world it lives in—a continuous, lifelong inflow of information and stimuli. So we cannot say that the origin of our impulses is purely within our heads. Our personalities are not dictated simply and entirely by our brain chemistry; the social factors which come into play when we contact the outside world also have an impact on our make-up. And if so, removing part of the brain of a criminal may not be addressing the real problem—the social circumstances which made him act as he did.

Unique and unrepeatable

It is just as well that our brains have this inbuilt unpredictability, since otherwise it might not be too difficult for an unscrupulous dictator with his team of neurosurgeons to dream of controlling his own world of mentally-doctored robots. But we are not so easily manipulated.

Nor are humans easy to duplicate. There has been a lot of talk about 'cloning': scientifically producing a replica of a human being by implanting the nucleus of one of his body cells in an unfertilized female egg. We could then, so it is said, produce hundreds of identical copies of Einstein, or Picasso, or Beethoven. There is no reason why such a technique should not one day be perfected. But would the replica really be a replica?

One writer has written: 'To produce another Mozart, we would need not only Wolfgang's genome but mother Mozart's uterus, father Mozart's music lessons, their friends and his, the state of music in eighteenth-century Austria, Haydn's patronage, and on and on, in ever-widening circles.' There can be no question that without Mozart's set of genes there would have been no Mozart. But, on the other hand, we have no right to assume the converse, that his genotype cultivated in another world at another time would have produced an equally creative musical genius. Cloning provides only part of a human being, and that quite drastically limits its alleged effectiveness.

Human beings are unique. The individual brain gives its owner a personal encounter with the world which cannot be copied by anyone else.

Nor can we make confident predictions about how someone else's thinking processes will work. Professor Keith Ward has remarked that the physicist Laplace (who taught that 'everything in the universe is completely predictable') could not in fact have predicted the very theory he came up with. And nor could anyone else:

Let us. . . pretend that we could predict the position and properties of all the quarks in Laplace's brain. Would we then know what he was thinking? We would obviously not—unless we knew a law stating that a certain state of his brain always correlates with, or causes the thought that, 'everything in the universe is completely predictable'. But how could we ever get such a law? We could not just magically intuit it out of the blue. We would have to get it, like all other laws of physics, from observation. But the plain fact is that we could never have observed the thought 'everything in the universe is completely predictable'. Because, until Laplace thought it, it had never occurred before, in the whole history of the universe.

Could Mozarts be mass-produced on a production line?

There is no getting away from it. There is a freedom and unpredictability about the brain and its thoughts which is of vital importance for human life. It means that we are not merely automata, driven by inexorable laws of brain chemistry. Words like choice, dignity, responsibility, still have a meaning.

Some thinkers have suggested that, if we adjusted our use of our brains, we would become better human beings, and solve all our problems. Arthur Koestler, for example, felt that we ought to limit the use of the cold, inhuman cortex, and let the warm, emotional, intuitive mid-brain have more say. Robert Ornstein believes that the two hemispheres of the cortex have different functions, and that we are not developing sufficiently the mystical abilities of the 'right brain'. And 'New Age' thinkers such as Nona Coxhead and Marilyn Ferguson argue that a transformation of our consciousness—through meditation, biofeedback, or other mental therapies—will expand our consciousness and produce a better world.

But these patent remedies are all implausible. Koestler fails to realize that it is the impulsive wilfulness of the mid-brain that causes problems for human beings, and that the cortex is actually what holds us back from being too aggressive and selfish. Ornstein's theory is a long way from proven; when a human being has one hemisphere removed under brain surgery, it does not seem to change the intellectual style in any marked way. And as far as a 'transformation of consciousness' is concerned, Steven Rose comments, 'Over the last three hundred years the most effective utilization of the human brain has been brought about by. . . the application of precisely those rational techniques of inquiry and observation concerning the universe which the "mystic experience" relegates to a secondary or inferior place'. Would a consciousness transformation take us forward—or backwards?

The problem with the human being is not the way the brain is used. There are no miracle cures for evil, depravity and violence to be found by tinkering with the circuitry. Human beings are free, responsible individuals, and if their lives fail to match up to the highest moral level, it isn't because of anything wrong in their internal wiring. The problem is of a different order.

And that's a subject for another chapter.

5

HOW MUCH MORE DON'T WE KNOW?

Uri Geller became famous in the 1970s as 'the spoon-bending man'. Was it genuine, or was it a trick?

Satya Sai Baba is a small, chubby Indian with a permanent beam and a shock of dark curly hair. He does not look at all extraordinary. Yet he claims to be able to produce objects from thin air—coins, crucifixes, flowers, even a mysterious 'holy ash' which is reputed to cure diseases when eaten. He is the most famous miracle-worker in India.

Rose Gladden is a mild-looking English lady from Hertfordshire. But her claims are extraordinary. She works as a healer, laying hands on sufferers and channelling energy by concentrating her mind to combat 'imbalances' and 'blockages' in the patient's body. (And not just the physical body, either. She claims to be able to see other dimensions of our existence in the shape of shadowy 'auras' surrounding the body, and to work on those.) 'We have dealt with most things over the years,' she remarks, 'arthritis, cancer, bad backs, epilepsy, multiple sclerosis, you name it and we've probably seen it.' There is no shortage of people who will testify that Rose Gladden has made them better.

Uri Geller rose to fame in the early 1970s as the man who could stop clocks and bend forks simply by using the strange powers of his mind. He is also reputed to have stopped a cable car in mid-journey, to have scored incredible results in dice-throwing ESP experiments, to have copied correctly drawings made by someone else out of sight. He was tested by American scientists at Stanford Research Institute, and the resulting report convinced many people that Geller was no trickster.

What is the explanation for stories like these? Is there a whole range of undiscovered abilities waiting to be discovered within each of us? Do human beings have unexplored powers which go far beyond what we normally expect to achieve?

Unusual people like Sai Baba, Rose Gladden and Uri Geller have appeared in every age of history. And often more ordinary people have done or experienced surprising things. Mothers with no great physical strength have succeeded in lifting cars so that children who have been run over could be freed from underneath; in the panic and anguish of the moment, it has not occurred to them that they are attempting the impossible. The most unlikely people have seen ghosts and apparitions. Are there things we still have to discover about ourselves?

Researching the paranormal

It was to explore this question that a group of scholars and scientists formed the Society for Physical Research. The SPR, which began in England in 1882, had among its founders some of the most eminent minds of the day, and included sceptics as well as those who were convinced that there really was something special to explore.

At first the quest seemed quite promising. Some impressive results were obtained from mediums and psychics who were tested. But a number of hopeful results turned out to be fraudulent, or at least dubious; and in the end public interest declined. The First World War was the turning point. 'By the time peace returned,' observes Brian Inglis, 'all prospect of psychical research establishing itself as an academic discipline had vanished.'

That was to remain true until 1927, when modern parapsychological research began in earnest at Duke University in North Carolina. J.B. Rhine, a member of the psychology faculty, had already been involved in some testing of strange abilities, and knew how easy it was to be fooled. So he tried to set up a rigorously scientific style of experimenting, based on three principles:

- The people tested must not be famous professional psychics, who might be adept at cheating, but unknown volunteers, often students;
- Test procedures should be simple and easily controlled (no darkened rooms or complicated methods);
- Results should be evaluated statistically by the most exacting standards possible.

J.B. Rhine, experimenter into the paranormal, works with a subject at Duke University.

Despite these high aims, Rhine's first experiments were still open to many criticisms. But he refined his methods and continued to work with dogged integrity. His obvious honesty and his determination to get to the bottom of the problems started to capture the imagination of other young researchers, and gradually 'parapsychology'—the study of unknown powers in the human mind—became a serious field of study. (Yet still it was not until 1969 that the Parapsychological Association was admitted to the American Association for the Advancement of Science—the ultimate recognition that a scientific discipline really *is* science.)

In the first years of Rhine's research, he found some exceptional subjects who produced quite amazing results. But in time they left university, or tired of being tested, or else seemed somehow to lose their abilities; and it proved quite difficult to find others who could produce the same effects. Interest in the subject waned again, until by 1960 less and less work was being done.

Then, suddenly, a new wave of 'star performers' brought the subject back to popular attention: people such as Ted Serios, who claimed to produce photographs by staring into a camera lens; Nina Kulagina, who was said to move objects from one side of a tray to the other by the power of thought; Uri Geller and

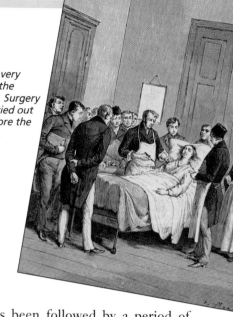

Hypnosis became a very popular pastime in the nineteenth century. Surgery was sometimes carried out under hypnosis before the days of anaesthetic.

Matthew Manning, whose strange energies interfered with electrical and mechanical equipment in dramatic ways. Television programmes and books fuelled popular interest, and an increasing number of colleges began to offer courses in parapsychology.

Much of this went outside the narrow field of interest to which Rhine's three principles had committed him. He had tested to find evidence of two abilities: 'ESP' (extra-sensory perception, the ability in a human being to perceive things which the normal senses could not perceive); and 'PK' (psychokinesis, the paranormal ability to affect the position and movement of objects). These terms were invented by Rhine, but parapsychologists now tend to use just one convenient word ('psi') to cover the field. 'Psi' simply stands for 'the unknown factor in psychic experiences'.

Today, parapsychology is regarded cautiously as a serious discipline by an increasing number of scientists, although many of them are reluctant to admit that anything definite has yet been proved. There are enthusiasts too; and there is a large, stubborn group of scientists (such as the members of the Committee for Scientific Investigation of Claims of the Paranormal) which resolutely refuses to believe there is anything real there at all.

And so the history of paranormal research has had three phases—the SPR period, the Rhine period, and the post-1960 period—each of which has had a curiously similar shape. At first there has been great excitement as a new crop of 'stars' have demonstrated unusual talents; this has been followed by a period of readjustment, in which testing has become more rigorous; then has come a tailing-off of results and a loss of interest. Supporters of 'psi' would say that this demonstrates what an elusive, unpredictable subject it is, and how much work we still need to do to be able to interpret what is going on. Opponents would argue that most of the impressive results were probably exaggerated or faked; especially since they seem to disappear when control procedures are tightened up. Who is right?

There are certainly good reasons for scepticism. In a Lloyd Roberts Lecture to the Royal College of Physicians in 1985, Professor Lewis Wolpert said:

I am frankly hostile to the paranormal, partly because it deals with such apparently trivial phenomena, but mainly because it is antiscience in that it stops serious thinking about the world. One of my objections to pseudo-science and the paranormal is that it is a way of getting knowledge on the cheap. Whereas conventional scientific knowledge is obtained in a very tedious and painstaking way, with breakthroughs and flashes of insight being rare events, it is characteristic of the paranormal that major knowledge is as easily obtained without any special knowledge.

An early exponent of hypnosis gives a demonstration to scientific journalists.

Perhaps this is not fair to the painstaking work of J.B. Rhine, but it is a valid criticism of many of the inflated claims made for 'star' performers. And it is noticeable that would-be psychics are much keener to be tested by scientists (who may know a lot about their own field, but are no experts in trickery) than by conjurors and professional illusionists. One sceptical magician is James Randi, who has promised to give $10,000 to anyone who can demonstrate genuine paranormal abilities to his satisfaction. In over twenty years he has had applications from people who have turned out to be charlatans, or self-deluded; but no one who has come near to winning the money.

George du Maurier's creation Svengali, in his 1894 novel 'Trilby', picked up on public fascination with hypnotic power over others.

It has to be admitted on the other side that psychics may have good reason not to trust illusionists too far. Within the history of theatrical magic there has been a long tradition of hostility to psychic claims, and both fair means and foul have been employed to discredit the psychics. When Houdini, the escapologist, tested psychic
he triumphantly produced blatant evidence of her cheating. Sadly, Houdini seems to have 'planted' the evidence himself.

And so one of the biggest problems with this subject is in knowing whom to trust. There have been eminent fakes. None was more notorious, or shattering, than Walter J. Levy Jr., who directed Rhine's own laboratory and was Rhine's intended successor. In 1974 he was found tampering with equipment to produce improved results. He had to resign, and years of completed work came under suspicion.

Rhine's greatest British contemporary was Professor S.G. Soal, who achieved some exciting results in the early forties with a photographer called Basil Shackleton. But when subjected to statistical analysis his records clearly seemed to have been tampered with. And a young assistant of Soal's confessed that she had caught him altering figures.

This does not mean that parapsychologists are necessarily more crooked than other kinds of scientist. It seems that some of the greatest names in science—Ptolemy, Galileo, Newton, Dalton, Mendel—may well have 'improved' some of their results. It is an easy temptation to fall into when you want to believe.

And, of course, such an attitude of mind also makes it easy for others to fool you. In 1979 two teenagers approached the new para-psychology laboratory at Washington University and offered to be tested. Their ability to bend metal, cause objects to move across surfaces, and affect articles which had been sealed into jars, impressed the researchers for three years. The laboratory director announced that 'these two kids are the most reliable of the people that we've studied'. However, in 1983 the two held a press conference and revealed that the whole thing had been a stunt.

Experimenters and their subjects

The most important problem psi investigators face is that there has never been a psychic experiment which could be demonstrated re-

Many stage performances have used the phenomenon of 'psi', as when Kuda Bux purported to read an unfamiliar newspaper while blindfolded.

peatedly. We know that something is scientifically established when it works in the same way, time after time, in a cause-and-effect manner. With the paranormal, this is just not so. A psychic may manifest great abilities on Monday, Tuesday and Wednesday—then lose them all, bafflingly, on Thursday. These strange abilities cannot be produced to order.

This is why people who try to make a living from their super-powers frequently end up looking ridiculous. Jeane Dixon, an American clairvoyant, may well have predicted the assassination of President Kennedy—but before that she had predicted that he would not be elected. The night before Jacqueline Kennedy married Aristotle Onassis, Jeane was confidently claiming that Mrs Kennedy 'had no thoughts of marriage'. Those who keep score of Jeane Dixon's utterances claim that throughout the seventies her record of accuracy slipped to abysmally low levels.

Sometimes it may be that a psychic will begin with something which is a genuine gift, and then, because it cannot be produced on demand, start cheating just to save face. Perhaps that is what happened to medium Arthur Ford, who by the end of his career was keeping extensive files on major figures in American public life—so that he could 'super-

DO THE STARS INFLUENCE OUR DESTINY?

In 1939 a Swiss mathematician wrote to the German Intelligence Service, explaining that he was a student of 'astro-biology', and had determined from the stars that Adolf Hitler's life would be in danger between 7 and 10 November. The letter was dismissed as the work of a crank. That is, until Hitler narrowly escaped death from a bomb on 8 November.

Suddenly the Swiss mathematician found himself very sought after indeed! And once the Nazi hierarchy had satisfied themselves that he had nothing to do with the bomb conspiracy, he became an unofficial prophet for the Nazi leaders.

It was a demonstration of one of the most pervasive beliefs human beings have ever had: that what

happens in the skies has some influence on human life. Astrology, the supposed science which studies this influence, has been with us for many centuries— arguably, claims Colin Wilson, for 100,000 years. And, he says, 'The labours of many serious investigators make it clear that it can no longer be dismissed as merely a manifestation of human gullibility.'

Certainly astrology is popular enough today. Most newspapers print horoscopes; the Faculty of Astrological Studies in London has no shortage of applicants for its diploma course; successful astrologers can become very wealthy people. But does it work?

R.B. Culver and P.A. Ianna spent several years collecting predictions from astrological

magazines, well-known astrologers, and other similar sources. In the end they amassed 3,011, of which only 338 came true. One correct guess in ten is not impressive—especially since some of the correct guesses could have been caused by shrewd guesswork, vague wording, or 'inside' information. It suggests that people tend to believe in astrology because one occasional correct answer makes a much more striking impression than eight or nine that didn't work out.

The astronomical basis for astrology is quite spurious. The idea that the sun spends a roughly equal length of

time in each 'house' of the Zodiac is just not true. Because of a phenomenon known as the 'precession of the equinoxes', the skies no longer look as they did when the dates were first worked out; and so if an astrologer tells you that your birth sign is Gemini or Scorpio or Libra, you may really be the next one along. And there is a thirteenth constellation (Ophiucus) which isn't taken into account by astrologers, since it was too faint to see with the naked eye when the original twelve were first discussed.

And yet it is true that many natural events do have an influence of some kind

naturally' produce information about them when required.

So the obstinate fact remains: repeatable evidence of the paranormal is extremely hard to find. John Beloff, once President of the Parapsychological Association and a researcher noted for his painstaking honesty, has commented, 'No experiment showing the clear existence of the paranormal has been consistently repeated by other investigators in other laboratories.'

So must we conclude that psi does not exist at all? Not necessarily. Even if we have no rock-solid evidence, there are enough partial indications to make it likely that *something* genuinely exists. Philosopher Antony Flew confessed his puzzlement after twenty-two years of looking for confirmation: 'There is still no reliably repeatable phenomenon, no particular solid-rock positive cases. Yet there still is

clearly too much there for us to dismiss the whole business.'

And perhaps there may be good reasons why evidence for psi is so unpredictable and elusive. An American psychologist, Professor Gardner Murphy, has pointed out how physicists have come to realize that we cannot understand the workings of things simply by looking at their constituent parts. Studying the behaviour of the individual particles in a field of energy does not necessarily tell us how the whole would behave: the whole is more than the sum of its parts. Perhaps we do not understand psi because we are studying individual human beings. Perhaps it has more to do with the relationships between human beings—and their minds—than with the single human considered alone. We may be talking about a 'psychic field' which links minds together, and in which—under unexpectedly favourable conditions—events may take place which are more than we would expect from studying the individual components who make up the field.

This is just one of many possible theories, and its development is hampered by the fact that no direct evidence supports it whatsoever. But it does show the possibility of conceiving plausible explanations for psi as a genuine phenomenon, yet one that behaves in strange ways.

Personally I am not convinced we will ever know for sure whether or not psi is real. There are just too many complicating factors which get in the way of research. One of these is the so-called 'sheep-goat effect'. This was first observed by a researcher called Gertrude Schmeidler. She carried out card-guessing tests on volunteers over a period of six years, and asked her subjects before testing them

on human life. It has been suggested that human blood is influenced by sunspot activity; that the human nervous system is affected by the earth's own magnetic field; that heart attacks and strokes are more likely at times of sunspot activity. So might there be influences from the planets—nearer to us than the sun—which affect human beings and help to make us the people we are?

Michel Gauquelin, a French psychologist and statistician, has produced some very carefully researched data which may well show that this is true. Those who excel in certain professions seem more likely to be born while certain planets are in clearly identified positions. Perhaps the personality trait that makes people rise to the top in athletics, for example, or military life, could have something to do with the precise moment of our birth?

It is too early to say. And Gauquelin emphasizes that this effect is one of character, not destiny. He has also studied athletes and soldiers whose careers were cut tragically short, and has found the same planetary positions for them; so the planets do not forecast our future. But they might just have a tiny part to play in determining the things we are good at in life.

whether they believed it was possible that they would demonstrate ESP in the test. If they said no, she classified them as 'goats'; if they thought ESP was possible, or if they were unsure, they were 'sheep'. The interesting thing was that 'sheep' scored consistently more correct guesses than they should have managed, simply by chance; and 'goats' scored many fewer. It was as if the beliefs of the subjects were affecting the phenomenon that was being tested. For the 'goats' were not simply scoring at a chance level; their score was well *under* what it should have been, as if something in their subconscious was deliberately guessing wrong!

As if this were not complicated enough, it was noticed that the doubters among the sheep (who were unsure whether or not it would work) scored better, not worse, than the totally convinced believers. Were the believers subconsciously trying too hard? There is no way of telling; all we can say is that if people's expectations can start fiddling with the results, it is going to be very hard to conduct valid tests.

Another problem for researchers is the 'experimenter effect'. It is well known that some researchers—especially those with a sympathetic attitude towards the possibility of psi—get consistently better results than others. Is this because they are cheating? Not necessarily; it could be that the attitude of the researcher as well as of the research-subject can affect the results of the experiment. If so, no wonder successful experiments tend to be unrepeatable; another researcher, with a slightly different attitude, could ruin the delicate balance necessary for success.

There are also other problems with the subjects who are tested. Some (as we have seen) will perform brilliantly for a while, and then their powers will seem to wane. They may guess correctly, time after time, which card is going to be turned up from the pack in the researcher's hand; and then twenty-four hours later get it all wrong. There is no ready explanation why powers vanish in this way. But it happens, and so another unpredictable element enters the situation. If I test a psychic who shows great abilities, say, in moving matches round a tray by the power of thought, and then hand her on to a colleague; and then

WHAT ARE BIORHYTHMS AND BIOFEEDBACK?

As the cells of our brain send out information to different parts of the body, by electrochemical impulses, they create wave patterns. Scientists have fitted electrodes to the scalps of volunteers and worked out what kinds of brain waves occur. Basically there are four types: alpha, which are produced when we are awake, but in a peaceful, relaxed frame of mind; beta, which occur at times of concentration and thought, and in normal daily alertness; theta, which are associated with the earliest stages of sleep, hallucination and creativity; and delta, characteristic during deep sleep.

In the late 1950s, an American psychophysiologist, Dr Joseph Kamiya, became fascinated with brain waves. He wondered whether people could be taught to discern their own brain rhythms, to sense what kind of waves they were producing at any given moment. And so he fitted electrodes to the scalps of some experimental subjects, monitored their brains, and asked them to guess at certain moments whether they were producing alpha waves or not.

At first guesses would be purely random. After an hour, the volunteer would be correct up to 60 per cent of the time. Two hours later, some people would be 80 per cent correct, and in the end a few volunteers would achieve 100 per cent results.

The next step was obvious. Could people be taught, not just to guess correctly, but to produce alpha waves on demand? Kamiya tested for this and, yes, it worked. Once people had learned to *recognize* their alpha waves, they could also *make them happen*.

When news of this dis-

all of a sudden the psychic can do nothing— what has happened? Have her powers somehow waned? Or is it the experimenter effect? Or have I just been easy to fool, while my colleague is more shrewd?

Then there are people who genuinely believe they have exceptional powers, when in fact they are fooling themselves. Randi comments that most of the applicants for his $10,000 fall into this category:

In the great majority of these cases, the persons involved have been convinced of their error, and

covery filtered out into the mass media, there was a great deal of excitement. Enterprising firms started to market devices to enable people at home to do their own 'alpha-training', and a variety of 'pop alpha' groups sprang up to offer new improved ways of producing alpha waves. It was claimed that the more alpha we can produce, the more we develop the powers of the psyche. Alpha waves were touted as the key to Eastern mysticism, as well as a revolutionary means to better health, prosperity, peace of

mind, better sleep, control of pain, and weight mastery.

Most of this is unproven and exaggerated, but 'biofeedback' has emerged from it all as a useful set of medical techniques. Bio-feedback is the process of giving people 'feedback' about processes in their bodies of which they are not normally aware—brainwave activity, muscle tension and heart rate, in particular—and then getting them to use that information to begin con-trolling the processes. In effect, this is a means of changing consciousness, since the mind and body are so intimately linked. To quote biofeedback pioneer Dr Elmer Green, 'Every change in the physiological state is accompanied by an appro-priate change in the mental-emotional state.'

Biofeedback certainly has a value in the treatment of hypertension, migraine, asthma and anxiety sym-ptoms; it can help to retrain the muscles after serious injury. But how much more it enables us to do is still an open question. Research continues.

Biorhythms are not to be confused with biofeedback. They are supposedly rhythmic periods through which we all pass regularly. Dr Wilhelm

Fliess, one of the pioneers, claimed that our bodies have a 'physical rhythm', a twenty-three-day cycle which determines how much strength, energy and physical confidence we will possess at any given time; and a 'sensitivity rhythm' a twenty-eight-day cycle which affects our creativity, mental co-ordination, and feelings of affection. It is also claimed that there is a thirty-three-day 'intellectual cycle' which controls our ability to think clearly and memorize.

Biorhythms had a brief phase of popularity in the early 1970s, but are now thought unproven and unlikely. 'In properly conducted studies,' says psychologist Hans Eysenck, '. . .none of the evidence supports the theory of biorhythms.'

'Watch me or I'll cheat; John King makes me cheat.' John King was the name she gave to the 'spirit' who directed her powers.

have retired gracefully. A good example is a lady in Italy who had produced hundreds of supposedly 'spiritual' photos with a Polaroid camera. She demonstrated for me via RAI-TV in Rome that she was simply not able to use the camera properly. . . test prints were sent to the Polaroid Corporation in the USA for their opinion, which agreed in every respect. These were problems that the company was familiar with, and which crossed desks there every day.

This particular case was easy to sort out. But what about those where the subject uncon-sciously cheats, while believing that genuine phenomena are being produced? The medium Eusapia Palladino used to warn researchers,

Is psi real?

All these factors mean that it can be genuinely impossible to tell what is really going on when someone claims a paranormal event has occurred. People who have strange experiences may be overwhelmed by them, and absolutely convinced that they are genuine; others may have different interpretations. For example, many hundreds of people have reported that, while they were undergoing major surgery, they 'died' for a few minutes and had the experience of tasting the afterlife. Typically, they report looking down on the operating room, and their own inert bodies, from a point near the ceiling; then they are drawn down a long, dark tunnel, and emerge at the other end into a place where they recognize figures whom they know to have died some time before. They receive interrogation from a 'being of light' who makes them re-evaluate their past life. Often people looking back on such an experience believe very strongly that they have crossed the barrier that separates this world from the next. But many scientists feel that they could simply be re-living the trauma of their own birth, in a confused way.

The interpretation is everything. Susan Blackmore was a student at Oxford when, under the influence of drugs, she had an 'out-of-the-body experience'—a sensation of leaving her physical body behind and travelling outside the room and building she was in. Now, after ten years' study of such experiences, she has come to believe that 'nothing leaves the body... Everything is seen from the person's own imagination.' The whole experience 'may be a process of exploring the contents of your own memory and imagination, brought to life by a new way of thinking in a special state of

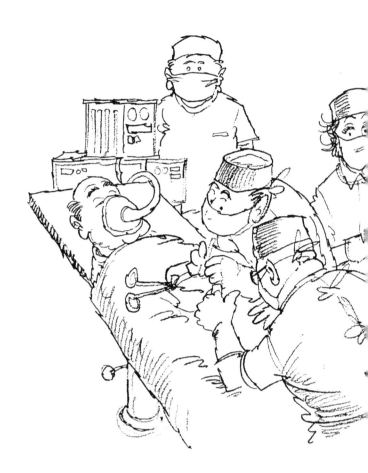

ARE THERE VAMPIRES AND WEREWOLVES?

Ever since Bram Stoker wrote his famous novel *Dracula* in 1897, people have been familiar with the idea of vampires. A creature that casts no shadow or reflection, with hypnotic powers and superhuman strength, rising from its grave each night to suck the blood of its victims with its pointed canine fangs. . . Surely nothing like this ever really happens? Wasn't it just a work of fiction?

Stoker's novel was certainly fiction. The real Dracula—a bloodthirsty tyrant known as Vlad the Impaler—was no vampire. But the tales about vampires come from many different cultures as far apart as China, Persia and Eastern Europe. And in the mid-eighteenth century there was an epidemic of vampire cases throughout Europe, which caused even the level-headed Jean-Jacques Rousseau to write, 'If ever there was in the world a warranted and proven history, it is that of vampires; nothing is lacking, official reports, testimonials of persons of standing, of surgeons, of clergymen, of judges; the judicial evidence is all-embracing.' Dom Augustine Calmet, a Benedictine scholar of repute who studied the cases, remarked, 'It seems

Some people who have been resuscitated after heart failure report that they became detached from themselves and looked down on their own bodies.

consciousness'. But for someone who has the experience, its reality seems quite undeniable.

Do human beings have unexpected powers? There seems to be no easy answer. Perhaps Uri Geller's abilities really are (as many people have alleged) nothing more than clever conjuring. Perhaps Rose Gladden heals people, not so much by psychic energy, as by implanting in them a strong belief that they will get better (though that idea raises many more questions again!). Perhaps Sai Baba, too, is a fake.

One thing seems clear. We know very little about the source and workings of psi; after a century of research none of the big questions have really been answered. Many researchers who have begun the study of parapsychology with great excitement have become quickly disillusioned with their lack of progress, and have dropped out to pursue a different branch of science. And if we know as little as this, it seems unlikely that we should pin our hopes on psi as a major prospect for human betterment. It seems unlikely that we shall become able to control and employ these odd abilities for any practical purpose. (And maybe it would not be good if we could; how would you like to live in a world where the man

impossible not to subscribe to the prevailing belief that these apparitions do actually come forth from their graves.'

One of these cases, in 1739, was that of Arnold Paul, who lived in Medreiga near the Turkish-Serbian border. It was reported that he had been sighted several times after his death and had done appalling damage. He was exhumed after forty days; his flesh was uncorrupted; the blood bubbled in his veins, and covered his whole body and shroud. When his heart was pierced with a stake, the vampire gave a horrible shriek.

What are we to make of this? Calmet pointed out that chemical substances in the soil could have conserved the corpse indefinitely, and nitre and sulphur in the earth can liquefy blood which has

clotted. A stake through the heart forces air out of the body, and so can produce sounds like shrieks. Interestingly, none of the vampire stories mention that the earth was disturbed around the grave; which would surely have happened if the body really had come out.

And Calmet pointed out that there was no proof of nocturnal visits, or of bloodsucking. 'The allegation that they returned to haunt and destroy the living has never been sufficiently proved. . .'

It seems, then, that there is no factual basis for vampire stories. What about werewolves?

A werewolf (from *wer*, 'man', and *wulf*, 'wolf') is a living person who changes into animal form—usually a wolf, but in some cultures a jackal, tiger or leopard—and becomes a killer and eater of human flesh. Usually this is

under cover of darkness, and the werewolf will change back to human form the next morning. Only a consecrated bullet, or a wound that draws blood, will cure a werewolf's strange disease.

Again, werewolves have been the subject of legends for centuries—from at least before the time of Christ. And two hundred years before the vampire 'epidemic', there was a period of the sixteenth century when werewolf stories abounded everywhere. But, as with vampires, there is no basis in fact. Insane people often *think* they are wild animals; but that is quite a different matter.

In this seventeenth-century woodcut, the devil marks a new disciple. Interest in personalized evil remains strong today.

DO HUMAN BEINGS LIVE MORE THAN O

Arnall Bloxham is a hypno-therapist who lives in Cardiff. He has made a speciality of hypnotizing people and taking them back to past lives. In other words, under hypnosis they will begin to come out with details of previous existences they have lived through. One person will speak as an eighteenth-century sailor, another as a twelfth-century Jewess, another a Victorian doctor. Does this prove that they really once were those people?

Eastern religions have taught 'reincarnation' (coming back from death to live another life) for many centuries. They have slightly different beliefs about it, but the central idea is clear. Something in us survives the death of the body; that something takes on a new bodily form, and then lives again. Reincarnation is now becoming a more-and-more popular belief in the West as well.

The problem is, as Don Cupitt comments, 'Reincarnation is unverifiable.' Just because some people can produce under hypnosis an incredibly detailed knowledge of certain historical facts, they have not necessarily gained the information by actually living through it. 'If the evidence exists by which you can verify the supposed memory, if, say, there is any means of checking. . . he could have got to know of it by telepathic or clairvoyant means.'

In fact, sometimes claims made under hypnosis have been checked out histor-ically and found to be a mixture of fact, plausible untruth and total fantasy. The problem is that our brain has a facility for weaving stories together in a compelling way, as we discover whenever we dream. The information may be true, but that does not mean it has come from the dead. The manufactured ghost 'Philip', mentioned in a previous chapter, some-times put his creators right about dates and historical facts. 'Philip' was always correct!

Professor Alan Gauld comments, 'I have strong

next door could read your thoughts?) Psi looks set to remain on the fringes of knowledge, as a curious, baffling enigma: never quite disproved, but resisting all attempts to prove it; never reliable enough to be used practically, but glamorous enough to provide a living for quacks and frauds of every description.

And there we could leave it—if the world were simply a closed system of cause-and-effect laws, natural properties, physical matter and nothing more. But Christians believe that there are other forces at work in the universe. The creating, sustaining activity of God, who holds the universe in being, and operates through the natural laws which scientists explore. But there is also, according to the Bible, an evil force at large in the world, which works for chaos and destruction, and can sometimes collide with the lives of human beings in a damaging, dangerous way.

Is it possible that this evil force is sometimes encountered in the search for paranormal abilities? The possibility has at least to be considered. Writing in the London *Times*, Clifford Longley commented that people still can become 'possessed' by evil in a way which science finds it impossible to explain:

Evil is now used as an emotive word to describe extremely inhumane or anti-social behaviour, not as a thing in itself. There is no conceptual language for talking about evil detached from personal behaviour, in the way that is implied by the term 'demon', or the idea of 'casting out'.

Yet the studies of the subject are all clear: what is being spoken about is not just changing behaviour. The 'possessed' condition is a radical change for the worse from normal, of which the best available analogy is of an invasion by something previously external, and which has to be made external again to restore normality. And the process of doing this invariably involves invoking another external image or entity, a supernatural God. . .

reservations about the hypnotic regression material. . . The hypnotic induction procedure seems to release powers of creative imagination that (the subjects) did not know they possessed.' It is not true that under hypnosis people will always tell the truth. They may lie or fabricate evidence without realizing it; they are certainly not helpless puppets who must inexorably do the will of their controller.

Another kind of evidence for reincarnation is sometimes called 'deja vu'. This is the experience of feeling that we have been in a certain place before, or done a certain thing, although we know that it was not in this lifetime. If this is so, it is argued, then we must have done it in some previous life.

The experience is very common, especially among children, epileptics, people who have undergone brain surgery and the semi-starved. That should make us suspect that perhaps it has more to do with the state of our body and mind than with our past lives; and indeed the most common explanation is that it is a functioning of the two halves of the brain out of rhythm with each other. This induces the feeling 'I've been here before', when really one side of the brain has simply perceived what we are seeing a split second before the other half has got there.

Peter Underwood has an alternative explanation. 'More likely it is the working of the subconscious mind triggered off on a particular course by an insignificant detail which escapes our conscious senses; and thus, reminding our unconscious mind of a similar incident or situation, persuading us that other details and happenings are also remembered.'

Either way, it makes little difference. There is no evidence to prove reincarnation.

Actress Shirley Maclaine has put forward a philosophy which claims to make sense of repeated incarnations.

IS ANYONE ELSE OUT THERE?

On 24 June 1947 a businessman called Kenneth Arnold was flying his private plane over the Rockies when he saw nine shining discs swerving in and out of the mountains with 'flipping, erratic movements'. He reported that they moved as a saucer might 'if you skipped it across the water'. The newspapers took it up, people started reporting similar sightings across America, and the term 'flying saucer' was born.

Interest grew. And it was fuelled enormously by the publication in 1953 of a sensational book, *Flying Saucers Have Landed*, by Desmond Leslie and George Adamski. Leslie's part of the book detailed historical records of flying-saucer sightings in previous ages; Adamski told the story of how he had actually met a Venusian in the Mohave Desert, and been allowed to photograph his spacecraft.

Unfortunately, Leslie's section was full of errors and mistaken claims, while Adamski's evidence—a picture of the spacecraft —failed to convince the experts that it was anything more than the top canister of a Hoover vacuum cleaner. But it made no difference: a new belief had been implanted into the public mind—that alien visitors have often visited earth.

What is the evidence? Certainly there have been some convincing claims of sightings, often made by people with no desire for publicity, who clearly believe they are telling the truth. On the other hand, the same is true of the 'giant airship' which was glimpsed by several hundred people above the United States in 1879 (its occupants\rather improbably singing 'Abide with me'). As far as we can tell, there was no such airship. And if so, honest eyewitnesses can be honestly wrong.

If there is any substance to the sighting claims, it could be, says Colin Wilson, 'a manifestation of the human unconscious. . . trying to prevent us from becoming jammed in a two-dimensional left-brain reality'. In other words, they are not objective reality, but the creation of our subconscious minds—a sort of 'super-poltergeist effect'.

It has been objected that if there are any beings out there, they are rather good at keeping quiet. Our planet is exceptionally noisy—our radio and TV transmissions must be capable of being picked up long distances away through space. But despite listening since 1948 we have never caught a snatch of an outer-space soap opera. And for all the thousands of sightings, no one item of outer-space origin has ever been found lying about afterwards. There have been claims; but nothing that could not have been explained away.

In fact we do not know whether there is anyone else there. Some scientists believe there probably is; more, it seems, believe there is not. The finely-balanced conditions which led to the miraculous emergence of life on earth may not have been duplicated anywhere else in the universe.

As well as walking on fire, some religious devotees push swords into themselves without apparent injury.

WALKING ON FIRE? RISING INTO THE AIR?

Some of the strange feats claimed for the human body sound quite impossible. Yet we find the same claims being made in culture after culture.

Take fire-walking, for instance. It was known before the time of Christ; Strabo, a Greek historian, wrote of priestesses in Cappadocia who could do it, and a tribe in Etruria were excused military service in the Roman legions if they could perform the feat. Fire-walking has also been part of religious festivals in India, Fiji, South Africa, Tahiti, Japan, the Philippines, and among American Indians. How is it done?

The answer is that nobody quite knows—although it indubitably happens, and even sceptical volunteers with no previous training have sometimes been able to walk across a bed of hot coals without any injury. One theory was put forward by psychic investigator Harry Price, who tested the ability of fire-walkers on beds of coals measured at up to 800 degrees Centigrade. He thought that the speed and confidence with which fire-walkers moved, and the low thermal conductivity of burning wood embers, protected the feet for just long enough.

Another theory is that perspiration on the feet of the fire-walkers forms a cushion of vapour which protects the sole of the foot from scorching. This was tested out by American scientist Mayne Reid Coe, who found he was able to stroke red-hot steel bars with the tip of his tongue without serious injury, dip his fingers into molten lead, and—as he had hoped—walk through a pit of burning embers.

Just in case anyone reading this should be inspired to try it out, we should note that many others who have tried to replicate these feats have been badly burned. Patience, caution and good fortune all seem to be required.

What about levitation— the ability to float in the air? It is reported that St Joseph of Copertino found himself frequently doing this, quite unwontedly, and on one occasion performed the feat in front of witnesses including the startled philosopher Leibniz. Last century a medium called Daniel Dunglas Home was famous for his ability to float in and out of windows; many theories have been advanced about how he might have faked it, but none yet sound convincing.

In our own day, graduates of the Transcendental Meditation 'siddhi' course claim the ability to levitate. Sceptics claim that their levitation is more like a series of short hops into the air and down again—and is probably caused by involuntary muscular action, propelling the meditator off the mat.

If poltergeist phenomena can make everyday objects float into the air, and even throw human beings out of bed, there may well be some sort of mechanism which we do not understand which would occasionally impel a human body to defy the force of gravity. All that we can say is that we do not know for certain.

Clergymen and others who have helped to deal with 'possessed' people have often found that they demonstrate involuntary paranormal powers—such as exceptional strength, flashes of precognition, or an ability to read thoughts. Is it possible, then, that occasionally the source of paranormal abilities may be evil from the supernatural realm? It is a possibility which must be taken seriously. Since we know so little about what psi actually is, it would be naive to laugh the idea out of court.

Tal Brooke, at least, has no doubts. He was one of the most intimate disciples of Sai Baba, with whom we opened this chapter. He saw at first hand the kind of supernatural feats which Baba was able to manifest. He was in no doubt about the reality of his guru's powers. But he came to believe that Sai Baba was more than a miracle-worker: he was tuned to a source of power which was ultimately destructive:

I will never forget my thoughts at that time. I had discovered an absolutely Satanic thing operating behind Sai Baba's veneer... Miracles, according to what I had just read in the Bible, were not infallible proof that one was divine, or in touch with God-consciousness. Or had transcended space. No. The powers of evil could work miracles...

Was Brooke right? Certainly, many of those who have tried most deliberately to harness supernatural power have ended as broken people, alcoholics, sexually deviant, incapable of sustaining real relationships with others. There are dangers in the pursuit of paranormal abilities. And whatever we believe about psi, we would be foolish to forget them.

Part III

People Together

6

WHY PEOPLE DO WHAT THEY DO

One of our problems in examining human beings is that we know only one person really well: ourselves. We observe everybody else from the outside. And that can be deceptive; people can wear masks, tell lies, create misleading impressions. Sometimes they will not even be conscious that they are doing it themselves. Others are always capable of surprising us; the final core of mystery remains, even after years of friendship or indeed marriage.

And do we really know even ourselves? When Sigmund Freud first started to write about the unconscious, and the effect it has on our actions, many people were indignant and amazed. We do not like to think that we are not wholly rational, logical, self-controlled individuals. But Freud suggested that many of our motives are obscure and our actions fulfil needs that we don't consciously understand. One contemporary professor, when Freud's theories were being mentioned, banged his fist on the table and shouted: 'This is not a topic for discussion at a scientific meeting; it is a matter for the police.'

This was in 1910. No wonder there was so much panic abroad; several currents of thought at that time seemed to threaten established rational and religious ideas.

It was less than fifty years since Darwin's ideas had become well known, and Western thinkers had been forced to start regarding human beings as part of the animal creation, with clear links back to lower forms of life. In Bordeaux a rabbi's-son-turned-atheist, Emile Durkheim, was teaching a university course on religion which maintained that the faiths of

Karl Marx and Sigmund Freud both put forward highly influential explanations of why people act as they do.

WHAT MAKES PEOPLE CRIMINALS?

When Richard Speck murdered eight nurses in Chicago, there was no question about his guilt. But his defence counsel hit on a brilliant idea. Speck, he claimed, had an extra Y-chromosome in his body, and since the Y-chromosome may be responsible for the aggression and combative-ness which characterizes men rather than women, a double dose might turn a man into a murderer. Speck was not responsible for his actions; his body had made him a criminal.

In fact, Speck did not have the extra chromosome, and it is by no means certain that men who do will inevitably end up as criminals. But this was just the modern version of an old game: the attempt to link criminal behaviour to some physical characteristic. A hundred years ago, the most famous name associated with this kind of thinking was that of an Italian physician, Cesare Lombroso.

Lombroso believed that evolution held the key to criminality. Evil-doers were people who had been unfortunate enough to be born with ape-like charac-teristics—as throwbacks to a more primitive state of human life. They had long arms, narrow foreheads, large ears, thick skulls and hairy chests. 'They are true savages,' he wrote, 'in the midst of our brilliant European civilization.' He recommended that they should be carefully mon-itored from birth, and then exiled for life whenever their criminal nature asserted itself. (His admirers often wanted a more severe solution. One wrote, 'There is all the more reason for destroying them when it has been proved that they will always remain orang-utans.')

Lombroso was wildly wrong. But is it possible that the cause of criminality lies somewhere in our biological make-up? We do know that more women commit crimes when suffering from pre-menstrual tension. And some-times brain surgery has removed deviant tendencies from men. Are criminals driven to their acts by their bodies?

The problem is that 'criminality' is not a scientific category. Criminal behaviour is criminal only because society says it is—and different societies have slightly different rules. And so some of the actions our society holds to be criminal may be committed because of some biological factor; but by no means all. Even Lombroso admitted that 60 per cent of criminal acts were nothing to do with evolution, but were the result of giving in to greed, jealousy and anger.

It is dangerous to try to impose biological answers. We need to look at all the factors which may be involved—social ones as well as physical. Soviet political dissenters have often been confined to mental hospitals because of their activities. Says Dr Gareth Jones, 'The use of psychiatry as a political weapon radically alters the nature both of political debate and of behaviour control: dissident behaviour becomes the product of an unbalanced mind—which is diagnosed solely on the basis of dissident behaviour.'

Human beings are people, and the motives behind their actions will be mixed. Some may be criminals because of their chemistry. Others will be criminals because of factors in their background, or because of the way society has treated them, or because they have been forced into criminal patterns of behaviour by the unjust structures of their

The soul-destroying life in prison can serve to reinforce people's anti-social behaviour.

society. For others, the only reason will be what the Bible calls 'sin'—an inbuilt bias all human beings have towards doing the wrong thing instead of the right, towards satisfying self rather than living for others.

And if we forget this final factor, we will never under-stand human nature.

humankind were important for reasons quite different from those officially claimed: the real ground of their strength and power was that they correspond to a hidden, unconscious need, deep within human beings. 'The reasons with which the faithful justify them may be, and generally are, erroneous,' he wrote. 'But the true reasons do not cease to exist, and it is the duty of science to discover them.'

It seemed as if the accepted picture of what a human being is—and how people arrive at their decisions and beliefs—was being turned completely upside-down.

As if all this were not enough, in 1910 the ideas of Karl Marx were gaining ground among intellectuals everywhere. In only seven years they would lead to the Russian Revolution. And Marx's claim was—once again—that human beings are not the free, responsible, rationally-choosing agents they fondly imagine themselves to be. Our actions and desires are dominated, according to Marx, by the economic circumstances of our lives; it is the sort of society we live in that makes us the people we are. Humans might feel themselves to be free, independent persons, but in reality we are shaped and conditioned by hidden factors over which we have no control, and to which we respond more or less blindly.

Over the last eighty years or so since 1910, we have grown more used to these ideas. We know that the deepest springs of a person's actions are often things that he knows nothing much about; and that human beings can be manipulated by forces outside themselves. We live in the century which has discovered subliminal advertising, political brainwashing, and even ways of selling religion by tapping the unconscious. Chris Elkins, who joined a religious cult as a result of the psychological techniques practised on him, reported afterwards that there is a '"process" that creates the "product" —that slow, almost imperceptible shifting of values, allegiances, and authority that transforms a person... into a member of a cult. This process is truly *subtle*,' he added, 'but rarely as *coercive* as some people would like to believe.'

All of this suggests another important dimension of human life which we need to investigate in this book. How do we know what makes people tick? Why do they do what they do?

ARE HUMAN BEINGS NATURALLY AGGRESSIVE?

In the 126 years between 1820 and 1945, it has been estimated that 59 million human beings died a violent death. This includes death through war, murder and fatal quarrels. And it is almost certainly an under-estimate.

Why are human beings so violent? It is calculated that in the last 2000 years we have enjoyed about 15 years of peace. Are we fated to be aggressive?

Some scientists blame it on the nature of our brain. Dr Paul MacLean points out that our brain can be divided into the two parts which come from reptilian or animal origins—and the part which is more deve-loped in humans than any other species. He suggests that the older two parts have animal tendencies which conflict with our new powers of logical reasoning, and drag us back into warlike behaviour.

However, human behaviour is much more complex than this; the centres of 'reason' and 'emotion' in our brain cannot be so easily dis-tinguished from one another. The brain does not operate in three competing bits, but as one functioning unit.

Violence can often seem totally futile and purposeless. What is it that makes people aggressive?

Other psychologists have held that human beings would lose their aggression if the frustrations were removed from the process of growing up. And so children should never be repri-manded or restrained. Unfortunately for a nice idea, children brought up under such a regime are often more aggressive and contentious than those who have been disciplined.

Certainly, aggression always seems to have been a part of human life. Even the most primitive societies show plenty of evidence of violent practices. And those who do not, usually live in the neighbourhood of much more violent neighbours, and seem to have developed a 'peace-at-any-price' stra-tegy of survival by sub-mission to their oppressors.

It is often claimed that men are more aggressive than women. This is borne out by studies of the games children play, and also by the crime statistics: men are several times more likely than women to be arrested for crimes of violence. What causes the difference?

Is it that the male is always more aggressive than the female, in any species? Not necessarily. This is often so, but there is a lot of vari-ation, and anyway to make generalizations from animals to humans is a risky business.

Could it be caused by the hormone testosterone, secreted in boys at puberty in larger quantities than happens in girls? Could there be a link between this hormone and aggressive behaviour? Again, the evidence is not clear-cut. Even if a link could be established, it would not provide a complete explanation. Greater male aggressiveness is visible at three years of age—many years before testosterone is secreted.

It seems more likely that male aggression has its origins in the expectations we have of male behaviour, as a boy is growing up. Perhaps if feminists succeed in shattering some of the easy assumptions we make about 'typical' male or female behaviour, and which we pass on uncon-sciously to our children, the difference in aggression between men and women will disappear.

But aggression hardly looks like disappearing from human life for a long time to come. And perhaps this is as it should be. Our history has been shaped by controversy and com-petition, and without obstinate struggles we could never have come as far as we have. Perhaps aggression is not an undesirable evolutionary residue, but the wise gift of a loving Creator who intends us to keep our aggressive qualities, but control and shape them to useful, non-destructive ends.

W.M. Krogman, an expert on child growth, has written: 'Man has absolutely the most protracted period of infancy, childhood and juvenility of all forms of life... Nearly 30 per cent of his entire lifespan is devoted to growing.' This important difference between ourselves and other forms of life is what makes us a socially dependent animal, incapable of being fully human (as we saw in chapter three) unless there are others around with whom we can mix. Biologist Stephen Jay Gould explains it this way:

But what is the adaptive significance of retarded development itself? The answer to this question probably lies in our social evolution. We are pre-eminently a learning animal... To enhance our learning, we have lengthened our childhood by delaying sexual maturation with its adolescent yearning for independence. Our children are tied for longer periods to their parents, thus increasing their own time of learning and strengthening family ties as well.

This means that human beings have a much more flexible, shifting, complicated relationship to their environment than other animals do. Sociologists Berger and Luckman comment that 'man's relationship to his environment is characterized by world-openness', that human beings do not live their lives according to the dictates of a bundle of instincts which were already predetermined before the day of their birth, but that after birth, 'the process of becoming man takes place in an interrelationship with an environment'. Even some biological developments which in animals take place within the mother's womb are delayed until after birth in human beings. At birth, the brain of a rhesus monkey is already 65 per cent of its fully-grown size; but our brains are only 23 per cent of their final size when we make our first appearance. And so when we emerge into the world we are not so rigidly complete as other species. Berger and Luckman comment:

There is no man-world in the sense that one may speak of a dog-world or a horse-world. Despite an area of individual learning and accumulation, the individual dog or the individual horse has a largely fixed relationship to its environment, which it shares with all other members of its respective species... The developing human being not only

interrelates with a particular natural environment, but with a specific cultural and social order, which is mediated to him by the significant others who have charge of him.

Human behaviour therefore depends very heavily on our relationships with other people. It is from others that we derive our original store of learning about the world: how we should cope with it, what we need to remember in order to survive, what society will and will not let us do. It is through others that we grow, receiving

ideas, mental stimulation, social pressure, examples to copy. It is with others that we encounter some of the major experiences of life—education, work, founding a family, belonging to a community. For most of us, solitary confinement is an unpleasant, even terrifying experience—it seems so unnatural. Human behaviour is social behaviour.

What brings people together?

What is it that encourages us to seek other people's company? Michael Argyle claims that there are at least seven basic drives, aimed at different goals, which spur us on to develop relationships with others. The simplest and most primitive kind is the drive which aims to satisfy biological or financial needs: sometimes people are drawn together in a common task in order to survive, or to live more successfully. That (as we shall see in chapter eight) was the origin of civilization: human beings in Mesopotamia clearly found that they could organize the irrigation of their fields much more effectively when they worked together, rather than competing for strips of land. From there it was a short step to the emergence of cities and more sophisticated forms of co-operation. And the same drive towards associa-

tion continues today when, for example, people form business partnerships with, or work alongside, others to whom they would not naturally be drawn.

The second main impulse towards social behaviour is something that begins very early in life: dependency. Children naturally develop dependency on their parents, in the first years of life, and then have to be gradually weaned away from it as they grow up ('Why don't you run along and play with the big boys?')—a process which (in Western society at least) tends to be especially emphasized with boys rather than girls. But the urge towards dependency can reassert itself, especially when we are in new and bewildering situations, or unsure of our acceptability. (This is why often a new student at college will link up with a more experienced one, and why a relatively plain girl will often make friends with a more attractive, assured and confident one.)

But why does the pretty girl want the plain one's company? Perhaps it is because of another of the drives: dominance. Many people have a need for power, or recognition, or achievement; to make contact with others who send back reassuring messages about our importance is a way of meeting these needs. Dominant people talk most in groups, develop strategies of getting their ideas considered, sometimes react with hostility to others who want to be dominant too. Not that everybody aims for dominance in the same way: someone who is a powerful public speaker, and derives great satisfaction from the authority he can wield over an audience, may be ill at ease and timid in a boisterous party.

Argyle called another of his seven drives 'the need for affiliation'. This means the hunger we all have for intimate relationships with close friends, the urge which propels us to strike up a friendship with strangers. This urge probably starts with childhood experiences of parental affection, too (psychopaths who have no under-standing of affection often have a background of very little maternal love). In Western culture girls often find it easier to indulge this urge than boys. Put together in the same room to accomplish some simple engineering task, a group of girls achieved very little, but by the end of the session knew all about one another; a group of boys in the same situation were still virtual strangers at the end of the session, but had worked much more effectively together.

The three remaining drives are: sex (which includes the urge to flirt, to find romance, to impress the opposite sex, to reassure oneself about one's self-worth by making casual 'con-quests'); aggression (which leads people to establish relationships with each other very quickly when, for instance, they crash into one another at traffic lights!); and self-esteem (the need to find approval in the reactions of others). All these factors draw human beings together.

But how do we behave when we actually meet?

When we first encounter another human being, both parties will have at least one of the motivations we have discussed, which will decide what they hope to gain from the encounter. Both will also possess a certain number of social skills: ways of acting towards

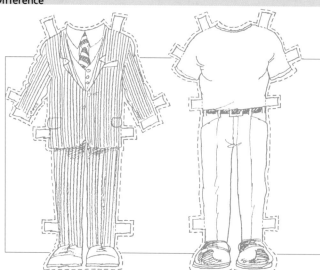

other people which they have gradually adapted, perfected and copied from others, through their years of growing up. Each will have learnt to perceive small cues in the other person's behaviour which give hints about how the relationship is developing; they will know how to use the right vocabulary and manner for the sort of relationship that is being built (you don't address your husband's employer as you would your hairdresser). Let's hope they understand how to talk in the right places, leave pauses of the right length, strike the right impression of interested attention without appearing too inquisitive. All these skills we naturally pick up as we go through life, without ever thinking too hard about them. What happens next is described by Michael Argyle:

A and B size each other up, in terms of their own private category systems, and select from their repertoire of social skills accordingly. It is almost certain that these two initial patterns of behaviour will not fit. . . it is very likely that one or both will find the other's behaviour not entirely satisfactory, in relation to his own need system. Both will be under some pressure to modify the state of affairs; they may change their own behaviour in order to synchronize better, or may attempt to change the other's behaviour. There is continual modification of behaviour until a state of equilibrium, more or less satisfactory to both parties, is arrived at.

What both A and B are doing here, as they chat with one another, is to think constantly: 'If I were him, what would I want me to say next? What would I expect?' George H. Mead has called this 'taking on the role of the other'. We say something which we think will elicit a certain response. If we get that response, we say something else along the same lines. If we don't, we swiftly change direction and try a different approach, until we find one which works. If everything we say brings a response we do not expect, we eventually retire baffled, and say to others, 'I really don't understand him.' We do not feel easy in our minds about our relationship with someone else until we can, at least partially, predict how that person is likely to react to what we say.

Mead points out that most human relationships are not simple two-way interactions. We do not take on the rest of the world one at a time. It is more like playing a game of football, where the man with the ball at his feet has to pay attention to the reactions of a whole number of different people at once—the opposing defenders, his own side, the goalkeeper ahead of him, the referee. And so our attitudes and actions become shaped, not by one person at one time, but by the normal, predictable reactions of all the people with whom we come into contact—what Mead calls the 'generalized other'. 'The attitude of the generalized other is the attitude of the whole community.'

So the behaviour of human beings is

What should I wear? It depends on what I plan to do, who I am going to meet ...

dominated, not just by their own free impulses, but by the reactions they expect to get from everyone else. This can affect even their deepest beliefs. Peter Berger has written of the 'plausibility structure' we all need to make our beliefs tenable. If there are others around me who believe as I do, I will not find it difficult to keep my views on life intact. But if suddenly I am plunged into a community that thinks differently and operates on different priorities (if, for instance, I am a Central African witchdoctor suddenly transplanted to New York, or a very young Christian in an army guardroom), I may suffer a tremendous shock to my whole mental system, and may in the end succumb to the ideas of those around me.

In 1830 four primitive South American Indians were brought back to England by the captain of the British exploring vessel *Beagle*. The aim was to 'civilize' them so that they could bring enlightened ways to their own people. Sure enough, with the exception of one who had died, the Indians returned completely altered, well dressed, proud of their immaculate appearance, and determined to settle in their former society with a new style.

A year later, when the *Beagle* returned to Tierra del Fuego, one of the 'civilized' Indians approached in his canoe. Charles Darwin, who was there, was amazed to see that he had become 'a thin haggard savage, with long disordered hair, and naked, except a bit of blanket around his waist... I never saw so complete and grievous a change'. None of the returned Indians had managed to retain their Europeanized ways. And some years later the 'savage' in the canoe was responsible for the massacre of six missionaries.

Putting on the style

If it is true that we act in ways which we think will please others, then obviously there is a certain amount of contrivance and pretence involved in our behaviour. Social anthropologist Erving Goffman has analyzed the 'personal front' which we all put forward to the world, in the hope that others will see what we want them to see, rather than what is really there.

The same woman who would die if anyone came to the door will look immaculate when she goes for a job interview.

95

We present quite differently, and feel different about ourselves, depending on our standing in comparison with the other person.

We want to manipulate their perception of us just a bit: to control the feelings that they will have about us. (And so the lady who has worked for hours to prepare a marvellous meal will strive to give the impression that it is 'just a few bits and pieces thrown together, really'; the boy who is quite capable of ironing his own shirts will pretend to be helpless in order to awaken his girlfriend's maternal instincts; and I will try to write this book in a smooth, flowing, effortless way that will totally conceal the sweat and agony that went into its construction.) Because we all know that others are playing the same game as ourselves, we accept the rules of the game. As Goffman puts it:

A tacit agreement is maintained between performers and audience to act as if a given degree of opposition and of accord existed between them. Typically, but not always, agreement is stressed and opposition is underplayed. . . Sometimes disruptions occur through unmeant gestures, faux pas, and scenes, thus discrediting or contradicting the definition of the situation that is being maintained. . . We find that performers, audience, and outsiders all utilize techniques for saving the show, whether by avoiding likely disruptions or correcting for unavoided ones, or by making it possible for others to do so.

This kind of 'performance' is not the same thing as the show put on by a confidence trickster, who is actually involved in a kind of double bluff—a performance of a performance. Goffman wryly comments, 'Perhaps the real crime of the confidence man is not that he takes money from his victims but that he robs all of us of the belief that middle-class manners and appearance can be sustained only by middle-class people.' Few of us are totally cynical about our 'performance', although this does happen occasionally, as when an obsequious waiter secretly despises his overbearing customers, or a *nouveau riche* rock star smashes up hotel rooms simply because that's what rock stars do. But then few of us are completely fooled by ourselves either; we know that we are presenting our 'best side'. And it is unsettling when we meet someone who 'believes his own publicity': the businessman, for example, who has surrounded himself with 'yes men' for so long that he now imagines he really is as dynamic, witty and brilliant as he pretends to be.

WHY DO WE WORK?

For most human beings in the Western world, work occupies nearly a third of our lives. Most of us need to work, to earn money to help us survive; but this is not the only reason we work. Unemployed people can feel a great emptiness in their lives as a result of having no work to do. Pools winners sometimes go back to their previous badly-paid jobs, even though they do not need the money any more, rather than exist without work. And management analysts who have explored ways of motivating people to work better tell us that more pay is not the answer. People do not work simply for money.

In his book *The Psychology of Work*, psychiatrist Donald Scott says that the true reasons are complex. 'Though man has the same basic drives as monkeys there are many other goals which are important. . . In addition his motives may often be mixed.' Scott distinguishes between conscious motives—such as achievement, self-assertiveness, mastery, gregariousness—and unconscious motives, fuelled by drives which we may not realize are there. For example, Freud saw the sex-drive as being extremely important in our functioning. Not all of it can be used up by 'love-objects'; in other words, the drive produces some spare energy which is left undirected. Scott explains that one way in which sexual energy can be used up is 'by sublimation, that is, it may be directed towards another end, so that states of high activity and high drive may appear'. Work is one way of using up the spare energy.

Some religious cults of the 1970s managed to extract astonishingly high work rates from some of their followers, by systematically focusing their attention on sex, and then frustrating their desires; so perhaps this theory is right. But whatever the psychological explanation, the Bible claims that work is something natural and necessary to humankind. In the Garden of Eden story, humans were involved in work activities before the Fall, that rebellion against God which brought disharmony into creation. Work is therefore part of God's good creation, not a 'necessary evil'. Christian psychologist Paul Tournier insists that 'the meaning of man's work is the satisfaction of the instinct for adventure that God has implanted in his heart'.

Work is not always like this for people today. Karl Marx complained that capitalist society has 'alienated' human beings from the true satisfaction they should feel in their work; he maintained that only revolution could alter this state of affairs. Work dehumanized people: 'The activity of the worker is not his own spontaneous activity. It belongs to another and is the loss of himself'. Communism, on the other hand, would be 'the re-integration or return of man into himself, the abolition of man's self-alienation'.

Christians would agree with much of Marx's critique of the modern industrial system. But they would raise three objections:

■ Socialist countries do not appear to be having much greater success than capitalist ones in making workers fulfilled through their labour. There are just as dreary, pointless lives of labour to be lived in Eastern Europe as anywhere else.

■ Although economic forces are important in determining the quality of human life, they are not the only things that matter. Work is important, but not ultimate.

■ Work needs to have a meaning which goes beyond this present world. It finds value only in the context of a relationship with a God of purpose and creativity. Says Tournier, 'Man is seen to be a spiritual being in the very act of his desire to understand the meaning of things, the meaning of the world, of life, and to understand the meaning of his own work so as to be able to see the part played in the whole, in the destiny of the world, by his own personal contribution.'

In fact most of us tend to oscillate between cynicism and sincerity, not quite confusing our 'performance' with our real selves, yet tending to become more convinced by it as time passes. Robert Park observes:

Everyone is always and everywhere, more or less consciously, playing a role... It is in these roles that we know each other; it is in these roles that we know ourselves.

In a sense, and in so far as this mask represents the conception we have formed of ourselves—the role we are striving to live up to—this mask is our truer self, the self we would like to be. In the end our conception of our role becomes second nature and an integral part of our personality. We come into the world as individuals, achieve character, and become persons.

When we encounter somebody else's performance, we will either warm to them or dislike them. What is it that makes us like people?

Physical attractiveness undeniably has a lot to do with it. We have higher expectations of good-looking people than of the unattractive. Two American researchers in 1972 discovered that this principle even affects the way teachers

WHY DO WE PLAY GAMES?

Games are pointless. There is nothing to be gained by propelling a small white ball over miles of grass so as to lodge it in tiny holes in the ground. For thirty intelligent professional people to devote their Saturday afternoons to hurling themselves at one another, rolling in the mud, all to move a leather ball from one end of a field to the other, is a remarkable waste of time. So why do we do it? What are games for?

'They recreate the freedom, the remembered perfection of childhood,' says Christopher Lasch, 'and mark it off from ordinary life with artificial boundaries, within which the only constraints are the rules to which the players freely submit. Games enlist skill and intelligence, the utmost concentration of purpose, on behalf of activities utterly useless. . .'

Games give us a chance to withdraw from daily life into an imaginary conflict, in which there are defeats, triumphs, miracles, tragedies, frustrations and panics —just like reality—except that none of it matters. The game allows full expression to all the emotions we are capable of—but also the knowledge that at the end of the afternoon, when the whistle is blown, we will not have to live with those emotional states any longer. Games are a holiday from everyday worries.

They can also help to prepare us for situations we have not met yet, or give us a chance to try out roles we cannot normally try out in life (it is not unknown for mild-mannered little men to turn into aggressive tigers when let loose on the football field). These are uses that we have had for games since our earliest years, according to psychologist Gordon Lowe.

Children take play seriously, so seriously that it has been described as the work of children. In play, the child moves from the known to the untried and unknown. Play involves risk, mastery by repetition and practice, and problem-solving. The child may use it as a vehicle for other feelings, such as self-assertion, the expression of otherwise forbidden impulses, and as a way of revealing his own nature. So far from being an idle pastime, play trains the child in social relationships.

Games can be found in human civilizations right back to the earliest days of history. At one time many of them were unrestricted by too many rules—about the number of players per side, for example, or the area within which the game must be played. Then came the nineteenth century, that great age of rule-making, when bodies were formed to run individual sports, and codes of rules were drawn up. Now, some would say, games are becoming more individual and unbounded in their emphasis: instead of staying within the confines of a court or a pitch, pitting themselves against other humans, twentieth-century people have taken to hang-gliding, wind-surfing, abseiling; pitting themselves against the elements—and against themselves.

Are we taking games too seriously? Jan Huizinga's famous book *Homo Ludens* claims that we are. Work, he maintains, has become routine drudgery for many people. It is abstract and impersonal, and any element of 'play' has dropped out of it. And so people turn to games with unusual intensity, seeking sensation and controversy. This is why there is football violence, and why tennis players become heroes by swearing at umpires. Games have been given an artificial, inflated importance, because we all need to play.

treat their pupils. 'Evidence seems to indicate,' they reported, 'that academic grades given to students are influenced by the attractiveness of the child.' And also: 'When shown a set of children's pictures and asked to identify the child who probably created the classroom disturbance (or some similar act of misconduct), adults were likely to select an unattractive child as the offender.'

Another factor is the amount of time people spend together. When people are thrown together over a period of time, working in the same office, for example, they may well become friendly enough to set up further chances to meet outside their normal meetings (going out on the town together once a year). Familiarity through exposure increases people's attractiveness, which is why boys marry the girl next door, and bosses fall for their secretaries. A few years ago, lectures at Oregon State University were attended by an unknown student encased in a large black sack, with only his feet showing. It was part of an attempt to investigate student attitudes. The outcome was that the demeanour of the other students changed, from initial hostility, to growing curiosity, to eventual friendship with the man in the bag. When he became a familiar sight, he was no longer a threat.

But the main reason for liking others is that in some way they offer us a reward. Their company may stimulate us, or flatter us; their interest in us and care for us may bolster our self-confidence; their sharing our opinions may make us feel more intelligent, more secure in what we believe. And so it is not surprising that we tend to be attracted most to people like ourselves. They can talk to us most interestingly about the things that mutually absorb us, and provide social support for our attitudes and views.

What about 'opposite poles attract'? This holds true only in some kinds of relationship: a friendship based on dominance and submission, for example (such as the shy girl and pretty girl we mentioned earlier). And even when onlookers see two people as 'opposites', they may in fact be conscious of great undetected similarities between them, on which they base their friendship. But people who genuinely are opposites tend to stay apart.

Falling in love

So much for liking. What about love? Most of us know the earth-shattering sensation of being hopelessly besotted with one other human being. It is estimated (I have no idea how) that at any one moment there will be 1,680,466,201 human beings in love, and 424 million more recovering from a past love affair. What is it based on? Why do we fall in love?

Clearly physical attraction has something to do with it, but different races and cultures look for different qualities. Fat calves, not a sign of beauty in Europe, are much prized among the Tiv of Nigeria. Kuwaitis like girls with a gap between their top front teeth. Black teeth attract the

Trobriand Islanders, and extremely big hips are a distinct asset in Hawaii. There seems to be no one generally-agreed human definition of attractiveness.

But the psychological mechanism involved in falling in love is the same everywhere. Psychoanalyst Theodor Reik says that love 'is not a crisis but the way out of a crisis which has arisen from a state of dissatisfaction with oneself'. In other words, we fall in love because we glimpse in the other person qualities we feel the lack of in ourselves. Forming a relationship with someone who has what we lack is a way of achieving wholeness for our lives.

And so love too, like friendship, is based on the idea of rewards. This also explains why people often fall out of love: the potential rewards in a love relationship are so great that it places a great strain on the couple's ability to relate their behaviour to one another. They need to synchronize their reactions very closely for the intimacy to continue, and of course few people get it right all the time. And so there are lovers' quarrels, episodes of kiss-and-make-up, cooling-off periods, and a general oscillation between intimacy and withdrawal as the relationship progresses. Engagement and marriage are useful social customs for one reason at least: they act as markers in an otherwise confusing, shifting situation, signalling to the couple concerned (and to everybody else) what stage the relationship has reached.

Something very like 'falling in love' happens in another major human behaviour upheaval: conversion. Why should someone's opinions suddenly go through a dramatic change of direction? No animal has ever had a Damascus Road experience, as the apostle Paul did; or left its settled background to live in a completely different way, like the Buddha. Yet human beings do have these sudden alterations of experience. A surprising number of people die as martyrs because of their Christian experience of conversion—something no other species will ever do. Why? Can we explain what is happening in conversion?

The answer is: yes and no. It is possible to see the human factors involved in a conversion to Hinduism, say, or Marxism or animal rights. But to explain such factors does nothing to invalidate the experience. We can examine the psychology of someone who has fallen in love, and find reasons to explain why it happened with that specific person at that precise time; but the data we collect will tell us nothing about whether the lover was *right* to attach himself to the object of his devotion. Whether or not he has made a mistake is something we will have to decide on other grounds.

In the same way, we can trace what human reasons were involved in a person's conversion to Islam, or fascism; but this does not tell us whether that person was right or wrong to embrace those beliefs. Christians claim (as we shall see in chapter nine) that when people become Christians, something supernatural takes place as God's power enters their lives. And even when we can see psychological reasons prompting a person's conversion to Christianity, there may still be another level of explanation: God revealing himself in that person's experience in an unmistakable way.

William Sergeant's famous book *Battle for the Mind* tried to link the mechanism of conversion with the kind of psychological conditioning to which Pavlov subjected his dogs. We saw in chapter four that this raises more questions than it answers; human brains are too complex to respond to simple stimuli in the same way as dogs. Although it is possible for dramatic, manipulative conversion techniques to 'condition' people for a while, by using such weapons as fear, excitement, exhaustion and repetitive indoctrination, no genuinely lasting results come in this way. (Chris Elkins, whom we quoted earlier, counsels the parents of cult members not to despair: 50 per cent of all members eventually leave the group, many walking away of their own free will. The 'harmony and blissful love is something that rarely lasts. Disillusionment is common. . .')

In fact, what happens in genuine conversion seems to be very close to the experience of falling in love. Social psychiatrist James Brown comments:

Religious conversion, considered from the psychological point of view, may take the form of filling a vacuum which has caused dissatisfaction with the existing personality in which case it supplies, as it were, the missing piece of the puzzle; or it may take the form of substitution of one piece for another which may have been lying dormant for years. . . The individual convert, in fact, is the man or woman in search of the system of beliefs which will integrate him more closely with what he regards as reality. They are not forced upon him by anybody, and the teacher is the occasion rather than the cause of his conversion.

Human beings are not robots who can easily be tinkered with. There is a genuine unpredictability about each individual we encounter. We can trace patterns in behaviour, as we have done in this chapter, and understand some of the mechanisms which make people act in society as they do. But however much we learn, there will always be the thrill of discovery and the anticipation of surprise whenever we meet a stranger. For every human being is different. And that is what makes social life so interesting.

7

WOMEN AND MEN

One of the most basic facts about human beings is sex. We come in two varieties. And in most cultures throughout history, the most important question deciding a baby's future destiny has been: is it a boy or a girl? Because we have very different roles in life for men and women to play.

Throughout history, it has usually been women who have had the worse of the arrangement. Men can be given so much power, so much attention, so much indulgence, that a woman starts to feel she has no real personality left. One has written:

When I am by myself, I am nothing. I only know that I exist because I am needed by someone who is real, my husband, and by my children. My husband goes out into the real world. Other people recognize him as real, and take him into account. He affects other people and events. He does things and changes things, which are different afterwards. I stay in this imaginary world in this house, doing jobs that I largely invent, and that no one cares about but myself. I do not change things. The work I do changes nothing; what I cook disappears, what I clean one day must be cleaned again the next. I seem to be involved in some sort of mysterious process rather than actions that have results.

And so one of the most important questions we must ask in this book is 'What are women *for?*' It is a question being asked with more and

Philippines' president Corrie Aquino has revealed an ability to touch the heart of a nation wounded by dictatorship. This spirituality, this sensitivity to emotion, is perhaps a gift women are particularly suited to bring to leadership.

Benazir Bhutto, Margaret Thatcher, Indira Gandhi — this generation has provided many national leaders who are women. Has this opened up greater opportunities for women in the nations they lead?

more urgency by women in Western society today.

The modern 'Women's Movement' owes a lot to a crusading book written in 1963 by Betty Friedan, a woman who had built her career out of writing for women and trying to interpret what they were really looking for. At first she had accepted the idea that women were most fulfilled when they followed the usual career path of marriage, motherhood, housewifery. Then she started to become aware of the existence of 'the problem that has no name'—the unspoken despair which existed among thousands of women who had done all the usual things and felt themselves losing touch with reality as a result. As one mother of four confessed to her:

I love the kids and Bob and my home. There's no problem you can even put a name to. But I'm desperate. I begin to feel I have no personality. I'm a server of food and a putter-on of pants and a bedmaker, somebody who can be called on when you want something. But who am I?

And so Betty Friedan wrote her book, *The Feminine Mystique*, to ask whether or not Western civilization had got it wrong. Since the Second World War it had been taught subtly by all the women's magazines, TV programmes and novels that a woman's real fulfilment lay in ministering to the needs of her husband and children; a glamorous 'mystique' had surrounded the role of housewife, which in fact was a boring, humdrum and often dehumanizing job, and it was time the 'mystique' was exposed for the lie it was. These kinds of societal arrangements were not the only way to carry on male-female relationships.

On that point at least, Betty Friedan was right. Anthropologists have shown that other human societies have sometimes had a different view of women, and would not accept the idea that women must be submissive, self-effacing, passive creatures. Margaret Mead, for example, studied three primitive societies which had very different notions. In one, the Arapesh, both men and women alike were 'feminine' and 'maternal' in personality; among the Mundugumor, both men and women were violent, aggressive, and 'masculine' in the way they behaved; and the Tchambuli expected the woman to be dominant and aggressive while the man was less responsible and emotionally dependent.

There are also societies in which the clear distinction of 'male' and 'female' is sometimes blurred. Among the Xaniths of Oman, for instance, there is almost a sense of being a 'third sex'. Xaniths are male homosexual prostitutes whose whole behaviour is female, and who are allowed by the rules of society to act in ways forbidden to other men—for example, talking freely to women in the street. Are they men or women? Biologically there is no doubt. Socially, it is not so easy to decide.

Telling them apart

Obviously we need to ask some very basic questions. Why are there sex differences anyway? What is a 'man', what is a 'woman', and precisely what differences are there between them?

When a baby is born, the first question people ask is about the child's sex. The way in which we tell is to examine the genitals. If a baby has a penis, it is a boy; if a vagina, it is a girl. Is this the way to distinguish 'male' and 'female'?

Not necessarily. There are plenty of species (birds, for example) in which the male has no penis. What is more, most of the time we cannot see one another's genitals—because clothes cover them up. Yet we have no difficulty in recognizing men from women. Clearly there is a complex set of signals and cues which allow us to work out the answer without inspecting each other's private parts.

In professional sporting events, men and women are sorted out by means of a 'sex test', which examines the sex chromosomes. All of us have forty-six chromosomes, of which all but two are organized into pairs. These two are called the sex chromosomes; in a woman they are identical, but in a man one is longer than the other.

Then are the chromosomes what finally distinguish male from female? Again, not always. Fish, amphibians and birds have the opposite arrangement: the male carries the identical chromosomes. And, confusingly, in some animals sex does not depend on chromosome differences at all, but on environment. A fish that would be female in some circumstances turns into a male when put somewhere else!

But there is one vital, general difference, which helps us to establish definitely what the difference is between male and female. It is a question of the 'germ cells' which an animal produces. If it produces a cell which contains food and is immobile, this is an 'egg cell' and the animal is female. If it produces a cell which is mobile, and contains no food resources, this is a 'sperm cell' and the animal is male.

The obvious question is: Why sex anyway? Plenty of living organisms reproduce by budding, or cloning, or hermaphroditical means (an individual creature producing both egg cells and sperm cells). Wouldn't this have been a better arrangement?

There are clearly lots of disadvantages in sexual reproduction. Budding or cloning produces a perfect copy of the parent; sex involves twice as much energy, from two individuals instead of one, and mixes up the genetic material contributed by both parents, creating a risk that the baby animal will suffer unexpected defects. And when we think about the time spent on courtship, the emotional and biological turmoil involved (for human beings at any rate), it all seems a complicated business.

Yet species that reproduce sexually have made much more progress and adapted to many more different conditions than others. So perhaps sex is actually an advantage to beings like us?

There are no definite answers. But many scientists point out that sex is a way of producing as much variation as possible in the next generation—and that means adaptability. If a species is to make itself at home in as many changing situations as possible, the more varied its offspring are the better. So sexual reproduction increases our chances of survival.

What is the difference?

It makes sense, then, that sex differences should exist. But are these differences just a matter of our role in reproduction? Or does

HOW DO I LOOK?

'I have this problem,' complains Professor Erica Abeel. 'Despite the consciousness revolution of the past five years, I still feel that I have to look beautiful. Men can look any old way.'

Why is this? Bertrand Russell once remarked that 'on the whole, women tend to love men for their character while men tend to love women for their appearance'. Men set a great deal of store by female beauty. (And they always have: psychologist Rita Freedman points out that even in the ancient ruins of Catal, in Asia Minor, we have found male burial sites full of weapons—and female burial sites full of jewellery and cosmetic devices.) This has created 'looksism'—'a form of social control that influences how people see themselves and how they are seen by others'. Women have to be pretty to make an impression on those around them. Otherwise, they have to be quite exceptional people.

This has been demonstrated in many ways. A 1966 survey of five hundred couples, who were asked the qualities they would look for in a 'date' and then paired up on that basis, showed that while women looked for a variety of qualities—good education, popularity, religious affinity—men insisted that their date must be good-looking.

Personnel interviewers tend subconsciously to grade women according to their looks, too. A number of them were shown the career details of a group of women, each with a photograph attached—in some cases before the woman concerned had undergone cosmetic treatment, and in some cases afterwards. It was found that the interviewer's

From Rubens nudes, through the covered Arab girl's face, to the fit young Western girl, the image of female attractiveness varies greatly from culture to culture.

being 'male' or 'female' affect our behaviour, so that we can expect boys and girls to show different traits and characteristics purely because of their sex?

Scientists are divided about this. Some claim that, yes, the biological differences do bring about inescapable personality differences along with them; boys are made differently from girls, and there is no way of escaping that. In

professional assessment of a woman's likely earning power would rise by as much as 12 per cent if the 'after' picture was studied rather than the 'before' one.

'Looksism' starts when we are children. Says Dr James Dobson, 'We adults respond very differently to an unusually beautiful child than to a particularly unattractive one, and that difference has a profound impact on a developing personality.' Thus appearance becomes desperately important even to a young girl. Clothes count for a lot; which is why a *New York Times* editorial asked in bewilderment, 'Why does a fourteen-year-old Brooklyn girl need to spend $40 on a manicure and $700 on pants,

sweaters, headbands and make-up to complete her back-to-school wardrobe?'

The effects of 'looksism' can vary enormously. It is feared by educationalists that many bright teenage girls subconsciously decide to underachieve at school, simply because being good at science or maths is not very 'feminine'. On the other hand, some will try harder for academic success as a compensation for lack of beauty: a study of remarkably successful women, all with six-figure incomes, showed that most of them had been embarrassed about their unattractiveness when they were girls.

An extremely serious modern psychological

problem is the 'slimmer's disease', *anorexia nervosa*, which has the highest mortality rate of any psychiatric illness, and is estimated to affect one female in a hundred between the ages of twelve and twenty-five. One psychologist explains what motivates anorexics in this way:

Their obsessive pursuit of thinness constitutes an acceptance of the feminine ideal, and an exaggerated striving to achieve it. Their attempts to control their physical appearance demonstrate a disproportionate concern with pleasing others, particularly men—a reliance on others to validate their sense of worth.

If our society cannot find ways of valuing people for what they are, rather than for the qualities they possess—whether beauty, brains or athletic ability —women will always be condemned to struggle against a stereotype which tries to shape their life. And for some of them, the struggle will end in death.

1972 John Money and A.A. Eerhardt claimed that sex hormones affect the brain before birth, and produce psychological differences which will show up in behaviour later. They claimed that a group of girls who had been exposed to the hormone testosterone before birth had become 'tomboys' with less maternal interests than other girls, and a streak of athletic competitiveness which made them enjoy playing with boys more than with girls.

But the way the researchers carried out these investigations has been criticized, and their results cannot be regarded as conclusive.

Other researchers would argue strongly that none of the differences between boys and girls are inbuilt and fundamental; the personality differences which emerge are merely a matter of the expectations of society. We all go through a variety of learning experiences—punishments and rewards, watching people whom we are encouraged to take as models, absorbing attitudes from our parents—which from our very earliest days give us a clear impression of the kind of behaviour society expects from a 'boy' or a 'girl'. It is because we live in such an environment that boys and girls turn out the way they do.

A third group of researchers would object that the first two both make the same mistake. They are treating the new human being as a totally passive object, simply driven by internal urges (in one version) or moulded by environment (in the other). But human beings come to understand their environment as they interact with it—trying out experiments, asking themselves questions, assessing messages that come from others. We arrive in the world with no set ideas about 'male' and 'female', but very quickly learn that there are two classifications of people. We use this fact as a way of making sense of the world, and deciding how we ourselves should act. And as we grow older, gradually the classification grows more and more elaborate, and we gain a more and more decided view of what it means to be 'a boy' or 'a girl'.

It all happens very quickly. When in 1978 some researchers gave 2–3-year-old children two paper dolls, one called Michael and the other Lisa, and asked them to imagine their activities and characteristics, they found that even at this early age the children had wide-

ranging ideas about which activities were 'right' for boys or girls, and how they would behave in a variety of situations.

There is no conclusive way of deciding between these three expert viewpoints. Perhaps each contains a part of the truth. There does seem to be some indication that at least some characteristics may be 'born into' the different sexes. An extra Y-chromosome can make men very aggressive, for instance, while an extra X-chromosome tends to undermine their masculinity. So it must be wrong to assume that all differences in attitudes and behaviour are the result of society imposing artificial sexual stereotypes.

Are girls and boys different by nature? Or are some of the differences caused by their parents' expectations?

Then what differences is it possible to trace between men and women? For one thing, men are 'less average' than women. In other words, it is in the male sex that extreme examples (of brilliance or idiocy, of tall or diminutive stature) are more likely to occur. And although males are generally bigger and stronger than females, women have a capacity for survival which men do not equal. Right throughout life—both in modern nations and developing countries, except where women have an extremely hard time—more males are dying than females of the same age. The United States census lists sixty-four specific causes of death. Of these, just two show a higher rate among females than among males, and five show about the same level; but for fifty-seven causes of death in the list, the toll of male deaths is greater than the female total.

Psychologically, there are only four traits where there seems to be a sex difference of some kind: girls have greater **verbal ability** than boys, although this does not show through until about the age of eleven; boys are better in **visual-spatial ability** than girls (for example, in seeing patterns in seemingly meaningless, unconnected lines on a piece of paper), and again this starts to appear in adolescence; teenage boys increase in **mathematical skills** faster than girls of the same age; and from the age of two onwards, males display more **aggression** and competitiveness than girls.

Women have a slightly different emotional make-up too, since the menstrual cycle each month can produce mood swings which men do not suffer. Too much can be made of this and it should never be used as an excuse to deny women jobs for which they are well qualified; it is not true that it impairs a woman's ability to think logically and make rational decisions. But 'pre-menstrual tension' is a reality. It is at this time in the monthly cycle that half of all females admitted to hospital will be taken there; that half of the females involved in serious accidents will have their mishap; and that most acts of suicide and violence committed by women will occur.

Are there other differences between men and women? Some would say that women are more responsive to sounds than men (mother will wake up when baby cries, father will snore peacefully through it all); and that men have a greater sexual *drive* (which makes them more impatient and hungry for gratification) while women have a greater sexual *capacity* (says Kate Millett, 'While the male's sexual potential is limited, the female's appears to be biologically almost inexhaustible'). But it has to be stressed that all these differences are relatively minor, and provide no excuse for the drastic judgments that have sometimes been made about the male-female divide. Socrates regarded a woman as an 'imperfect' man; St Thomas Aquinas said that a woman was 'defective and misbegotten', and that the birth of girl babies could sometimes be explained by the hostile influence of an adverse south wind!)

Why males dominate

It is noticeable, however, that throughout history men have tended to dominate women. There are plenty of examples of societies in which men have treated women as inferior menials; there are few examples of 'matriarchies', that is, societies in which the positions of leadership and authority are given to women rather than men. Even cases which seem to be exceptions turn out, on closer inspection, to prove the rule. Among the Iroquois Indians, it is true, the women played a central role in the selection of a chief; but the chief was always a man. In ancient Egypt, Queen Hatshepsut ruled the country just like a king; but in her sculptured portrait she is shown wearing a beard—as if to underline the fact that she was not acting as a woman but as an 'honorary man'. Mrs Thatcher has been one of the strongest British Prime Ministers of the twentieth century, but by far the majority of her cabinet have been males, and she has made it clear she prefers it that way.

Why do males dominate? Is it because they are bigger and stronger, and therefore capable of more strenuous, worthwhile activity? This may explain male dominance in ape societies, where there is a massive difference in size and weight between male and female, but among humans the difference is not so great, and anyway, in some male-dominated societies the women do much more arduous work. Another

A woman executive has to work harder to maintain her position.

explanation which has been suggested is the economic one: primitive males were the hunters, and so controlled the food supply, which allowed them to assume authority over all the affairs of the tribe. But in many societies where women are treated as inferior, they—not the men—are the producers of most of the food.

There are lots of theories (Peter Farb speculates that men proved better than women at hand-to-hand combat, and so tribes in which men were dominant survived while others did not) but no certain answers. Yet the fact remains that throughout most of the history of Western society, women have been kept in a subordinate role, and have gradually

DO ALL HUMAN SOCIETIES PRACTISE MARRIAGE?

Human beings are unpredictable. Other animals may have a great variety of different mating arrangements—some coupling together just for the season, others staying together for life, others finding many mates, some even eating their mates after intercourse —but within the species we can usually expect to find absolutely uniform behaviour. Not with humans, however. We have evolved a startling variety of different customs.

In some societies one woman will have several husbands; in other societies the reverse will be true. Some cultures expect a liaison between a man and a woman to last for life; in others the arrangement will be much less permanent. Some couples are allowed to choose one another; elsewhere the family does the choosing, and the couple may not meet until the day they begin living together.

However, one thing remains true. Every single human society recognizes the need for some sort of established system to regulate relationships between men and women. There is no society in the world where promiscuity is the rule; that would threaten the proper care of the young, and gradually lead to the extermination of the society itself.

There is no culture in the world where the family does not exist, and all attempts to eliminate it have failed. In the early days of the Russian Revolution, an experiment in allowing people to form limited-term contracts with one another in place of marriage—for a few years, a few weeks, or even a single day—had to be abandoned when it was found that gangs of unwanted de-

linquent children were beginning to form. In an Israeli kibbutz, the children are cared for communally, and close family ties are discouraged; but even here natural family preferences keep on obstinately re-asserting themselves.

Really only two forms of marriage—monogamy (one man, one woman) and polygamy (or more precisely 'polygyny': one man, several women) are common. It is

sometimes claimed that polygyny has a lot of advantages: it takes care of any surplus of females in society; it provides a socially useful way of flaunting one's wealth (taking on an extra wife is better for society than buying a new Rolls Royce); and it allows socially superior males to father more children than the incompetent, who naturally cannot afford as many wives. But this theoretical picture does not work in practice. Most polygamous societies do not in fact have a 'surplus female' problem; polyamy simply causes jealousy and inequality among men, and unfair treatment for women; and the males who are likeliest to have most wives are the

old, whose powers of reproduction are failing, but who have had time to amass enough money to afford more women.

In fact, monogamy is by far the most widespread form of marriage, because it offers benefits no other system does. It allows social stability and protection of the young, unlike a casual 'living together' arrangement. It allows the maximum number of individuals to be

The Unification Church (the 'Moonies') believe in arranged marriage, and sometimes huge numbers are wed in one ceremony. Can this take away from the truth that one man and one woman commit themselves to each other when they marry?

involved in marriage—unlike polygyny or polyandry (one woman, several men). It minimizes sexual jealousy and allows an intensity of relationship between two people which cannot be found anywhere else; and it simplifies inheritance, property and kinship problems. That is probably why—even in an age of marriage stress and increasing divorce figures—so many people still instinctively feel it is the best solution.

The Bible's prescription for marriage is that a man should 'leave his father and mother and be united to his wife, and they will become one flesh'. It still makes sense.

been struggling towards equality. As far back as 1700, Mary Astel wrote:

If all Men are born free, how is it that all Women are born slaves? As they must be if the being subjected to the inconstant, uncertain, unknown, arbitrary Will of Men, be the perfect Condition of Slavery?

Even in a society where there is theoretically equality of opportunity for men and women, the unseen pressures of our social environment can condition us to behave in certain accepted, safe, unequal ways. As Betty Friedan has written:

When girls are invited to undertake domestic chores 'just like Mummy', the utensils on offer—half-sized irons, cookers, vacuum cleaners—supply no scope for the management, marshalling and manipulation which are implicit in the public character of the boys' equivalents: toy soldiers, model railways, garages and race tracks. While boys explore an expanding range of possibilities, girls serve a brief, narrow, private apprenticeship.

Often the literature provided for children reinforces the stereotyped ideas of male domin-

ance and female submission with which we have lived for so many centuries:

Peter has a red ball. He plays with the boys with the red ball. Jane looks on. That was good, Peter, says Jane.

Jim quite enjoyed balancing on the metal rail. Susy stood and watched him with her hand to her mouth. Susy rarely did anything else when she was with him.

'Sex stereotyping' has a profound impact on the working careers of men and women. In Britain in the late 1970s, men outnumbered women in the professions at every level. Women made up 27 per cent of practising doctors, 8 per cent of all barristers (but only 4 per cent of solicitors), 2 per cent of engineers and 1 per cent of scientists and technicians. In America the figures were even lower. In the mid-eighties Diane Souhami reported:

'Seventy-five of the seventy-eight High Court judges are men, and the Civil Service is remarkable for its concentration of women in the lowest grades. In 1984 the gross weekly earnings of women in the Civil Service averaged 66 per cent of men's. No Permanent Secretaries are women, only 4 per cent

WHERE DOES HOMOSEXUALITY COME FROM?

Until Dr A.C. Kinsey, nobody realized just how many homosexuals there were. Kinsey was an American researcher who produced two reports, *Sexual Behaviour in the Human Male* (1948) and *Sexual Behaviour in the Human Female* (1952), based on over 18,000 interviews in which he questioned people about their sexual practices. He showed conclusively that homosexuality—harbouring a sexual preference for people of the same sex as oneself—was remarkably widespread. Only 4 per cent of men were exclusively homosexual, but many men carried on homosexual and

heterosexual relationships at the same time, and in all, 37 per cent of the men surveyed had had at least one homosexual experience in their adult lives.

Kinsey's findings helped to change public perceptions of homosexuality. Previously it had been dismissed as a fairly minor problem; now it came to be realized that a large proportion of the human race has homosexual inclinations. Not surprisingly, since Kinsey there have been great changes in the laws regulating homosexuality in many Western countries.

In fact not all cultures have traditionally condemned homosexual activity; in

many it has been an accepted part of life. C.S. Ford and F.A. Beach surveyed anthropological literature and discovered that out of seventy-six primitive societies which were described, forty-nine condoned some form of homosexual activity. The Siwan tribe in North Africa even thought a man peculiar if he did not sleep with both males and females; and the Aranda of Australia had a custom of homosexual 'marriage' which lasted for a few years until the older partner went off and found a female instead.

What makes someone homosexual? Many homo-

sexuals claim that they have always felt that way, that their sexuality has been with them since birth. This could mean that those who are exclusively homosexual are **born** that way, perhaps through some genetic factor; or that hormonal imbalances in their body make them **grow up** that way; or that early experiences in life **predisposed** them to become homosexuals, before they were aware of sex at all.

The search for a genetic factor has been unsuccessful. Homosexuals rarely suffer from abnormalities in their sex chromosomes, and it has not been possible to detect any linking factor in the thousands of different homosexuals who have been studied. As for hormonal imbalances, experiments have been tried in which sex offenders in prison have been dosed with androgens (male hormones) in an attempt to change their

of Deputy Secretaries, 5 per cent of Under Secretaries and 10 per cent of Principals. Unsurprisingly, however, women make up 77 per cent of clerical assistants.'

The story of feminism

It is facts such as these that have given birth to the movement known as 'feminism'—an attempt to achieve genuine equality of opportunity and status for women. Feminism has risen to prominence twice in recent history. The first time was the late nineteenth century when on both sides of the Atlantic women campaigned for the right to vote, equality of educational opportunity, and equal status before the law. It was a long, hard fight, on both sides of the Atlantic. In America, in 1872, a group of Rochester women went to register and vote, believing that the Fifteenth Amendment to the Constitution allowed them to do so. They were promptly arrested.

Anger and resentment grew, and by the early years of the twentieth century parades,

sexual orientation. The effect was certainly to increase their desire for sex—but sex of the same kind to which they were already accustomed! There was no change to hetero-sexuality.

It looks at the moment, then, as if the most likely cause of homosexuality is psychological. Perhaps certain home circumstances and life-shaping events conspire together to produce in some of us a desire for our own sex. Developmental psychologist Elizabeth Moberly describes the process as 'an intra-psychic wound, borne repressed within the personality since early childhood, which has checked a vital aspect of the normal process of psycho-logical growth since that point of time'. Whatever the cause, homosexual feelings cannot easily be removed.

Different religions have different stances towards homosexuality. The Christian tradition has always rejected homosexual *conduct*, but the Bible does not condemn the homosexual *nature* —which is something that the individual can't help. Most Christians (apart from a small and vocal minority in the Gay Christian Move-ment) believe that God's plan for sexual life is heterosexuality, the comple-mentarity of male and female, and therefore homosexual acts are a distortion of the sexuality God intended.

picket signs, automobile rallies and speech burnings were attracting wide attention to the cause. In Britain, the Women's Social and Political Union was formed in 1905 by Mrs Emmeline Pankhurst and her two daughters. The movement became notorious for its dramatic and even violent methods: smashing windows, pouring acid into post boxes, setting fire to empty houses, women chaining themselves to railings. When imprisoned, they refused to eat. One 'suffragette', Emily Davison, made her way to the Derby race meeting in 1913 and flung herself to her death in front of the King's horse. Christabel Pankhurst wrote in a WSPU pamphlet:

It is only simple justice that women demand. . . For fifty years they have been striving and have met with nothing but trickery and betrayal at the hands of politicians. Cabinet Ministers have taunted them with their reluctance to use the violent methods that were being used by men before they won the extension of the franchise in 1829, in 1832 and in 1867. They have used women's dislike of violence as a reason for withholding from them the rights of citizenship. . . The message of the broken pane is that women are determined that the lives of their sisters shall no longer be broken, and that in future those who have to obey the law shall have a voice in saying what the law shall be.

By the end of the First World War, the valuable part played by women in roles which had never been open to them in peacetime had convinced many people that their cause was right. Votes for women (over the age of thirty, at least) arrived in Britain in 1918, and the United States followed suit in 1920 when finally thirty-six states passed the proposed legislation.

The next wave of feminism did not arrive until the 1960s, and it was provoked by Betty Friedan's book, which we have already mentioned. (An earlier book— *The Second Sex* by Simone de Beauvoir—had helped to prepare the ground a decade before.) Betty Friedan put into words what many thousands of women had been feeling: that despite the supposed equality which now existed, society was silently coercing women into accepting a narrow, reduced view of their potential in life, by squeezing them into the mould of 'housewife and mother'. The depression and emptiness they felt was 'the problem that had no name'. She suggested it was a direct result of the Second World War:

A pent-up hunger for marriage, home and children was felt simultaneously by several different generations; a hunger which, in the prosperity of post-war America, everyone could suddenly satisfy...

For the girls, these lonely (wartime) years added an extra urgency to their search for love. Those who married in the thirties saw their husbands off to war; those who grew up in the forties were afraid, with reason, that they might never have the love, the homes, and children which few women would willingly miss. When the men came back there was a headlong rush into marriage.

Was Friedan right? Her ideas have been much criticized since. Marxist feminists complain, justly, that 'she excludes working-class women from the terms of reference and never penetrates the manifestations of women's oppression through the material structure of society'. Jonathan Gathorne-Hardy points out that her analysis of what happened after the war fits America much more convincingly than other countries; there had to be more factors at work than she claims. His idea is that Betty Friedan's popularity came because society was now intensely concerned with personal fulfilment and success in living as it never had been before:

The developments of the 1950s should be viewed as the expression of a generation—the Privilege Bulge Generation—brought up under the ever-growing influence of psychoanalytic ideas and in search, therefore, of personal happiness and fulfilment...

What, in a general way, has happened is that, for all ages, growth has joined sex and much else as the point of any relationship, including the most important relationship—marriage.

Be that as it may, Betty Friedan's work led very rapidly to the growth of a new network of women's organizations, including consciousness-raising groups, women's publishing companies, theatre companies, counselling services for rape victims, and refuges for battered wives. Much faster than the early feminists, today's activists have made an impact on the law: the US Congress passed an Equal Rights Amendment in 1972, and the British Sex Discrimination Act of 1975 set up an Equal Opportunities Commission to ensure fairness in employment.

Broadly speaking, there are now three main groups of feminist thinkers. One is the **liberal** feminists, of whom Friedan is one. These feminists want equality, but believe they can achieve it without any fundamental changes to the status quo in society. Elaine Storkey says about them:

Liberal feminists today would still argue that emancipation can be fully achieved without any major alteration to the economic structures of contemporary capitalist democracies. Nor would we expect to find any major challenge to the patriarchal system from 'mainstream' liberal feminism. For the problem is not with systems per se—class or patriarchal. It remains at a deep level as one of individual freedom...

Marxist feminists see the problem of female equality as being deeply embedded in the repressive structures of capitalism. Women will not be equal until we achieve socialism. But many of them point out that male Marxists have often failed to take female concerns into their thinking: Sheila Rowbotham argues:

In order for Marxism to prove useful as a revolutionary weapon for women, we have at once to encounter it in its existing form and fashion it to fit our particular oppression. This means extending it into areas in which men have been unable to take it by distilling it through the particularities of our own experience.

Finally, there are **radical** feminists, for whom the problem lies deeper than the economic argument between capitalism and socialism. Even supposing we had a revolution, they argue, we would just replace a male-dominated capitalist regime with a male-dominated socialist one. The real problem is patriarchy—the oppressive attitude to women which has permeated all society's arrangements throughout history. How is patriarchy to be eradicated? Some feminists see the answer as biological (women's bodies must be freed from the responsibility of giving birth, by artificial means of reproduction); others see it as legal (increasing the protection of women against rape, the massive potential threat which has always allowed men to keep women in fear and submission); others claim it is cultural (unpicking the threads of male-dominated educational systems, and rewriting history, sociology and

Women protesting about missiles at England's Greenham Common, mothers demanding the return of their vanished children in the then military dictatorship of Argentina — a leading role in modern peacemaking and human rights is played by women.

psychology from a female perspective).

Feminists disagree with one another about a great deal, but on one topic many of them are united. They see the Bible as anti-feminist, and Christianity as a system of reaction and oppression. Are they right?

Women and the Bible

Certainly it cannot be denied that some Christian leaders have been strongly convinced of the inferiority of women. 'The woman herself alone is not the image of God,' taught Saint Augustine, 'whereas the man alone is the image of God as fully and completely as when the woman is joined with him.' 'You are the devil's gateway,' growled Tertullian, to women in general; 'you are she who first violated the forbidden tree and broke the law of God.' But statements like this are not found in the Bible itself. Indeed the Old Testament contains a memorable picture of a fulfilled, successful, creative woman (in Proverbs chapter 31), and holds her up as an example of God's ideal. And in the New Testament, Jesus gave women a place of importance among his followers which was frankly scandalous to the orthodox teachers of his day.

Some feminists have charged the Bible with anti-feminism because it presents a God who is a Father. This is patriarchal, they argue. Why not a Mother Goddess? Plenty of the nations surrounding Israel worshipped female deities. But that was the problem, argues Mary Hayter: the idea of a goddess was tied up with ecstatic fertility religions of a kind which trivialized and cheapened the Israelite understanding of God:

To them, it seemed that the only way to purge the nation of the obsessive fertility cult was to remove all notions of a Goddess from Yahwistic religion, for in the ancient Near Eastern milieu any form of Goddess worship meant opening the door to the unequivocally sensual character of the vegetation

deities... Veneration of a Goddess alongside Yahweh involved ideas and actions which thoughtful Hebrews no longer found compatible with the nature of their faith in a unique and transcendent God... Therefore, the objective of Old Testament writers was... to avoid, as far as possible, any projection of human sexuality on to their God. They believed Yahweh to be neither male nor female but supra-sexual.

It is clear from a passage in one of the apostle Paul's letters that women were allowed to pray aloud and prophesy in public in the early Christian church—an astounding liberty which would not have been allowed in the Jewish synagogues from which some of them had come. And in his letter to the Galatians, Paul recites a formula which was probably repeated at baptismal services, when a new Christian was welcomed into the Christian church:

There is neither Jew nor Greek, slave nor free, male nor female, for you are all one in Christ Jesus.

Each morning an orthodox Jew would say the *beraka*—a special prayer in which he thanked God for not making him a Gentile, a slave, or a woman. Now the Christians were saying that these kinds of distinctions—racial, economic *and sexual*—had no meaning any longer. Women and men are equals. No wonder many Christians were involved with the early feminist movements; Betty Friedan quotes a black feminist named Sojourner Truth:

Look at my arm! I have ploughed and planted and gathered into barns... and ain't I a woman? I could work as much and eat as much as a man—when I could get it—and bear the lash as well... I have borne thirteen children and seen most of 'em sold into slavery, and when I cried out with my mother's grief, none but Jesus helped me... and ain't I a woman?

Christians are not anti-feminist—or they should not be. But they would want to say to liberal feminists like Betty Friedan: are you so sure that true fulfilment comes with equal opportunity, or is it possible that the emptiness you discern in women's lives needs a deeper fulfilment yet? And to Marxists they would want to say: where is the evidence that revolution will bring female equality? Aren't the radicals right in alleging that Marxist movements so far have shown no signs of an end to male chauvinism? And to the radicals, in the words of Elaine Storkey: 'Crucial to a woman-centred utopia must be love. Self-giving, sharing and caring, patience and joy are the very building blocks of the new future... But radical feminism can provide no basis for these qualities. If gender characteristics are all socially constructed, how can any such qualities be inherent in womanhood?'

In short, equality of men and women is important, desperately important. But it will not solve all the problems of the human race in one fell swoop; nor will it be achieved by the natural goodness and altruism of human beings. It will take a transformation of human character to make it possible.

And there, Christians feel, they have some unique solutions to suggest.

8

THE HUMAN RECORD

If an alien in a UFO had been skimming over the surface of Planet Earth 5,000 years ago, looking for signs of civilization, he might not have been very impressed by what he found. There would have been signs of life in several places, and evidence that human beings were learning to control their environment: dogs, pigs and cattle were being domesticated, crops were being grown. Our alien would have noted groups of people on the move in search of better agricultural land and living conditions. He would have noted flat-roofed mud houses in Bulgaria, and thatched villages in Holland. Stone-built tombs were scattered across the face of Europe. But civilization in any real sense had still to arrive.

If he had come back two thousand years later, the alien would have found a lot of changes. He would see evidence of extensive city building around Egypt, the Mediterranean, India and China. The 'Fertile Crescent' in the Middle East would have presented a hive of activity—with thousands of people building, travelling, fighting, trading. Altogether, he'd be much more impressed, and slightly amazed that so much was now happening in so many places unconnected with one another.

Two thousand years after that, the contrast would be even more startling. Now human civilization could be found, not just in a few important areas, but almost everywhere on the earth's surface. The Great Wall of China would already have been straggling across the map for three centuries. Great civilizations would have risen and fallen in Africa, and even in South America—quite uninfluenced by what humans were doing anywhere else. Roman and Greek architecture could be spotted in countries whole continents apart from one another. Persia, Ethiopia, Japan, Northern Europe—

wherever he looked, our alien observer would find human beings leaving their mark on the environment. Few parts of the world would have been left undisturbed by progress.

Let's imagine that our alien was overcome with curiosity and timed his next visit for only a thousand years thereafter. What would he find today? That a revolution in agriculture, science and technology has transformed the face of this planet even more. He would see more change in this last thousand years than on any of his previous trips. And he'd note that the buildings and human artefacts on different continents showed much more similarity than ever before: that the whole of human culture has become much more unified. He would see evidence, too, that we are preparing for another major change in our control of the environment: launching pads on at least two continents, showing that human beings have developed the ability to leave their home planet and travel into space. As he flew past drifting clouds of acid rain, and glimpsed polluted lakes thick with industrial effluent, the alien would also realize that another change has taken place. Human beings have now achieved so much control of their environment that they can destroy it, too. . .

The human race has come a long way in just over five thousand years. And the story has been one of gradual acceleration; at first the changes came slowly and steadily, but bit by bit the pace of change has quickened until now it is so rapid that human beings find it hard to adjust to. Alvin Toffler has written:

Take an individual out of his own culture and set him down suddenly in an environment sharply different from his own, with a different set of cues to react to—different conceptions of time, space, work, love, religion, sex, and everything else—then cut him off from any hope of retreat to a more familiar landscape, and the dislocation he suffers is doubly severe. Moreover, if this new culture is itself in constant turmoil, and if—worse yet—its values are incessantly changing, the sense of disorientation will be still further intensified. . .

Now imagine not merely an individual but an entire society, an entire generation—including its weakest, least intelligent, and most irrational members—suddenly transported into this new world. The result is mass disorientation, future shock on a grand scale.

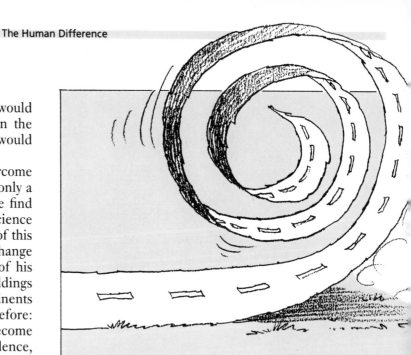

FROM AGRICULTURE TO INDUSTRY

According to an ancient Sumerian text, 'When the human species appeared, it did not know bread or cloth. Man walked on hands and feet. He ate grass with the mouth as animals do, and he drank the water of the stream.'

Just a mythical story, of course, but reminding us of something important: life has not always been this way. Human beings have gradually taken more and more command of the planet, and altered their own lives significantly in the process.

It has been claimed that 'for all but one per cent of our known existence' humanity lived by primitive hunting and gathering—relying for our survival on whatever we could find lying about. This all began to change some time after the tenth millennium BC, when human beings began living in villages, domesticating animals, and actively trying to make plants grow instead of just picking berries. This was the Agricultural Revolution, which started in the Near East and spread all over the world. Farming became the style of life of most human beings, and hunting decreased in popularity, until in the eighteenth century something new happened which made both hunting and farming secondary occupations.

This time it was the Industrial Revolution, which began in England, but in the twentieth century has affected most parts of the world. More than 80 per cent of the world's active population was engaged in agriculture in 1750. Two hundred years later it was around 60 per cent —and falling steadily.

The Industrial Revolution drew people into large towns and cities, and gave them jobs centred round machinery which increased human power over the environment to a staggering new degree. Not that everyone was involved directly in industry: unlike an agricultural society, an industrial society involves far less of its members in actual 'industry'. Instead, the industrialization allows the growth of a 'tertiary sector' of service activities—banking, insurance, government, the liberal professions.

These Revolutions were

more than just twists and turns in history. They marked significant jumps ahead in the way people lived. Life changed almost overnight in the most bewildering fashion.

For one thing, the total amount of energy under human control increased enormously. Agriculture meant human control of 'chemical energy from edible plants and animals, heat from plants, power from draught animals. . . Populations expanded in size beyond any former "ceiling". . . Certain groups and classes at least became free of the continuous search for food. Specialization became possible and also higher forms of activity and leisurely speculation.' Industrialization meant completely new sources of energy—not just plants, animals and human labour—and expanded the possibilities for human life to an unimagined degree. In 1800 the world produced about 15 million tons of coal each year; by 1950 it was producing about 1,454 million tons.

All of this meant that life expectancy changed dramatically too. From what we know of pre-agricultural life, we can deduce that there was a very low density of population, with infanticide, war, headhunting and starvation frequent causes of death. In the 'agricultural' period, things were a little better, although life expectancy at birth was no more than twenty to thirty-five years, and the growth of population was slowed by recurrent waves of epidemics—clear evidence that humans had not yet completely gained control of their environment. In industrial society, famine and epidemic diseases have been successfully combatted, and the population of the world has risen dramatically. It took until 1830 for world population to reach one billion. By 1930 it had reached two billion. Now there are five billion of us, and more arriving every minute.

This is the prospect that man now faces. Change is avalanching upon our heads and most people are grotesquely unprepared to cope with it.

The story of human progress becomes even more startling if we look at the age of the earth we live on. We have really appeared very recently within history. Francis Crick has remarked that if we equate the age of the earth with a single week, 'Modern man would have appeared in the last ten seconds and agriculture in the last one or two. Odysseus would have lived only half a second before the present time.'

How have we reached our present position? Where did human civilization come from—and how has it grown? The story is almost impossible to condense into a short chapter such as this one. But perhaps we can have a look at some of its main outlines.

The first human civilizations

Around 3300BC southern Mesopotamia was a very wet place to live. Its fertile plain was bounded by two great rivers which often overflowed their banks, and the drainage from annual flooding made the soil more productive than anywhere else in the Near East. Not that life was easy; the constant peril of flooding, and the need to keep crops well irrigated when rain was infrequent, meant that systems of banking and channelling water had to be worked out with ever-increasing complexity. The land was fertile: it produced enough food to free some of the population from the necessity of working in agriculture. And irrigation channels were needed, and this forced people to work together on a large scale. Perhaps it was these two factors which led to the growth of cities, and a sophisticated pattern of life, earlier here than anywhere else.

For about a thousand years, the history of Sumer (an ancient name for the region) was a confused story of internal battles between city states led by warrior kings. But eventually— between 2400 and 2350BC—one great leader, Sargon I, conquered all the cities one by one and welded them into a unified empire. Sargon had trading links with countries as distant as the Levant and Syria, was rumoured to have sent his soldiers as far as Egypt and Ethiopia, and is said to have had 5,400 soldiers eating in his palace. The empire he built lasted for two centuries, until his great-grandson was overthrown. But Sumerian civilization continued until about 2000BC, when the central city of Ur was overthrown by invading Elamites.

The Sumerians achieved a great deal: an increasingly sophisticated system of writing; massive temples, palaces, and ziggurats; a remarkably well-thought-out legal system; and the first organized educational system in the world. But just as important was the effect they had on their neighbours. Sumerian civilization sparked off change in nations round about. One immediate result was the neighbouring empire of Babylon, which around 1792BC produced one of the greatest law-givers of ancient times, Hammurabi.

But things were stirring further west as well. Only a century or so after the rise of Sumer, a king called Menes succeeded in unifying the whole of Egypt—carving out for himself a kingdom six hundred miles long. This was the beginning of a civilization which was to last for two thousand years and span twenty dynasties of rulers.

Egyptian civilization was centred on the importance of the king. He was the supreme landowner, the source of all law, and also a divine figure. 'He is a god by whose dealings one lives, the father and mother of all men, alone by himself, without an equal,' wrote an Egyptian civil servant around 1500BC. But the king could not have kept his position without the civil service. Another Egyptian achievement was the building of an impressive bureaucracy to keep the state running, involving thousands of scribes, trained in history, writing, law, surveying and accountancy.

Writing (which took the form of hieroglyphics, much harder to learn than Sumerian cuneiform) was a skill jealously kept for the initiated few, like a trade secret. The Egyptians can take the credit for inventing papyrus, which took writing into new realms of flexibility that clay or stone tablets would not allow; without it we might never have had the modern book. But what most people remember the Egyptians for is their massive public buildings—the palaces and pyramids of the Pharaohs.

The pyramids are not actually remarkable for the technical skill employed in their construction. The Egyptians did not use winches or pulleys, just levers, and their feats were achieved by employing thousands of slaves to manhandle the gigantic blocks physically into place. The Great Pyramid of Cheops, for instance—which contains 2.5 million stones weighing from 2.5 to 15 tons—employed around 100,000 unskilled labourers as well as craftsmen and quarrymen. It took twenty years to complete.

About two centuries after Egypt became a nation, other civilizations burst into flower further north. On the small Mediterranean island of Crete, the Minoans were establishing a rich culture based on craftsmanship and trade—tin from Spain, gold and pearls from Egypt, ivory from Syria and North Africa. The Minoans produced complex metalwork, glazed faience earthenware, and gold jewellery. The sense of colour, the appreciation of nature and the exuberant joy of living which emerges from Minoan records is unlike anything else in the world of their day.

Just as Minoan civilization was ending (probably through the devastation caused by violent volcanic eruptions in 1400BC), another style of life was evolving in China. A tribe called the Shang became the rulers of about 40,000 square miles of territory, and built there a sophisticated culture with a common currency, ambitious building projects and a complex system of government. Eventually they were deposed by another tribe, the Chou; but the structure they had built remained, and helped to form the shape of later Chinese civilization. Order in society, the importance of the family, specified social roles for every citizen—these ideas were taken up later in the sixth century by China's great thinker, Confucius, whose influential teaching was to dominate the thinking of the Chinese for the next two thousand years.

Shortly after this came the first real African civilization south of Egypt—the kingdom of Kush (which in fact conquered Egypt and ruled it for some years)—and the beginnings of Indian culture with its caste system and elaborate religious philosophy. So far, civilization had sprung up on almost every continent, but little had happened in Europe. But that was about to change.

The great age of Greece and Rome

Somewhere around 1200BC, the country we now call Greece was invaded by a people from the north, who drove the original inhabitants out of their lands to take refuge in a few key cities and in islands around the Aegean. Four hundred years later, both the invaders and the original inhabitants were starting to think of themselves as one nation—and Greece was born.

Greek civilization was formed around the city-state—a small area of country ruled and administered by a city set within it. The cities were not large (few had over 20,000 inhabitants) but were self-contained centres with their own distinctive character. It is not surprising that the idea of democracy began in Greece, where every citizen could readily feel he had a vital part to play in the development of his own tiny state.

The first three hundred years of Greek life, the 'Archaic period', laid the foundations of Greek art. Lyric poetry started to be written, and intricate, beautifully decorated ceramic art was produced. Sculpture, too: and the Greeks specialized in realistic portrayal of the human body, in a quite unprecedented, startlingly lifelike way. The perfectly formed human body was thought to be the ultimate in beauty, and Greek fascination with it led to some amazing artistic achievements.

The Greeks also began the attempt to understand the workings of life and the universe by rational means. Philosophy, the 'love of wisdom', was another Greek innovation —and the foundations were laid in the Archaic period.

But it was in the following century—the fifth century BC—that Greece reached its golden age of poetry, drama, art and history. Herodotus, the writer who began historical analysis of an objective kind, was born in 480BC. Just ten years later appeared Socrates, most famous of philosophers—and close behind him came Plato and Aristotle. There seemed no end to the talent and genius emerging from the cities of fifth-century Greece. Medicine and science flourished alongside philosophy. Astronomy and geology made advances.

In the north of Greece, a warrior statesman called Philip of Macedon began to dream of

unifying the whole of Greece under one central government. If he could do this, he reasoned, he could lead a Greek army into Asia and take over new lands on which to settle Greek people. And despite Athenian opposition he succeeded in bringing Greece together, but then died unexpectedly before he could lead the army to Asia. Undeterred, Philip's son Alexander took over, and by his series of victories, all achieved before his early death at thirty-two, he managed to spread Greek culture widely over the ancient world.

Alexandria, a city established in Egypt by the Greeks, became the centre of this cultural diffusion: its massive port attracted ships from many countries, and its great library brought together the key literature of the ancient world. Alexandria was the place where Euclid worked out the foundational principles of geometry, and where Aristarchus of Samos calculated (centuries before Copernicus) that the earth goes round the sun.

Just as the Archaic period was beginning in Greece, a neighbouring civilization was establishing itself in Northern Italy. The Etruscans were spread over an area from the valley of the river Po down to the south beyond Rome—a fertile area with extensive reserves of iron, copper and wood. We know little for certain about Etruscan civilization (they left no history behind, although we know that they kept records). We have to guess about their life from the detail in their colourful paintings. They seem to have been keen on trying to foretell the future, using elaborate means of divination from the entrails of animals; a practice the Romans later copied. And they speculated a great deal about what happens after death. They also prized excellent craftsmanship, especially in bronze.

Then Rome itself broke free from the Etruscan grip, and started annexing more and more Etruscan territory. By 200BC Etruscan civilization was more or less over. Now it was the turn of the Romans to found an empire which would dominate the ancient world for half a millennium, and leave an indelible impression on the languages and even the landscape of Western Europe.

After breaking away from their previous Etruscan rulers, the Romans started to attract the loyalty of other small states in Italy. Eventually they became strong enough to challenge the might of another ambitious Mediterranean city—Carthage, in North Africa —and decisively win the contest. After that, they turned their attention to Greece: 150 years after Alexander the Great, Macedonia itself fell to Roman dominance.

The Romans continued to spread their influence further and further, and by the second century AD were holding together an awesome collection of nations and subject peoples in one vast empire. The *Pax Romana*, or 'Roman Peace', which linked together countries who would otherwise have fought unproductive wars against one another, enabled trade and the arts to flourish, and an increased standard of living.

What were the Romans' main achievements? They developed a new building material, concrete, which allowed them to construct durable architecture on an awesome scale. They built straight roads and aqueducts with a sure grasp of complicated engineering principles. The need to hold together an empire of very different peoples brought about the foundations of international law. Their literature and art may not have quite the disarming beauty of Greek culture, but it built on the achievements of the Greeks, and added some memorable works of genius.

Health care, sanitation, military thinking, town planning, the calendar—to list all the achievements of the Romans would take the rest of this chapter. One very important but quite unexpected (and at first unwanted) benefit of the *Pax Romana* was the growth of the religious faith which was to influence more people than any other in the world's history: Christianity.

Jesus Christ was born in a small province ruled by the Roman empire. The Jewish nation to which he belonged was small, but possessed

an impressive cultural history of its own. The Jews had a startlingly sophisticated religious tradition of faith in one Creator God, and the writings of their prophets and poets had developed their picture of the God they worshipped to a subtlety unmatched in any of the comparatively crude myths of their neighbours. Their belief in this one God had matured and deepened during traumatic periods of national disaster and years of captivity and exile.

Jews and Christians today would claim that the unusual religious grasp of this small tribe was no accident, but came from God's choice of Israel as his chosen people, to whom he planned to reveal himself gradually through the centuries. Christians would go on to say that his revelation reached completion when the time came for the arrival within that nation of God's own son. Jesus Christ was the fulfilment of that plan.

The early Christians, convinced that their leader had risen from the dead, spread the message about him throughout the ancient world. And here the *Pax Romana* proved extremely useful. Christian missionaries were able to travel with comparative ease from one country to another, and spread their ideas through the trading routes and cultural centres of the empire. They were so successful that despite fierce opposition the Roman empire itself eventually surrendered to them; Christianity became the state religion of the empire from AD329.

Greece and Rome were in many ways the most impressive civilizations of this period of history; but they were not the only ones. Two hundred years before Greece became a nation, settlers had moved into the area of Persia and set up two rival kingdoms—Media and Parsa. Four hundred years later they were one nation, united by Cyrus the Great, king of Parsa. And by 546BC his empire included Assyria, Babylonia, part of central Asia and lands in India. Twenty years later, Egypt too was part of this empire.

Cyrus planned carefully to hold his empire together. He was unusually tolerant of the religious faiths of his subject peoples (the Jews, for example, were given permission to rebuild the city of Jerusalem and re-establish temple worship—something their previous conquerors had not permitted). The legal system which operated throughout the empire was famous.

Administratively, the whole territory was divided into twenty provinces, and a taxation system set up; the Persians invented the first internationally-used monetary system so that taxes could be paid in money rather than goods. A long 'Royal Road' ran right across the empire for 1,600 miles, up to the royal palace at Susa.

The Persian empire did not remain strong. It was conquered by Alexander the Great in 334–31BC; then the Parthians took it over in AD261; then Bedouins captured it in the seventh century and the Persian city of Baghdad became the centre of an Islamic empire. But Persia showed a peculiar capacity for winning over her invaders. Alexander married a Persian, and alarmed his advisors by proposing to re-structure Greece along Persian lines; Islamic culture was to owe most of its shape to Persian cultural achievements, and its administrative arrangements to Persian ways of doing things.

India; the Pacific rim

While all this was going on, very different civilizations were taking shape further away. At the same time as Greek society was emerging, the foundations of Indian culture were being laid too. As Greece reached its 'golden age', India already had a system of kings ruling small areas, a caste system which divided people into sharply defined social groups, and an elaborate religious system, in which priests wielded enormous power over everyone else. Around 500BC their position was attacked by a series of reformers—of whom the greatest was Gautama Buddha, the founder of a new philosophy which sent its missionaries all over the East at the same time that Christian missionaries were evangelizing the West.

Most of north and central India was united in the third century BC, and the impact of Buddhism was soon felt when the third emperor Ashoka became converted (after a military campaign which sickened him because of the loss of life involved). As a Buddhist, Ashoka renounced war as a means of conquering his enemies, instituted medical services and social support systems, banned the killing of animals for sacrifice, and insisted that justice must be even-handed, treating the poor identically with the rich. Ashoka taught that kings were responsible to their people, as well as vice versa—a revolutionary thought for his day, and one that was to have no influence elsewhere for many centuries to come.

Under Ashoka, Buddhist teachers spread their message southwards, and won a growing following. Hinduism was not to take the initiative again until the emergence of the Gupta dynasty, around AD319. Their cultural influence (which included developments in painting, pottery, dance, and an appreciation of sexual skills—the *Kama Sutra* comes from this period) re-established traditional Indian ways of looking at life. Their policy of building new villages threatened the supremacy of the Buddhist monasteries, which by now were wealthy and confined to major centres.

In the end Buddhism was to lose the battle for India, but make its most important impact on other Asian cultures. One of those was China. After the Shang dynasty, which we have already mentioned, and the Chou who followed them, China splintered into a collection of warring states, and was not brought together again until the Qin dynasty imposed their authority in 221BC. They were harsh rulers, who lost popularity among the intellectuals by trying to stamp out all literature which was privately owned, and lost the favour of ordinary people by the suffering they exposed them to during the building of the Great Wall. Not surprisingly, there was a revolt, and the Han dynasty took over. Their four hundred years of rule, roughly parallel in time to the emergence of Rome, saw the beginnings of history writing; the invention of paper; an understanding of magnetism and the compass; and widespread use of cast iron (eighteen hundred years before Europe discovered it). But they proved incapable of holding their territory together, and from AD220 onwards China went through some very unsettled years.

But this was just the time when Japanese culture began to spring into life. A chieftain called Jimmu succeeded in conquering most of the country around AD300, and his victory made it possible for a Japanese society to emerge, closely copying Chinese culture, thinking, sculpture and architecture. (Even today the Japanese system of writing is unwieldy, involving 1,800 separate characters—which is because it did not emerge naturally within Japan, but was simply adopted from the Chinese system.)

Buddhism, which had penetrated China during the Han period, arrived in Japan in the sixth century AD, and was adopted alongside the traditional Shinto religion.

Other things were beginning to stir. Across the Pacific ocean, in South America, the great city of Teotihuacan flourished from the time of Christ until six hundred years or so later. It was a major trading centre with a massive complex of religious and public buildings attached, and had a population of more than 100,000 people. It bestowed an enormous legacy on later South American civilizations, even after it had been mysteriously besieged and burnt in 750BC by unknown attackers.

One of the great civilizations to follow Teotihuacan was that of the Maya, who centred themselves on what is now Guatemala and south-east Mexico. The Maya built great architectural monuments in elaborate complexes, but did not actually live in them. These places were only for the priests and the leaders; the rest of the people lived in temporary forest huts, and moved to a new home every second year or so. This was because their fairly primitive agricultural methods exhausted the soil's capacity quickly, and they had to move on to new fields.

Despite these and other limitations (they never discovered the wheel, for example), the Maya achieved some startling things. Their elaborate calendar, based on careful astronomical work, gave them a grasp of the immensity of time which was superior to that of any other ancient people. The Mayans were able to imagine a prehistory of hundreds of thousands of years. Their greatest period was between AD600 and 900; but the last Mayan city did not fall to the Spaniards until 1699.

Mayan civilization was just beginning, and Jimmu was just conquering Japan, when the Roman empire underwent a dramatic shift. Constantine, the emperor who had embraced Christianity, decided that Rome was not a suitable place for the capital of a new Christian empire. It had too many traditional associations with the old gods. And so he moved his capital to Byzantium, an old Greek trading town on the Bosphorus, creating within six years a major city which came to be called (after him) Constantinople. He chose the site with care—it stood strategically on some of the most important trade routes in the world—and planned the city ambitiously. Byzantium became the focus of a fabulous amount of wealth and artistic enterprise.

The Byzantine empire lasted until 1453, when Mehmet II, a young Ottoman Sultan, conquered the city of Constantinople and turned it into an Islamic centre. But for all its long life it enjoyed scarcely a single year of peace. It was constantly under attack from envious neighbours; and within Byzantium itself there was an atmosphere of intrigue and suspicion. No less than twenty-nine of its eighty-eight emperors died violent deaths.

Byzantium was the centre of world Christianity for a while, and hosted some of the great councils in which disputed matters of Christian faith were resolved and creeds formulated. The Byzantine emperor was regarded as the earthly head of the Christian church, until AD800, when Pope Leo III crowned Charles, King of the Franks, as Emperor of the Holy Roman Empire. This split between two versions of Christianity—the Western and the Eastern—later had ruinous consequences, when in 1204 an army of Western Crusaders attacked Constantinople.

However it was excused, the primary motive for this sudden devastation was simple greed: the Crusaders wanted the wealth of the city for themselves. They had little appreciation of Byzantium's unique culture. The city was stripped bare of every kind of item of value, even ancient Christian relics. The shock to Byzantium's system was one from which she never completely managed to rally; and two centuries later Mehmet II ended eleven hundred years of illustrious empire.

But where had the Ottomans come from? And the Crusaders? To trace the story of their civilizations, we need to move back to a period five hundred years before.

This Hindu holy man has taken a vow never again to lie down. He sleeps supported by ropes. The holy men of India stand in one of the longest religious traditions in the world.

The barbarians and afterwards

Between the years AD300 and 500, it might have seemed to our alien observer that human civilization was going into reverse. For waves of nomads began to sweep through the most significant civilizations of the world, looting and ravaging as they went. Rome was raided and sacked in 410 by the Visigoths; the Gupta empire in India was destroyed by Huns in 465; the Ostrogoths terrorized Italy, and the Vandals roamed over Spain and North Africa (also descending on Rome, in 455). Not just to aliens in spacecraft, but also to ordinary people in the frightened West, these events seemed inexplicable and bewildering; and one of the greatest books in the history of the Christian church—Augustine's *City of God*—was written to try to explain from a Christian perspective what was happening to the old civilization.

In less troubled areas, however, good things were still happening. The Maya in South America were steadily building towards their greatest years. The Sasanid empire in Persia was bringing Persian art and learning to one of its most notable periods of greatness. And even the barbarians soon settled down—adopting Roman law and even Christianity. A new, independent, Germanic culture began to take shape.

But the biggest surprise was to come from the Arabian deserts—a strip of unpromising land significant for nothing but a few warring tribes and grazing herds. This was where the prophet Muhammad began at the beginning of the seventh century to preach a new faith—an urgent appeal to human beings to put away evil, submit to God's rules for living, and live in a brotherhood with other believers. The new faith was simple, compelling and authoritative; it rapidly won a following, and eager Arab converts began to overrun neighbouring countries. Less than a century after the death of Muhammad, their empire stretched from Spain almost to India; a hundred years later they were established in India itself, and two hundred years after that the great African kingdom of Ghana was conquered by Muslim warriors. It was an astonishing achievement—based, for once, not on an outstanding military leader but on the power of religious conviction.

The Islamic empire used the different skills of its subject peoples, and the commercial links it could establish with other areas, to build a rich, colourful and distinctive culture. Works of science and philosophy—all the scholarly achievements of the ancient world—were translated into Arabic, and Arab scholars made important discoveries in medicine, mathematics and science. Poetry, weaving, metalworking—in the arts as well as the sciences Arab culture advanced.

Meanwhile in China the Han dynasty had collapsed within the third century, and the country was plunged once again into a confused period of short-lived governments. But just as the Arabs were beginning to listen to the voice of Muhammad, another great dynasty—the Tang—arrived on the scene. Their achievement was to link China much more closely with the cultural achievements of other nations: through trade and travel, the Chinese of the Tang dynasty developed an appreciation for the best of what was happening abroad, and it created a new cosmopolitan style in art and literature. Pottery and landscape painting reached new standards of attainment. Alien visitors would not have noticed a wealthier (or indeed larger)

city anywhere on the earth's surface than the Tang capital Ch'ang-an.

After the Tang began to lose their power, the country was re-united by a new dynasty, the Song. During their three hundred years of power, artistic masterpieces continued to be produced, but learning also began to be much more widespread. This had something to do with the fact that the Song had discovered the art of printing, which allowed them to diffuse ideas much more rapidly. In addition, they put the administration of the nation into the hands of civil servants who qualified for their jobs by passing examinations based on the Confucian classics. (This examination system continued until 1905.)

Human civilization had now reached the point where most different civilizations were at least aware of some of the others. Few were totally isolated any more. Civilization in Russia, for example, started around this time when Vladimir, Grand Prince of Kiev, sent envoys to look at various other countries to decide which religion the Russians should embrace. They investigated Jews, Muslims, Catholic and Orthodox Christians before selecting the brand they preferred—something that could not have happened a few centuries before!

But there were still some isolated spots on earth. And there, too, the human cultural enterprise was continuing.

Africa and America

Mali today is one of the poorest countries in the world. This certainly was not the case in the thirteenth century, when it absorbed the ancient kingdom of Ghana and spread to cover an area of West Africa measuring a thousand miles across. The ruler of Mali is said to have had ten thousand horses in his stables. Europeans who later came into contact with Mali's capital Timbuktu expressed shocked astonishment that a nation so far removed from the rest of the world should have produced such wealth and splendour.

Not that Mali was totally remote. Its rulers adopted Islam (although most of their subjects seem to have clung on to tribal religions) and in 1307 one of them caused a sensation when

ARE WE DESTROYING OUR PLANET?

'Human beings now have to live on a planet whose carrying capacity for all practical purposes is irreversibly less now than it was previously. Unless concerted action is taken immediately, there will be a further decline in the planet's capacity to support its population. Subsequent generations will be left a sorry heritage: less productive land; less diversity; less room for manoeuvre; fewer options; more people.'

These claims are made by Robert Allen, senior policy advisor at the Swiss-based International Union for Conservation of Nature and Natural Resources. He produces some arresting figures to back his argument. The world's deserts are expanding at a rate of 23,000 square miles per year—twice the area of Belgium. India loses 6,000 million tonnes of fertile soil annually. In North America, 4,800 square kilometres of excellent farming land disappear under concrete and tarmac every year.

Tropical rain forests are the richest land environments on this planet. Yet their trees are toppling at a rate of fifty acres *every minute*. By the end of this century, we will have just half the amount of un-logged productive tropical rain forest which exists at the moment. What are we doing to ourselves?

Then there are pesticides. When Professor Ralph Dougherty took semen samples from a test group of healthy students, he was startled to find that in every cubic centimetre there were only two-thirds as many sperm cells as in samples taken in 1929. He tested further, and found that the students' genitals contained chemicals that should not have been there. Particularly DDT—which has been banned since 1972, but is almost indestructible and clearly has not gone away.

At the time of writing, concern is rising about what we may be doing to the ozone layer of the upper atmosphere. Some types of aerosol spray have been shown to damage it. And that could be disastrous for human life—the ozone layer protects us from deadly solar ultra-violet rays, which produce (among other things) skin cancers.

It all sounds very gloomy! Yet Robert Allen's book is entitled *How to Save the World*. He believes that there is still time, provided we make the right kind of efforts quickly, to preserve a planet fit for our children and grandchildren to live on. Dr Ian Blair, of the Atomic Energy Research Establishment at Harwell, England, comments, 'The reality of the ecological crisis is becoming more visible with every passing day, and one therefore has reason to hope that necessity, together with that other human characteristic, self-preservation, may impose general acceptance of what Christians have been proclaiming for many centuries—that man is the custodian and steward of the earth and not its outright owner.'

The accident at the Chernobyl nuclear reactor in the Ukraine alerted humanity to the fearsome dangers inherent in modern technology. Are such technologies justified when the damage could be so great?

he made a pilgrimage to Mecca. In a much more remote part of the world, two civilizations were beginning their independent rise to greatness at this same time—and they would remain completely unknown until the first Spanish explorers landed in their part of South America.

In the twelfth century, the Inca tribe of Peru began to carve out a small empire for themselves by taking over neighbouring peoples. The Incas had little cultural originality of their own, but they knew how to adapt the skills of the people they conquered, and use them for their own ends. And between 1400 and 1530—a period tragically cut short by the depredations of the European invaders—the Inca empire reached heights of unexpected greatness.

The Incas lived in an area which combined, in a most unpromising way, deserts and snow-capped peaks, fertile valleys and bare crags, hot arid zones and wet tropical regions. Only a people with an extraordinary degree of engineering skill could have built an empire there; and the Incas met the challenge. They built 10,000 miles of roads, as well as suspension bridges, terraces on hillsides to increase land available for cultivation, and a royal palace with its blocks of stone joined so perfectly that no mortar was necessary to knit them together.

The Incas' craftsmanship in gold, silver and precious metals reached an extraordinary degree of perfection. This was made easier by the fact that all produce legally belonged to the state, and commerce did not exist. The highly-organized civil service kept a tight control on the lives of the people—restricting population movements, organizing marriages, and administering compulsory labour schemes. Individual freedom was a foreign idea; the good of the state was all that mattered.

The Incas rarely practised human sacrifice (although it did happen at times of crisis), but the other great South American civilization—that of the Aztecs—was built on it. One of the first Europeans to visit the Aztec capital, Tenochtitlan, reported seeing a massive rack standing beside the city's temple which contained 136,000 skulls. Aztec civilization was profligate of human life (the annual ceremony in honour of the maize goddess involved beheading young women as they danced; 20,000 captives were sacrificed to celebrate the dedication of a temple). But for all that it was a tremendous achievement.

The Aztecs (who inhabited central Mexico) were highly skilled in agriculture and in craftsmanship involving precious metals. Tenochtitlan covered an area of almost five square miles; it was built as an island, intersected by a network of canals, served with fresh water through a system of ramps. Inside a walled precinct at the heart of the city were massive temples and soaring terraces. The first Europeans to reach it had never seen anything like it in their lives.

While these civilizations had been growing, much had happened elsewhere. Hinduism had reasserted itself over Buddhism in India, and great temple cities had been built before Muslim invaders arrived in the thirteenth century. Their conquests had the effect of pushing Hindu peoples into new areas, where fresh centres of art and culture developed. The conflict between Islam and Hinduism produced several new religious developments. Guru Nanak (1469–1530) began a new religious philosophy—Sikhism—when he proclaimed, 'There is no Hindu, there is no Muslim.' It was just the message that many people, weary of conflict, wanted to hear; and the fact that Sikhism abolished caste distinctions gave it an immediate appeal to the poorer classes.

This was to lead to the establishment of a new empire in India: the Mogul empire, dating from 1556. The Moguls set out to be neither Hindu nor Muslim, but simply Indian. They produced art and buildings of great beauty—notably the Taj Mahal, which incorporates Hindu and Muslim styles with breathtaking elegance.

While Sikhism was gathering force in India, Western civilization was adjusting to several bewildering changes. Byzantium disappeared in 1453. Russia began to be unified in 1480. Around the same time, the invention of movable type made printing easy and quick, and allowed books to spread knowledge quickly and widely. And then in 1492 the Arabs were finally expelled from Spain; the long association of Muslim culture with Europe was over.

But something else happened in 1492—Columbus landed in America. And that heralded the real start of a new world. European sea

The Taj Mahal, legacy of sixteenth-century India, points to the serenity of a world beyond.

explorers were pushing back the frontiers of the unknown further and further, and drawing world history together.

European thinkers were beginning to rediscover the riches of classical Greek writers such as Aristotle and Hippocrates. The rise of universities had helped the new ideas to spread: now there were learned communities in all the major countries of the West (fifty-six universities were flourishing by 1400) which could store, teach and develop important thinking.

The name given to this gradual rebirth of classical learning—which actually spread over three centuries or so—is the Renaissance. It led to a new view of human beings and their relationship to the universe. Scientific discoveries were part of this: Copernicus, a Polish monk, shocked the church by suggesting in 1543 that the earth was not the centre of the universe; within a century Galileo and Kepler had proved him right. Artists started to develop a new realistic style. Literature began to be written in modern languages as well as classical. The Renaissance encouraged human beings to examine the whole world afresh and see what was really there.

One important outcome of the Renaissance was the Reformation. All the new learning was beginning to challenge the authority of the church, and to emphasize the importance of individuals forming their own opinions carefully

by scrutinizing the facts. The Reformation started with a realization that the church had grown corrupt, tradition-bound and unbiblical in its teaching. Martin Luther challenged the authority of the church by preaching that a person's relationship with God depends on faith alone—and not on any other conditions invented by church authority. The Reformation spread quickly from Germany to Scandinavia, Switzerland, Holland, France and Scotland. The Church of England broke away from the authority of the Pope.

The following century saw the rise of modern science and philosophy. Newton discovered gravity, Harvey the circulation of the blood. Descartes revolutionized philosophy by insisting that serious thinking about the world must start with no hidden assumptions: a philosopher must systematically question each of his premises. The method of examining the world carefully, taking nothing for granted, was yielding exciting new areas of knowledge. Human beings had never understood their environment so well.

Meanwhile, elsewhere

The growth of European culture was to prove the most important force determining future world history. But there were other things happening, too. In Japan, as far back as the eleventh century, an aristocratic court society with few duties had had the time to produce sophisticated novels and poetry. By the fourteenth century, Japan's own form of drama—the *no* play—was fully developed. And when in 1603 Tokugawa Ieyasu became *shogun* (the officer given authority by the emperor to rule the country), a period of stable government started which allowed all the arts to flourish.

But the Tokugawa family became convinced that contact with Westerners could only be harmful to Japanese culture. And so they expelled the Portuguese and Spanish missionaries who had been in Japan since 1542, and condemned Japan to centuries of cultural isolation, which ended only in 1853 when America sent four warships to demand the

For all its faults, the United Nations is a historically unique attempt to bring all nations into co-operation for the benefit of all humanity.

important city and royal capital from about 1400, until in 1830 it was destroyed by another African people. Ruins of a palace, a temple, and the great wall which encircled the city can still be seen today.

Two thousand miles away, the kingdom of Benin (in what is now Nigeria) had taken bronze sculpture to a high degree of refinement. Benin's heyday lasted from the fifteenth to the seventeenth centuries.

But by the seventeenth century the future lay very definitely with Western Europe. And so we must go back there to conclude the story.

The enlightenment and beyond

Seventeenth-century science had led to some amazing advances. And consequently many people in the following century felt a tremendous optimism about the future of the human enterprise. Reason and careful examination were the only keys needed to unlock the secrets of the universe; at last we were discovering the regular principles by which everything fitted together. Human happiness could be arrived at by applying reason to life; the unprovable dogmas of religion were no longer necessary. Paul Hazard has crystallized the intellectual mood:

Religion; revealed religion, that was what stood in the way; that was the major adversary. Once

opening of the country and the signing of a commercial agreement.

Christian missionaries had also arrived in China in the sixteenth century. They found there a well-developed culture, producing a fantastic array of luxury goods and priceless art works, under the rulership of the Ming dynasty. The missionaries were able to advise the emperors about such subjects as mathematics and astronomy; but the Chinese had very little interest in what they could gain from outsiders. Chinese society was self-sufficient and culturally superior to every other. What could they learn from Europe?

That remained the Chinese attitude right through to the end of the nineteenth century, when it became painfully obvious that the West was outstripping China in technological progress. Many of the political problems which have beset China this century can be traced back to the crisis of confidence which Chinese society underwent when it suddenly realized that it was not, after all, leading the world.

At the same time as the European Renaissance and the rise of the Incas, another great civilization arose mysteriously in southern Africa. The mystery stems from the fact that this civilization, Zimbabwe, never developed the ability to read and write, and so records are scanty. But we do know that Zimbabwe was an

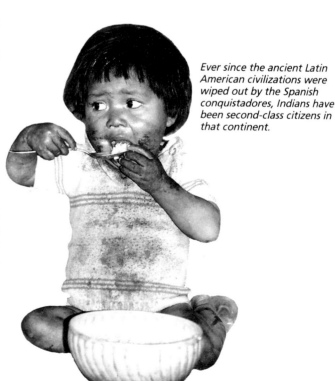

Ever since the ancient Latin American civilizations were wiped out by the Spanish conquistadores, Indians have been second-class citizens in that continent.

make it clear that, from the nature of the case, there could be no such thing. . . then the philosophers could go ahead. . . Every belief must be based on reason; to reason, even the Supreme Being himself is compelled to defer.

The Enlightenment, as this period of thought was called, produced a great deal of valuable philosophy, literature and political thinking; but its easy certainties were soon rendered obsolete by bewildering changes which transformed the face of the world.

The most obvious was the Industrial Revolution, which altered the economic relationships of human beings more dramatically (and more rapidly) than any previous change in history. Industrialization meant the growth of cities (London's population shot up from 875,000 to 5 million between 1800 and 1900), a new wealth and power concentrated in the hands of factory owners rather than the old aristocrats, and the emergence of a working class which (Karl Marx pointed out) was poorer than anyone in history before. For, he said, even the poorest weaver or peasant of the eighteenth century owned the tools he worked with; but the industrial labourer, working on somebody else's machine in somebody else's factory, owned nothing—not even his labour.

Industrialization also meant an increased quality of life for those who gained from it. More goods were available, at cheaper prices, and of more reliable quality. It also meant that Europe dominated the world — more successful in producing wealth and dominating world affairs than any previous culture.

Here we reach our own century, in which the Western style of thinking and technological development has left its impact on one society after another, all over the world; in which the 'super-powers', the Soviet Union and the United States, have emerged in place of Europe to dominate the international scene; in which our alien observer would have noticed the gunsmoke of two greater wars than the world has ever seen, and the mushroom clouds rising from the explosion of the first nuclear weapons.

What conclusions can we reach after surveying the human achievement so far?

SHOULD WE STOP BUILDING BOMBS?

When the first atomic bomb dropped on the Japanese city of Hiroshima in 1945, it was the biggest explosion the world had ever seen. Today it is estimated that both the United States and the Soviet Union have armaments capable of producing 500,000 explosions the size of the Hiroshima blast. And even Britain, not the world's greatest nuclear power, has enough for 11,600.

One frightening aspect of nuclear weapons is simply how much they cost. It has been calculated that to feed, educate and house the underprivileged of the world would cost $14 billion per year. An enormous sum—but no more than the world spends on armaments *every two weeks*. In other words, if we could stop the arms race for a fortnight, we could conquer world hunger.

Then there is the effect of nuclear weapons. In a one-megaton attack on Leningrad, 890,000 people would die 'promptly' (which means within thirty days), and 1,260,000 would be injured. A majority of them would die young as a result. A counter-attack on American military bases would produce between two and twenty-two million 'prompt' deaths. But if the Russians decided on an all-out attack, between 35 and 77 per cent of the American population would die 'promptly'. This is the terror we are building for ourselves. Why do we do it?

Small wonder that Christian pacifist Alan Kreider argues, 'Because of their tremendous explosive power, because of their radiation and fallout, because of the improbability of arresting escalation, because of the incredible problems of communication, command and control, nuclear weapons are a new phenomenon in the history of warfare. They are intrinsically indiscriminate, and thus intrinsically unjust.'

But not all Christians agree. Dr Delmar Bergen is a leading scientist at Los Alamos National Laboratory in the United States, actively designing and testing nuclear weapons. He says, 'People tend to focus on the nuclear wars aspect of nuclear weapons, but I am more interested in how science can create a situation where war cannot be considered as the solution to any problem. I believe nuclear weapons have done this by preventing wars. They have prevented major conflicts, I think, for the last forty years.'

There are no easy answers. Nuclear weapons are here, and they cannot be dis-invented; they give us an opportunity to do more spectacular harm to the human race than any generation before us. The real problem was analyzed accurately right at the start of the nuclear arms race, in 1948, when Dr Albert Einstein remarked: 'The true problem lies in the hearts and thoughts of men. It is not a physical problem, but an ethical one. . . What terrifies us is not the explosive force of the atomic bomb, but the power of the wickedness of the human heart, its explosive power for evil.'

IS THIS PLANET OVERCROWDED?

Someone has estimated that more than half the people who have ever lived are alive today. Only a century and a half ago, the world's total population was one-fifth of what it is now. How many more can we take? Is this planet overcrowded?

Scientists have made mind-boggling projections for the future. Physicist J.H. Fremlin, calculating that the world's population is doubling once every thirty-five years, worked out that if things were to continue at that rate for about 900 years, there would be a hundred people standing on every square yard of the earth's surface (including the oceans!)—a total of

60,000,000,000,000,000 people in all. He commented that if they were all housed in a continuous 2,000-storey building, covering the entire planet, it might be possible to give them all three or four yards of floor space each.

Could we send them all off to the stars instead? Not unless things change dramatically. Professor Garrett Hardin estimates that if Americans were to cut down their standard of living to 18 per cent of its present level, they would save enough in a year to finance the sending of *one day's* population increase to the stars.

'An equilibrium must be reached,' says Professor Carlo Cipolla. 'But when will it be reached? And how?' We have no answers to this question. What we can say confidently is that at the moment we are a long way

from such a frightening situation. There is more than enough food and space for everyone on earth; in 1984, for example, the world produced four times as much grain as it needed to feed its population. Yet over half the world's population is malnourished. Why?

The problem is not one of population, but exploitation. Those of us who live in Western countries make up only 5 per cent of the world's population; yet we consume over 40 per cent of the world's resources. It doesn't leave a lot for others.

And the truly poor are being concentrated in the wrong places. By the end of the century, we are told,

three-quarters of all Latin Americans and one-third of all Asians and Africans will be living in cities. Today there are six hundred million landless poor in Africa, Asia and Latin America; by the turn of the century there will be a thousand million. Their first reaction will be to head for the city. How can stretched urban resources cope with this sort of influx?

Planet earth is not overcrowded—yet. But unless something is done, it soon will be. And even now we have a problem of distribution, as the poorest humans flock to places where they are least likely to receive help. If we are ever going to feed the world, we need to try a little harder.

Human beings plainly have an inbuilt urge to find out answers, to solve problems, to build, create and produce, which marks them apart from any other kind of animal on earth. For all the parallels with other species, there remains a huge and obvious difference.

But there are some problems which human beings have never solved—because they are problems inside human beings themselves. The same 'inhumanity' which led to the Aztecs torturing children in their rain ceremonies, or to the total extinction of Carthage by the Romans, has produced in our own time the awful massacre of Kampuchea, the ghastly experiments Mengele carried out at Auschwitz, the bloody purges of Stalin. The idea that human beings can perfect themselves, and produce a trouble-free planet, seems more and more of an illusion with every newspaper we read.

Today's world presents us with more urgent problems than ever before. We now have the technology to devastate the whole world if we choose. International trade and massive third-world debt can produce inequalities which result in mass starvation—on a planet well capable of feeding its entire population, three or four times over. The over-consumption of the world's resources by a tiny minority in the rich countries is leaving a large proportion of the world's population destitute. But there seems no way to change the situation.

Modernity itself is a threatening thing. It gives us more options than we have ever had before—as to what foods we will eat, how we will spend our time, what career we will

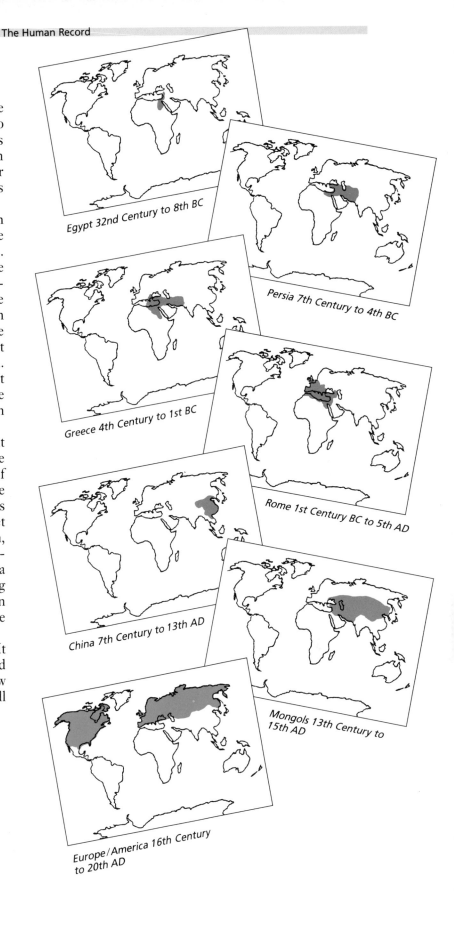

Egypt 32nd Century to 8th BC

Persia 7th Century to 4th BC

Greece 4th Century to 1st BC

Rome 1st Century BC to 5th AD

China 7th Century to 13th AD

Mongols 13th Century to 15th AD

Europe/America 16th Century to 20th AD

133

follow, what our beliefs will be. And so, says sociologist Peter Berger, we have the anxious task of making all the important decisions for ourselves:

Put simply, the individual is faced with a number of alternative careers, especially in his younger years, and therefore must make decisions about these available options. It is possible for the individual to imagine himself as having different biographies. . . it increases the likelihood of frustration regarding specific careers. . . This frustration will be linked with feelings of regret or even guilt if the individual believes that he has missed some options or made some wrong decisions in the past. The frustration will be linked to anxiety regarding present or future decisions.

And so Berger concludes that 'modern man has suffered from a deepening condition of "homelessness"'. We understand our world better than any previous civilization has done; but we feel less settled within it. We are painfully conscious of the imperfections in ourselves (and the discoveries of Darwin and Freud have served to underline how humble we need to be about our own potential). As we look to the future, we see mounting problems to which there are no immediate answers.

One wonders about the alien visitor, as he speeds away in his flying saucer and marks down 2100 in his diary for the date of his next visit.

Would he fly away feeling optimistic about our future—or the opposite?

Part IV

The Meaning of a Person

9

WHAT HAVE THE GREAT FAITHS TO SAY?

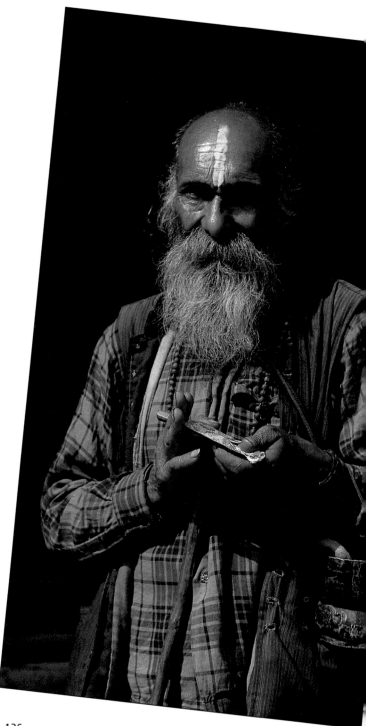

The most Northern tribes of the White Nile are the Dinkas, Shilooks, Nuehr, Kytch, Bohr, Aliab and Shir... Without any exception they are without a belief in a Supreme Being, neither have they any form of worship or idolatry; nor is the darkness of their minds enlightened by even a ray of superstition.

This was the blunt conclusion that Sir Samuel Baker, the Victorian explorer, announced to the Ethnological Society in London in July 1866. He had found people who had no religion. Not a trace of supernatural belief could be found in their culture. They had no gods.

But Samuel Baker was wrong—wildly and spectacularly wrong. All these tribes had their own religious systems, and some of them remarkably sophisticated; especially the Nuehr and the Dinka. It was just that their beliefs were so different to Baker's own that he failed to identify them. And so he lived among them in order to study them without ever noticing how religious they were.

Baker is one example of many people in history who have tried to find evidence of

Gurus enjoyed a surge of popularity in the West in the 1970s. It was part of a come-back for the religions, which had seemed to be in decline.

human beings who are religion-free. And all have failed. There is not a single human culture where some form of religious worship has not been known. Even in civilizations that developed in complete isolation from one another—such as the South American cultures, and the great empires of Africa—we find exactly the same basic questions about human life being asked, the same sense of 'something else out there' being expressed, that we find in our own culture and those closest to it.

Human beings have always been religious animals. And there seems no sign, at the end of the twentieth century, that this is about to end. Even in the Soviet Union, after almost a century of atheist propaganda, there are calculated to be 97 million Christians—more than there were before the Revolution. In China, when the harsh repressions of the Cultural Revolution came to an end and churches reopened, far more people were found to be Christians than at the time when China turned communist.

Other religions are surging back as well. The growth of Buddhism in the West this century has been quite a success story. And fundamentalist Islam has added a whole new dimension to the political jigsaw of the Middle East. Clearly, what Muhammad started over 1,300 years ago is still potent enough for thousands of people to be willing to give their lives in its service.

And in the West, even those who do not see themselves as conventionally religious people often have guiding beliefs that shape their lives. The growth of astrology, mind-control therapies, yoga systems and Tarot reading has demonstrated clearly that people still have religious longings which need to be satisfied somehow. Successful actresses credit their success to the wise advice given by spirit beings who are 'channelled' by mediums in a trance. Businessmen take off their shoes and sit before an altar meditating, or chanting a phrase in Japanese, so as to attune themselves to the universe and change their lives for the better. And not long ago, all over the Western world, there was a wave of new religious movements—The Unification Church, the Children of God, Scientology, the Rajneeshis—all showing an alarming propensity to dominate the minds of young people and persuade them to make a violent

break with their previous lifestyle. Just how far these new religions could go, in their power over adherents, was demonstrated when 900 people committed suicide one afternoon in a forest clearing in Guyana. Their group leader had told them to.

How did human beings first become religious animals? The question is important because, again, this is one of the things which marks us off from the rest of the animal creation. No monkey ever said a prayer, no beaver ever built a church. Yet wherever one looks throughout human civilization, the signs of religion are unmistakable—temples, mosques, ziggurats, shrines, altars, standing stones. How did it all begin?

How did religion begin?

The great psychologist Sigmund Freud believed that religion began when people lived in a tribe ruled by one male, the father of the group. This ruler would have had a large number of wives, and the younger men would have been forced out of the tribe to find mates for themselves. Finding this intolerable, they must have revolted, murdered the father—and then been so ashamed by what they had done that they had to find ways to ease their crippling feelings of guilt.

Freud conjectures that they took an animal to act as a symbol of the dead father, and honoured it throughout the year, giving it the kind of respect once paid to the murdered leader. And then, on the anniversary of the murder, they would kill the animal as a sort of recreation of their crime—thus assuaging their guilt, and also celebrating their new freedom.

In this way, says Freud, came about the basic ideas of religious ritual, sacrifice, symbols, guilt and forgiveness. It is a plausible theory. But is it correct?

Plainly no proof can be found for the truth of such a story, either for or against. But Freud's whole case depends on the idea that human primitive societies have a lot of similarities to ape societies, and we now know that this is just not true. What is more, enough data has been discovered about the origins of symbols and ceremonies to be fairly sure he was wrong about them. And did he really believe his own theory anyway? David Stafford Clark, a leading expert on Freud's thought, is not convinced.

Did Freud believe this to be a historical account? The answer to this is that he did and at the same time he didn't. He writes about the possibilities and probabilities, the unlikelihood and at the same time the certainty that this was part of the original mental inheritance of the human race. In a sense, he tends at this stage both to display ambivalence and to plead poetic licence. . . Freud the mythmaker has come a long way from Freud the scientist.

Freud's theory might just fit with religions which place a lot of emphasis on guilt and forgiveness—such as Judaism and Christianity. But it has little relevance to other faiths (Shinto, say, or Buddhism) which are concerned with very different things. It looks as though Freud was wrong. We have to look elsewhere for the origins of religion.

Another influential view is that human religion began with dreams. When we dream, people appear in our mind's eye in a peculiar, disembodied fashion; and that may have given primitive man the idea (said E.B. Tylor, whose theory this originally was) that souls can exist apart from bodies. From this, it was just a short step to ancestor worship (fearing and respecting those souls which had broken free of their bodies); then to attributing to spirits the power to control rain, fire, fertility and other natural events; then to worshipping a whole variety of different gods; then finally to narrowing everything down to the worship of just one supreme God.

What about this theory? First, again there is no direct proof. Other researchers into primitive religions saw the chain of events a little differently. J.G. Frazer argued that it all started, not with dreams, but with magic; Herbert Spencer thought it began with ancestor worship, and goes back no further than that. Also, as Ninian Smart has observed, 'It makes primitive man very logical in his approach to religious belief.' The process of development from one step to another involves a fairly sophisticated use of reason and inference. We know that developments in human culture are not usually quite so neat. Were human beings really so remorselessly rational?

There is another possibility, advanced by anthropologist Wilhelm Schmidt. He reverses Tylor's sequence, by claiming that there is evidence, all over the world, that the original belief of humanity was in one High God; and that only later on did this primal conviction become distorted by polytheism and 'animism' (or spirit-worship). This idea would seem to fit well with the apostle Paul's account of how religion developed:

Since the creation of the world God's invisible qualities—his eternal power and divine nature— have been clearly seen, being understood from what has been made, so that men are without excuse.

For although they knew God, they neither glorified him as God nor gave thanks to him, but their thinking became futile and their foolish hearts were darkened. Although they claimed to be wise, they became fools and exchanged the glory of the immortal God for images made to look like mortal man and birds and animals and reptiles.

'In any event,' agrees Ninian Smart, 'it is a striking fact that many primitive cultures have a belief in some sort of High God, even though very often there is no specific ritual directed toward such a being.'

Inward and outward religion

We may not be sure where religion started from, but we can trace its major developments through history with some assurance. One period of three hundred years was most important. Just before 800BC, in most major civilizations, religious worship had become bureaucratized. It was the preserve of a body of officially-appointed priests, with elaborate rituals and centralized administration. And then over three centuries, quite suddenly in culture after culture, came challenges to the established power of the priesthood, which led to some of the most creative and brilliant developments in human religious history.

In India, for instance, where there were already some sacred scriptures connected to priestly worship, a new kind of writing arose— devoted to explaining the inner, personal meaning of faith. The older scriptures had stressed the existence of several gods and the

Statues of the Buddha carry the serene expression of one who both taught and practised renouncing earthly desires.

importance of sacrifice; they had taught that in a sacrifice a certain power is released, called Brahman, which can help the worshipper. Now these new scriptures were claiming much more: that Brahman was not just a kind of energy, but the very energy which lies behind the world itself, and holds it all together. The old belief in several gods was beginning to lose its grip. Perhaps there was just one vital force with which people had to do?

The Indian writings are called the Upanishads. In Hebrew culture too, this was the time when the prophets tried to understand God's feelings about his chosen people and their behaviour. The picture painted by the prophets of a God who was unique, unrivalled and endlessly caring for his creation, laid the basis for no less than three world faiths: Christianity, Islam and Judaism.

Another development in India at this time was the emergence of two unusual men with genuinely original ideas. Gautama Buddha, the 'Enlightened One', cut through all religious complication by announcing a direct and clear philosophy: Life is unhappy when we are in the grip of earthly desires; losing these desires is the way to true freedom, integration and wholeness. The Buddha's 'Eightfold Path' is the way to learn how to eradicate earthly desires. Vardhamana Mahavir, on the other hand, stressed the need to do good: that would destroy the evil of the human heart, harmonize with the inbuilt moral order of the universe, and win salvation for the individual. The recipes were different, but both teachers agreed about one thing. Priests and sacrifices were unnecessary; the response of the individual to the forces at work in the universe—that was what religion should be about.

Meanwhile in Persia a religious teacher called Zoroaster (or more correctly Zarathustra) was upsetting old ideas too. Unlike the other great teachers of this period, he actually was a priest. But he taught that before God all human beings stand on an equal basis; that

Buddhist young men often undergo a period of training as monks.

ARE RELIGIOUS EXPERIENCES FOR EVERYONE?

Over the last three centuries, scientific advances have completely transformed our world. It's not surprising that many people in Western society now see scientific facts as somehow more 'real' than others. If a claim cannot be tested in a laboratory—analyzed, photographed and documented—how do we know it is true? If something cannot be measured and explained in cause-and-effect terms—how do we know it is happening?

This has led, claims Lesslie Newbigin, to a split in the minds of many human beings between the 'public world' of hard, objective, scientific fact, and the 'private world' of values, opinions and prejudices. In the 'public world' you have to believe the same facts as everyone else—that two and two make four— but in the 'private world' you can believe whatever you like. There is no proof.

And so many people look sceptically at religious experience, and doubt those who claim to have had an encounter with God. Is it all a private fantasy? Or does it have any objective meaning in the 'public world'?

Religious experience seems to be just as common as ever it was. In many industrialized countries, churchgoing has slumped dramatically this century. This has been explained as the inevitable outworking of 'secularization', as industrial people lose their need for religious faith. But, as Harvie Conn points out, this is not universal; there are signs that 'religion seems alive and fresh in the secular city'. And even if there is a seeming lack of interest in religion, it may simply mean that the religious impulse is taking another direction: people still need answers to the basic questions of life and death, and still build their lives on religious assumptions, whether or not they go to church.

David Hay of Nottingham University conducted interviews with a random sample of adults, most of whom did not belong to an organized religious group. He found that a surprisingly large percentage spoke of sensing a power or presence in their lives which was greater than themselves. Many of them said that they had never told anyone else about their experience.

Hay became convinced that 'religious experience is something biologically natural to man'. He added: 'The common testimony of the religious traditions and of those who have spoken to us is that they normally lead in the direction of personal integration and just behaviour towards fellow human beings.'

This may show that religious experience is natural to human beings, but how do we know if it is true? Some religions simply state flatly that it is, but make no attempt to justify their assertion. Christians claim that it is possible to go beyond this instinctive awareness of a greater power, and establish a personal relationship with God himself, which provides the ultimate proof of his reality. The final chapter of this book describes the experience in more detail.

ARE ALL RELIGIONS SAYING THE SAME THING?

Human beings follow many different religious paths. And even within major religions, there can be bewildering numbers of competing denominations and sub-groups. Within Islam there is profound disagreement between Shi'ite and Sunni Muslims, and Sufis have sometimes been so unorthodox as to be suspected of not being Muslims at all. In Buddhism, the Hinayana and Mahayana schools have very different viewpoints, and fringe groups such as the influential Nichiren Shoshu actually believe very little that the Buddha would have approved of. Hindu personalists and impersonalists argue with one another; Christianity is estimated to have 21,780 denominations and sub-groups within it. It seems that human beings have an infinite capacity for falling out with one another over metaphysical questions. But is it possible that, for all the disagreement, everyone is saying the same thing?

Over the last century there have been many 'syncretistic' movements, which have tried to harmonize the claims of different religions. An important landmark was the World Parliament of Religions, held in Chicago in 1893, when leaders of a colourful assortment of faiths came together to share their perspectives. The academic discipline of Comparative Religion, which began at about the same period, provided a method of evaluating world religions without making any prior assumptions about which—if any—was true. It became much more attractive than ever before to believe 'All religions lead to God', or 'Every great faith boils down to the same essential truth'.

However, if one wants to believe this, there are some problems to be faced. For one thing, different syncretistic movements have very different ideas about what the essential core of all religions actually is. Theosophy locates it in the 'theosophia', a collection of arcane esoteric knowledge and wisdom. Transcendental Meditation claims (without any historical evidence whatsoever) that it is the meditation technique which TM promotes. The Baha'i Faith claims that it is the shared vision of a group of strategic prophets who taught a basically Islamic view of God. Others say that the core is a bundle of shared ethical viewpoints, such as 'Do as you would be done by' and 'Love your neighbour as yourself'. Which is right?

Another problem is: how do we define a 'religion'? The word covers all sorts of different practices—from the ethical idealism of Guru Nanak to the murderous insanity of Charles Manson and the debased magic of Aleister Crowley. Do all these paths lead in the same direction? Or do we exclude some? If so, which?

Again, syncretists often underestimate the real divergences in the world view of different faiths. Is God one or are there many gods? Is he a person, or is it a thing? Do men live once, or reincarnate? How do we achieve union with God? Where did evil come from? To all these questions, and many others, the great religions return radically different answers. It leads to one simple conclusion: if all religions lead to God, then none of them tells us very much about him. Their competing claims cancel one another out.

Finally, there are those religions which claim to be unique. Christianity claims to be a once-for-all revelation from God, which applies to human beings of every culture and background: 'God now commands all men everywhere to repent.' We can reject this claim, or accept it; but we cannot ignore it. Either Christianity is the unique faith it claims to be or it stands condemned as an over-ambitious mistake.

Hindus bathe in the waters of the holy river Ganges at Varanasi.

they have a personal moral duty to choose good and shun evil. Zoroastrianism was to become, by the time of Christ, the most powerful religion of the known world; then slowly to sink into the background, surviving today only as the religion of the Parsis in India, and a small group of about 17,000 believers in Iran.

In China too, these were important times for religious development. Just eight years or so after the birth of the Buddha, the great teacher Confucius was born. Confucius (or K'ung Fu'Tzu, to give him his proper name) argued that it was wrong to focus one's attention on the next life: here and now there are duties and responsibilities to be observed. It was not that Confucius did not believe in the gods; but he stressed (just like the Buddha, the Hebrew prophets and Zoroaster) that sacrifice on its own will not achieve much; that it is much more important to examine carefully one's own moral life, and check that one's conduct is all it should be. As we saw in chapter eight, Confucius' teaching about ethics and relationships in society became the foundation of Chinese society for 2,500 years.

But Confucius was not the only Chinese religious genius. There was also Lao-Tse, born at around the same time. Just like the

Upanishad writers and Mahavir, Lao-Tse conceived ideas about one energy source which holds the universe together. But where the Upanishad scholars talked of Brahman and Mahavir described the moral power of the universe, Lao-Tse spoke of the 'Tao', the Divine Principle which explains and comprehends all reality:

The Tao that can be expressed is not the eternal Tao; The name that can be defined is not the unchanging name. Non-existence is called the antecedent of heaven and earth; Existence is the mother of all things. From eternal non-existence, therefore, We serenely observe the mysterious beginning of the universe; From eternal existence we clearly see the apparent distinctions. These two are the same in source and become different when manifested.

This is not remarkably clear. But at least one thing is obvious from it: Lao-Tse saw reality as made up of two balancing forces, a harmony of opposites. Later Taoism developed the idea of the Yin and the Yang—two great forces which interact with one another. (It is interesting that a Christian fringe religion today, the Unification Church, uses the idea of Yin and Yang in its theology, and actually calls its sacred book *Divine Principle*. It owes more to the Taoist background of its Korean founders than many of its Western followers realize.)

Taoists never believed that the Tao could be talked of as a personal God: 'How can the Creator have a conscious mind?' And some Upanishads take a similar view. Equally, the Buddha declared himself unsure about whether the gods existed or not. Certainly we could expect no direct help from them; human beings needed the Eightfold Path because they had to struggle with the issues of life unaided. Clearly the trend in many of these major religious developments was towards a concept of God which saw him as a force, a remote essence, incapable of being communicated with in a personal relationship.

And so in many ways it was going against

Jews have a high reverence for the 'Torah', the Law of Moses. Readings form part of synagogue worship. Here the book of the law is raised to show its pre-eminence.

the grain of world religious development for the Hebrew prophets to insist stubbornly that God was personal, and can be known in a personal way:

When you pass through the waters, I will be with you; and when you pass through the rivers, they will not sweep over you. When you walk through the fire, you will not be burned... Since you are precious and honoured in my sight, and because I love you, I will give men in exchange for you, and people in exchange for your life.

But in the end it was their concept of God which was to have the biggest impact on the world. Indeed, the other religions started to show signs of needing the same kind of God. As Buddhism developed and spread, more and more of a need came to be felt for some supernatural figure to which the worshipper could relate; and (not surprisingly) the Buddha himself became an object of worship. Nowadays we have all seen statues of the Buddha; every antique shop has a few. But those statues did not generally exist before the first century BC. That was when *bhakti*, personal feelings of love and devotion to the Buddha, became popular. (This has led to a situation today in which there are two rival schools of Buddhism in the world: one stressing the element of personal devotion, the other largely ignoring it.)

In Hinduism, there was a similar change of direction. In the second century BC (or perhaps a little later) appeared the most famous Hindu scripture of all: the *Bhagavad Gita*, 'the Song of the Lord'. It takes the form of a poem in which Arjuna, a warrior prince facing a dangerous battle, receives a vision of the god Krishna himself, and begins to understand the vital importance of personal love and devotion to him. The *Gita* does not deny the earlier teaching about Brahman, but suggests that Brahman can take personal form in the shape of one of the gods, such as Krishna; and that devotion to a god might achieve forgiveness of sin and eventual salvation.

(Today the well-known Hare Krishna cult bases its entire faith on a literal reading of the *Gita*. Hare Krishna disciples devote themselves utterly to the person of Krishna, worship him with chants and meditation, and shave off all their hair except for a top-knot—which is retained, by tradition, so that Krishna can use it to haul the deserving disciple up to heaven.)

But from the heart of the truly personal faith—Judaism—sprang the most amazing surge of religious enterprise in world history. When Jesus Christ died on the cross in Jerusalem, he had only 120 followers, all of whom had fled and left him to die. Within a short space afterwards, they were travelling all over the ancient world boldly proclaiming their message, and founding churches as they went. What had happened? J.M. Roberts, a historian who is not a Christian, says of Jesus' teachings:

Though they were effective in his lifetime, they seemed to die with him. At his death his followers were only one tiny Jewish sect among many. But they believed that a unique thing had happened. They believed that Christ had risen from the dead...

Christians established themselves in Europe, North Africa and the Middle East, and indeed became so numerous that the Roman emperor Constantine finally decided to make Christianity the state religion of the empire.

This access to power and influence was not all good for Christianity. For less than three hundred years later, 'Christians' in the Arabian peninsula were leading such hypocritical lives that a young merchant was shocked. He came to believe that if God is all-high and all-holy, then Christians must have distorted the Scriptures to make life comfortable for themselves; for they did not show God any real respect. When one day the young trader, Muhammad, heard voices in his ears telling him to write, he obeyed; and so (in time) came about the Qur'an, the sacred book of the Islamic faith.

'Islam' simply means 'submission', 'Muslim' means 'one who submits'. The whole basis of Islam is that God has set rules for living, which when observed bring happiness and success, and when ignored bring chaos and disillusionment. Muslims do not talk of a God of 'love' as Christians do. God is the all-merciful; but nothing more than that. He is so highly exalted above humanity that it is blasphemous to speak of him in a familiar way.

Muhammad was a persuasive teacher, and the vision of brotherhood he offered to the Arabs made instant headway. Within fifty years Islam was the dominant faith of North Africa, much of Spain, parts of Central Asia, and almost the whole of the Middle East. Later it

Such figures as the Ayatollah Khomeini and Yasser Arafat are symbols of Islam's high political profile. Religious fundamentalism, of several different kinds, has a strong following today.

was to penetrate Africa further south, parts of Central Asia.

However, there were often violent clashes between Hindus and Muslims in India, and that was what provoked Guru Nanak (1469–1538) to begin a new religious grouping which would combine the best of Hinduism and Islam. The new religion has come to be called Sikhism.

Sikhs combine a Hindu view of life—such as a belief in rebirth after death—with the Muslim view of one highly exalted but personal God. Nanak was convinced that good insights could be had within each tradition; that the saints of Hinduism and Islam genuinely had, each in their own way, made contact with God. It was folly to stand apart and criticize the other belief.

Unfortunately, Sikhs found themselves cut off from both the Hindu and the Muslim communities. Rather than being a bridge between the two, they were forced to become a grouping on their own; and to defend themselves militarily, which involved doing some things which were against the strict code of *ahimsa* (non-violence) which they had been taught. Sikhs in India today feel themselves a beleaguered minority, threatened by the large groups around them.

Is there a god?

Many centuries before Christ, a Hebrew psalmist wrote, 'The fool has said in his heart that there is no God.' It has always been possible to be a complete unbeliever, at almost any stage of history; atheism is not an entirely new development. The ancient Greek philosopher Epicurus, for example, taught that the universe was simply a material object, that human beings were accidental, and the gods non-existent. But it is true that over the last two hundred years unbelief has become more popular in the West than it has ever been anywhere.

There are many causes for this. One is the movement of thought in the eighteenth century, called the Enlightenment (see chapter eight), when after a century of religious wars European thinkers despaired of ever making sense of religion and instead tried to reason their way to sensible principles of living. If God was still allowed to exist, he was thought of simply as the First Mover, the craftsman who had made everything and set it in motion; but impossibly remote from practical concerns on a day-to-day basis.

Then came the rapid industrialization of the following century. People were torn from their former community life and jammed together into city streets where the old certainties, the former symbols, did not seem to apply any more. Churchgoing dropped steadily, and the Western world started to see the beginnings of 'secularization'—the word sociologists use for the way in which modern styles of living are rendering religion peripheral to the lives of an increasing number of people.

Another pull against traditional beliefs was exerted by nineteenth-century scientific discoveries which seemed to call in question the claims of the Bible. When Charles Darwin finally published *Origin of Species* in 1859 (after sitting on it for over twenty years, scared of the reaction it would provoke), he appeared to be challenging the accuracy of the book of Genesis. Some defenders of the Bible were ill-informed, illogical and abusive, and many people started to assume that science was now undermining the foundations of Christian faith.

A major expression of unbelief gathering momentum at about this time was 'humanism',

WHEN DID ATHEISM BEGIN?

It is sometimes thought that in previous ages everyone was superstitious and credulous, and so believed in supernatural powers of all kinds. Only recently, on this view, in our more enlightened times, did humans dare to start believing, 'There is no God.' In fact this is not true.

■ We know that some of the great Greek philosophers were unbelievers: they cautioned their disciples to observe all the religious rites which society expected of them, so as not to scandalize the public and make trouble for themselves, but in fact thinkers such as Democritus of Abdera (c460–c370BC) were thoroughgoing materialists. Others such as Epicurus (341–270BC) did not deny the existence of the gods, but did deny that there is any divine providence or purpose, any supernatural intervention in this life or punishment hereafter, and any existence of the human soul after death. In fact, the gods had so little to do in his scheme of things that for all practical purposes they did not exist.

■ One of the founders of the great world religions was undecided about the gods. The Buddha was content to remain unsure whether or not they existed. Only one thing was certain about the gods, he taught: they were not going to help human beings. Buddhism is an applied philosophy to help human beings live their lives without supernatural assistance.

■ Atheism in the West started to become much more attractive after the rise of science, which showed that natural features of the physical world could be explained in terms of natural law, without any direct intervention from God or gods. Science had not disproved or undermined religious faith; but it had removed one 'proof' on which many people had naively built their faith 'There could not be a world like this unless God was constantly pulling strings to make things happen.' And so when Napoleon asked the astronomer Laplace what part God played in the *System of the World* Laplace had put together, he was told 'Sire, I have had no need to make use of that hypothesis.'

It needs to be remembered that many of the great scientists (such as Galileo and Newton) and the philosophers who struggled with the implications of their discoveries (such as Descartes and Kant) were convinced Christians. But their work opened the door to new possibilities for human minds, and atheism was one of them.

One influential figure was the eighteenth century philosopher Georg Hegel (1770–1831), who believed that God was the 'world-spirit' whom we encounter in the processes of the world—not an independent figure. 'Without the world God is not God.' Hegel influenced Ludwig Feuerbach (1804–72), who was more radical: for him, religion was just 'the dream of the human mind', and talking about God was simply a coded way of talking about what humanity wanted to be like. God did not exist at all.

The stage was set for the arrival of nineteenth- and twentieth-century atheism, which has taken too many different forms to describe. Three have been particularly influential. **Marxism** took its lead from Hegel and Feuerbach. They argued that the force which they saw running through history, was not to be identified with God; religion was simply 'opium for the people'. **Humanism**, which emerged from the thought of men such as Thomas Huxley and Leslie Stephen, who insisted that this is the only world there is, and human welfare within it must be our prime concern. **Atheistic existentialism**, which centred on French thinkers Jean-Paul Sartre and Albert Camus, claimed we must face the fact that we are living in an absurd universe, and bravely reckon with the contradictions and frustrations we cannot escape. 'Atheism is a cruel, long-term business,' Sartre wrote, 'I believe I have gone through it to the end.'

a school of thought which claimed that humanity could find true dignity in life only by facing up to the fact that we are alone in the universe, and must try to solve our problems for ourselves. Some of the humanists were brilliant people, such as the philosopher Bertrand Russell, who summed up the humanist viewpoint memorably in one famous statement:

That Man is the product of causes which had no prevision of the end they were achieving; that his origin, his growth, his hopes and fears, his loves and his beliefs, are but the outcome of accidental collocations of atoms; that no fire, no heroism, no intensity of thought and feeling, can preserve an individual life beyond the grave; that all the labour of the ages, all the devotion, all the inspiration, all the noonday brightness of human genius, are destined to extinction in the vast death of the solar system, and that the whole temple of Man's achievement must inevitably be buried beneath the debris of a universe in ruins—all these things, if not quite beyond dispute, are yet so nearly certain, that no philosophy which rejects them can hope to stand.

Interestingly, Russell's own daughter returned to religious belief; she became a Christian. Later she wrote:

I would have liked to convince my father that I had found what he had been looking for, the ineffable something he had longed for all his life. I would have liked to persuade him that the search for God does not have to be in vain. But it was hopeless. He had known too many blind Christians, bleak moralists who sucked the joy from life and persecuted their opponents; he would never have been able to see the truth they were hiding.

The other influential form of unbelief was Marxism, the faith which today controls the lives of millions of people worldwide. Karl Marx believed that religion was an instrument used by the ruling classes to keep the workers in their place; it had no objective reality, and must be fought as strenuously as possible.

Marx drew his ideas about religion from German philosopher Ludwig Feuerbach, who claimed that human beings create God in their own image—in other words, that the statements we make about God (God is good, God is loving, and so on) are really just declarations of our own ideals. The more we think about God, the less able we will be to progress. Said Marx, 'The more man puts into God, the less he retains himself.'

Can we accept this as a fair account of what religion is about? David Hay, a researcher into religious experience, thinks not. He remarks:

Convinced atheists like Freud and Marx certainly felt they had explained religion away, yet their criticisms. . . are purely functional: religion is false consciousness, or a neurosis, and leads to the diminishment of man.

. . .The evidence collected over the past two decades suggests that these attacks, partly determined by a nineteenth-century positivism which had already dismissed religion before examining it in details, were too sweeping. All recent studies of the 'experiential' dimension of religion show that it is typically associated with personal integration, a sense of meaningfulness in life, and concern for social justice.

THE FAITH THAT GREW AND GREW

Which religious teacher has had most impact on the human race? The answer has got to be: Jesus Christ. He started with no conventional advantages; he was not born in a prominent place geographically, nor was he a member of an important family, nor did he receive an extensive education. And he died at an early age compared with the founders of other religions. Yet Jesus has had a staggering impact on human history. He left behind no writings or even a visible organization; his committed followers, numbering about 120 when he died, are said to have lost their courage and deserted him at his death.

Yet today the Christian church exists in virtually every country in the world—including hostile societies such as Albania, where Christianity has officially been exterminated but secret fellowships are still known to meet. After seventy years of atheistic propaganda in the Soviet Union, the number of Christians there has actually increased. At the time of writing, the Soviet government is changing its policy, and seeking closer links with Christian churches instead of trying to undermine their activities.

Almost one-third of human beings today are associated with Christianity, at least to the extent of keeping the membership qualifications of a church. It has been estimated that 63 thousand people each week become Christians.

The amazing spread of Christianity is sometimes attributed to the fact that it is a religion of the West, and Western civilization has carried it throughout the world. But Christianity showed signs of unexpected vitality long before it became an accepted Western faith. In its earliest days, for example, Christians were severely penalized and persecuted by the Roman Empire, and there was every reason to expect that the faith would die out—or at least go underground as an esoteric minority belief. In fact Christianity had become so widespread within three centuries that the Roman emperor Constantine gave up trying to fight the inevitable, and established Christianity as the state religion of the empire. After many centuries of Roman state religion, this was a striking about-turn, and would not have happened unless Christianity's power to spread seemed quite invincible.

Christians attribute the impact of Christianity to the uniqueness of its founder. Jesus Christ made claims which are quite unprecedented in the history of religion. His followers said that he claimed to be the Son of God—a title which denoted an intimate special relationship with God which no other human being has ever had. He taught that through his death human beings could find forgiveness for their wrongdoing, and come to know God's presence in their lives as Father, guide and king.

His claims were not the only unusual thing about him. From the earliest times, Christians have asserted that Jesus was a worker of miracles, and that he rose from his grave after burial, since death could not defeat the Son of God. These ideas have often been derided as impossible, and yet there is a great deal of suggestive evidence which has often convinced sceptics. If Jesus did not do what Christians claim he did, there is a historical puzzle to be solved.

But all of this would not be sufficient to explain Jesus' impact. Early Christians believed that 'if anyone is in Christ, he is a new creation; the old has gone, the new has come!' And this experience of transformation, of 'new life', has been the clinching factor for many millions of people down through the centuries.

Christianity has spread further and faster than any other religion. One reason is the imagination and energy with which it has been made known. Here a street drama gives emotional impact to a Gospel story.

Can God be known?

Ultimately there are three positions we can take with regard to religious experience:

■ We can simply say, 'Religious experience is not real or helpful.' This is Marx's position, and also the position of J.G. Frazer, whom we discussed earlier. Frazer believed that it was possible to trace the same symbols and myths— for example, of the dying and rising God—in a variety of different religious traditions, and therefore that we were not to think of *any* of the stories as literally true. At one stage of his life C.S. Lewis was an admirer of Frazer. Then he came to believe that there was a difference between Christian claims and the other myths:

Now the story of Christ is simply a true myth: a myth working on us in the same way as the others, but with this tremendous difference that it really happened.

■ Or we can say, 'Religious experience is real, and it happens to just about everyone.' This is David Hay's position. He has studied for several years the claims made by ordinary people who feel that they have encountered God. He has found that these kinds of experiences happen over and over again:

Something woke me up. There was something or somebody by my bed; I wasn't frightened. Within ten minutes the torment I'd felt, for some strange reason left me. I think I had more peace then than I'd had for a very long time... I have enough knowledge to know that there's somebody there, to know that I need never be so alone again...

I began praying, not really sure that there was a God. At one particular time after a great deal of thought a relaxation came upon my mind and everything fitted together. It only lasted for a moment, perhaps four to five seconds... I really felt God was communicating with me.

This sounds like the sort of thing which the Bible predicts should happen:

From one nation God made every nation of men, that they should inhabit the whole earth; and he determined the times set for them and the exact places where they should live. God did this so that men would seek him and perhaps reach out for him and find him, though he is not far from each one of us.

■ Perhaps these fleeting experiences are all we can ever know of God. Or perhaps there is a third possibility? This would be to say, 'Religious experience is real, and can be a signpost towards God; but a *deeper* relationship with God is possible too.'

Jesus Christ is on record as saying, 'I am the way, truth and life; no one comes to the Father except through me.' One of the distinctive things about Jesus' teaching was the way he constantly referred to God as 'the Father'—an emphasis not much explored in Judaism, despite its strong belief in a personal, caring God. It was as if he was saying that it is possible for human beings to approach God more closely—to have an individual relationship with him which is as intimate as a father-child relationship. And that the only way to establish such a connection is 'through' Jesus.

We will examine this claim more closely in another chapter. But here we should note that what seems like the apparent staggering arrogance of his statement immediately sets Jesus Christ apart from other religious leaders. He was not content to be a prophet or a rabbi, a Guru Nanak or a Lao-Tse; he said he was the one direct route to God. And today, two thousand years later, almost a quarter of the human race claims to follow him and believe the claim.

Could he have been telling the truth? Let C.S. Lewis have the last word.

On the one side clear, definite moral teaching. On the other, claims which, if not true, are those of a megalomaniac, compared with whom Hitler was the most sane and humble of men. There is no half-way house and there is no parallel in other religions... The idea of a great moral teacher saying what Christ said is out of the question. In my opinion, the only person who can say that sort of thing is either God or a complete lunatic suffering from that form of delusion which undermines the whole mind of man.

10

THE HEART OF IT ALL

Human beings have a seemingly incurable habit of looking for patterns. You can test this by sprinkling ink blots at random on a piece of paper, and then showing it to some friends, asking them what they see. They may come up with different ideas, but most will be able to see some sort of picture there. The same is true of imagining faces in the clouds or melted snow, or guessing the next number in a sequence, or sensing a connection in the events that happen to you from day to day. (Which is why humans are often easily persuaded by the claims of astrologers and fortune tellers; and why we have to be careful with claims of answers to prayer.) The human mind does not like randomness; it always looks for meaning. Presented with a pile of bits of information, it instinctively sets about sorting them into an organized pattern.

And one thing we have discovered about patterns is that the whole can be more than the sum of the parts. You can describe a piece of wood in terms of its chemical composition, the pigment adhering to it, and the position of the molecules involved; but until you have also stated that it is a signpost bearing the message *Trespassers Will be Shot*, you have certainly not exhausted its meaning! Similarly, as we have seen, you can count up the chemical constituents of human life, and put them in a fairly accurate list, right down to the last traces of selenium and molybdenum. But you have not even started to assess the importance and meaning of human life.

In a famous book called *Holism and Evolution*, written in 1923, South African premier Jan Christian Smuts claimed that analyzing the elements of things would never give us the truth about the universe. He insisted that if we do not look at wholes, and appreciate the drive towards higher organization which is present in nature itself, we will never understand the significance of the isolated discoveries we make.

Examining the track is no way to discover what a railroad is for! We need to learn to see life whole.

149

More recently, a new approach known as General Systems Theory has taught that the component parts of any system are so intimately related in their interactions that it is dangerously misleading to consider them separately. A single variable can be both cause and effect within the system. We have to understand the whole, not just aspects of the parts. 'General Systems Theory is symptomatic of a change in our world view,' says Ludwig von Bertalanffy. 'No longer do we see the world in a blind play of atoms, but rather a great organization.'

The whole and the parts. . . This book about human beings has concerned itself with the 'parts'. We have explored the body, the brain, the personality, the successes and failures, the social life and sexual differences, of *Homo sapiens sapiens*. We have looked at fringe possibilities—extra-sensory powers, contact with alien races, fire-walking, vampirism, levitation. And even in our survey of the parts, we have left out a shamefully large amount. I am conscious, for example, that a Marxist would object that I have paid scant attention to the way in which economic forces shape society; and a mystic would look in vain for an adequate treatment of ecstatic experience, altered levels of consciousness, meditation and asceticism. I would personally like to have spent more time on hypnotism, yoga, the development of philosophical thought, sexual behaviour, the significance of clothes, body language, human ritual. But the list is endless. In no way can one book address all the aspects of the rich, variegated, paradoxical jumble of human life.

However, it has been on the 'parts' rather than the 'whole' that we have focused. Now I want to redress the balance a little, before the end of the book. And I need to do this for a very important reason: anyone who writes about the 'parts' will tend to do so in a way that reflects his view of the 'whole'. All writers make assumptions about the meaning and significance of their subject. I am no exception.

I have a suspicion that if this book had been written by, say, David Attenborough or Desmond Morris, it would have come out rather differently. This is because I am assuming a view of human life which is a little different from theirs, because I am a Christian. And although I have tried to be fair, and to present only facts which I can be sure are true, my starting point is inevitably going to colour the way I write.

And so it is time to tie all the loose ends together. What is the 'whole', where human life is concerned? What is the ultimate significance, the point and purpose, of this endlessly fascinating development in an otherwise lonely universe?

The point of life

As we have seen, some thinkers find no point in life. Our existence is merely absurd; we are a chance accident in space (admittedly a most improbable one), and there is no continuing meaning in what happens to us day by day. Death ends everything; there is no Creator in charge, and we could well end our own history by blowing ourselves up.

This does not mean that such thinkers merely opt out of life with nerveless resignation. Jean-Paul Sartre spoke of the need to achieve 'authentic existence', not just passively accepting whatever the universe happened to do to us. And some of the great humanists have been tireless workers for social justice and human liberties. But it does mean, that in the end, as humanist Kit Mouat put it, 'If it is necessary, humanists would rather state flatly that they have no final cut-and-dried reason why they believe that Man must live a good and constructive life.'

Other people teach that our present life is not the final truth about us. Indeed, this life is basically illusion: the real 'us' belongs somewhere else, as part of the great creative force which underlies everything and breathes through all life. And so the point of life is to realize that we do not belong here, that this world is not ultimately real, that only when we lose our individuality and stop being personally differentiated will we at last achieve integration and harmony.

This is the position of some of the great Eastern religions. But there are problems with this claim. C.E.M. Joad complained, in a famous passage, that it did not make much sense for 'me' to aspire towards a condition in which 'I' would cease to exist! I can believe, if I like, that this world is not real, and that my personality is basically illusory; but while I am on this planet, I have to live *as if* it is real and *as if* I am an individual. All the experiences of life supply me with evidence that this is actually true. If I want to believe it is not, I take a step of faith on the basis of no evidence whatsoever.

Christians like myself have a different view from either of these two. Looking at human beings, Christians see that one of the most significant things about us is that we are social animals: we exist in relationship to others, and it is through others that most of the important experiences of life come to us. Now there is nothing specifically Christian about this insight; Matthew Arnold, for instance, saw human relationships as the one source of meaning human beings can find:

Ah love, let us be true
To one another! for the world, which seems
To lie before us like a land of dreams,
So various, so beautiful, so new,
Hath really neither joy, nor love, nor light,
Nor certitude, nor peace, nor help for pain. . .

Paul Simon has expressed the same idea more starkly:

And so you see I have come to doubt
All that I once held was true
I stand alone without beliefs;
The only truth I know is you.

But to build our whole lives on the important relationships we have with other people is to risk disappointment, and in the end futility. The Western world is full of older people whose partners have died, and who consequently, although they are physically healthy enough to last for another twenty years, have no further reason for living. And since divorce rates have climbed so steeply in recent years,

Darwin's theory of evolution made people rethink their belief in God's creation; the positivist philosophy of Bertrand Russell and the existentialism of Jean Paul Sartre were both avowedly atheistic. Christianity has taken some knocks in the last century, but it is still very much alive.

151

many sociologists have started to ask: is it because we look for too much from marriage nowadays? If we are looking to human relationships to supply the ultimate meaning of our lives, are we placing on them a strain they cannot bear? The words of a pop star's deserted wife—herself an intelligent, articulate actress—are instructive:

Ever since I was a little girl, I thought marriage was what comes at the end of the rainbow. Maybe I just put too much stress on it.

Christians claim that humans were created to be dependent on relationships, not just with other human beings—but also with God himself. And only in this permanent, unfailing relationship can true meaning and purpose be found. Paul the apostle wrote:

I am convinced that neither death nor life, neither angels nor demons, neither the present nor the future, nor any powers, neither height nor depth, not anything else in all creation, will be able to separate us from the love of God that is in Christ Jesus our Lord.

God is therefore not an impersonal force (as some religions believe) nor a remote lawgiver (as others see him). Neither is he a distant, mysterious figure who may have created us, but is now unknowable and beyond our grasp.

God, if the Bible is correct, stands ready to establish a relationship of love and trust with any of his creatures who is willing to encounter him.

This is what the Bible means when it says that humanity was made 'in the image of God'. The resemblance is not physical; God is not a physical entity. Nor can we fix on one key quality of human beings (reason, or morality, or creativity) and say that is especially like something in God. Rather, says philosopher Arthur Holmes, it means:

A human being's relationship to God, seen both in dependency on God and in bearing God's image in the world, makes us all at heart religious beings. Our highest end, our all-inclusive supreme good, is to glorify God and enjoy him forever. . . . As dependent, we must seek God in all we are and do. As responsible image-bearers, we represent the Creator in all of it, too.

Human relationships

'Representing the Creator' means that our relationship with God will affect all the other relationships we have in our lives.

■ **It will affect our relationship to nature.** If we are creatures of the dust of the earth,

Alexander Solzhenitsyn is one of a galaxy of great men and women who have maintained Christian faith and values, often against great odds.

dependent on nature for our continuing existence, and yet responsible to God for the way we treat it, then there are certain things we cannot do. We cannot treat the world as if it does not matter. Christians take the human body seriously (and the rest of the natural creation as well), because they cannot accept the teaching that this world is basically evil or illusory. It is the real creation of a good God, and must be given its full value.

On the other hand, neither can Christians treat the world as if it is all-important. The kind of naturalistic, materialist viewpoint which reduces humanity to just one fortuitous component of nature—this cannot be a Christian attitude. Christians are always conscious that there is something beyond the physical; we are more than hapless machines. Our bodies and brains are subject to physical influences and conditioning, but there is still a real human freedom and responsibility which remains uneroded by the speculations of Pavlov, Skinner, Desmond Morris.

And so when it comes to ecology, Christians line themselves up with those who want to preserve the environment and protect our vital ecosystem. God's creation must be safeguarded, and we are responsible for that. On the other hand, there is a strain of nature mysticism running through the thinking of many campaigners for the environment—as if the world were some kind of deity in itself. Christians want no part of that. The world is God's creation; that makes it very important, but not somehow worshipped in itself.

■ **Living in the image of God also affects our relationship to other people.** If all other humans are made in the image of God, as I am, then I cannot manipulate or abuse them; I cannot treat them as mere objects. Every human life matters, however useless or unproductive it may seem to be. I cannot 'write off' those I do not like, taking refuge in the thought that they are just accidents in the cosmos, or evanescent incarnations who will live again many times.

Of course, Christians have no monopoly on the idea that 'every life matters'. But if human beings are *not* the individual, personal creations of a loving God, such a belief becomes unexpectedly hard to justify. Humanists would unanimously condemn Hitler for the slaughter of six million Jews; but, as we have seen Kit Mouat admit, 'for no final cut-and-dried reason'. Mahatma Ghandi is a marvellous example of a Hindu who was motivated by infinite concern for other individual human beings; but there was no justification for his attitude within his philosophical system.

■ **The image of God also leaves its mark on our relationship with ourselves.** On the one hand, we are created beings, operated on by an awesome variety of physical forces, which condition and shape us definitively. That should give us a proper humility, and an awareness of our own limitations.

This kind of humility has often been forgotten in Western culture. It happened during the Enlightenment of the eighteenth century, when reason seemed to be the key to all life's mysteries and the means by which the planet could be brought to perfection:

The shades of ignorance, of intellectual night Will fade and flee before the coming light.

It happened again in the mid-nineteenth century optimism of 'social Darwinism', when thinkers such as Herbert Spencer were proclaiming that 'progress is not an accident, but a necessity... It is the law of nature'. It happened again in the rise of humanistic psychology in the twentieth century, and the 'New Age' movement of the 1970s, with its belief that the human race was entering the 'Age of Aquarius', an era of staggering new potentials, cosmic powers and worldwide peace.

The history of the human being, and the way we are made, does not warrant any such optimism. Christianity focuses clearly on the smallness and dependence of human beings. As one of the Psalms puts is:

When I consider your heavens, the work of your fingers, the moon and the stars, which you have set in place, what is man that you are mindful of him, the son of man that you care for him?

It is a good question, and the answer is: 'You made him a little lower than the heavenly beings and crowned him with glory and honour'. The Christian view of human nature includes a realization that our lives have a real dignity and purpose. Human individuality matters, and I am responsible to shape my life by my own choices and calculations. I am not the plaything of fate; I am a free being.

Sometimes people have complained that the Bible's attitude is excessively gloomy. Christians have been criticized for talking too much about guilt and sin, for producing a cult of self-abasement which denies human beings the chance to stand on their own feet and take legitimate pride in their own achievements. Now certainly some Christianity has erred in this direction. There are some startlingly spineless hymns:

O to be nothing, nothing!
Simply to lie at his feet...

But this is not the Bible's picture of a free, responsible figure of dignity, 'crowned... with glory and honour'. Our relationship with ourselves need to be realistic, and humble; but not negative or dismissive.

In all of these ways, then—our relationship with nature, other people, and ourselves—it makes a tremendous difference to believe that we are made 'in the image of God'. But why *should* anyone believe it? Are there good grounds for believing that it is true?

know for sure? Only by putting God to the test: 'Find out for yourself how good the Lord is,' urges the Psalmist. The early Christians were confident that something had happened to them which had altered their experience of life permanently, and introduced them to the friendship of God.

But if this is so, why are we not experiencing it already? Because human beings are not automata, but have responsibility for their own actions. Arthur Holmes comments, 'To be responsible... implies that I can do something that will make the relationship different.' And the Bible asserts that this is exactly what has happened. The human race has misused its freedom and turned its back on God, preferring to live life independently. To quote the Psalms again:

There is no one who is righteous, no one who is wise or who worships God.

Writing in 1948, just after the discovery of the atomic bomb, Albert Einstein remarked, 'What terrifies us is not the explosive force of the atomic bomb, but the power of the wickedness

Knowing for sure

Christians believe that much of the objective evidence about humankind points in the direction of a Creator God. For one thing, the chance of life emerging on earth at all was vanishingly small; it is hard to believe that something as complex and sophisticated as the human being should have emerged through mere accident. And if the highest form of life we know on earth is personal, it is reasonable to suppose that anything higher than ourselves might also be personal—and might attach as much importance to relationships as we do ourselves. Christians also look at the evidence about Jesus Christ, who claimed to be the ultimate revelation of God's nature, and find there things which cannot be explained unless Jesus was exactly who he claimed to be.

Considerations such as these are strong indications that God is real; they give good, but not conclusive, evidences. Is there a way we can

Who should we follow? There is a wide choice of blind guides. Are they a good bet?

154

HUMAN LIFE AS THE WRITERS DESCRIBE IT

*But man, proud man,
Drest in a little brief authority,
Most ignorant of what he's
    most assur'd,
His glassy essence, like an
    angry ape,
Plays such fantastic tricks
    before high heaven
As make the angels weep.*
Shakespeare, *Measure for
Measure*

*Glory to Man in the
highest! for Man is the
master of things.*
Algernon Swinburne

*The life of man, solitary,
poor, nasty, brutish, and
short.*
Thomas Hobbes, *Leviathan*

*But trailing clouds of glory
    do we come
From God, who is our home;
Heaven lies about us in our
    infancy!*
William Wordsworth

*Human life is everywhere a
state in which much is to be
endured, and little to be
enjoyed.*
Samuel Johnson

*Created half to rise, and
    half to fall;
Great lord of all things, yet a
    prey to all;
Sole judge of truth, in
    endless error hurled;
The glory, jest, and riddle, of
    the world!*
Alexander Pope

*Man is only a reed, the
weakest thing in nature; but
he is a thinking reed.*
Blaise Pascal

*I am a man; I count
nothing human alien from
me.*
Terence

*Man is by nature a political
animal.*
Aristotle

*If we may believe our
logicians, man is
distinguished from all other
creatures by the faculty of
laughter.*
Joseph Addison

*In a short while the tribes
of living things are changed,
and like runners hand on
the torch of life.*
Lucretius

*If God does not exist. . .
man is in consequence
forlorn, for he cannot find
anything to depend on,
either within or outside
himself.*
Jean-Paul Sartre

*What is man that you are
    mindful of him,
the son of man that you care
    for him?
You made him a little lower
    than the heavenly beings
and crowned him with glory
    and honour.
You made him ruler over the
    works of your hands;
you put everything under his
    feet. . .*
Psalm 8

of the human heart, its explosive power for evil.' The greatest problem of humankind is the problem of our own moral failure—what the Bible calls sin. The history of our race demonstrates clearly just how fallible we are. And, as I have tried to argue in the chapter on the workings of our brains, we cannot blame our failures on our conditioning; we are free to choose for ourselves.

Sin affects all the relationships which human beings were created to enjoy. Our relationship with the world, for example; we are misusing the resources of our planet. Our relationship with other people is affected, too: racism, genocide, social and caste barriers are all evidence of the divisions that sin has brought between us. Our relationship with ourselves suffers: we feel guilty and annoyed with ourselves when we do now live as we feel we should, and we cannot make sense of our own existence. Rock singer Bruce Springsteen has been treated as a contemporary messiah by many young people today; yet he says, 'I don't have the answer to anyone's life, including my own. We're all just thumbing through the darkness looking for that bright spot.'

God's solution

All these broken relationships are serious. But the worst effect of sin on the human race is that it shuts us in to an existence without God, an empty universe in which contact has been broken with the infinite. Small wonder that existentialists such as conclude that God is just not there:

Up till now, man derived his coherence from his Creator. But from the moment that he consecrates his rupture with him, he finds himself delivered over to the fleeting moment, to the passing days, and to wasted sensibility.

Yet Christians insist that God has not left us, that the 'rupture' need not be final; that in fact God has taken the initiative and found a way of breaking through the barrier between human beings and himself. This way is, to use New Testament words, 'through the coming of our Saviour, Jesus Christ'. How did Jesus' coming make a difference?

When Jesus Christ died he took the brunt of the penalty we deserved—to pay for our sins and rebellion against God. He stood in our place and accepted our blame. As a result of his death, we can go free.

Because of Jesus' death for us, human beings are faced with another choice: to continue ignoring God, and live life in proud independence; or to accept forgiveness gladly and begin to experience the friendship of God. One man who chose the second option, while on the run from the American authorities, was Black Panther leader Eldridge Cleaver. He wrote of his experience:

That night I slept the most peaceful sleep I have ever known in my life. I woke up the next morning with a start, as though someone had touched me, and I could see in my mind the way, all the way back home, just as clear as I've ever seen anything. . . I had it within my power to get back home by taking that first step, by surrendering; and it was a certainty that everything was going to be all right. I just knew that—that was the solution, and I would be all right if I would take that step.

And so this is the 'whole' which Christians believe—I believe—makes sense of the fascinating 'parts' we have examined in this book. Human beings can 'get back home'. They can find, just as Eldridge Cleaver did, a relationship with God which unifies and integrates and intensifies and deepens all that it means to be truly human.

All the rest of this book remains true and valid, whether or not the reader accepts the truth of this closing personal statement of faith.

But it would be strange indeed to collect all kinds of data about the human experience, and yet not take time to weigh up the claims of Jesus which many people have found make sense of everything else. This is what it is all about. This is the ultimate meaning of humankind.

Today's young people look on into an uncertain future. What kind of life will they choose to live?

Books quoted in 'The Human Difference'

John Archer and Barbara Lloyd, *Sex and Gender*, Pelican 1982

Robert Ardrey, *The Social Contract*, Fontana 1970

Michael Argyle, *The Psychology of Interpersonal Behaviour*, Pelican 1972

Isaac Asimov, *The Universe: From Flat Earth to Quasar*, Pelican 1971

Peter Berger, *Facing Up to Modernity*, Basic Books 1977

Peter Berger, *The Social Reality of Religion*, Penguin 1973

P. Berger and T. Luckman, *The Social Construction of Reality*, Penguin 1971

P. Berger, B. Berger and H. Kellner, *The Homeless Mind*, Pelican 1974

H. J. Blackman and others, *Objections to Humanism*, Pelican 1965

M. Bolt and D. G. Myers, *The Human Connection: How People Change People*, Hodder 1984

Tal Brooke, *Riders of the Cosmic Circuit*, Lion 1986

J. A. C. Brown, *Techniques of Persuasion: from Propaganda to Brainwashing*, Pelican 1975

Carlos Castaneda, *A Separate Reality*, Penguin 1973

C. M. Cipolla, *The Economic History of World Population*, Pelican 1965

Eldridge Cleaver, *Soul on Fire*, Word 1978

Vernon Coleman, *Stress Control*, Pan 1980

C. W. Colson, *Born Again*, Hodder 1976

David Cook, *Blind Alley Beliefs*, Pickering and Inglis 1979

Francis Crick, *Life Itself: Its Origins and Nature*, Futura 1982

Richard Dawkins, *The Blind Watchmaker*, Penguin 1988

Richard Dawkins, *The Selfish Gene*, Oxford 1976

M. W. Dempsey, ed, *Everyman's Factfinder*, Galley 1988

Maya Deren, *The Voodoo Gods*, Paladin 1975

John Drane, *Jesus and the Four Gospels*, Lion 1979

Hoyt, Edge and others, *Foundations of Parapsychology*, Routledge and Kegan Paul 1986

Martin Esslin, *The Theatre of the Absurd*, Pelican 1968

Mary Evans, *Women in the Bible*, Paternoster 1983

C. Stephen Evans, *The Quest for Faith*, IVP 1986

H. J. Eysenck and D. K. B. Nias, *Astrology: Science and Superstition?*, Pelican 1982

Peter Farb, *Humankind*, Granada 1978

Marilyn Ferguson, *The Aquarian Conspiracy*, Routledge and Kegan Paul 1981

Antony Flew, *Darwinian Evolution*, Paladin 1984

George Frankl, *The Failure of the Sexual Revolution*, NEL 1975

Betty Friedan, *The Feminine Mystique*, Pelican 1986

Martin Gardner, *The Whys of a Philosophical Scrivener*, Oxford 1983

Martin Gardner, *Science: Good, Bad and Bogus*, Oxford 1983

Erving Goffman, *The Presentation of Self in Everyday Life*, Pelican 1987

Stephen Jay Gould, *Ever Since Darwin: Reflections in Natural History*, Pelican 1980

John Grant, *A Directory of Discarded Ideas*, Corgi 1983

J. A. Hadfield, *Childhood and Adolescence*, Pelican 1975

David Hay, *Exploring Inner Space*, Pelican 1982

Mary Hayter, *The New Eve in Christ*, SPCK 1987

Paul Hazard, *European Thought in the Eighteenth Century*, Pelican 1965

Paul Hazard, *The European Mind 1680–1715*, Pelican 1964

Arthur F. Holmes, *Contours of a World View*, IVP 1983

H. Stuart Hughes, *Consciousness and Society*, Paladin 1974

Morton Hunt, *The Universe Within*, Corgi 1984

Roger F. Hurding, *Roots and Shoots*, Hodder 1986

William Jones, *The Varieties of Religious Experience*, Fontana 1960

D. Gareth Jones, *Brave New People: Ethical Issues at the Commencement of Life*, IVP 1984

H. T. Kerr and J. M. Mulder, eds, *Conversions*, Hodder 1984

Leszek Kolakowski, *Religion*, Fontana 1982

Harold S. Kushner, *When All You've Ever Wanted Isn't Enough*, Pan 1987

Harold S. Kushner, *When Bad Things Happen to Good People*, Pan 1982

Christopher Lasch, *The Culture of Narcissism*, Abacus 1980

The Last Two Million Years, Reader's Digest Association/Hodder 1986

C. S. Lewis, *God in the Dock*, Fount 1979

C. S. Lewis, *Mere Christianity*, Fount 1979

C. S. Lewis, *Miracles*, Fount 1981

C. S. Lewis, *Surprised by Joy*, Fontana 1974

Gordon R. Lowe, *The Growth of Personality*, Pelican 1972

David Lyon, *The Steeple's Shadow*, SPCK 1985

Donald Mackay, *Human Science and Human Dignity*, Hodder 1979

Marshall McLuhan, *The Gutenberg Galaxy*, Routledge and Kegan Paul 1962

Marshall McLuhan, *Understanding Media*, Sphere 1969

I. Howard Marshall, *I Believe in the Historical Jesus*, Hodder 1977

Patrick Masterson, *Atheism and Alienation*, Gill and Macmillan 1971

Katinka Matson, *The Encyclopedia of Reality*, Paladin 1979

Margaret Mead, *Culture and Commitment*, Panther 1972

George Melly, *Revolt into Style: the Pop Arts in Britain*, Penguin 1970

John J. Mitchell, *Human Life: The Early Adolescent Years*, Holt, Rinehart and Winston (Toronto) 1974

Juliet Mitchell, *Psychoanalysis and Feminism*, Pelican 1975

Elizabeth Moberly, *Homosexuality: A New Christian Ethic*, James Clarke 1983

R. A. Moody, *Life After Life*, Corgi 1976

Stephen Neill, *Crises of Belief*, Hodder 1984

Lesslie Newbigin, *Foolishness to the Greeks*, SPCK 1986

Oliver O'Donovan, *Begotten or Made?*, Oxford 1984

Vance Packard, *The Hidden Persuaders*, Pelican 1974

M. Scott Peck, *People of the Lie*, Rider 1983

Clark H. Pinnock, *Reason Enough: A Case for the Christian Faith*, Paternoster 1980

J. M. Roberts, *The Pelican History of the World*, Pelican 1980

Steven Rose, *The Conscious Brain*, Pelican 1976

Sheila Rowbotham, *Women's Consciousness, Man's World*, Penguin 1973

C. I. Sandstrom, *Psychology of Childhood and Adolescence*, Pelican 1968

Donald Scott, *The Psychology of Work*, Duckworth 1970

W. J. H. Sprott, *Human Groups*, Pelican 1977

G. Rattray Taylor, *The Natural History of the Mind*, Secker & Warburg 1979

William Sargant, *Battle for the Mind*, Pan 1970

Ninian Smart, *The Religious Experience of Mankind*, Fount 1977

Anthony Smith, *The Body*, Pelican 1985

David Stafford-Clark, *What Freud Really Said*, Pelican 1983

Elaine Storkey, *What's Right with Feminism*, SPCK 1985

J. R. W. Scott, *Issues Facing Christians Today*, Marshalls 1984

John G. Strelan, *Search for Salvation*, Lutheran Publishing House (Adelaide) 1977

Gay Talese, *Thy Neighbour's Wife*, Pan 1981

Robert Thomson, *The Psychology of Thinking*, Pelican 1977

Alvin Toffler, *The Third Wave*, Pan 1981

Paul Tournier, *The Adventure of Living*, SCM 1966

Paul Tournier, *Learning to Grow Old*, Highland 1985

Peter Tyrer, *Stress*, Sheldon Press 1980

Peter Underwood, *Dictionary of the Supernatural*, Harrap 1978

Adrian Wilson, *Family*, Tavistock Publications 1985

Colin Wilson, *Poltergeist!*, NEL 1981

Robert Wrenn and Reed Mencke, *Being: A Psychology of Self*, Science Research Associates 1975

Index

Acknowledgments

B & C Alexander, page 50; All Sport Photographic Ltd, pages 37, 40 (top), 41, 46 (bottom); APA/Holger Holleman, page 48 (bottom); Associated Press, pages 10, 28, 67, 69 (right), 90/91, 111, 115 (bottom), 127, 144; Howard Barlow, pages 87, 153; Barnaby's Picture Library, pages 7, 25, 32, 39 (both), 58, 59, 82, 100/101, 108/109, 125, 131; Steve Benbow, page 104 (bottom); Bridgeman Art Library, page 107; Susanna Burton, pages 4 (top right), 36; Camera Press, pages 26, 27, 61, 74, 85, 103, 104 (top), 130 (bottom), 132, 152; Church Missionary Society, page 34 (left); Richard Dean, pages 4 (bottom right), 14, 15 (centre), 17, 23, 57, 97 (top), 98/99, 135; Mary Evans Picture Library, pages 75, 76 (both), 77 (both), 84, 88 (both), 151 (top and centre);

Format Photographers, pages 40 (bottom), 89, 97 (bottom); Hulton Picture Company, pages 24/25, 64 (both), 151 (bottom); Hutchison Photographic Library, pages 42 (both), 43, 56, 78, 106 (top), 115 (top), 129, 130 (top), 142; Lion Publishing: David Alexander, page 55 (bottom)/Fritz Frankhauser, page 54/David Townsend, pages 5, 55 (centre); London City Mission/Peter Trainer, pages 146/47; Richard Opei, page 104 (centre); Photo Co-op/Vicky White, page 30; Picture Point, page 140; Popperfoto, pages 68, 69 (left); Rex Features, pages 4 (centre left), 48 (top); Gerald Rogers, page 12; Nick Rous, page 33; Science Photo Library, pages 80/81; David Simson, page 15 (top); Tony Stone Worldwide Photolibrary, pages 3, 9; David Townsend Photography, pages 34 (right), 35, 55 (top), 94, 95; Janine Wiedel, page 19; Zefa (UK) Ltd, pages 16, 45, 46 (top), 51, 86, 106 (bottom), 109, 110, 121, 136, 139, 141